EVOLUTION:
REDUCTIO AD ABSURDUM,
AND ITS MEANING FOR PUBLIC EDUCATION

MIKE PINCHER

EVOLUTION
Reductio Ad Absurdum, and its Meaning for Public Education
Copyright © 2023 by Mike Pincher

Library of Congress Control Number: 2023910089
ISBN-13: Paperback: 978-1-64749-902-0
          Epub: 978-1-64749-923-5

All rights reserved. No part of this publication may be reproduced, distributed, or transmitted in any form or by any means, including photocopying, recording, or other electronic or mechanical methods, without the prior written permission of the publisher or author, except in the case of brief quotations embodied in critical reviews and certain other noncommercial uses permitted by copyright law.

Although every precaution has been taken to verify the accuracy of the information contained herein, the author and publisher assume no responsibility for any errors or omissions. No liability is assumed for damages that may result from the use of information contained within.

Printed in the United States of America

GoTo Publish

GoToPublish LLC
1-888-337-1724
www.gotopublish.com
info@gotopublish.com

CONTENTS

Dedicated to vii
Prologue and Acknowledgements 1
    A.   Why this Treatment? 1
    B.   The Operative Premise 14
    C.   Church Atrocities and Doctrinal Dogma as a Stimulus For an Alternative. 15
    D.   Philosophical Underpinning 16
    E.   Chapter Breakdown 17
    F.   A Word on References and Citations 21
    G.   Further Notes on Nomenclature 24
    H.   The Ultimate Premises 24
    I.   Acknowledgements 25
Chapter One Perversion as Persuasion 29
    A.   The Copernican Principle of Mediocrity is Not Even Copernican 29
    B.   Archaeopteryx is Not A Transitional Fossil And is Decidedly A Bird 36
    C.   Haeckel's Fraudulent Embryonic Wood Carvings And Drawings Are Still In Public School Textbooks Today 39
    D.   The Apostle Paul Did Not Teach That Faith Alone Equals Salvation, Nor Does The New Testament .. 44
    E.   An Adverse Reaction To Religious Atrocities And Extremism Is Not Proof Of A Contrary Theory 48
    F.   To Say That The Designer Could Have Done A Better Job Is Intellectually Cheating 53
    G.   The Horse Series That Wasn't (And Still Isn't) 55
    H.   The Adventures Of Piltdown Man 62

Chapter Two A Precept In Need Of A Poster Child 63
    A.   Macro's Contemporary Advocates Needed A Mouth-Piece 63
    B.   The Legend That Huxley Had Rather Come From An Ape Than A Bishop 65
    C.   Contemporaries "Managed" Darwin's Success 67
    D.   A More Complete View Shows That Darwin Was An Atheist 75
    E.   How Unique Was Darwin's Theory? 80
    F.   Darwin Compared To Scientific Greats 89
    G.   The Question Of Darwin's Health And Other Physical Problems 104
    H.   Darwin Married His First Cousin 108
    I.   An Unjust God Is Not Proof Of The Absence of One 110

Chapter Three Macro's Biased Foundation 113
    A.   Eliminating The Supernatural As An Explanation Ab Initio Is Neither Good Science Nor Good Logic 113
    B.   Intellectual Honesty Demands An Evidentiarily Rebuttable Presumption Of Design, Maybe Even Res Ipsa Loquitur, And Design Inclusion Would Have Been Favored By Our Founding Fathers 116
    C.   The Evidence Is Replete With Suppression Of Both Human Origins And Size Because It Doesn't Fit Macro's Theory 133
    D.   There Is No Complete Stratigraphic Column Anywhere On Earth 148
    E.   Fossils At Contradictory Stratigraphic Levels Are Arbitrarily Explained Away, And Dating Is Determined By Circular Reasoning (Logical Fallacy) 149
    F.   Radioisotope Dating Methods Are Unreliable 151
    G.   The Modern Suppressors Of Truth, Who They Are, And Why They Would Fail With A Properly Presented Case To The U.S. Supreme Court, Consistent With Edwards V. Aguillard 160

Chapter Four 179
    It Is A Physical And Chemical Impossibility For Life To Originate Without A Pre-Programmed, Closed

System, Which Could Not Happen By Accident ... 179
Chapter Five 183
    The Genetic Code Speaks Against Strict Macro, Not For It, And Has Deep Philosophical Implications (The Flight Of Sir Antony Flew), Especially When Combined With Reproductive First Cause 183
Chapter Six 197
    Macro Theory Begs For Asexual Reproduction Over Sexual, Simplicity Over Complexity, And Uniformity In Life, Not Diversity, And Faces The Further Problem Of Multiple Creations 197
Chapter Seven 203
    Undirected, Nature Proceeds From Greater Programming To Lesser, And The Second Law Of Thermodynamics Militates Against Macro 203
Chapter Eight 211
    Intelligent Design And Creation Science Have Notable Distinctions, And Intelligent Design Is A Science 211
Chapter Nine 219
    Macro As Religion 219
Chapter Ten 231
    The Models Compared 231
Chapter Eleven 249
    From The Mouths Of Hypocrites 249
Chapter Twelve 261
    Is There An Ulterior, Insidious Motive Behind The Macro Agenda? 261
Chapter Thirteen 265
    Macro Must Deal With The Declining Longevity And Size Issues Of Man, Fauna And Probably Flora 265
Chapter Fourteen 273
    The Question Of Starlight 273
Epilogue 277
Bibliography 289
Index 303

DEDICATED TO

My loving parents, Michael H. and Mary A. Pincher, who always taught me that setting and reaching goals are still secondary to the integrity of <u>how</u> you go about them.

PROLOGUE AND ACKNOWLEDGEMENTS

It seems fair to say that evolutionary theory reached a full public consciousness with the November, 1859 publication of that provocative book by British naturalist Charles Darwin (1809-1882), On The Origin of Species By Means of Natural Selection, or the Preservation of Favoured Races in the Struggle for Life. While various modified aspects of it surface the mainstream, it is Darwin's theory that is traced and dealt with here as the linchpin for all that followed, and modifications thereto will be appropriately addressed. But it remains key to the entire Creation (generically, as it is Intelligent Design that is being advocated herein) v. Evolution dispute, and it is aspects of both his and his theory's rise to prominence that are targeted herein. While Darwin made advances toward disproving fixity of species as wrongly espoused by prime advocates Georges Cuvier (1769-1873) and Louis Agassiz (1807-1883—Cuvier's protégé), who did so without legitimate biblical authority, his principle of natural selection cannot account for transmutation among Scriptural kinds.

A. Why this Treatment?

The reader is advised that this work was originally published back in 2010 by self-publisher Publish America, who after various name changes eventually went out of business. For every topic originally covered, while countless discoveries and claims in all scientific disciplines have been made since then by both the evolutionary and Intelligent Design camps, the disagreements between them have only widened, with no knockout blow having been delivered by either side. Now there are even further claims of transmutation from dino to bird being made based on recent discoveries and technological advances, that new dinosaur species are seemingly discovered daily, that the James Webb telescope has opened up the cosmos to an even greater extent than did its Hubble telescope predecessor, that the human genome has been far greater unraveled than previously, that paleontological and archaeological finds have greatly increased through both greater technology and greater interest than ever before with more interdisciplinary involvement, that further time dilation theories have been proposed by young earth creationists addressing the distant starlight issue, and the list goes on and on.

But the only end result of this heightened activity has been for both sides to dig their heels in even deeper in defense of their own positions without any dispositive concessions having been made by either. So the point-counterpoint pedagogy concerning evolution and Intelligent Design originally posed back in 2010 remains a chronic and unaddressed need regardless of the changes since original publication. So rather than update the time period between 2010 and now with all of these events, the original work is simply being republished because there has been no change in the reason for the pedagogy and if anything, it has been further confirmed to be necessary due to the controversy widening rather than abating since its original publication. Further, some advocates on both sides have died or been replaced by successors since 2010 but still the same principles remain, so said deaths or successors usually are not reported in this update because irrelevant to the overall theme of this work.

This book has five targets: (1) reducing macro evolution's ("macro") tenets to logical absurdity (in Latin, "reductio ad absurdum"); (2) showing that micro-evolution under any evolutionary label is a misnomer for adaptation and variation because while genetic information is involved in each, that change is pre-programmed through design by a designer rather than being random; (3) creating a basis for the teaching of Intelligent Design (this phrase and its monogram of "ID" will be used interchangeably throughout) principles and other scientific theories in the public school system in counterpoint to Darwinian macro evolutionary precepts; (4) showing how the philosophies and legislative intent of our Founding Fathers not only permit such a teaching method for science instruction, but further make it federally <u>un</u>constitutional not to, and thus mandate ID principle inclusion, and (5) establishing that macro evolution is impossible because it is chemically impossible in natural law to create even a single cell living organism in any host (but especially water) without having a highly programmed, <u>fully-formed</u> closed system to begin with. Such is unaccountable in evolutionary terms.

While the fourth target relates to the third, it is separated here because it is one thing to say that Intelligent Design principles can allowably be taught under the First Amendment Establishment Clause, and quite another to say that it is <u>mandated</u> (the latter of which I find to be true). If we are to follow the vision that the Constitutional framers such as Madison, Jefferson (in his influence of Madison), and probably even Hamilton had in mind for this country, and their concern for the full flow of information to be provided to the public, Intelligent Design principles MUST be taught. As will be shown, such a dissemination was so important to Jefferson, he said that if he had to choose between either a free press or government, he would <u>abandon government altogether</u>! That's pretty powerful stuff!

Argumentatively, too little emphasis has been placed upon examining transmutational evolution (macro) through critical thinking by testing it against logical fallacies. Virtually all other avenues have been diligently pursued; limited examples being the mathematical impossibility of evolution on the macro-level, the inherent unreliability of the various "scientific" dating devices used, the inconsistency of its premises with the existing interdisciplinary scientific evidence (including the dubious stratigraphic fossil record), and the paleontological frauds and farces perpetrated by its proponents such as Piltdown ("orangutan jaw and chimpanzee teeth") Man and Nebraska ("pig's tooth") Man. I deem all of these points to be valid criticisms to varying degrees.

Nonetheless, they lead to an endless point and counter-point <u>outside</u> polemic based upon interpretation of the evidence, leading to the basic quagmire depicted by author Andrew Lang, who said of an opponent: "He used statistics as a drunken man uses lampposts; for support rather than illumination."[1] Like stats, scientific "evidence" and data are too often interpreted "through the eyes of the beholder," inevitably infusing subjectivity rather than objectivity. The danger (if undirected) is that

---

[1] http://quotationsbook.com/quote/37341. [8/1/09.]

the reader is left unduly influenced by the limited sample presented because not properly exposed to all serious scientific positions in more clinical fashion and in one reference work. It presents a quagmired puzzle with too many pieces to coherently find and fit together.

This reality, in fact, is one of the linchpins of this work. As will be shown upon examination of the intent of our American Constitutional framers, a proper (and absolutely critical!) public education is consideration of many scientific views, with no pre-screening of academic merit (censorship) being made by biased book content arbiters. Knowledge is freedom both academically and politically, and the tasks often merge in the communication thereof. Liberty under any reasonable label cannot prevail under a suppressed, obstructionist environment, where interested parties flagrantly use their bias and prejudice to control intellectual data flow.

So why bother trying to reduce macro to absurdity? Why not just argue for full scientific information and disclosure? Because there are macro organizational forces out there today such as the American Institute of Biological Sciences ("AIBS"), National Center for Science Education ("NCSE") and the National Academy of Sciences ("NAS") that are very well organized and hell-bent on preventing that from happening. They do not want to see American public school children receive an unbiased, un<u>brainwashed</u> education that enables them to think for themselves, instead of being mental puppets manipulated by purveyors of prejudicially controlled input. It is my task to show that what is being "pre-screened" from public schools by allegedly "scientific" textbooks (again, <u>censored</u>) is not based on the goal that the Founding Fathers envisioned as the ideal education to quality assure that students are taught objective science. Rather, it is unethically and immorally (as well as unconstitutionally) devised to promote one form of dangerous dogmatism over another. Thus, liberty of both mind and body are imperiled in today's society, and we as concerned parents and American citizens must act now to help return it to the democratic-republic standards envisioned by our forefathers and for which much blood has already been shed.

I am not a blind, chauvinistic flag-waver exhorting, "My country, right or wrong!" Far from it! In fact, I could not think of a more irresponsible credo, which betrays the very citizenry that the government is supposed to serve. Rather, I submit, "The truth shall set you free;" not only for its obvious religious connotation, but for its secular as well. It was a cornerstone in the Constitutional mentality and architecture of the Establishment Clause, part of the very fabric and rubric of its being, as will be explained in this work. The framers strove to make government a public servant, with the people themselves the ultimate arbiter of how they should be governed. Events since then have taken us away from that fundamental principle, and this book poses a means of returning to that paradigm by giving our schoolchildren the liberty of mind that intimately walks hand and hand with that of body. Abusively controlling our means of information is an invitation to tyranny, which the framers were acutely aware of and specifically legislated to guard against.

Thus, the second linchpin of this book is established; to expose macro for its fraud both in the inducement and in its execution, and the argumentatively weak logical foundation upon which it rests. Only then will the full extent of its exclusive imposition upon an unsuspecting public and its threat to our Constitutional liberty be fully appreciated, and hopefully prompt immediate corrective action. One means of exposing the fraud is by examining the history of the purported supporting evidence for it, hence considering Piltdown Man, Nebraska Man, Lucy (Australopithecus afarensis), Haeckel's fraudulent anatomical drawings, Archaeopteryx, and the stratigraphic record, among other examples. This fraud was perpetrated not just through obvious phony examples, but also in misrepresenting the quality of the evidence, and in drawing conclusions based on dubious, unproven (ASSUMED) premises.

Thus we segue into a second means of revealing the fraud, by showing the logically erroneous argumentative grounds supporting it through logical fallacies, presented mostly by unproven postulates supported by circular reasoning (or tautology). Logical fallacies are failures in the method of reasoning, arriving at premature conclusions not justified by the presented evidence. Even statements which end up being true can sometimes be arrived at improperly, but we must not arrive at them by that route, because in so doing, we drastically compound our chances for error. I have not seen this combined approach used against macro before, at least not on the scale that I use it, and most certainly not targeted for the purpose I use it for.

There is a third but related means of exposing the fraud utilized herein, and that is by tracing the historical, politico-social context wherein macro arose. Again, a response against repressive church dogmatism is not only justifiable, but in fact, necessary. But <u>not</u> when it is used as a ruse for a transition of power for selfish, greedy purposes, wherein one form of abuse is surreptitiously replaced by another. A fair question is: Are transmutational evolutionary (macro) tactics "smoke screens," or mere ways to reveal the truth by manufacturing situations that best put the truth on display? Unfortunately, it is submitted that the former, rather than the latter, is the case.

A review of some of the opening second Paragraph above arguments will even be done here, but very quickly so that the concentration is on how these relate to the whole theme. It is the social and political context that helps reveal the fallacy, that makes the matter transcend the mere point and counterpoint between competing doctrines, and helps explain why the overall false edifice is being promulgated to begin with. We learn the derivation and "why" behind the fraud.

The political and historical implications are another reason why this is not simply a work on Intelligent Design, though it would be oxymoronic (from this writer's perch) to be a Creationist without acknowledging Intelligent Design. All Creationist proofs necessarily entail ID as a component, whether of the Christian variety, or otherwise. As for politics and history, however, they are unavoidable areas because an integral part of why macro is erroneous involves showing how politics and history have played out to promote the sham and scam of macro. While the dubious macro background would not by itself vitiate its authenticity (if the reality of 3 + 4 equals 7 arose under forced circumstances, that would not negate the fact that it is still true), the additional fact that the scientific method of testing and retesting was abandoned to fit the theory is a valid <u>combined</u> reason for discrediting it. Even that, however, does not paint the total picture.

A fourth means of exposing the fraud is the more basic physical reality that the very natural laws that macro apotheosizes (in this case, chemistry) make it impossible for life to originate in water (and any other medium, for that matter) by pure chance. A purposefully <u>directed</u>, pre-programmed, fully pre-formed, closed system is required.

Since the totally unbiased, clinical analyst exists only in the mind of a very fertile imagination, rather than in practice, I warn you of my bias. I am a Christian Creationist who unabashedly believes in a literal six-day (24-hour day) Creation week of the heavens and the earth, and supports the Young Earth hypothesis. But hopefully the reader will see that I have not permitted it to taint my objectivity. I do not capitalize macro, but only because since it does not acknowledge a higher power as its agency, or present any other other form of intelligent agency source or basis (not even extraterrestrial) for upper case treatment of its first letter, it has no proper ground for it.

Since it implies some kind of a creative intervention for design to be present, I have also capitalized Intelligent Design, but again, that intervention is simply by an agency we are not necessarily yet familiar with, and not necessarily divine in character. It is more emblematic here of a programmed <u>intelligent</u> agent and is capitalized deferentially in that sense only. Darwinism is capitalized because linked to a specific person, and for no other reason. Since Deism and Theistic macro also assert a supernatural assistance, they too are often capitalized, even though neither represents my personal outlook. Faith is an element for all forms of Creationism (<u>an indispensable one in fact</u>), but it is logically foundationed rather than blind. Like the search for truth generally, BOTH the Creationist and macro positions require faith, and hence are both religions. I can hear the evolutionary screams from here, but it's true, as is discussed throughout this book.

Again, however, Creationism is not the goal here, just evidences of Intelligent Design, which itself can lead the student to numerous conclusions as to its framer (only one alternative of which is a Christian God). Bear in mind that even any extraterrestrial third party agency (as well as in any other form we can or cannot contemplate) can be an Intelligent Designer. The key is simply in what teaching method (pedagogy) is used to most effectively negate bias and prejudice and yet allow full disclosure of relevant facts.

However, the purpose is not to target Intelligent Design as the only answer but rather, as a viable alternative. It is among that informational database that must be presented to the student for his consideration before he reaches his own decision on origins or the nature of certain scientific phenomena. Are change and certain other processes random or directed? The more reliable the data for the student to consider, the sounder the decision will be. Allowing, also, of course, for non-committal if the student can argumentatively show why the information is insufficient for him to decide. ID proponents pronounce, "Teach the controversy!" While there are many ways in which that phrase coincides with my message, I prefer to express it as "teach the competing evidentiary facts and supporting arguments." To me, that more completely removes bias and, perhaps even more subtly and importantly, the suggestion of it (especially where the theme of "teaching" the "controversy" adopts the phraseology of teaching the "strengths and weaknesses of evolution"), and more precisely targets the objective, clinical approach that needs to be taken with this issue.

For further background, I am a concerned American citizen first and practicing California civil attorney second who has spent at least ten years researching the Creation-Evolution controversy overall and its ill-treatment by the judiciary as a portion thereof. As already alluded to, my position is that it would be federally unconstitutional to NOT teach Intelligent Design (again, note the absence of Creationism, which is totally intended) alongside macro in the public schools in the sense of presenting a point and counterpoint to the evolutionary thesis presented the student. While I personally consider transmutational macro evolution unproven and even disprovable (and have stronger words for it privately), the interjection of personal opinions or bias into classroom instruction is not only "not" the purpose of a true education, but is antithetical to it. The scientific establishment of the day holds to transmutational macro evolution (rightly or wrongly) with growing minority opposition, but the purpose of education is to imbue the student with the applicable data so that a decision can be made for himself (used generically) as to what his stand on origins should be, undiluted by undue influence.

The history of the First Amendment Establishment Clause DEMANDS the freest possible flow of scientific information unfiltered by bias or agenda, and it will be shown how our forefathers, such as Jefferson, Madison, and probably even Hamilton, would have insisted upon total disclosure. More specifically, the Establishment Clause in large part is in response to a particular form of power struggle and control exercised by the church-state (whether Anglican, Catholic, or otherwise), but its essence is avoidance of abuse by <u>any</u> power group. This is regardless of which Madisonian "factional" power, interest or pressure group it ends up being (for which his Federalist Paper no. 10 is highly informative and should be required reading in any American History course). The only preventative measure against this abuse is a total disclosure of the facts, nothing more or less, constrained only by practicality but otherwise totally uncensored.

Since macro itself is a religion, an argument could be made that the issue could well be off the table if a pure, hard-line approach is applied based on the letter of the law rather than its spirit and intent. But this is negated by the purpose of an education being to present the global facts for decision-making by the student when there are at least several sides to an issue, as is the case with origins and the derivation of certain scientific phenomena. That is all education should seek to do, and not openly advocate any particular religion because the goal is to get students to do critical thinking. <u>This is the fundamental essence of the First Amendment, though the need for truly "critical" thinking transcends even that consideration</u>. The promotion of critical thinking would have both practical and idealistic value whether the First Amendment existed or not, but the provision significantly adds value by codifying an available legal forum.

To buttress this approach, I use two arguments that I have not seen used anywhere else, at least not in book-length form. I first assert that the burden of proof to establish its scientific theory lies with macro, not Intelligent Design, in that we should start out based on the evidence acknowledging an inference of design. Second, I maintain that there is such a powerful inference of design that it should be presumed to be true until shown otherwise. With these assertions, we would expect ID to be emphasized in public school textbooks and macro minimized. But I do not actually suggest this application for two reasons: (1) based on the legislative intent of the Constitutional framers of the Establishment Clause, it is wrong to emphasize either position over another. The conclusion must be based on a comparison of empirical data and <u>established</u> observational facts, and (2) also due to such legislative intent, that very conclusion must be made by the student and no one else. It cannot be force or spoon-fed.

The inference of design and its logical corollaries and legal impact as argued herein are intended only to show WHY ID must be injected into the public school education curriculum. It must be part of the format but not <u>dictate</u> the format. By presenting a point and counterpoint approach under one roof, starting off with a macro premise (such deference only being due to convention rather than proof), we approach origins and its related topics with a purely secular purpose, where anything construable as religious in character is an intellectual decision made by the reader uninfluenced by curriculum bias and prejudice. Even an agnostic or atheistic conclusion is possible under this scenario from the purely intellectual, argumentative point of view.

The U.S. Supreme Court case of <u>Edwards v. Aguillard</u> (1987) 482 US 578 will be reviewed to illustrate the validity of this approach, as well as to serve the obvious purpose of showing that it does not violate the Establishment Clause when placed under legal scrutiny.

In this book, evolution is referred to mostly on the transmutational macro-level (where dinosaurs purportedly become birds, e.g.) and whole new "kinds" of creatures (to borrow from Scripture) are formed (even though their derivatives changed only through the micro and remain alive to this day. Why they are simply not wiped away in toto to achieve yet higher statuses of being is a MAJOR problem for evolutionists). Man, of course, is a primate-mammal derived from the same flawed process under this "theory." The deeply flawed traditional sequence is bacteria to metazoa to fish to amphibian to reptile (and in some circles, dinosaur to bird) to mammal to man.

I use the word macro for transmutational macro-evolution for more than just convenient short-hand purposes. I avoid saying "evolution" except where the context demands it because there is far too great a tendency to link macro as a logical and inevitably foregone complement to <u>micro</u>-evolution (herein called "adaptation" or "variation"). I know of no serious Creation advocate who denies adaptation or variation (which is totally consistent with the DNA/RNA genome), <u>though he would take serious issue (as do I) with the notion that the process is random rather than pre-programmed</u>.

Further, it appears that <u>neither</u> camp fully dichotomizes the two concepts, so that too often the two forms are referenced as if interchangeable, though they are not. They are, in fact, as distantly different in scope and implication as is the size differential between a single molecule and a star mass. The felony is compounded by macro proponents ("macros"), which for them, the very word "micro-evolution" <u>improperly</u> implies a near Pavlovian, a priori concession (blind "conditioned coat-tailing," if you will) that the process inevitably leads to macro. That kind of invisible rope (tagline) will not be afforded them here. There are other reasons for this that will become clear with the application of the "natural selection" principle, which is greatly dependent upon whether viewed as a programmed process or simply as an end result.

Also, when used herein, the words "micro-world" will discuss atomic and sub-atomic parts, spelled out so as to differentiate it and avoid connection of this use of "micro" with adaptation and variation.

There is <u>no conscious</u> attempted slant in analyzing the evidence itself, though my pre-disposition is clear. We will abide by Socrates and trace where the evidence leads, which in this case, it is submitted is Creationism and by extension, ID. If there was not a starting bias, I wouldn't hold any position at all, so what is important is that I show how my bias is hopefully offset by objectivity in handling the evidence. Christian Creationism is not unduly emphasized except in the context of showing how Scripture is misrepresented by macros. Scripture will never be quoted or utilized for any other purpose except in Chapter 13 (where I discuss longevity and size decrease in both man and animal) and in the context of Darwin not considering his seminary training in aspects where he obviously should have. It is submitted that within the scope of this book, intellectually a Creationist conclusion is inevitable (i.e., that there is a maker in some shape, manner or form), but that is as specific as it gets, and is still not a forced one. The reader can still disagree, and whether he expands that to Christian Creationism or not (or concludes Creationism at all) is his own prerogative.

Conversion to that specific form is not the purpose herein. In fact, what I am depicting is what I feel your conclusion will be. This would never be arrived at in the same way in a school curriculum because I am doing one thing for this work that a public school system must not be allowed to do; to try to objectively use evidence but for the subjective purpose of hoping you will turn to a particular position. I directly attack macro through the evidence in trying to convince you that as a scientific theory it doesn't cut it. In doing that I am still advocating for a particular position. A public school curriculum cannot and should not do that. It has to be more reportorial, presenting the extant facts and theories, from the pool of which the student then draws his own conclusion. That is why it must be presented in a stated position (point) and then opposing positions (counterpoint) format. So do not consider the layout of this work as an example of how the issue should be approached in a public school textbook. I am simply <u>trying to get you to see WHY it must be presented in point and counterpoint fashion: by showing that macro is far from an established scientific reality, and therefore must be subjected to objective examination and testing</u>. I am advocating a curriculum format that I think is best designed to eliminate, to the extent possible, human bias and prejudice from the presentation of the facts.

Again, as Socrates would say, simply let the evidence lead you where it will, but be intellectually honest enough to consider the "actual" and not contrived evidence from either direction. I have been intellectually honest enough to tell you I am a young-earth, Christian Creationist. There are also self-proclaimed, old-earth, Christian Creationists. You be the judge as to whether I have successfully avoided allowing this slant to prejudice my analysis. In either event, follow the evidence to where it leads and ONLY there. And if you remain a macro at heart and conviction after all of my toil, then that's the luck of the draw. I'll live with that. But I still hope you will work to change the public school curriculum format (another reason for stressing the dissemination of information objectives of our forefathers). Its presentation of "alleged" scientific fact is far too skewed. There is still a legitimate controversy that must be dealt with.

What you will find in reading this work is that I do openly attack the <u>practices</u> of the macro community in terms of suppression and castigating those who disagree with them. That has nothing to do with the macro doctrine itself, although I do argue that it is part of an agenda by macros, in this case partly to hide the weaknesses of the doctrine in order to artificially and argumentatively sustain its power play. But that is still a practitioner's issue. If I were to condition my Christian beliefs to the scrutiny of how some of its alleged proponents practice or have practiced it (e.g., the undeniable foreign church and church-state abuses), I would not be a Christian at all. <u>Remember always that no matter how much I attack some of the practices of the macros, I never once advocate that macro not be taught in the public schools</u>. It simply is to be tested by empirical evidence and theory like any other submitted scientific theory and not irresponsibly taken as a given like it is now, violating numerous logical fallacies in so doing.

But a further crucial point must essentially be made here. Regardless of whether I literally render macro in the reader's mind as reductio ad absurdum or not, it is hoped that he will be convinced enough of the potential viability for Intelligent Design in nature to concede there is a GENUINE SCIENTIFIC CONTROVERSY AS TO ORIGINS, AS WELL GENERALLY AS TO HOW NATURE FUNCTIONS, as to merit a full disclosure of the facts. Note also that I propose this disclosure, including macro theory, regardless of the decision the reader reaches as to macro's reality, even if it is concluded that it is a total fiction or must be intellectually challenged. The student, for his own edification, needs to consider it regardless of the ultimate conclusion, if any, because it has become such a thread in our scientific history, part of an imposed worldview. Even if it were to be totally discredited, e.g., it would then serve as a good example of how we must avoid logical fallacies in considering scientific data, which is a further reason why certain logical fallacies, the bugaboo of critical thinking, are discussed herein.

A final note as to science application is that I do not consider the word "law" a fitting appellation for the physical phenomena we describe with that label; "observation" appears to be the far superior term. Law connotes immutability, which is hardly the case when evaluating such phenomena, which may (and usu. does) vary when the surrounding milieu changes. Gravity, e.g., is affected by elevation, as is time itself. The word "observation" connotes that certain given conditions must co-exist to make that specific observation operative. It calls for a more targeted description of when the observed phenomenon applies and when it does not. This is a closer, more accurate depiction of the scientific phenomena we describe. We must not forget that we as humans are not, when it comes to physical observations, law-givers but rather, at best, law discoverers; we are interpreters and describers, and our initial impressions (interpretations) are not necessarily (and usually simply are not) the most complete and accurate ones. They are subject to continuing re-evaluation.

B. The Operative Premise

It is submitted that macro has no valid scientific foundation when subjected to unbiased critical thinking. Analogized mathematically, when the theory is reduced to its lowest ideological fraction, its operative premises are too demonstratively fallacious to be scientifically valid.

In supporting this hypothesis, scientific principles and theories are discussed only to the extent necessary to test macro's scientific foundation. It is submitted that scientific <u>expertise</u> is not needed to reduce evolutionary precepts from first logical implausibility to then impossibility. Some knowledge of science, of course, is necessary to establish the premises for discussion and to properly evaluate them. At no point, however, will this work transform into a scientific textbook, which not only is beyond the expertise of this writer, but is also unnecessary and diverting. The theme throughout is that there is sufficient evidence to dictate that macro is far from an established fact, and hence challenges to its premises must be freely included in public school textbooks. The differing viewpoint is submitted and it is up to the student to determine whether or not this is a macro weakness or strength.

Still further, the genetic code is not perceived herein as a micro-evolutionary function but rather a sophisticated data response, which some organisms are more capable of generating than others, depending on the programming. "Natural selection" is a conclusionary description rather than a distinct process, an end observation at best, and holds a current power in our so-called scientific approach that is totally unwarranted by the evidence. As you will see, Alfred Russel Wallace concluded that as well (which it is submitted is one of the more compelling reasons why Darwinian macro is nominated rather than the "Darwin-Wallace" theory). It is not a clipped convenience, but an actual avoidance of macro's glaring weaknesses rather than Darwin's being the superior version). A rejection of the bad traits and acceptance or adoption of the good is far too simplistic and broad-brushed to have scientific meaning (and it also, when carried out to its logical conclusion, fallacious). The general knowledge that man must breathe oxygen for survival qualifies no one to start up his own medical practice. It is submitted that DNA and RNA are impossible results of purely materialistic natural forces and are only reconcilable via a formal "programming" inexorably requiring a "programmer."

What does "programming" mean in this context? As I use it, it is the highly sophisticated division of labor of cells (as communicated by information and then carried out in accordance thereof) dependent upon precise synchronization that is a condition precedent to the accomplishment of the tasks assigned to the respective cells. This far transcends mere "order" but shows a definite Intelligent Design for which the absence of precise and deliberate orchestration would be fatal. It is submitted that order as we commonly use the term can SOMETIMES be accidental, but programming cannot. While often used separately in discussions, I submit that true "complexity" necessarily involves programming. Just recognize for now, however, that when many books and articles discuss complexity as not proving Intelligent Design, it is not being referred to in the sophisticated manner that I refer to programming.

An overriding theme of this work is that the greatest refutation of macro belongs to the integrated cellular division of labor in the micro-world, of which DNA and RNA are integral components. All of the general themes are listed below at the end of this Prologue.

C. Church Atrocities and Doctrinal Dogma As a Stimulus For an Alternative.

It will be shown that church-state or state abuses committed under heavy church influence, ranging from utter mind control and subjugation (even slavery) to outright extermination, <u>inundate</u> World History, and were well-known during Darwin's time. It was also, however, a period of transition through new power players, those who controlled the means of production and mass transportation as opposed to the clergy and nobility (large landholders).

D. Philosophical Underpinning

Christianity and all other Supernatural religions ascribe a divine act for Creation. Macro poses an unplanned, fortuitous process as an alternative. The implications of each are monumentally divergent. If macro submits otherwise, it is granting organization without an organizer in a way totally violating the Second Law of Thermodynamics. Morality is defined by an omniscient, omnipotent lawgiver in one, and by ideology in the other. The first is definitive because issued from an Ultimate Author clearly superior to us. If He is indeed the Creator of everything, including us and all else both observable and unobservable, then He is so vastly superior to us in every way that whatever He directs of us is inherently authoritative, and the final word on the subject. The AUTHORITY has spoken, though we are given free will to analyze and determine just what that <u>Authority</u> actually said and means.

If pure macro is true, then we have no special place in the ultimate scheme of things, but are simply the by-product of an unplanned, accidental process—a fluke, if you will. In turn, we are accountable to no higher order. As will be shown, that lack of accountability has been a compelling motivation for most macros, as generations of Huxleys have attested to. Obviously, humanism can result in humanitarianism and philanthropy, but does it make sense that mere mortals can ultimately and exclusively decide what ethics and morality ought to be? Especially when that can vary markedly from culture to culture as well as one's political, social and economic upbringing and status?

Under Christianity and the Decalogue, we are told not to kill. End of story. We know a priori it is wrong. We are obviously speaking of cold-blooded or even heat of passion murder or manslaughter as opposed to self-defense. This is implicit in Christ's instruction that it is alright to do good on the Sabbath, or to rescue a calf that has fallen into a pit. Under non-Theistic systems, it is a reasoned conclusion, though often reached. However, the room for costly human error enters the picture, which almost inevitably leads to tragedy.

It is submitted that whether or not there is an Omnipotent Being by which our governance is overseen or some other form of ultimate authority is so paramount a question that there should be a mechanism for resolving the matter relatively early in life. If "yes," then the higher and far more consequential question must be asked (be it a supernatural power): "Is He a just God?" Whether we are dealing with a benevolent, malevolent or median adjudicator takes center-stage. In terms of this book, however, that is a discussion for another day.

Even without that question, however, life's target is defined early on. Fellowship in Christ requires an attitudinal "we," whereas no accountability allows and even encourages a "me" way of thinking. How a target is identified guides conduct. Conduct is dictated by whether the target is "selfless" or "selfish". While mistakes are made following either course, the direction of fallibility changes, even though its status remains.

E. Chapter Breakdown

Chapter One, "Perversion as a Means of Persuasion," attempts to show the misrepresentations about their theory that the macros have passed on to an unsuspecting general public, as well as to many in the scientific community. Persons or groups that resort to such deception must be held immediately suspect. There is no excuse for intellectual dishonesty. Chapter Two is, "A Precept in Need of a Poster Child," and basically shows how Darwin was in the right place at the right time concerning the politico-social climate, and had the very characteristics needed for others to control how his theory was presented. It is astounding how hardened adherents had so little scientific basis to grab onto. A strong case for Darwin being a game-player is laid out, and his status as an atheist exposed, as opposed to being a Theist or agnostic as he announced in different circles. When the reasons for the spotlighting of macro theory are revealed, their overall integrity becomes highly suspect. It was not the brainchild of a clinical, objective approach. It is easy to see that somebody is not playing fairly here—neither intellectually, nor morally nor ethically. Bottom line: Objectivity is not being striven for by the macros, but merely an agenda under a false, contrived objectivity umbrella.

Chapter Three, "Macro's Biased Foundation," delves into the fundamental errors of logic that macro indulges in, and the falsified and contrived evidence it relies on. Theistic macro is also discussed, concerning the growing awareness among highly credentialed scholars and scientists, of the limitations that a purely naturalistic explanation for the development of life's organisms offers. Chapter Four, "It is a Physical and Chemical Impossibility For Life to Originate Without a Pre-Programmed, Closed System, Which Could Not Happen By Accident," presents a solid scientific reason why pure, unassisted, naturalistic macro is not even possible following the very laws of nature that macro extols and even deifies beyond all rationality, and proves that macro cannot account for the First Cause, the origin of life itself. This was one of the reasons for the conversion of Sir Antony Flew, perhaps the world's most notorious atheist, to Deism.

Chapter Five is called "The Genetic Code Speaks Against Macro, Not for It, And Has Deep Philosophical Implications (The Flight of Sir Antony Flew), Especially When Combined With Reproductive First Cause," and conveys that the programming behind the DNA/RNA machinery is beyond the scope of Darwinian capability, a major ground upon which philosophers have been rethinking the irrationality of a purely naturalistic macro theory. Chapter Six, "Macro Theory Begs for Asexual Reproduction Over Sexual, Simplicity Over Complexity, and Uniformity Over Diversity, and Faces the Further Problem of Multiple Creations," portrays the irrationality of trying to build systems of any sophistication at all in a random manner. It particularly probes the illogic of diversity of life based on a common progenitor.

Chapter Seven, "Undirected, Nature Proceeds From Greater Programming to Lesser, and The Second Law of Thermodynamics Militates Against Macro," shows the implausibility of matter directing itself in a random manner to achieve life as we know it because, again, it directly contradicts the very natural law that macros revere. Chapter Eight, "Intelligent Design and Creation Science Have Notable Distinctions, and Intelligent Design Is a Science," shows ID is far from simply backdoor Creationism, and merits true scientific recognition. Chapter Nine, "Macro as Religion," reveals that macro is every bit as much a religion as any of the formal public religions ever thought of being. Instead, however, of teaching neither macro nor ID principles in the classroom, both should be taught in the context of fulfilling a secular purpose without promoting the religious aspects of either.

Chapter Ten, "The Models Compared," shows how the Creation model is so much better suited to explain the scientific phenomena observed than macro is. What are being compared are scientific facts and observations in terms of point and counterpoint to macro for purposes of public education curriculum. This hints at Intelligent Design, and that for the purely secular purpose of dealing with origins and related issues. Then the student can make up his individual mind as to his own conclusion rather than being force-fed or spoon-fed it contrary to the aspirations of our Constitutional framers when the First Amendment was espoused.

Chapter Eleven is "From the Mouths of Hypocrites," and shows how the AIBS, NCSE, and NAS (who exert tremendous influence on the education system of this country) work to suppress a true scientific study by censoring the facts that might lead to an Intelligent Design inference from our nation's students on a state by state basis. Chapter Twelve asks, "Is There an Ulterior, Sinister Motive Behind the Macro Agenda?" and their behavior certainly suggests that, and Chapter Thirteen is called, "Macro Must Deal With the Declining Longevity and Size Issues." This constitutes a serious challenge to issues that macros ignore, which betrays that on the surface they have something to hide by declining to properly investigate. It is submitted that this is so because a sincere study would undermine their principles of improving change in nature, among other things. Finally, Chapter 14, which I have labeled "The Question of Starlight," broaches the issue of how, if the earth is truly young as young-earthers postulate, we see starlight that apparently emanates from millions of light years away.

Hopefully, these chapters help to show that the overall macro movement epitomizes the words of Nietzsche (1844-1900): "It is no small discipline and preparation of the intellect on its road to final "objectivity" to see things for once through the wrong end of the telescope."[2] (Emphasis added.) Tragically, through lies and censorship, it threatens the liberty of America by attempting to take away its ability to ascertain the truth.

As will be seen by exploring the intent of key members of our Declaration of Independence champions and Constitutional framers, what they ultimately wanted to protect was the dissemination of all information to the public so they can best ascertain truth for themselves under the greatest knowledge database possible. Favoring or endorsing any particular religion would defeat that purpose, subject

---

[2]   Frederick Nietzsche, On the Genealogy of Morals, a Polemical Tract.

the governed to possible subjugation, and hence defeat liberty. But it is important to realize that even absent that, favoring religious dogma over empirical truth is still a threat to intellectual liberty, whether violence or dictatorial oppression accompanies it or not. An old TV ad used to say, "A mind is a terrible thing to waste," but that is precisely what is happening in our American society today.

They were alluded to above, and Thomas Jefferson and James Madison are indeed oft quoted in this work, but for good reason. Both not only were main architects of two of the most seminal documents in American history, Jefferson receiving most of the authorship credit for the Declaration of Independence, and Madison for the U.S. Constitution (it was mostly formally written by Governeur Morris of Pennsylvania from the Committee of Style),[3] but they also greatly influenced one another. Jefferson, being the older of the two, was often considered Madison's mentor, and greatly influenced the drafting of the Constitution, but was not technically one of its framers.[4] They co-founded the Democratic-Republican Party as an alternative to the Federalist Party. Madison was at first opposed to a Bill of Rights, but Jefferson (though not singularly persuasive, as politics had a lot to do with it) influenced his reconsideration and eventual approval and support of it.[5] Madison helped fund Jefferson's University of Virginia. And, of course, both are former Presidents of the United States, succeeding one another, with Jefferson 3rd and Madison 4th. It is difficult to find two other men who were so pro-active in achieving the initial independence of this nation, and yet so fully also shaped the political and social landscape, both philosophically and participatorily, as they did for the years after that independence was achieved. Their respective influences are very hard to exaggerate. No treatment of this subject could be broached without dealing with their several and joint influences. Arguably, they weighed in the most heavily of our forefathers considering the totality of the relevant topics under consideration in this work.

Hamilton, besides his obvious influence on the economic side of our history, deserves inclusion herein on the basis of Federalist paper no. 1

---

[3] WikiAnswers – Who Wrote the Constitution;" http://wiki.answers.com/Q/Who_wrote_the_US_Constitution, at p. 3 of 5. [1/26/10.]
[4] Ibid.
[5] See, e.g., Jefferson's 3/15/1789 letter to Madison; this is an exhibit to "First Federal Congress: Amendments to the Constitution" at http://www.gwu.edu/~ffcp/exhibit/p7_1text.html, 5 pages. [1/26/10.]

alone, besides his other Constitutional influence. His identification of ill motives for even those on the proverbial "right side of the fence" on any given political issue says volumes for the incentive for the "factions" advocacy that Madison in Federalist paper no. 10 made so famous, as well as for "checks and balances" generally.

F. A Word on References and Citations

I am trying to establish that there are substantial challenges to macro (enough to overcome it completely and debunk it in my view), though that is unimportant and secondary to the recognition that there is a definite controversy (as qualified above) in scientific circles that the public school system needs to address. Thus, the bulk of the references will by necessity be to Creationist and Intelligent Design sources, with notable exceptions. I also occasionally quote from those who are convicted macros but nonetheless have doubts about the completeness of Darwinian theory, and acknowledge that it cannot explain all of life's phenomena. I also quote from some converts (notably former atheist Sir Antony Flew) who, following the evidence clinically and objectively, have been compelled to depart from strict macro, usually in the direction of Deism, and sometimes Theistic macro. There is a very impressive list of those who have gone in those latter directions, a partial one of which will be referred here throughout. Men such as Flew, Morris, Gingerich and Tipler are very highly credentialed, and their doubts should certainly showcase the seriousness of the stakes involved in this education issue.

I have read a number of books on this basic controversy and almost all argumentative aspects of what is raised via Internet references I have also seen in these books. There is information garnered, however, that nonetheless I was first exposed to via the Internet, such as for Sir Antony Flew, Simon Conway Morris and Owen Gingerich. So for the Internet references, I have placed, when available, the date I downloaded these sources following their URL locations, so that they can be checked out by the reader and compared for recent changes in text, or used to evaluate my interpretation of them. I have enclosed the access dates in brackets rather than parentheses, a personal preference because I feel they stand out better that way. Of course, some of these sites will eventually be deleted or moved from their indicated location from the time I reference them.

There is nothing especially illuminating to be garnered from the dates of these references in terms of priority of importance. The more recent in time have no connection whatsoever with when their respective subject matter was deemed important. They do not suggest any hierarchy of ideas but when I felt that more timely and targeted authority was needed for insertion. As will be seen, I use them in the context of their having been reviewed by others unless there is a complete text from the web source itself, upon which I make my own independent analysis. This is particularly apropos because I am trying to portray a controversy that is to be explored by all public school students, so that where the answer lies is not as important as being provided the necessary information database and having read and absorbed its content by the individual student. This is an approach that Jefferson in particular would have highly approved of.

The reader will observe that though footnotes are used extensively, there are some sources that I do not do that with when their identity is deemed important enough to be included in the main text so as to not interrupt the flow, or to alert the reader as to their significance. It is also recognized that sometimes the reader does not wish to break the continuity of the reading by straying the eyes away from the main body of the text. With one exception, biblical sources are given in the main body contained within brackets for easy reference for the reader, particularly when misconceptions concerning the apostle Paul and divine grace are discussed. They also appear incidentally for a few other points, such as when effort is made to make the reader aware that the appellate decision on the Scopes Monkey trial is available on the Internet by giving the URL there. The same is done for legal references such as court case citations or code references, which are treated as a lawyer would reference them in a legal brief. The attempt was made here to maintain the flow as best manageable while preserving key moments or making key points without the eyes needing to stray for the authority supporting those moments or points. Footnotes were chosen over endnotes so that the eye could remain on the immediate page being read. They were also chosen over author and page references keyed to the bibliography for that same reason.

Creationism has a growing institutional base, with probably the most prominent being the Institute for Creation Research ("ICR"), headquartered in Dallas, TX after many years in CA, whose primary publication is Acts & Facts. Significant others include Answers in Genesis, out of Florence, KY, which publishes the magazine Creation ex nihilo, and the Creation Research Society, located in St. Joseph, MO, which puts out the Creation Research Society Quarterly.

Probably the two most renowned modern Creationist debaters have come out of ICR, the late Dr. Duane Gish and the late Dr. Henry M. Morris. ICR faculty have authored numerous books and made extensive videos. All three named above have websites and Answers in Genesis has an extensive Creationist series of outlines on the Internet. A simple Google or other engine search reveals a number of other websites that can be referenced for Creationism, as well as ID. The Discovery Institute in Washington State is the largest and best known of the Intelligent Design organizations.

The ICR has a creationist museum in Santee, CA (now run by the Life and Light Foundation since ICR's move to TX), but probably the largest in the country is the Creation Museum and Family Research Center near Cincinnati, OH. There is also the 70,000 square foot Creation Museum in Petersburg, KY run by Answers in Genesis. There are numerous other Creationist locations in many states of the U.S., as well as around the world.

Even more importantly, poll after poll shows either the majority of Americans supporting some form of Creationism or ID over Evolution (and often the teaching of both in the public schools), or simply not believing in evolutionary theory. E.g., a 2/11/09 Gallup Poll showed that only 39% of Americans believed in the theory of evolution, with about 25% claiming they do not believe in it, and another 36% expressing no opinion on the subject.[6]

What this translates into is that our school curriculum, within Constitutional boundaries, must stop emphasizing a theory to the exclusion of others that not only is much more hotly disputed in scientific circles than is indicated in the news media, but also is not accepted by the public at large. There is enough public support for a change to prompt responsible action in that direction. It is also almost

---

[6] Frank Newport, "On Darwin's Birthday, Only 4 in 10 Believe in Evolution," February 11, 2009, Gallup Poll, http://www.gallup.com/poll/ 114544/darwin-birthday-believe-evolution.aspx, at p. 1 of 6. [9/25/09.]

inevitable that if the general public were fully informed as to macro's campaign of misinformation, disinformation and outright deceit, these support numbers for full disclosure would be much higher. And this only serves as further motivation to adjust the teaching of scientific theories on origin and related issues to reflect the full knowledge database so that the purely secular purpose of allowing students to reach their own conclusions can be best effectuated.

G. Further Notes on Nomenclature

There are technical distinctions between "hypothesis" and "theory." Under the definition of a hypothesis being "an educated guess based on observation" as opposed to a theory being based on a hypothesis or group of hypotheses confirmed by repeated testing,[7] I would agree that macro is technically closer to a hypothesis than a theory in actual practice, especially since some of macro's historical positions cannot be tested. However, macro is foundationally supported and allegedly "tested" by many flawed evidentiary sources that have been fraudulently used to falsely confirm its hypotheses. Thus, it qualifies in the public domain as a theory and will be referred to here throughout that way. The intent of this book, of course, is to falsify that theory. Macro theory is a fiction, but so is the word "hypothesis" when premised upon fraud.

When I use the word "transitionals," it refers to fossil characteristics that are intended to indicate steps toward eventual transformation from one Scriptural kind to another, which instead of teeming as macro would presuppose, are nonexistent. Finally, it is recognized that macro claims that our modern apes and humans both have common ape-like ancestry rather than man directly descending from an exact ape lineage, such as, e.g., from the gorilla or chimpanzee.

H. The Ultimate Premises

They are:

1. Macro should be working toward perfection but it is not.
2. If there really were a common progenitor, there should be resulting sameness, not diversity.
3. Macro cannot adequately explain predation.

---

[7] Anne Marie Helmenstine, Ph.D., "Scientific Hypothesis, Theory, Law Definitions: Learn the Language of Science," http://chemistry.about.com/od/ chemistry101/a/lawtheory.htm, at p. 1 of 2. [9/13/09.]

4. Macro cannot explain thinking, creativity, and the performing arts.
5. Sexual selection is illogical.
6. Naturalness cannot explain programming.
7. It is a physical impossibility for life without a pre-programmed closed system, which evolution cannot provide.
8. Macro isolates disciplines so that the global picture is unjustly (and deliberately) ignored.
9. It violates the First Amendment of the U.S. Constitution not to teach Intelligent Design principles in our public school system in a manner best calculated to provide the most complete factual basis for students to determine origins and related topics for themselves.
10. The balance of nature between predator and prey and their respective fecundities, as well as between fauna and flora, is demonstrative of design rather than of being an a priori given.
11. The argument that a light-time dilemma for starlight to have reached earth (horizon problem) precludes a young earth is not scientifically established and there are alternative theories that address it that allow for a young earth that must be further considered. The extant "big bang" theory also suffers from the same horizon problem.
12. Haldane's Dilemma, which basically postulates that vertebrate reproduction does not occur at a sufficient rate to accommodate macro, must be thoroughly analyzed in point-counterpoint fashion in any public school science curriculum.
13. Mutations are caused by loss of genetic information which precludes transmutation.
14. Though not the predominant theme of this work, under the law, even religious advancement is allowed in a proper context, and that proper context exists in our present society.
15. The history of written communication suggests a young age for the earth.

I. Acknowledgements

Kudos are owed to many for their contributions to this work. I must start off, however, with acknowledgement of my dear friend, Richard Pittack, B.A., M. DIV, who first alerted me to the dynamics of the controversy between the Creationist and macro camps. Prior to him, I regarded the age of the earth as conventionally touted not all that important of an issue, and he edified me considerably concerning the unscientific assumptions made by the macros in that and other relevant areas of Creationism vs. macro ramifications. He also encouraged me to become active in the polemic of it, and his guidance has been immeasurably helpful, indispensable and inspirational in seeing that through. He himself has authored books in the field, among them The Archaeopteryx Controversy and Was Darwin Wrong? YES, both of those published by Walden's Computer Services. The Archaeopteryx Controversy is also a cited reference in this book. Rich also gave me his invaluable insights and suggestions after reviewing this work for me. Thank you Rich. This book would not even have been possible without you. You'll always be my "go to" guy. Rich's inspiration caused me to do extensive Internet research (in addition to plain old book reading), wherein I found, among other groups, the ICR. I receive their Acts & Facts publications monthly and continue to be impressed with their scholarship and integrity. They make a genuine effort to present both sides of an issue and be fair and even-handed in their presentation. More than any other organization, ICR made me acutely aware of the arguments for a young earth, as have some of their tapes and DVDs. It is organizations like this that help those of faith (here, Christian Creationism) realize that they have a solid scientific foundation for it. I have always found ICR to be very well researched and well argued, even in those situations where I have disagreed with their conclusions.

While I have authored other kinds of written pieces prior, such as co-authorship with Roy L. Schaeffer of the article, "The Case for Zapruder Film Tampering—The Blink Pattern" in the well respected, Assassination Science—Experts Speak Out on the Death of JFK (Catfeet Press), as well as "The Zapruder Film—No to Copyright Protection" for the Assassination Science website, I have never written a book before. This has been a totally unique experience, both in the magnitude of the undertaking, and in the fact that regardless of the kind of writing I had previously undertaken, the editing and getting matters to print parts were always done by somebody else. I simply submitted my relatively short pieces and rode off into the sunset to let them figure out the logistics and who would handle them. We all need help along the way, and that showed me the necessity and value of teamwork.

I am also indebted to Gus Calderon, without whose expertise in computers, this work LITERALLY would have never seen the light of day. Cyberspace would have eaten me alive if not for his irreplaceable assistance in getting this to the publisher. Gus, I couldn't have done this without you guy. Thank you profusely!

CHAPTER ONE

PERVERSION AS PERSUASION

A. THE COPERNICAN PRINCIPLE OF MEDIOCRITY IS NOT EVEN COPERNICAN

Copernicus (1473-1543) himself was a convicted Creationist and did not greet his own heliocentric discovery of the earth and other planets revolving around the sun as a disclaimer of Creation, but rather, as the crowning glory of it. To reduce to mediocrity the earth's status as not being special (even though untrue) and link that to Copernicus as the macros do is itself a deception. Without investigating, one would think that Copernicus sought a relegation of God and espoused that position, whereas quite the opposite is true. In fact, he felt a heliocentric solar system was a logical corollary to the sun being the source of light and life.[8]

There is no Scriptural support for the sun revolving around the earth, the text being silent on the matter. Because the sun was made later in the Creation scenario (4th day) is certainly no ground for such a presumption. That sunlight and starlight serve the earth does not logically allow the leap that celestial bodies providing them revolve around the earth. That religious zealots (who had their own agenda to begin with) proposed such is evidentiary of nothing but predisposed bias and prejudice. That man was made last among the living creatures did not make him subservient to them, as Scripture makes the opposite clear.

---

[8] "Development of the Heliocentric Solar System; Key points: Why Copernicus developed a new theory; whether his approach was a success," http://ircamera.as.arizona.edu/NatSci102/NatSci102/lectures/ Copernicus.htm, at p. 4 of 7. [7/24/09.]

Instead of mediocrity, it could be argued that earth's placement in its own solar system makes it the best host for scientific observation. Astronomer Guillermo Gonzalez and philosopher and theologian Jay W. Richards, co-authors of The Privileged Planet: How Our Place in the Cosmos is Designed for Discovery (Washington, D.C.: Regnery Publishing, Inc., 2004), have compiled a number of scientific facts lending to the inference of design and that our planet's placement was intentionally best calculated for both purposes of sustaining life and for making scientific observations. I have only seen the VCR video (there is also a DVD, of course), but I find the points highly persuasive. Fine-tuning is fully explored, and, with little margin for deviational error, the various forces such as gravity, etc. work in marvelous balance to both allow and sustain life. And the "beyond coincidence" status of the most habitable planet being the same planet in the best position to make scientific observations is quite compelling.

The size and juxtaposition of the moon in relation to the earth and sun so that the earth has just the right tilt and is positioned for a perfect solar eclipse to take place does seem to belie pure chance. That the moon is 1/400th the sun's size but the sun is 400 times further from the earth than the moon to allow such an event, does not seem accidental, either. Besides these factors, there must also be a straight line in space for these aspects to conjoin for an observable eclipse, and there is. The significance is that the total eclipse factor allows for an analysis of the sun's corona so that we can learn its internal composition in a manner unattainable and immeasurable otherwise. And the stars' roles as hot balls of gas are therefore also verifiable. It has also confirmed Einstein's general relativity prediction that light bends due to gravitational pull. The moon's precise size and position, in relation to the sun and its gravitational pull, also allow proper ocean tide management to just the right ocean temperature to sustain complex life (within a very painfully small margin of error). The precise percentage of nitrogen in the air also allows a transparent atmosphere for visible spectrum light and observation.[9] These are just a few of the intricate number of facts raised by the authors.

---

[9] Dr. Ray Bohlin (Fellow of the Discovery Institute's Center for Science and Culture), Probe Ministries, "The Privileged Planet," http://www.probe.org/site/c.fdKEIMNsEoG/b.4218193/ k.5BFC/The_Privileged_Planet.htm, at p. 3 of 7. [7/24/09.]

In a more general sense, Gonzalez and Richards laundry list some of the requirements for a habitable planet to be: (1) Right terrestrial planet; (2) Stabilizing moon; (3) Plate tectonics; (4) Right atmosphere; (5) Right planetary neighbors; (6) Right single star; (7) Right galaxy; (8) Galactic location; (9) Right cosmic time, and (10) Universe fine-tuned for life. The book fills in the vitals for all of these requirements, as to an extent, so does the video.[10]

As one might expect from the macros, the book was not received with universal warmth. Victor Stenger wrote a brief film review and concluded: "Of course, Gonzalez and Richards are entitled to their views, but this tale provides yet another illustration of the stealthy nature of the strategy behind the Discovery campaign to 'renew science and culture.' The Privileged Planet represents a new, cosmic wedge in the Discovery arsenal. (Why can't one have an arsenal of wedges?) It joins with Intelligent Design as another form of stealth creationism, claiming to be science but motivated by religion. We can only wonder why a group of people who claim a special pipeline to the source of truth and morality feel they can't be honest with the rest of us." (Emphasis added.) Talk about the pot calling the kettle black! (author of The Comprehensible Cosmos: Where Do the Laws of Physics Come from?)[11]

Stenger's remarks are professionally irresponsible. Assuming for the sake of argument only a purely religious motivation (I see a much more scientific than religious one), since when is motivation by religion condemnatory, and why would that connote intellectual dishonesty? Stenger's bias is clearly shown by his remark, "We can only wonder why a group of people who claim a special pipeline ..." Just where is it that a "special pipeline" is being claimed by the authors? Observations made and reported on by sweat equity hardly qualify as a "special pipeline," just a richly deserved perspective acquired by diligent and thoughtful scientific exploration. All researchers should demand of themselves that kind of "special pipeline."

Instead, what is clear is that as long as the empirical facts are reported honestly and accurately, and the conclusions follow logically from properly framed premises, it matters not what the motivation is. As

---
10 [The Privileged Planet, supra, cited by Reasons to Believe's 2003 Conference, Session 6 (Internet, no URL given).]
11 Victor J. Stenger, "Reality Check, The Privileged Planet," Committee for Skeptical Inquiry, http://www.csicop.org/sb/2005-09/reality-check.html, at p. 3 of 3. [7/24/09.]

will be shown, macro is backdoor atheism, and the motivation is to promote that Godless philosophy. Does that predisposition by itself disqualify macro from presenting the facts and the logical inferences to be drawn from them? Argumentatively speaking, certainly not (though in practice, they fail to deliver on that item). Logical fallacies are covered later, but the specific fallacies involved with that logic are "Guilt by Association" and "Genetic Fallacy." But the point is that an atheistic attitude going in should not be argumentatively considered a solider foundation than a theistic one (the religious implications for Constitutional purposes being displaced for now).

The <u>Privileged Planet</u> film was much more favorably received by Ray Bohlin of Probe Ministries, who is not a macro.[12] Based upon his viewing at the Smithsonian Institute, and after describing many of the facts presented by the video, he wrote: "The film does an excellent job of taking sometimes complex scientific concepts and communicating them in a way that most anybody can appreciate. This film deserves as wide a distribution as possible. [New Para.] But because much of the scientific community remains locked in a purely naturalistic worldview, the perspective of purpose and design will continue to be resisted. <u>However, parents and educators can readily use this excellent resource to simply investigate the facts and help to eventually gain Intelligent Design a much deserved place at the roundtable of scientific inquiry.</u>"[13] (Emphasis added.) Bohlin reiterates the message propounded here—"investigate the facts," and don't presuppose the results.

Some mention should be made of Bohlin's credentials. While he is President of Probe Ministries and a Research Fellow in 1997-1998 and 2000 of the Discovery Institute's Center for the Renewal of Science and Culture (the world's largest ID institute), his doctorate is not in divinity, but in molecular biology, and he also has an M.S. in population genetics, and B.S. in zoology. In sum, he is a well-rounded scholar. It is another of the great myths perpetrated by the macros that all modern creation scientists are second-rate scientists with dubious credentials from dubious institutions of learning. The evidence reveals the contrary.

---

12 Bohlin, Ray, "<u>The Privileged Planet</u>: An Unwanted Premiere!," http://www.probe.org/site/ c.fdKEIMNsEOG/ b.4218193/k.5BFC/The_Privileged_Planet.htm. [7/24/09.]
13 Id., at p. 5 of 7

In fact, it would be difficult to attack the credentials of especially two of the noted commentators on The Privileged Planet dust jacket, Simon Conway Morris and Owen Gingerich. Morris is a Professor of Evolutionary Palaeobiology in the Department of Earth Sciences at the University of Cambridge and is the author of Life's Solution: Inevitable Humans in a Lonely Universe. Gingerich is a retired Research Professor of Astronomy and of the History of Science at Harvard University, as well as a senior astronomer emeritus at the Smithsonian Astrophysical Observatory, and author of The Book Nobody Read: Chasing the Revolutions of Nicolas Copernicus. Both are properly regarded as Theistic evolutionists (which I feel is an incompatibility. Morris even identifies himself as a Christian—but that is the beauty of this controversy, that learned scholars can come from different philosophical and etiological backgrounds and argue different implications from the same facts). If taught uncompromisingly in terms of the facts, without a pre-disposed slant, there is no telling in what direction the students' minds might individually and aggregately go. It is indeed difficult to find two universities any more reputable than Cambridge and Harvard. This is by no means suggesting that these facilities alone hold the keys to learning to the exclusion of other very fine institutions. It is simply saying that these universities have indisputably established reputations as academic bastions.

Morris poses these questions on the book jacket: "Is our universe a blind concatenation of atoms, evolution a random walk across a meaningless landscape, and our sense of purpose a pathetic shield against a supremely indifferent world? Or does the universe and our place within it click, repeatedly? These starkly different views open up immense metaphysical and theological questions, and at least part of the answer must come from science and the unfolding triumphs of cosmology, astronomy, and evolution. [New Para.] In a book of magnificent sweep and daring Guillermo Gonzalez and Jay Richards drive home the arguments that the old cliché of no place like home is eerily true of Earth. Not only that, but if the scientific method was to emerge anywhere, the Earth is about as suitable as you can get. Gonzalez and Richards have flung down the gauntlet. Let the debate begin; it is a question that involves us all." (Emphasis added.)

Indeed, this is a question of origins, which it will be demonstrated is very allowable as a classroom inquiry per the U.S. Supreme Court case of Edwards v. Aguillard (1987) 482 U.S. 578. While construable on one level as a theological question (as Aguillard well points out), it is also a highly secular one, in that the student is entitled to know the scientific data and theories addressing the issue. That the twain does meet in that limited sense does not disqualify the enterprise. I agree with Morris; let the debate begin (his statement), using the public schools as a forum in a carefully presented scientific curriculum showing no allegiance to any "religion" (theism or atheism, or anything in between—my statement).

Says Gingerich of Privileged Planet: "This thoughtful, delightfully contrarian book will rile up those who believe the Copernican principle is an essential philosophical component of modern science. Is our universe designedly congenial to intelligent, observing life: Passionate advocates of the search for extraterrestrial intelligence (SETI) will find much to ponder in this carefully documented analysis."

For now, suffice it to say that macros should not be labeling a principle around a scientist who did not apply his discovery in the same manner that they do, and who felt that that reality was well reconcilable with his Christian faith. Considering the factors making the earth the most prominent place for observation in the solar system and the only body within it capable of sustaining complex life, its not being in the physical center of the solar system is totally irrelevant, either secularly or Scripturally. It is man's traditional (and probably vain) notion that assumed the sun and planets rotated around the earth (geocentrically) as opposed to the actual heliocentric truth. As noted, Scripture in no way either expressly states that or even implies it. As always, the traditions of men often interfere with an accurate assessment of Scriptural truth. That was Christ's point with the Scribes and Pharisees, and it is as true today as well as at numerous periods in historical progression as it was at that time.[14]

There are two other historical points to mention concerning Privileged Planet, each having alarming ramifications. Despite the laudatory comments above by Morris and Gingerich, as well as others, there

---

14 Matthew 23:2-33, but esp. 2-9 in this context (Scribes and Pharisees); see also, Colossians 2:8 (human traditions) & Matthew 15:1-9 (tradition of elders) (Revised Standard Version).

is substantial evidence for Gonzalez not getting his tenure at Iowa State University because of that very work (showing discriminatory bias and prejudice in the alleged "academic" community), and also that the Smithsonian has a scientific mission precluding any evidence of Intelligent Design. Bohlin's article gets into the latter. I have seen a website describing Gonzalez's hatchet job as Scientific McCarthyism. It is difficult to quarrel with this assessment. According to the website, Gonzalez has written about 70 peer-reviewed articles, and his research has led to the discovery of two new planets.[15] Both of these websites are by the Discovery Institute, the most influential ID organization out there, but it is hard to dispute the argumentation. The contrarian position is also footnoted below.[16] Besides the glowing reviews by Morris and Gingerich, Gonzalez's additional credentials hardly portray a man devoid of scientific acumen. It does portray a man, however, in the midst of a vicious power play and "scientific" culture that not only censors contrarian literature, but also those who write it. As will be seen, this would have upset Jefferson, Madison and probably Hamilton very greatly.

Highly respected scientists in their fields consider origins and presentations like Privileged Planet worthy of academic discussion. So do I. As the Aguillard treatment will point out, a discourse on origins can address a highly secular purpose and be a valid curriculum in the public school system. That the points raised in Privileged Planet address origins is also stated in its dust jacket by Henry F. Schaefer III, Graham Perdue Professor of Chemistry, Director, Center for Computational Quantum Chemistry, University of Georgia, Five-Time Nobel Prize Nominee: "This new book is an excellent and timely contribution to the broadening and increasingly important discussion of origins."

This kind of macro behavior should not be historically surprising. In an act of academic cannibalism, they think nothing of turning on even their own kind when they sense betrayal, which in this case can merely mean departure from the macro dogma (regardless of soundness of reasoning or degree of departure). One such victim is Dean Kenyon, Professor Emeritus at San Francisco State University. As will be seen

---

15 Uncommon Descent: Serving the Intelligent Design Community, http://www.uncommondescent.com/intelligent-design/habitable-zone-astronomer-guillermo-... [7/27/09.] See also http://www.evolutionnews // www.evolutionnewsorg/gg-bckgrndr.final.pdf. [7/27/09.]
16 see www.expelledexposed.com/index.php/the-truth/crocker. [7/27/09.]

below, to a lesser extent, the same happened to de Perthes and J.D. Whitney (the latter of Mount Whitney, CA fame). As for Kenyon, he and co-author Gary Steinman were the toast of the macro town for their work <u>Biochemical Predestination</u>, McGraw Hill text (January, 1969), which championed natural chemical evolutionary origins. But in 1976, Kenyon had a change of heart after being given a book by one of his students authored by A.E. Wilder-Smith called <u>The Creation of Life: A Cybernetic Approach to Evolution</u>, which featured objections to <u>Biochemical Predestination</u> that Kenyon felt he could not satisfactorily address. Based on this and his reading of some other works, he eventually became a Creationist and Intelligent Design advocate.

After the <u>Aguillard</u> decision, he and co-author Percival Davis changed language in their book <u>Of Pandas and People: The Central Question of Biological Origins</u>, Foundation for Thought and Ethics; 2d ed. (Sept., 1993), converting references to Creationism into Intelligent Design, marking for many the birth of the modern ID movement. Kenyon became a macro pariah after that, but to his credit, has stuck to his guns. Of course, he had taught evolutionary biology for 16 years prior to his conversion, and unlike Gonzalez, was already tenured. He is illustrative of major macro figures who, when presented with the evidence and receiving it with an open mind, have found that <u>intellectual honesty</u> compelled a conversion of allegiance. Sir Antony Flew, e.g. (treated below), has gone from an atheistic legend to a Deistic direction. While there have been converts the other way (much fewer in number), it is submitted that they had much less conviction to begin with than men such as Kenyon and Flew, who were highly committed until contrary evidence caused them to re-evaluate and adjust their positions accordingly.

B. ARCHAEOPTERYX IS NOT A TRANSITIONAL FOSSIL AND IS DECIDEDLY A BIRD

Perhaps the most fascinating and controversial fossil finds to date revolve around how to treat that specimen known as Archaeopteryx. Archaeopteryx has been vigorously debated as to whether it is a full-fledged bird or reptile-bird transitional form (which is the macro position). It consists of 7 finds at the following dates and locations based on its ultimate recognition of being an Archaeopteryx fossil, with one unfortunately lost to posterity: (1) <u>1861</u>-Germany-the London specimen; (2) <u>1877</u>-Germany-the Berlin specimen; (3) <u>1951</u>-was either a new genus or a juvenile; (4) <u>1958</u>-Germany-this is the one that was lost-when its discoverer, Eduard Opitsch, died in 1992 and the fossil thereafter disappeared; (5) <u>1960s</u>—near Eichstatt, Germany; (6) 1970-at Teyler Museum in Haarlem, Netherlands by John Ostrom where the fossil, initially discovered in 1855, had been mislabeled as a pterosaur; and (7) <u>April, 1993</u>-significant in that a specimen was found with a full sternum, substantiating that it could fly like virtually any modern bird.[17]

The following factors distinguish it as a bird: (1) primary feathers—nothing primitive; (2) all its teeth lack serrations; (3) 2 jaw bones (reptiles' jaws are single-boned); (4) a furcula (wishbone); (5) long external nostrils; (6) perching feet; (7) shallow breast bone (like a hoatzin, which is definitely a bird); (8) wings, and (9) the tailbone (while long) has feathers similar to swans.[18]

While Archaeopteryx did have claws, so do the modern hoatzin of South America and touraco of Africa have claws on their wings when they are young. The modern mature ostrich also has three claws on its wings. As for having teeth per se, there not only were earlier, ancient birds with teeth, but also "every subclass of vertebrates has some with teeth and some without."[19] Thus, that no modern birds have teeth is inconsequential.

Nor is Archaeopteryx necessarily in the proper stratigraphic fossil order to be the progenitor ancestral bird as macros often exhort. There are indications of birds being found in <u>lower</u> stratigraphic layers than Archaeopteryx. The apparent first indication was a false alarm. In 1977, Brigham Young University geologist James A. Jensen purportedly found a bird fossil in the Dry Mesa quarry in Western Colorado in the Lower Jurassic strata that preceded Archaeopteryx by some 60 million years.[20] This Jensen reported in 1981. By 1989, though, Jensen and

---

17 Richard B. Pittack, <u>The Archaeopteryx Controversy</u> (2007), Walden Computer Services, ISBN 978-0-6151-8232-3, pp. 116&117.
18 Id., at p. 114.
19 Luther Sutherland, <u>Darwin's Enigma</u>, p. 75, quoted by <u>Archaeopteryx Controversy</u>, id., at p. 104.
20 Id., at p. 108.

co-author Kevin Padian re-identified this specimen as the theropod Deinonychus.[21]

However, in 1983, Sankar Chatterjee and two of his Texas Tech University co-workers found a fossil consisting of a group of delicate white bones with small bumps (connoting feather insertions) and a single hole in the skull, all indicating a bird antecedent to Archaeopteryx by 75 million years which they called Protoavis (primordial bird), early enough to co-exist with the dinosaurs themselves (whom macros like to say morphed into birds).[22] Unlike Jensen with his discovery, Chatterjee has held fast to his assertion of earlier birds than Archaeopteryx. In his book, The Rise of Birds: 225 Million Years of Evolution (1997) The Johns Hopkins University Press, Baltimore, Chatterjee continues to assert the legitimacy of his Protoavis discovery and its preceding Archaeopteryx by about 75 million years, despite Archaeopteryx being a more primitive bird than Protoavis is. From the purely Archaeopteryx perspective, it's hard to co-exist with and descend from alleged ancestors at the same time. Even David Copperfield would be "handcuffed" trying to escape from that conundrum.

It must be mentioned that Chatterjee himself still believes in a dinosaur-to-bird evolution, that coming from earlier protoavian dinosaurs, the most likely transition being from theropod to coelurosaur to miniraptor to bird, though he theorizes this from a cladogram rather than showing direct empirical evidence, which is still lacking.[23] He considers Archaeopteryx itself to be a "living fossil" of the late Jurassic; as Covey phrases it, "an evolutionary side branch, a dead-end with no descendants."[24] Thus, dinosaur to bird is a controversy among scientists that is still going on, and it is highly significant that the integrity of Archaeopteryx as a transitional fossil is, at best, very much "up in the air" (with the better view being it is completely grounded), as is any lineage attempting to link dinosaur to bird, regardless of its singular source, be it Chatterjee or anyone else. It is interesting how many macros do not understand how controversial Archaeopteryx really is,

---

21 J. A. Jensen and K. Padian, "Small pterosaurs and dinosaurs from the Uncompahgre fauna," (1989), Journal of Paleontology, 63:372, cited by "Archaeopteryx: Answering the Challenge of the Fossil Record," The TalkOrigins Archive, http:www.talkorigins.org/faqs/archaeopteryx/challenge/html., at p. 11&12 of 14. [10/12/09.]
22 The Archaeopteryx Controversy, supra, at p. 50.
23 Jon Covey, "The Rise of Birds," B.A., MT (ASCP), edited by Anita K. Millen, M.D., M.P.H., M.A., South Bay Creation Science Association, http://www.creationinthecrossfire.com/Articles/ The%20Rise%20of%20Birds.html, at p. 2 of 3. [10/12/09.]
24 Id., at p. 1.

as will be illustrated with Kathleen Hunt and her article on transitional fossils from the TalkOrigins website further below.

A prominent point needs to be made. It is submitted that if intermediaries indeed existed, with the millions of fossils that have been uncovered even since Darwin's day, lithology would be TEEMING with their examples. Creationists have been arguing that for years, and I agree with them. There should not be isolated cases of such fossils in the stratigraphic record but rather, a plethora of them. It is because of this acknowledged lack that noted macros Stephen Jay Gould and Niles Eldredge came up with "punctuated equilibrium" to try to account for this void.

Likewise, Archaeopteryx is to be considered, at most, a fascinating mosaic, which by itself does not amount to macro. The duck-billed platypus (qualities of both mammal and reptile) and the gnu or wildebeest (qualities of both ox and horse) are both mosaics, but there is no serious contention made by macros as to their "missing link" qualities or general progenitorship. There is nothing preceding Archaeopteryx that precurses any of its qualities or any subsequent transitionals that more closely approximate pure birds. It stands complete and by itself.

The true bottom line to all of this is that there is a consensus among leading macros and certainly leading ornithological authorities both past and present that there is substantial evidence for Archaeopteryx being a bird and not a transitional.

C. HAECKEL'S FRAUDULENT EMBRYONIC WOOD CARVINGS AND DRAWINGS ARE STILL IN PUBLIC SCHOOL TEXTBOOKS TODAY

Anatomist Ernst Haeckel (1834-1919) was, in his time (unjustifiably), the world's most influential macro theorist. Unjustifiably because he would think nothing of taking severe dramatic (and also in his case, artistic) license to manipulate others into accepting macro theory through fraudulent drawings that he even admitted were such in 1909. He was a professor in Jena, Germany, a prestigious university town that also housed renowned polymaths like Schiller, Goethe and Hegel. He strongly advocated racist eugenics, undoubtedly influencing Hitler and other luminaries of his ilk. He is most famous for his "law of biogenics (or biogenetics)" introduced in 1866, wherein came the expression "ontogeny [development of an individual from a fertilized ovum to maturity] recapitulates [repeats] phylogeny [the development over time of a species, genus, or group]." It is the biological equivalent of, "Past is prologue."

Translated, the theory holds that the various embryonic stages of the human embryo mimic its macro development from the past; herein, from fish to chicken to dog to man. <u>Therefore, our historical macro pattern is traceable by observing the various maturing patterns of the embryo</u>. The various forms allegedly resemble a "Chicken Sac" (really our first blood-making organ, which is initially necessary because we start off without bones, which subsequently manufacture our blood, so that we first need blood made by this sac-like organ to eventually make the bones that take over as the source to make the blood), "Lizard Tail," (really an important spinal part, and produced by the fact that at conception, the spine is actually longer than the body) and "Fish Gills or Slits" (really just the folds for our middle ear, parathyroids, and thymus, which do not even remotely function like fish gills or slits).

True recapitulation of development of our heart chambers consistent with development from lower life forms would be a straight-line sequence of one to two to three to four chambers, when in reality, it is from two to one to four.[25]

Even hardened macro Stephen J. Gould repeatedly acknowledged the fraudulent aspect of the Haeckel drawings: "Those phony embryos were recently discovered persisting in textbooks, and creationists have blustered about finding Haeckel's skeleton in the closet of evolution ever since. See, for example, M.K. Richardson et al., "Haeckel, Embryos, and Evolution," <u>Science</u> 280:983-985 (1998). Haeckel's dogma of recapitulation had lost its luster on any terms by 1910 or so, when it became 'unfashionable in practice, following the rise of experimental embryology, and untenable in theory, following scientific change in a related field (Mendelian genetics).' Stephen Jay Gould, <u>Ontogeny and Phylogeny</u> (Cambridge: Belknap Press, 1977), p. 77."[26]

---

[25] <u>Pathlights</u>, http://www.pathlights.com/ ce_encyclopedia/Encyclopedia/17rec01.htm, pp. 1-4. [7/3/09.]
[26] Stephen Jay Gould, "This View of Life," <u>Natural History</u>, March 2000, cited by David Brody in "Ernst Haeckel and the Microbial Baroque," <u>Cabinet Magazine</u>, Issue 7 Summer 2002 FAILURE, at p. 6 of 9. http://www.cabinetmagazine.org/issues/7/ernsthaeckel.php. [7/3/09.]

Other macros have also noted: "The core scientific issue remains unchanged: Haeckel's drawings in 1874 are substantially fabricated. In support of his view, I note that his oldest 'fish' image is made up of bits and pieces from different animals-some of them mythical. It is not unreasonable to characterize this as "faking".... Sadly, it is the discredited 1874 drawings that are used in so many British and American textbooks today."[27] (Emphasis added.) The two-row chart appearing on page 3 of 4 from this last footnoted angelfire reference is particularly probing in that the top row shows how Haeckel drew the embryos for the fish, salamander, turtle, chicken, rabbit and human, respectively. The bottom row has pictures of the actual embryos for each, and they stand in STARK CONTRAST.

Also, at p. 3 of 4, Angelfire very effectively quotes from another macro as to why such a fatally defective viewpoint was nonetheless perpetuated long after it was first strongly suspected and then KNOWN TO BE FRAUDULENT: "In seeking to understand why the Haeckelian view persisted so long, we have also to consider the alternatives. We often are highly conservative and will hold to a viewpoint longer than is justified when there is no alternative or, worse, when the logical alternative upsets the rest of our world view."[28] (Emphasis added.) That alternative, of course, is at least a Deistic if not Theistic or Christian God whose very specter terrifies the macros down to the core. Further, it is outright cowardice and fraud to lie about the status of sources because the advocate has nothing to currently draw on.

But it is submitted that this is so typical of macro behavior. As will be seen, it is also antithetical to the search for truth that hallmarked the writings of Jefferson and Madison both generally speaking and as to education specifically. This is ADMITTED SUPPRESSION AND MISREPRESENTATION and should be responded to accordingly. Yet, as will be also revealed, the same behavior is performed by the macros generically to this very day. E.g., there is no complete stratigraphic column in existence today or ever has been, but that is usually not even mentioned. Skeletal fragments from even thousands of miles from one another may be used to articulate a specimen and

---

27 Macro Mik Richardson's letter to Science (5381); 1289 Aug. 28, 1998 titled "Haeckel's Embryos, continued"; "Haeckel's Lie: Ontogeny Recapitulates Phylogeny," http://www.angelfire.com/ mi/dinosaurs/ontogeny.html, p. 4 of 4. [7/3/09.]
28 Keith Stewart Thomson, "Marginalia Ontogeny and phylogeny recapitulated," American Scientist Vol. 76, May-June 1988, p. 274.

is complete guesswork, yet is passed off as conclusive evidence of their position.

Skeletal remains of humans are suppressed because their suspected ages don't square with the hypothetical time line macros want the public to swallow hook, line and sinker to convince us that man and dinosaur or even other fauna that wouldn't fit in their macro progression did not coexist. As will be further seen, horse fossils are suppressed when inconsistent with the projected, hypothetical story posited by the macros. Fossils are frequently found out of sequence of lithological order but the most preposterous theories are "conveniently" presented in attempts to explain it away.

There is a definite hyprocrisy when noted macros like the late Gould decry phonies like Haeckel (which, on its superficial face, is commendable) yet fully approve and often suppress tactics that are known to be based on world view rather than empirical evidence. If Haeckel were alive today, he could rightly say, "Talk about the pot calling the kettle black!" Hmm, that's my second use of that phrase already!

Gould and Richardson are not alone in Haeckel's condemnation. Ian Quigley writes: "There are a number of flaws with Haeckel's theory. For example, Haeckel confused a fish embryo with a young human one. Haeckel's drawings strongly suggest that a variety of vertebrates share a common developmental phase, but he does not account for the entire process of development, nor does he compensate for size differences. His drawings were grossly oversimplified and ignored or obfuscated many salient differences. This did not stop Haeckel's law from being widely accepted for the majority of the twentieth century. Many otherwise up-to-date textbooks, such as Molecular Biology of the Cell, written by Nobel laureate James Watson and National Academy of Sciences President Bruce Alberts, continue to cite Haeckel."[29] (Emphasis added.) It seems especially tragic and deceitful that men of the caliber underscored would either deliberately or be so badly out of the loop as to continue to print such a travesty. Insightfully, however, it is not atypical behavior for proponents of a fiction to not always be in synch in perpetuating it.

---

29 Quigley, Ian, "Haeckel's Law of Recapitulation," Animal Sciences/2002, appearing at http://www.Encyclopedia.com/doc/1G2-3400500182.html, at p. 2 of 6. [7/3/09.]

Quigley continues: "Despite mainstream acceptance of Haeckel's ideas, gastraea [author's note: this was Haeckel's label for an organism he postulated existed that resembled gastrula cells that develop soon after fertilization and was thus the ancestor of all vertebrates] do not exist. Nor does evolution advance by adding traits to developing embryos. While there are definite similarities among developing vertebrates, Haeckel's famous utterance can be safely dismissed. <u>Despite the acceptance he found elsewhere, scientists in Haeckel's native Germany considered his findings suspect. He was accused of academic fraud and pled guilty, claiming that many of his drawings were reproduced from memory</u>. When comparing photographs of actual embryos to the drawings, however, one could conclude that Haeckel remembered only one embryo and claimed that all vertebrates looked just like it. As Michael Richardson said, 'These are fakes. In the paper, we call them 'misleading and inaccurate,' but that is just polite scientific language.' (Times London, August 11, 1997)."[30] (Emphasis added.)

Eugene R. Worth, MD, has also commented: "Ernst Haeckel propounded the theory of embryonic recapitulation in 1866. His conclusion ... was "Ontogeny recapitulates phylogeny." <u>However, Haeckl lacked evidence supporting his views so he fraudulently changed some of the drawings of other scientists in order to increase the resemblance between species and to hide dissimilarities</u>. Haeckel's deception was exposed by one of his peers (Wilhelm His, Sr.) <u>in 1874</u>, and <u>Haeckel himself admitted such in 1909</u>.[31] (Emphasis added.)

Just to show the depths of the coverup behind Haeckel's fraudulent recapitulation theory, despite its exposure by His, Sr. 21 years earlier and by others, he was made the namesake of a mountain as part of the Evolution Group <u>in 1895</u> by Theodore Solomons. A professor of mathematics at Stanford, Solomons was plotting a route from Yosemite to Mt. Whitney (now part of the John Muir Trail) and decided to honor macro "greats" by naming peaks after them en route. These peaks were also named by E.C. Bonner of the U.S. Geological Survey. Besides <u>Mt. Haeckel</u>, also named were Mt. Darwin, Mt. Spencer (Herbert Spencer [1820-1903], who coined "survival of

---

30   Id., at p. 3 of 6.
31   Pennisi, E., "Haeckel's embryos: fraud rediscovered," Science 1997; cited by Eugene R. Worth, MD, Med, Department of Anesthiosology and Perioperative Medicine, Health Sciences Center, University of Missouri-Columbia Hospital and Clinics, Columbia, MO, Letters to the Editor, "Haeckel's Recapitulation Theory Should Not be Used as a Defense of the ASA Difficult Airway Algorithm," http://www.anesthesia-analgesia.org/cgi/content/full/98/4/1192, at p. 1 of 3.

the fittest" and is considered the father of Social Darwinism), Mt. Wallace, Mt. Fiske (John (James) Fiske [1842-1901], who is credited with founding "Theistic evolution," though in some ways that honor could also go to Wallace or perhaps Asa Gray as discussed below), Mt. Lamarck and Mt. Mendel (more will be made of this later).[32] It is small wonder that textbooks are infiltrated with the "recapitulation" lie when formal public recognitions like this are made. While Solomons and Bonner are understandably faultless, why was no name change forthcoming after Haeckel's own confession in 1909 and certainly after the recognition of the fraud by the legendary Gould and others of more recent vintage?!

D. THE APOSTLE PAUL DID NOT TEACH THAT FAITH ALONE EQUALS SALVATION, NOR DOES THE NEW TESTAMENT

Macros butcher the Bible as well. Instead, what Paul taught was that <u>good works alone, without faith,</u> fall short of salvation. As stated in Romans 10, 2-4 (all references herein are to the Revised Standard Version): "I bear them witness that they have a zeal for God, but it is not enlightened. For, being ignorant of the righteousness that comes from God, <u>and seeking to establish their own</u>, they did not submit to God's righteousness. For God is the end of the law, that every one who has faith may be justified." (Emphasis added). Good works for the sake of self-aggrandizement and laudation is what is being targeted, not lack of good works. Doing the prescribed right things for the wrong reasons simply doesn't cut it. God sees through that. That is why Paul asserted at Romans 9:30-32: "What shall we say, then? That Gentiles who did not pursue righteousness have attained it, that is, righteousness through faith; but that Israel who pursued the righteousness which is based on law did not succeed in fulfilling the law. Why? <u>Because they did not pursue it through faith, but as if it were based on works.</u>" (Emphasis added.) Otherwise put, "…None is righteous, no, not one; no one understands, no one seeks for God. All have turned aside, together they have gone wrong; no one does good, not even one." [Romans 3:10-12.]

But we are also judged by our works, make no mistake about it. An ivory tower pedantic simply espousing faith has no hope. At Romans

---

32 http://www.summitpost.org/area/range/183633/evolution-group.html, pp. 1-6.

2:6-11, it is said: "For he will render to every man <u>according to his works</u>; to those who have <u>by patience in well-doing</u> seek for glory and honor and immortality, he will give eternal life; but for those who are factious and do not obey the truth, but obey wickedness, there will be wrath and fury. There will be tribulation and distress for every human being who does evil, the Jew first and also the Greek, but glory and honor and peace for every one who does good, the Jew first and also the Greek. For God shows no partiality." (Emphasis added). Clear enough? The law must still be followed.

At Romans 3:31, it is written: "<u>Do we thus overthrow the law by this faith? By no means! On the contrary, we uphold the law.</u>" (Emphasis added.) At Romans 6:1,2, we find: "What shall we say then? Are we to continue in sin that grace may abound? By no means! How can we who died to sin still live in it?" At Romans 6:15, Paul states: "What then? Are we to sin because we are not under law but under grace? By no means!" The law is not removed through faith, it is simply that man is not worthy enough by his own merits to enter heaven. No amount of good works makes him worthy of entry without the grace of God. Otherwise, as Paul points out at Galatians 2:21: "I do not nullify the grace of God; for if justification were through the law, then Christ died to no purpose."

At Galatians 5:19-21, Paul admonishes: "Now the works of the flesh are plain: immorality, impurity, licentiousness, idolatry, sorcery, enmity, jealousy, anger, selfishness, dissension, party spirit, envy, drunkenness, carousing, and the like. I warn you, as I warned you before, that those who do such things shall not inherit the kingdom of God." Why would this be said if faith were the only barometer? At Galatians 9:9,10, Paul adds: "And let us not grow weary in well-doing, for in due season we shall reap, if we do not lose heart. So then, as we have opportunity, <u>let us do good to all men</u>, and especially to those who are of the household of faith." (Emphasis added). In 2 Thessalonians 2:10-13, Paul counsels: "For even when we were with you, we gave you this command: <u>If any one will not work, let him not eat. For we hear that some of you are living in idleness, mere busy-bodies, not doing any work</u>. Now such persons we command and exhort in the name of Lord Jesus Christ to do their work in quietness and to earn their own living. <u>Brethren, do not be weary in well-doing.</u>" (Emphasis added.)

Put another way, "For we are his workmanship, <u>created in Christ Jesus for good works</u>, which God prepared beforehand, that we should walk in them." [Ephesians 2:10.] (Emphasis added.)

Thus, it is through faith plus good works (through which faith is effectively and meaningfully expressed) that are to be fulfilled by men of faith to glorify God, rather than themselves, that salvation is achieved. So is faith alone enough to do the trick and does that serve as a rubberstamp for otherwise proscribed wrongdoing?—not a chance! Though not a letter from Paul, New Testament scripture drives this point home at James, 2:17-26: "<u>So faith by itself is dead</u>. But some one will say, 'You have faith and I have works.' Show me your faith apart from your works, and I by my works will show you my faith. … <u>Do you want to be shown, you foolish fellow, that faith apart from works is barren</u>? Was not Abraham our father justified by his works, when he offered his son Isaac upon the altar? <u>You see that faith was active along with his works,</u> and the scripture was fulfilled which says, 'Abraham believed God, and it was reckoned to him as righteousness'; and he was called the friend of God. <u>You see that a man is justified by works and not by faith alone.</u> … For as the body apart from the spirit is dead, so <u>faith apart from works is dead</u>." (Emphasis added.)

But what of men who use force to punish those not religiously correct toward God? This is also forbidden. At Romans 12:14-21, Paul states: "<u>Bless those who persecute you; bless and do not curse them</u>. Rejoice with those who rejoice, weep with those who weep. Live in harmony with one another, do not be haughty, but associate with the lowly; never be conceited. Repay no one evil for evil, but take thought for what is noble in the sight of all. If possible, so far as it depends upon you, live peaceably with all. <u>Beloved, never avenge yourselves, but leave it to the wrath of God</u>; for it is written, 'Vengeance is mine, I will repay, says the Lord.' No, 'if your enemy is hungry, feed him; if he is thirsty, give him drink; for by so doing you will heap burning coals upon his head.' <u>Do not be overcome by evil, but overcome evil with good.</u>" (Emphasis added).

At 1 Corinthians 13:1-2, Paul proclaimed: "If I speak in the tongues of men and of angels, but have not love, I am a noisy gong or a clanging cymbal. And if I have prophetic powers, and understand all mysteries and all knowledge, and if I have all faith, so as to remove mountains, but have not love, I have nothing." At 1 Corinthians 13, 13, he said: "So faith, hope, love abide, these three; but the greatest of these is love." Why the enduring with these three qualities if there is rubber-stamp authority to kill? [2 Corinthians 6:3-10]. In his letter to Titus at Chapter 2, verses 7 & 8, Paul instructed: "Show yourself in all respects a <u>model of good deeds</u>, and in your teaching show integrity, gravity, and sound speech that cannot be censured, so that an opponent may be put to shame, having nothing evil to say of us." Elsewhere, he also advises: "Let no evil talk come out of your mouths, but only such as is good for edifying, as fits the occasion, that it may impart grace to those who hear." [Ephesians 3:29.]

In sum, even under Paulian and other New Testament philosophy, those who disagree with Christianity are not to be slaughtered but to be tolerated, to be rebuked gently by example. Faith calls for earnest fulfillment of the law, not rebellion or disobedience. <u>If one does not follow the law, he does not have faith, for one with faith does not commit the very wrongs his heavenly Father advises against</u>. There is no place in heaven for those who violate God's commandments, regardless of the veneer through which the transgressions are committed. Vengeance is the Lord's, not man's. Applied, the mass slaughters throughout recorded history (as acknowledged below) may have been hypocritically done under the banner of the Lord's name, but not under His authority, nor under any reasonable reading of the Apostle Paul, nor anywhere else in the New Testament and attributed to him.

Macros have a beef all right, but with phonies under the guise of allegiance with God, flawed human beings, not God Himself. They cannot properly gain an argumentative advantage with deliberate misrepresentation of Christian doctrine. Yet they do it all the time to try to show the alleged irrelevance of Scripture.

E. AN ADVERSE REACTION TO RELIGIOUS ATROCITIES AND EXTREMISM IS NOT PROOF OF A CONTRARY THEORY

History is replete with atrocities committed by religious organizations, be they Catholic, Protestant, Mohammedan, etc., under the alleged banner of religion. The Founding Fathers were well aware of that, and <u>Christianity was not exempt from their retrospection and condemnation</u>, as Madison wrote: "During almost fifteen centuries has the legal establishment of Christianity been on trial. What have been its fruits? <u>More or less in all places, pride and indolence in the Church, ignorance and servility in the laity, in both, superstition, bigotry and persecution.</u>"[33] (Emphasis added.)

The church generally, throughout history, was a considerable source of wealth and land-holding power. Once again, Madison admonishes against it in his Detached Memoranda, and includes a caveat against <u>all corporations (ecclesiastical and secular)</u> re an over-accumulation of property and therefore power: "But besides the danger of a direct mixture of Religion and civil Government, <u>there is an evil which to be guarded agst [against] in the indefinite accumulation of property from the capacity of holding it in perpetuity by ecclesiastical corporations</u>. The power of <u>all</u> corporations, ought to be limited in this respect. <u>The growing wealth accumulated by them never fails to be a source of abuses</u>. [Author's note: again, this includes SECULAR.] A warning on this subject is emphatically given in the example of the various Charitable establishments in G.B. [Great Britain] the management of which has been lately scrutinized. The excessive wealth of ecclesiastical Corporations and the misuse of it in many Countries of Europe has Long been a topic of complaint. <u>In some of them the Church has amassed half perhaps the property of the nation</u>. When the reformation took place, an event promoted if not caused, by chat disordered state of things, <u>how enormous were treasures of religious societies and how gross the corruptions engendered by them</u>; so enormous & so gross as to produce in the Cabinets & Councils of the Protestant states in disregard, of all the pleas of the interested party drawn from the sanctions of the law, and the <u>sacredness of property held in the religious trust</u>."[34] (Emphasis added.)

The Madison Detached Memoranda are considered particularly probing in that analysts consider them to have been written as a collection between 1817 and 1832, even after his presidency from 1809-1817. They were found among the paperwork of Madison

---

[33] James Madison, "Memorial and Remonstrance Against Religious Assessments" (6/20/1785), quoted by Devin Bent, "Epilogue: James Madison and the Separation of Church and State," http://www.ungardesign.com/websites/madison/main_pages/Madison_archives/constit_confe..., at p.1 of 3. [6/13/09.]

[34] <u>Detached Memoranda</u> excerpt from Pfeffer, Leo, "Madison's 'Detached Memoranda': Then and Now,' <u>The Virginia Statute for Religious Freedom, Its Evolution and Consequences in American History</u>, Edited by Merrill D. Peterson and Robert C. Vaughan, Cambridge University Press (1988) pp. 286, 287.

biographer William Cabel Rives circa 1946 and were published in their entirety by Elizabeth Fleet in the William & Mary Quarterly of October, 1946.

From the Christian perspective, there can be no doubt that both these atrocities and obscene wealth accumulation would have been abhorrent to Christ Himself for reasons discussed below. Regardless, and UNDERSTANDABLY, they formed a basis for which people linking these actions with divine right concepts (be it of kings, of Popes being divine vicars on earth, whatever) would be looking for alternatives as a release from bondage and tyranny, be it physical, philosophical, psychological, ideological, or any combination thereof. That search in and of itself is not condemnatory, but it is submitted that that has been exploited by the overly financially powerful to subjugate the masses.

What is submitted here is that taking that reality at face value and as a given does not justify intellectual dishonesty by forcing another viewpoint for its own sake, thereby "begging the question" if you will. You can't defensibly force-feed a falsehood to try to expose another falsehood. Nothing less than truth as the saber will do. In fact, that is not all that has been done here--something quite the opposite and far darker is revealed than just that. One power play has simply been replaced by another, with just as great a set of abuses under the successor as its predecessor.

In other words (and this is recapped in the Epilogue), in revolting against denominational religion or religious configuration in any form, blame the pupil and not the Teacher. Correct and rebuke the pupil but do not replace one hegemony and oligarchy with another, which is exactly what has happened with the lobbies and moneyed interest (pressure) groups we have today. As will be revealed, these include the National Center for Science Education (NCSE), American Institute for Biological Sciences (AIBS) and the National Academy of Sciences (NAS) that were referenced in the Prologue.

The biblical God never operated on that level himself. The Noahic flood was preceded by Noah's warning about it for 120 years. [Genesis 6:1-3.] Efforts were made to try to save Sodom and Gomorrah before they were consumed. People were instructed by Scripture to be rebuked gently, not forcibly, when it came to issues of religious intolerance and defending the Christian belief system. What macros attempt to do now (through humanism as well as pseudo-science, which will be expanded upon later) is dominate the mind with logical absurdities and unscientific conclusions to justify that man alone determines his own destiny and is UNACCOUNTABLE FOR HIS ACTIONS along the way. Therefore, laissez-faire and moneyed interests become the name of the game, and the Golden Rule is recharacterized as, "He who has the gold, rules." The churches have used their power position in an abusive manner, unquestionably. But the same goes for the capitalist evolutionaries (as will be seen later, calling them evolutionaries rather than revolutionaries is deliberate). It is basically the Machiavellian principle with whatever power group that enjoys control of the day; power corrupts and absolute power corrupts absolutely. One means of power is replaced with another. Abraham Lincoln is quoted later as having recognized that.

Strict quasi-religious dogma is a precursor to both dissolution of faith and violence. Part of Christ's mission was to show that God was to be worshipped and the Sabbath observed in <u>accordance with Scripture rather than the traditions of men</u>. Hence, He exposed the first power play <u>in this discussion</u> as evidenced by the quotes earlier in this work. When social and political gain became prioritized over true religious conviction even in the days of the Scribes and Pharisees, the quasi-religious atrocities that were to follow were predictable in event if not in scale. <u>Again, the beauty of the Detached Memoranda Madison quote is the recognition, however, that corporate abuse by getting too big and acquiring too much wealth is a danger regardless of affiliation, RELIGIOUS or SECULAR</u>.

There can be no doubt that separation of church and state in the American Constitution was predicated upon the reality that it is impossible to have the same body mutually exercise ecclesiastical and secular power without dictatorial and even mortal abuse (in this sense, our Founding Fathers truly did their homework and were indisputably historical scholars). Of course, that is because said organizations depart from God rather than unify under Him. <u>The perverted Word is an excuse for dominance and suppression, an expression of power rather than religious conviction</u>. They cannot quote Scripture to justify their actions without pervertedly taking it out of context. <u>Of course,</u>

the Bible itself was deprived to the masses in the early church days, an obvious power play in and of itself.

Today, the power play is different but similarly applied. Separation of church and state is perverted to mean that macro can be taught but not only must the evidence for ID be suppressed (censored), but even the multitudinous weaknesses of macro as well. Despite credible evidence for a young earth of anywhere from 6,000 to 50,000 years duration being weighed by a student jury against the submitted older earth evidence, it is totally suppressed and it is absolutely "assumed" that the earth is at least millions and perhaps billions of years old. Thus, Eugenie Scott and the NCSE are perpetrating a fraud upon the public in presenting as scientific fact that which is unproven (and in this case, unprovable because false). Proof of micro changes is adaptation, which no Creationist would even think of denying because it is consistent with divine or other interventionist programming.

It is astounding how easily religious doctrine gets perverted. The basis of the atrocities listed in the website referenced below is that these purported Christians were "allegedly" acting under the Paulian principle of Atonement, which to them states that as long as faith is present, salvation is achieved and bad deeds are swept under the rug. That interpretation is a gross perversion of Paul's message. [Chapter One, Subchapter D].

So why is this subject matter mentioned in a treatment emphasizing logic? Because logic depends on the integrity of its premises and those are never adopted in a social, political or otherwise environmental vacuum. When ideological alternatives are sought as an escape from the bondage or undue influence of quasi-religious extremism, it is likelier to be found than under more comfortable circumstances (along the lines of necessity being the mother of invention). When the premises are tainted, so is the conclusion, or at least that conclusion must be subjected to stricter scrutiny.

As already shown, the Founding Fathers were very well aware of religious atrocities in Europe, and were diligent to see to it that that kind of tyranny did not take place in the United States by enacting separation of church and state. They were well to take heed. E.g, in 8/23-24/1572 (and for several months afterward), approximately

70,000 Huguenots (French Protestants), starting with Admiral Gaspard de Coligny, were slaughtered under Catholic queen Catherine de Medici during the St. Bartholemew's Day Massacre.[35] Apparently independent of that, Pope Pius V ordered 20,000 Huguenots killed in that same year.[36] At the Battle of Belgrad in 1456, 80,000 Turks were killed.[37] In the 17th Century, about 30,000 Protestants were killed.[38] During the 1648 Chmielnitzki massacres, about 200,000 Jews were slain in Poland.[39] This represents but a small smattering of what the Constitution drafters were well aware of and, to the extent possible, wanted to guard against (I, of course, based on section (D), do not attribute these actions to any proper assertion of Christian atonement, regardless of the purported motives of the perpetrators).

However, we are dealing now with issues of science and public information and the best ways to pursue truth, the vanguard of a true democratic republic. That aim is not met by simply adopting the contrarian view of vital life issues so that abusive state or religious practices are attacked. Often in earlier days, the ecclesiastical state was dominant. There is no denying that in this context, the goal of separation of church and state is inevitable and necessary. No political and social entity can survive without it. Human nature seeks to dominate. But that remains to be done through other means, such as exposure, e.g., of those power plays wherein authority has been abused for more devious secular ends having nothing to do with Christianity or virtually any other true form of religion. It is not properly accomplished by presenting something new to offer while disregarding the appropriateness of what that new thing is. It still needs to be based on truth and tolerance and nothing else. Sincere macros have lost sight of that.

F. TO SAY THAT THE DESIGNER COULD HAVE DONE A BETTER JOB IS INTELLECTUALLY CHEATING

This is the classic example of what this writer calls the ignoring of the "integration" principle discussed below. It also suffers logically in two

---

[35] Harry Kollatz, Jr., "The Huguenots-They fled their homes for religious freedom," Richmond Magazine, April 2003; http://Huguenot-manakin.org/kollatz.htm, at p. 1 of 2.
[36] "Victims of the Christian Atonement Theory," The Flaw of Atonement; http://www.themodernreligion.com/comparative/christ/christ_foa.htm
[37] Id., at p. 1 of 12.
[38] Id., at p. 4 of 12.
[39] Ibid.

ways: (1) While there were dozens of proposed vestigial organs for the human body decades ago, almost all have been debunked today. Criticisms of design are subject to re-evaluation when the benefits of the alleged "vestigial" organs are considered. The bottom line is that our state of knowledge only enhances the ingenuity demonstrated by the functioning of these organs and (2) The human body is an overall monument to engineering, with thousands of miles of veins and arteries in the body, one hundred trillion cells, the intricate movement of the heart chambers, the elaborate electrical nerve networking through the spinal cord and spinal column, etc.

Our bodily stream of hemoglobin is a wonderment surpassing the greatest terrestrial rivers we have and capable of responding to the vastly different stimuli presented. Susan Schiefelbein of the National Geographic Society reports that: "Within the human body flows a river unlike any other earthly river—a crimson stream that courses through every organ, twists past every cell on a journey that stretches sixty thousand miles, enough to circle the planet two and a half times. Earthly rivers refresh the land with water; the body's stream nourishes and cleanses, delivering food and oxygen to every cell, removing waters, regulating the human environment. Earth's rivers flow through inorganic rock and sand; the body's river travels through living tissue. The powerful heart that propels this stream and the vessels that guide it are all alive. The human river can regulate its own velocity, its banks widening or narrowing to control the shifting tides. And it can change its own course, instantly channeling its swift currents to meet new demands: Swimming or sleeping, contemplating, celebrating, running a race or rocking an infant—each alters the flow of this powerful river."[40] (Emphasis added.) While a person's DNA genome could be stretched about six feet, in another example of engineering marvel, it is nonetheless compacted into $1/2500^{th}$ of an inch within the cell's nucleus.[41]

Schiefelbein writes of a cycling-recycling sequence of our body's red blood cells in enormous quantity: "Deep within the bone marrow, primitive cells [Schiefelbein's opinion is that they are primitive, not mine] called erythroblasts continually divide. The resulting pair of

---

[40] Susan Schiefelbein, "The Powerful River," The Incredible Machine, 1992 (Third Printing), National Geographic Society, at p. 99.
[41] Id., Susan Schiefelbein, "Beginning the Journey," at p. 15.

cells in turn divides until each has produced 16 red blood cells. As it matures, a red blood cell expels its nucleus, thereby giving up the ability to repair or reproduce itself. Launched into the bloodstream, each cell will live only 4 months, traveling between the lungs and other tissues <u>75,000 times</u> before returning to the blood marrow to die. <u>In the second it takes to turn a page of this book, we will each lose about 3 million red cells. Yet during that second the marrow will have produced the same number.</u>"[42] (Emphasis added.)

The compaction factor is of primary significance for the cell itself, let alone its manifestation in terms of what host it is functioning in. Writes molecular biologist Michael Denton of the cell: "It is astonishing to think that this remarkable piece of machinery, which possesses the ultimate capacity to construct every living thing that ever existed on Earth, from giant redwood to the human brain, can construct all its own components in a matter of minutes and weigh less than 10 to the minus 16th power grams. It is of the order of several thousand million million times smaller than the smallest piece of functional machinery ever constructed by man."[43] The programmed engineering of this process is utterly astonishing. One has to seriously contemplate the likelihood that such a powerhouse of energy so minutely programmed to perform Herculean tasks could possibly be the end product of random events. When prospectively viewed like that, randomness does defy logic.

Here, the theme is that our further knowledge only enhances the grandeur of our entire human system. The Palais de Versailles, that French masterpiece of baroque architecture (which this author had the pleasure of visiting circa 1992 as part of his spoils from a Wheel of Fortune appearance), is not as elaborate. It is so intricate and complex that its overall functioning would be properly described as a "miracle" if the thought of that word didn't terrify the macros so much. Under their mode of thinking, Mt. Everest should be criticized for not being an inch higher and the speed of light should be chastised for being a mere 186,000 thousand miles per second in a vacuum. It ought to be much faster.

---

42 Id., Susan Schiefelbein, "The Powerful River," at p. 100.
43 Michael Denton, Molecular Biologist. <u>Evolution: A Theory in Crisis</u>. Adler and Adler, cited by <u>Evolution Is Dead. com</u>, http://www.evolutionisdead.com/quotes.php?QID=070. [8/8/09.]

From the integration point of view, it ducks the question. Biblical adherents say that the Fall of Man made everything that was originally so highly advanced denigrate. To the degree that the human body is physiologically or anatomically imperfect from a pure craftsman-like point of view (assuming arguendo only that this is true because it is a marvel of technical engineering) could well be because of the consequences of the Fall. Thus, this kind of objection adds nothing to and improperly diverts from the debate. It is among the plethora of examples wherein the macros have been intellectually dishonest. There is something disingenuous about criticizing for lack of absolute perfection when what IS before us is of unparalleled human engineering.

G. THE HORSE SERIES THAT WASN'T (AND STILL ISN'T)

Creationists sometimes refer to this issue as "The Second Piltdown man of Paleontology." This to me is a misnomer for a number of reasons, not the least of which is that its efforts well preceded Piltdown Man (treated below), going back to the 1870s. Its purpose was also far broader in scope—to try to demonstrate how the extant fossil record showed a clear development to the modern horse, Equus. At first, it was presented as a clear orthogenetic (straight-line) progression. But as further "information" came in, it was also determined that the lineage was traceable yet not nearly as clear-cut as before. So "adaptive radiation" (a split-off from main ancestry with eventual co-existence—cladogenesis) was also featured which at least in evolutionary terms was more explosive, while other branches of its ancestry did show "anagenesis" (gradual transformation).

Geologic time scales are measured in terms of Eons (not often referenced), Eras, Periods, Epochs and Ages. Basically, the Eras are divided, from most recent to oldest, into the Cenozoic ("Age of Mammals"-64 million yrs.), Mesozoic ("Age of Dinosaurs"-183.2 million yrs., from over 64 million yrs. ago to 247.2 million yrs. ago), and Paleozoic ("Age of Invertebrates"-281 million yrs., from over 247 million yrs. ago to 528 million yrs. ago). The Cenozoic Era is further divided into a two Periods (Quaternary [two sub-Periods (Neogene and Paleogene)] and Tertiary), and then the following Epochs from most recent to oldest are: (1) Holocene; (2) Pleistocene; (3) Pliocene;

(4) Miocene; (5) Oligocene; (6) Eocene and (7) Paleocene. The Mesozoic Era is further divided into the Cretaceous, Jurassic and Triassic Periods. The Paleozoic Era is divided into the Carboniferous, Devonian, Silurian, Ordovician and Cambrian Periods.[44]

For an explanation as to the derivation of many of these names, particularly for eras, see the U.S. Geological Survey at [http://pubs.usgs.gov/gip/geotime/divisions.html, at p. 1 of 1.] [7/2/09.] There is the more generic bottom Era called the Precambrian. According to the USGS, this traces from the earth's birth to "the appearance of complex forms of life," which, according to them, comprises over 80% of our planet's estimated age of 4.5 billion years. [Ibid.]

Among the major Creationist objections to the horse series are: (1) So called vestiges of the outer two toes on the rear foot are not matched by any vestiges of the outer three toes of the front foot; (2) North American ungulates allegedly evolved their rear foot from 3 toes to a single hoof, but South American ungulates CONTEMPORANEOUSLY allegedly evolved a single hoof to four toes; (3) The three-toed Neohipparion lived CONTEMPORANEOUSLY in the fossil record with the one-toed Pliohippus; (4) The stratigraphic record does not offer a horse sequence in successive time layers (there is a very uneven distribution therein) but the sequence is contrived by macros trying to force-feed such a series; (5) The Hyracotherium (Eohippus), except for the skull and tail, is almost morphologically identical in other detail to the modern living Hyrax (sometimes referred to as a "rock hare," and hardly bearing any resemblance to a horse); (6) No pattern of progression can be chronologically ascertained based on tooth count, size of the animal, vertebrae count and rib count; (7) Modern Equus and Hyracotherium lived CONTEMPORANEOUSLY because they are very often found in the same rock layers; (8) The fossils have been arranged in varied and contradictory ways and (9) That Miocene fossil known as "Moropus" is excluded from the sequence because it contradicts the hypothesis that there was a gradual increase in the size of the sequential fossils (which is immediately suspect anyway, as diminution is mostly observed in animal development through the succeeding geologic ages rather than an increase in size). Moropus was

---

44   Jeff Poling, "Geologic Ages of Earth History," (chronological graphic), http://www.dinosauria.com/ dml/history/htm, pp. 1-4. [7/2/09.]

bigger than even the Clydesdales of today at two meters in height, which also exceeded that of its contemporaries, the Meryhippuston horses.[45]

"The sequence in the series which presents transitional forms between small, many-toed forms and large, one-toed forms, has absolutely no fossil record evidence."[46] Or as G. A. Kerkut (British zoologist and physiologist, 1927-2004) put it: "In some ways it looks as if the pattern of horse evolution might be even as chaotic as that proposed by Osborn (1937, 1943) for the evolution of the Proboscidea, where 'in almost no instance is any known form considered to be a descendant from any other known form; every subordinate grouping is assumed to have sprung, quite separately and usually without any known intermediate stage, from hypothetical common ancestors in the Early Eocene or Late Cretaceous.' (Romer 1949)."[47]

Just how imaginative do the horse-toters get in promoting their fiction? They even take fossils from distant locations to one another to contrive (reconstruct) specimens. Macro Francis Hitching even observed: "A complete series of horse fossils is not found in any one place in the world arranged in rock strata in the proper evolutionary order from bottom to top. <u>The sequence depends on arranging Old World and New World fossils side by side, and there is considerable dispute as to what order they should go in.</u>"[48]

As Kerkut reminds us: "At present, however, it is a <u>matter of faith</u> that the textbook pictures are true or even that they are the best representations of the truth that are available to us at the present time. ... It makes quite a difference whether a name on a diagram represents a whole skeleton or just a tooth, ..."[49] (Emphasis added.) Obviously, the "reconstructions" can get quite creative and doubtlessly reflect the bias of the macros. Putting Old World and New World fossils side by side for these reconstructions? Is this not a stretch, besides being scandalously dishonest?!

---

45 Extracted primarily from "Textbook Fraud: Hyracotherium "dawn horse" eohippus, mesohippus, meryhippus," "Scientific Evidence for Creation," www.bible.ca, http://www.bible.ca/tracks/textbook-fraud-dawn-horse-eohippus.htm, pp. 1-36 & 5-10 of 36, especially 1 & 2 & 5-10. [7/2/09.]
46   John Moore, and Harold S. Slusher, Eds., <u>Biology: A Search for Order in Complexity</u>, Zondervan Publishing House, Grand Rapids, Michigan, 1970, p. 548, cited by "Textbook Fraud," id., at p. 4 of 36.
47   G.A. Kerkut, <u>Implications of Evolution</u>, New York: Pergamon Press, 1960, p. 149, quoted by "Textbook Fraud," id., at pp. 8 & 9 of 36.
48   Francis Hitching, <u>The Neck of the Giraffe – Where Darwin Went Wrong</u>, (New York: Ticknor and Fields, 1982), pp. 28-30, quoted by "CREATION BITS No. 24. Evolution(?) of the Horse," http://www.rae.org/bits24.htmm, at p. 1 of 3.] (Emphasis added.) [7/2/09.]
49   <u>Implications of Evolution</u>, supra., at pp. 141-149, quoted by CREATION BITS, ibid.

The objective observer has to ask: What's the difference between this brand of dogma and religious dogma? The honest answer is: not a thing!

Size differential has definitely been a contrived criterion demonstrating nothing concerning evolution and really is meaningless when considering the horse family (Equidae) as a whole. Just as there are tremendous size differences between the Chihuahua or the Toy Bulldog and the Saint Bernard or Bull Mastiff among dogs (and no one would argue an evolutionary sequence there), it is also true of our modern living horses, ranging in today's world from the Clydesdale to the Fallabella (17 inches; 43 cm. tall).[50] It is fair to say, however, that this tortuous, contorted attempt to show a non-existent progression of size among horses is a concession of the devolution that is a fact in nature and militates against basic Darwinian principles and is a <u>failed</u> effort at trying to debunk it or mollifying its import.

The Equidae family is part of a larger order of hoofed mammals, including rhinos and tapirs and maybe even hyraxes, referred to as perissodactyls because they bear their weight on a central 3rd toe.

Modern efforts to defend the horse series invariably fall short. Such is the case with the Internet entry "Horse Evolution" by Kathleen Hunt that appears at TalkOrigins.com.[51] She does proceed by admitting the evolutionary line was not orthogenetic (purposeful) but also makes this very interesting remark: "… horse evolution was not smooth and gradual. Different traits evolved at different rates, didn't always evolve together, and <u>occasionally reversed direction</u>."[52] (Emphasis added.] How can anyone advocate for something that is so chaotic and tortuous? It doesn't even make sense from the natural selection standpoint, where there is no apparent advantage to the shifting back and forth. She also extends the caveat that it would be wrong to think that Equus was a <u>target</u> of evolution because there are so many other major branches of the horse tree (things must remain undirected, remember).

Hunt treats the Miocene in interesting fashion, which saw three major groups emanate from "merychippine radiation," namely, the hipparions,

---

50 "Horse Evolution—Did horses evolve from a small fox-like animal?"-<u>Christian Answers.Net</u>, http://www.christiananswers.net/q-aig/aig/-c016.html, at p. 3 (numeral 4) of 4. [7/2/09.]
51 http://www.talkorigins.org/faqs/horses/horse_evol.html, pp. 1-15, last updated 1/4/95. [7/2/09.]
52 Id., at p. 2 of 15.

protohippines and "true equines." This latter group is described as follows: "A line of 'true equines' in which the side toes sometimes began to decrease in size. In this flurry of evolution, Merychippus primus gave rise to two later merychippines called M. sejunctus and M. isonesus, who had a mixture of "primitive" (Parahippus-like), hipparion, and equine features. They, in turn, gave rise to M. intermontanus, which begat M. stylodontus and M. carrizoensis. These last two looked quite "horsey" and gave rise to a set of larger three-toed and one-toed horses know as the 'true equines.' ... <u>Crystal clear, right?</u>"[53] (Emphasis added.) Again, there is no honest inquiry into the rhyme or reason—just a blind obedience to this tortuous direction, despite an admission of it being as clear as mud. Could this quandary as to how they arise be a clue that in an evolutionary sense, they didn't <u>arise</u> at all?!

The chaos behind this whole process is best shown in her Summary, which in pertinent part states: "Tracing a line of descent from Hyracotherisum to Equus reveals several apparent trends: reduction of toe number, increase in size of cheek teeth, lengthening of the face, increase in body size. <u>But these trends are not seen in all of the horse lines. On the whole, horses got larger, but some horses (Archeohippus, Calippus) then got smaller again. Many recent horses evolved complex facial pits, and then some of their descendants lost them again. Most of the recent (5-10 My) horses were three-toed, not one-toed, and we see a "trend" to one toe only because all the three-toed lines have recently become extinct.</u>"[54] (Emphasis added.) Again, doesn't this randomness and aimlessness clue that maybe this process called transmutational evolution is so arbitrary as to be a meaningless and inaccurate construct and artifice rather than a process at all?

Yet, Hunt shows her ignorance of the overall issues involved in posing a challenge to Creationists: "A Question for Creationists: Creationists who wish to deny the evidence of horse evolution should carefully consider this: **how else can you explain the sequence of horse fossils?** Even if creationists insist on ignoring the transitional fossils (many of which **have** been found), again, how can the unmistakable **sequence** of these fossils be explained? Did God create Hyracotherium, then kill off Hyracotherium and create some Hyracotherium-Orohippus intermediates, then kill off the intermediates and create Orohippus,

---

53   Id., at p. 7 of 15.
54   Id., at p. 11 of 15.

then kill off Orohippus and create Epihippus, then allow Epihippus to "microevolve" into Duchesnehippus, then kill off Duchesnehippus and create Mesohippus, then create some Mesohippus-Miohippus intermediates, then create Miohippus, then kill off Mesohippus, etc. … each species coincidentally similar to the species that came just before and came just after? [new Para.] Creationism utterly fails to explain the sequence of known horse fossils from the last 50 million years. That is, without invoking the "God Created Everything to **Look Just Like Evolution Happened**" Theory."[55] (Emphasis original.)

Is this tortuous concatenation that Hunt just relayed meant to impress, because it was lost on this end? Instead, it betrays her contradictoriness. She at one point earlier <u>admits</u> that the sequences are as clear as mud, and at the other turn tries to put Creationists on the defensive for it when the macros need account for its randomness, not the Creationists. There are enough leaps and bounds in her last immediate passage to force a kangaroo into rest periods. A contortionist would envy her.

Ms. Hunt's last remark ignores Francisco J. Ayala (who is treated below) and other macros (who like all macros are acutely aware of the horse series) who have extolled how Darwin's theory permits them to show that an otherwise "appearance" of design is still not design. Their theme is that macro happened even though on the face of it, it looks from the stratigraphic record like it did not happen. This, of course, segues into my later developed point that the burden of proof under ordinary rules of evidence when the true history and foundation of macro is placed before the objective observer places the burden on the macros and not the other way around. Far more egregiously, however, Hunt makes no effort to relate or otherwise address the <u>objection</u> of how this so-called "obvious" fossil sequence of hers is the construct of the macros, and that said arrangement (even in her muddled form) is highly controversial even among her own colleagues, and that <u>nowhere</u> in the <u>real world</u> is there an actual lithological representation of this. Nor does she address any of the other Creationist (and sometimes other macros') objections above, <u>even though she otherwise calls out</u> the Creationists. This imputes upon her a duty to know the entire controversy and she fails the exam. This betrays total ignorance of the true issues or total indoctrination by the education system or

---

55 Ibid.

intellectual dishonesty or any combination of these factors. The indoctrination aspect of the education system (the brainwashing, of which Ms. Hunt appears to be a clear victim) is precisely what it is the theme of this book to expose and remove.

Hunt also has a URL at TalkOrigins wherein she discusses the "true" transitional fossil evidence.[56] Unfortunately for her and her cause, it is at least as mortally wounded as her horse transitional treatment. I don't feel I could improve upon the Darwin Papers extensive critique on this treatment and so advise your reading both sites and drawing your own conclusions. Macro, it is submitted on this writer's end, comes out on the very poor end of the stick. The Darwin Papers URL is footnoted below.[57] In that same piece, Author James M. Foard also critiques Joseph Boxhorn's FAQ, "Observed Instances of Speciation" with like devastating results for macro theory.[58]

While his style sometimes comes across to me as too condescending, Foard nonetheless makes excellent points concerning the fallacies of Hunt's analysis, fully exposing the dearth of her actual evidence. He also makes clear that the morphological hurdles for specific areas of transmutation, while themselves formidable, are only part of the problem. Just as substantial, if not more so, are the physiological ones, such as, e.g. (without being exhaustive), the required transition of the soft gelatinous-like amphibian egg transitioning into the hard-shelled amniotic reptilian egg (he quotes Denton from his Evolution: A Theory in Crisis at pp. 218-219 as presenting eight obstacles to be overcome in making such a transition), as well as no apparent accountability for the chiasmic difference between the hearts of the two forms, a gap transmutational macro theory has not come close to bridging.[59]

As devastating as his overall treatment is, Foard hyperlinks still other websites where the assault could be continued, as well as the previous chapter of his own Darwin Papers work, "The Fossil Record." He promises to add more evidence "showing Ms. Hunt's fabrications" as his website continues its construction over the ensuing year.[60] The only

---

56   http://www.talkorigins.org/faqs/faq-transitional.html. [9/5/09.]
57   http://www.thedarwinpapers.com/oldsite/number6/number6.htm, "Evidence for Evolution from Talk Origins," at, for Hunt transitional fossil commentary, pp. 7-30 of 40. [9/5/09.]
58   Id., at pp. 30-32 of 40.
59   Id., at pp. 21-23 of 40.
60   Id., at pp. 29 & 30 of 40. [9/5/09.]

reason I am not salivating is that how many times can you re-kill an already dead horse (pun intended)?

H. THE ADVENTURES OF PILTDOWN MAN

Perhaps the most celebrated singular hoax in paleontological history was Piltdown (orangutan with chimpanzee teeth) Man, a supposed "transitional" missing link from ape lineage to man. A skull and jawbone from a Piltdown village gravel pit near Uckfield, East Sussex, England were discovered in 1912 by Charles Dawson and was thus designated as Eoanthropus dawsoni ("Dawson's dawn-man"). <u>It was to further establish that the brain developed sooner than the jaw in the macro chain, as the cranium more closely resembled humans and the jaw that of an ape.</u> As it turned out, the find really was of a <u>modern human cranium</u> and the jaw was definitely not from a transitional ape but rather, as has already been alluded to, from a <u>500 year old Sarawak orangutan with chimpanzee teeth that had been filed down</u>. Another set of fragments from a purportedly second skull (Piltdown II), circa two miles from the original finds, were discovered by Dawson in 1915. Nonetheless, the exhibit was not officially exposed as a fraud until 1953.[61]

It seems strange indeed that under any circumstances a fraudulent exhibit of that significance could remain unexposed for that length of time without foul play being the reason. Still further, in 1923, anatomist Franz Weidenreich inspected the specimens and made the exact same findings as made in 1953 with the possible exception of the teeth being a chimpanzee's. The aging effect of the bones was created by staining them with chromic acid and an iron solution. Allegedly, the specimen was not challenged because it confirmed the prevailing belief of the brain being modified prior to the jaw.[62]

---

[61] Roger Lewin, Bones of Contention (1987), (http://www.clarku.edu/~piltdown/map_expose/ chain_of_fraud.html), cited by "Piltdown Man"-Wikipedia, the free encyclopedia; http://en.wikipedia.org/ wiki/Piltdown_Man, at pp. 1&2 of 7. [6/19/09.]
[62] "Piltdown Man," Wikipedia, id., at http://www.tiac.net/~cri_a/piltdown/piltdown.html, at p.5 of 23. [6/19/09.]

CHAPTER TWO

A PRECEPT IN NEED OF A POSTER CHILD

A. MACRO'S CONTEMPORARY ADVOCATES NEEDED A MOUTH-PIECE

As a backdrop, the influence upon macro of history and politics should be mentioned. Historically, the landholders were the first power brokers. The entire feudal system rested on that basis. While various forms of currency always existed (even if only in the form of barter in determining equivalencies, but here the emphasis is on fiat money), he who held and controlled the most balanced strategic and quantitative property held the keys to power. The church was always more than a religious institution; it was a powerful landholder, a true power player. The feudal period was a system of hierarchy based on a form of rental occupancy by the servants (peasants) to the lord, who in turn served the king, who controlled the landholding. While there was always a Royal Palace Guard network, the lords were still expected to serve and protect the king.

Enter the Industrial Revolution which, depending upon the source, was prevalent from perhaps 1750 through 1850, maybe even into the early 1900s. Primarily, production was accomplished through machines, both for transportation and manufacture (mass production—beyond the scope of artisans and craftsmen). With such an expansion, a convenient means of exchange in the form of paper money came into being.[63] From this growth arose a new source of power—money and production capacity that transcends mere ownership by creating more

---

63 "Industrial Revolution"-Wiki, the free encyclopedia; http://en.wikipedia/Industrial_Revolution, at p. 1 of 31. [11/21/08.]

ways of generating the means of exchange and increasing transactions—again, paper money. Sustenance was no longer dependent upon the lord of the manor but the means of acquiring money, which added to the ways of becoming more independent.[64]

Landholding is certainly still a very viable means of earning money, but so are the mass manufacturers who can provide goods and generate moneyed income, which is a dramatic change from before. The same holds true for the mass transportation providers to a far more dramatic degree than before. Trade expansion was an inevitable result. Of course, entertainers (actors, musicians, athletes, etc.) and perhaps the entertainment industry specifically can generate similar income as well, but that varies with popularity and the social climate. Those things that address necessities will always be successful and profitable as long as adequately managed.

The bottom line is that multiple transactions occur, so that far more money is generated by those controlling the means of mass production, transportation and communication than ever before. There were hence new means of wealth involved; more specifically, new means of generating the quantity of the means of exchange via multiple transactions.

Perhaps this can be even more greatly appreciated when it is understood how totally immersed the Anglican Church initially was in secular affairs, from the very top of Parliament to the grass-roots village level. Even in part of Darwin's time, a nominal adherence to its teachings was a prerequisite for admission to the elite universities, Cambridge and Oxford. Graduation from these prestigious citadels was more or less a condition precedent to gaining a foothold into the leading professions of the day. One such profession was the clergy, so most of the clergy were Cambridge or Oxford graduates who were also associated with the English gentry. The clergy by itself was less expensive to pursue than say, law or medicine, but it also paid less. So usually, additional means of support were necessary. In fact, Darwin's mentor, John Stevens Henslow, was a clergyman-naturalist, as was his cousin and friend, William Darwin Fox. Besides Parliament and the universities, the Church controlled municipal corporations and grammar schools. At one time, to illustrate the connection with the

---

64 Id., at p. 17.

gentry, the local squire as a landholder virtually owned the parish, built the church, and brought in only clergymen he personally approved of. The clergy and landed gentry were virtually wedded together into the English social and economic fabric.

While there was a residual of this power and influence during Darwin's time, changes were taking place that arguably gave Darwinism a more hospitable environment. Between 1800 and 1870, the Anglican Church started losing its stranglehold on the state, and gradually became relegated to the status of merely one denomination among many, so that dissenters (including the Roman Catholics) could occupy Parliament and be admitted into universities, grammar schools and municipal corporations. The secular state became more and more involved in aiding the poor and in administering education and justice. This poured-over into the small villages, and from the 1850s to the 1880s, the clerical roles became more and more dissociated from the secular, and the Church of England started stressing its own denomination rather than more public concerns. As a result, non-Conformist preachers were gaining congregations. The Darwins themselves were impressed with Non-conformist evangelist J.W.C. Fegan. With the grasp of the church's tentacles loosening, change was definitely in the wind in this manner as well, precursing a further social context for the 1859 welcoming of Origin.[65]

B. THE LEGEND THAT HUXLEY HAD RATHER COME FROM AN APE THAN A BISHOP

It is well known that Huxley had an animus toward anatomist Richard Owen, and was greatly influenced by the "Darwinism" of Ernst Haeckel of the infamous woodcarvings and drawings falsely depicting ontogeny recapitulating phylogeny. Recapitulation has been thoroughly discredited by serious science, with even noted macro Gould and others being well aware of its hoax. But Huxley is also credited in folklore with a retort on June 30, 1860 to Samuel Wilberforce, Bishop of Oxford, that legend says goes like this, and became a rallying point for the macros: Wilberforce: "Is it on your grandfather's or grandmother's side that you claim descent from the apes?" Huxley: "I would rather be descended from an ape than a bishop." It is conceded even by macros

---

[65] http://www.darwinproject.ac.uk/content/view/152/144/, "Darwin Correspondence Project – Darwin and the church: historical essay," pp. 1-3, 5, & 8 of 9. [3/28/09.]

that this legendary account is almost certainly not true, no more than Nero literally fiddling while Rome was burning. In fact, it is not even clear what actually was said, but it seems to have gone along the lines of: Wilberforce asked if it was Huxley's grandfather or grandmother that descended from a monkey, and Huxley responded that he was not ashamed to have a monkey for an ancestor, but he would be ashamed to be connected with a man who used great gifts to obscure the truth. This was taken to be a personal attack against Wilberforce.[66]

Obviously, almost any retort of substance at all would have carried great force at that moment at such a public meeting with tensions naturally running high, and it is virtually certain that Huxley did come up with something at least catchy. It is even somewhat controversial whether that was immediately good or bad for the cause, but it grew in stature as the years went by. I consider Lucas's treatment of the subject quite even-handed. I disagree entirely with his assertions of how science has verified Darwin since, as I believe quite the opposite is true, but his treatment of the encounter itself is fair enough and well articulated.

But macro's resort to this fiction involves another logical fallacy, that of "Appeal to Ridicule" (which is something that Dawkins is reputed to resort to rather consistently).[67] It is also called the "Appeal to Mockery" and the "Horse Laugh." Mocking a claim is not evidence of its falsity. Many might argue that this more properly belongs in the Ad Hominem "against the man" personal attack category[68] (also known as Ad Hominem Abusive), but I see it as more to "Ridicule" and an attack on clergy generally, as well as the traditions and dogmas of the church generally. It seems more targeted at what Wilberforce represented as a Bishop than on a direct personal level. As Lucas points out in his article, people wanted to hear about macro. In that sense, revolution was in the air.

As the macros have used the incident (including contemporarily), it is also an "Appeal to Spotlight,"[69] and further evidence of the revolutionary fervor that over-magnified a single incident into such

---

66 J R Lucas, "Wilberforce & Huxley: A Legendary Encounter;" http://users.ox.oc.uk/; ~jrlucas/ legend.html. [1/30/10.]
67 http://www.nizkor.org/features/ fallacies/appeal-to-ridicule.html. [9/5/09.]
68 http://www.nizkor.org/features/ fallacies/ad-hominem.html. [1/30/10.]
69 http://www.nizkor.org/features/fallacies/spotlight.html. [7/14/09.]

large notoriety. Perhaps the more precise applicable logical fallacy is "Appeal to Novelty."[70] The public as well as scientists were ready to go in another direction. Anything remotely making sense or seemingly plausible was preferred to ecclesiastical rigidity. Regardless, the incident itself must not argumentatively form the basis by which the merits of this controversy should be approached.

C. CONTEMPORARIES "MANAGED" DARWIN'S SUCCESS

Darwin's notoriety was overblown and nurtured virtually ab initio (from the beginning). Mount Darwin was named to commemorate Darwin's 25th birthday during the Beagle voyage by Captain FitzRoy—not to be confused with the Mount Darwin in California of Solomons and Bonner fame.[71] Darwin submitted Alfred Russel Wallace's own evolutionary thesis, which he received on 6/18/1858 to Lyell, who in turn shared it with Hooker. The 7/1/1858 Linnean Society joint presentation by Lyell and Hooker soon followed showcasing both Darwin and Wallace, with a marginal reception. Origin was published by John Murray on 11/22/1859, which was arranged by Lyell.

An important inquiry is why Darwin was chosen as the vanguard over Wallace (1823-1913). It would seem that his general unavailability for personal appearances (whether for genuine health reasons, that he was psychosomatic, that his demeanor was not commanding enough, or for other reasons or a combination of those stated) would play a dramatic role in that choice. While Wallace became a notorious spiritualist, that was not in earnest until circa 1868, and at least on the basis of the evidence I have seen, he tinkered with the notion for only a few years before then.[72] Of course, Wallace was much younger than Darwin, who was already famous and well placed in societal circles. Likewise, Darwin had been developing his theory for many years before Wallace and was presumably further along in its nuances.

But Darwin's pre-notoriety is worthy of some exploration. The issue is: Why was he coddled to begin with? His Beagle "exploits" were widely publicized in scientific circles by John Stevens Henslow, his

---
70   http://www.nizkor.org/features/fallacies/appeal-to-novelty.html. [1/30/10.]
71   http://en.wikipedia.org/ wiki/Mount_Darwin_(California), at p. 1 of 2. [8/18/09]
72   Ross A. Slotten, <u>The Heretic in Darwin's Court: The Life of Alfred Russel Wallace</u> (2004), p. 231, cited by Alfred Russell Wallace-Wikipedia, the Free Encyclopedia, http://en.wikipedia.org/wiki/ Alfred_Russel_Wallace, at p. 13 of 24. [2/14/09.]

college biology instructor. Just like his contemporaries jumped on Darwin's bandwagon, the same could have been for Wallace, whose thinking could have been "guided" along the way. Doubtless the best explanation (at least initially) was with the historical Darwin name and lineage. Grandfather Erasmus Darwin (1731-1802) was a highly respected physician, as well as Macro proponent who wrote Zoonomia. This would have been the impetus for Darwin's initial grooming, along with his other manipulable traits shown during his college days.

In fact, it would appear that Wallace was dangerous to the macro rebels. He had definite socialist leanings in advocating state ownership of land to be leased to those whose use would be for the most utilitarian good, and was critical of the impact that English free trade policies had on the working class. His criticisms of British society in his 1869 book, The Malay Archipelago, favorably got John Stuart Mill's attention, prompting Mill to have him join his Land Tenure Reform Association, which dissolved after Mill's 1873 death. In 1881, Wallace was elected first president of the Land Nationalisation Society, and in 1882, he published Land Nationalisation: Its Necessity and Its Aims. In 1889, after reading Looking Backward by Edward Bellamy, Wallace even declared himself a socialist, and openly opposed Social Darwinism and eugenics, claiming society was too corrupt to make an objective determination of who was fit or unfit. These are not capitalist rallying points. He also wrote on the wastefulness of militarism, another handy capitalist means for profit.[73]

Further, Wallace did not accept sexual selection [defined by Darwin in The Descent of Man and Selection in Relation to Sex (1871) as the effects of the "struggle between the individuals of one sex, generally the males, for the possession of the other sex,"[74] deeming it instead a logical consequence of natural selection. Roughly contemporaneous with his becoming a spiritualist, he said that neither wit nor humor nor mathematical, musical or artistic genius could be accounted for by natural selection, though he supported "natural selection" in other capacities. And the origin of life itself from inorganic matter required "the unseen universe of spirit," as also did the infusion of consciousness

---

[73] Heretic in Darwin's Court, id., at pp. 365-72, 436, 453, 487-488, and Michael Shermer, In Darwin's Shadow: The Life and Science of Alfred Russel Wallace (2002), pp. 23, 279, both cited by Wallace, Wikipedia, supra, at p. 6 of 24.

[74] quoted by "Sexual selection"-Wikipedia, the free encyclopedia, http://en.wikipedia.org/wiki/ Sexual_selection, at p. 1 of 12. [9/24/09.]

in higher animals as well as all higher mental faculties for man. This, of course, suggests divine intervention, the bane of all Darwinists. <u>Also, he thought that the development of the human spirit was the overall purpose for the universe</u>. This, too, imputes a direction in life, a very unDarwinian premise.[75]

While these attitudes were exposed post-<u>Origin of Species</u>, one wonders if these kinds of influences kept him from greater contemporary recognition promoting macro and from getting greater credit afterward. The politico-socio-economic climate conspired to place Wallace in a secondary position, at least on the macro scenario, although not entirely. His "Wallace effect" to explain how natural selection would tend to militate against hybrids, they being less well adapted than either parent form, was a substantial contribution and this principle is still seriously considered today.[76] Also recognized in this area is his theory of warning colouration (particularly protective colouration) in animals.[77] To the objective observer, this lends credence to his observations of macro's limitations even within the macro realm; but as already noted, this would lead to uncomfortable conclusions for the general macros. In other arenas he was highly respected, such as being regarded as the foremost expert on the geographical distribution of animal species, sometimes being called the "father of biogeography."[78]

To the third party objective observer, Wallace's approach has its compelling points. Darwin's "sexual selection" in terms of musical talent is certainly suspect. [Charles Darwin, <u>The Descent of Man</u>, 1871: "I conclude that musical notes and rhythm were first acquired by the males or female progenitors of mankind for the sake of charming the opposite sex."[79] Assuming his wife's influence in his making that determination (see footnote), how are orientations made blindly to accommodate composing music and devising a piano, let

---

75 Wallace, Wikipedia, supra, at p. 11 of 24.
76 <u>Heretic in Darwin's Court</u>, supra, pp. 413-415, cited by Wallace, Wikipedia, ibid.
77 <u>Heretic in Darwin's Court</u>, id., pp. 251-254, cited by Wallace, Wikipedia, ibid.
78 Charles H. Smith, "Alfred Russel Wallace: Evolution of an Evolutionist Introduction," http://www.wku.edu/~smithch/wallace/chsarwin.htm, a website known as the Alfred Russel Wallace Page is hosted by Western Kentucky University, cited by Wallace, Wikipedia, id., at p. 1 of 24.
79 quoted by Jennifer Viegas of Discovery News from the Discovery Channel, "Darwin's pianist wife influenced theories—Love of music played larger role than many think in shaping his work," (3/3/09), Technology & science, <u>Darwin's pianist wife influenced theories – Discovery.com- msnbc.com</u>, commenting on a paper for the journal Endeavour written by Julian Derry of the Institute of Evolutionary Biology at the University of Edinburgh, http://www.msnbc.msn.com/id/29492764/, at p. 2 of 5 (the article itself is at Endeavour, Vol. 33, Issue 1, March 2009, pp. 35-38.) [9/24/09.]

alone developing the dexterity and musical sensibility to play it? It is a non sequitur. <u>A desire to attract the opposite sex through any form of musicality would have no connection whatsoever with the mechanisms required to achieve musicality</u>. Regardless of the degree of Emma's actual contribution to his theory (Darwin did delight in her music, but he enjoyed music even prior to his marriage), this same challenge to the accreditation of music as part of sexual selection (a connection Darwin unequivocally made) can be asserted. Wallace, to his credit, realized this and knew the answer had to lie elsewhere.

In fact, it is quite eye-popping that two men who independently came up with the "natural selection" concept could diverge so dramatically as to key precepts of macro generally, and even as to the overall dynamic of "natural selection." Especially since Wallace was so very gifted in many arenas in his own right. In fact, some of his notions have a ring of familiarity in another context. He could have easily been designated the "father of theistic or progressive evolution" in the sense of his instances of "divine intervention" if you will (he would surely express it differently) in the progressive steps of macro. Doubtless, his "God" would be more of a Spinoza-like one, similar probably to Einstein. As far as compatibility with Scripture and macro generally, from a Creationist perspective, that in itself is not only different than Wallace's approach, but was not unique even in Wallace's time. American botanist Asa Gray, a Darwin advocate, embraced that with Darwin's approval in his own pamphlet, whose distribution Darwin half-financed, "Natural Selection is not Inconsistent with Natural Theology."[80]

However, while the mechanism of "natural selection" was largely complementary between Darwin and Wallace, its conceptual framework most certainly was not. For Darwin, it was a living, breathing mechanism with a virtual life of its own, a Zeitgeist-like force, a kind of natural dialectic if you will that constituted its own

---

[80] "Darwin and Design: Historical Essay," *Darwin Correspondence Project*, 2007, [http://www.darwinproject.ac.uk/content/view/110/104/] & Sara Joan Miles, "Charles Darwin and Asa Gray Discuss Teleology and Design" (2001), (http://www.asa3.org/ASA/PSCF/2001/PSCF9-01Miles.html), *Perspectives on Science and Christian Faith*, 53:196-201, http://www.asa3.org/ASA.PSCF/2001/PSCF9-01Miles.html, both cited by Charles Darwin-Wikipedia-id., at pp. 11&12.] [3/28/09.]; see also, "Reaction to Darwin's theory"-Wikipedia, the free encyclopedia; http://en.wikipedia.org/wiki/Reaction_to_Darwin's_theory, at p. 10 of 15. [3/28/09.]

"creative force." For Wallace, it was merely a descriptive end-result.[81] Logically, the Wallace conception could arguably allow for a pre-programmed, genetic Creational variation theme in reaction to the environment, but he remained macro.

For Darwin, natural selection revolved around intra-species competition to survive and reproduce, whereas for Wallace, it was a matter of environmental and biogeographical pressure among both species and varieties to adapt to the local environment.[82] Wallace kept macro as a servant to final causes, which was certainly antithetical to Darwin.[83] That would be far too directed and targeted for Darwin's liking. Wallace obviously did not disqualify God, but simply made him a more passive observer until the interventionist points mentioned above, although these are certainly considerable, and would seemingly make him Theistic as opposed to Deistic. The latter suggests more of an entity setting things in motion and letting the chips fall where they may, with no pro-activity with human affairs after man was created. Darwin eliminated him totally, at least in terms of any active involvement in the affairs of men, though technically labeling himself an agnostic. This would be a compelling reason to separate the two men and keep Wallace in the background in terms of macro.

A word on Darwin himself extending a helping hand to Wallace must be mentioned. He was well aware of Wallace's serious money issues and, in 1879, began paving the way for his getting a government pension despite great initial opposition from people like Joseph Hooker, who deeply held Wallace's associations with Spiritualism and how he tried to have it discussed at a British association sectional meeting against him (though he later withdrew his opposition).[84] On a personal level, Darwin greatly respected Wallace's ideas and held

---

81 Charles H. Smith, Guest Editorial: "Alfred Russel Wallace, Past and Future," Journal of Biogeography 32(9): 1509-1515 (September, 2005), read verbatim at the bicentennial meeting of International Biography Society—"...Wallace only reasoned that the whole of the process passed through the natural selection filter, and not that natural selection itself *initiated* it."] (Emphasis original.) http://www.wku.edu/~smithch/essays/SMITH05.htm, at p.4 of 11; as opposed to Darwin, "By contrast, in Wallace's model of natural selection—even after 1858—there actually is no implied *process* of adaptation: there is only the logical *result* of being adapted," at p.3 of 11.] [9/24/09.] (Emphasis original.)
82 Edward Larson, Evolution: The Remarkable History of Scientific Theory (2004) Modern Library. ISBN 0-679-64288-9, p. 75 & Peter J. Bowler & Iwas Rhys Morus, Making Modern Science (2005), The University of Chicago Press. ISBN 0-226-06861-7, p. 149, both cited by Wallace, Wikipedia, supra, at p. 10 of 24.
83 "Alfred Russel Wallace, Past and Future," supra, at p. 5 of 11 ("Recall that Wallace seems to have had in mind an evolutionary process subservient to final causes. In his own words, the 'changes in organic forms' are 'to keep them in harmony with the changed conditions' (i.e., the environment, characterized very generally) (Wallace, 1870, p. 302)," at p. 5 of 11. (Emphasis added.)
84 Heretic in Darwin's Court, supra, pp. 357-358, 362, quoted and cited by Wallace, Wikipedia, supra, at p. 13 of 24.

private correspondence with him.[85] It would be a great falsehood to suggest that Darwin himself wanted to trivialize or suppress Wallace in any way, and that is certainly not being suggested here. The macro movement most certainly did that, however, both during and after Wallace's lifetime.

Eliminating God from the picture best minimized the church from the capitalist perspective, which would make Darwin the preponderantly more appealing macro. He fit far better into their felicific calculus than did his younger contemporary. The very next section discusses whether or not Darwin was a Deist as some people think, or a Theist or agnostic as he at different times described himself. This author concludes that he was for the better part of his life an atheist.

There were other social reasons as well for the macro society generally avoiding Wallace in macro priority. Darwin's wife Emma Wedgwood's grandfather Josiah was a major player of the Industrial Revolution in the manufacture of pottery. He was commissioned by such dignitaries as Queen Charlotte of England and Empress Catherine of Russia, the latter still on display at the Hermitage Museum.[86] While Josiah was himself a humanitarian and a vocal slavery abolitionist,[87] he was well connected in terms of the capitalistic, machine-age establishment (even inventing the pyrometer to measure oven temperatures)[88] from which socialism and Marxism[89] and socialism in other contexts arose out of protest.[90] Some even designate Wedgwood as the first tycoon.[91] And Darwin (whose own father was wealthy) was hence well funded from both sides of the family. The Wedgwood family was also nonconformist and members of the Unitarian church.[92] They were part of that group that felt a need to break away from Anglican Church dominance, as well as the foothold of the landed aristocracy.

---

[85] In Darwin's Shadow, supra, p. 149, cited by Wallace, Wikipedia, id., at p. 12 of 24.
[86] Hermitage Museum, http://www/hermitagemuseum.org/html_En/03/hm3_3_2_4b.html, cited by "Josiah Wedgwood," Wikipedia, the free encyclopedia; http://en.wikipedia.org/wiki/Josiah_Wedgwood, at p. 1 of 4. 2/14/09.
[87] Id., at p. 3.
[88] BBC-History-Josiah Wedgwood (1730-1795), http://www.bbc.co.uk/history/historic_figures/wedgwood_josiah.shtml, at p. 1 of 1.
[89] "Karl Marx: Communist as Religious Eschatologist," http://www.mises.org/journals/rae/pdf/rae4_1_5.pdf, cited by "Industrial Revolution," Wikipedia, the free encyclopedia, at p. 25 of 31.]
[90] "Industrial Revolution," Wikipedia, id., at pp. 20 (British Labour Party, created from merger of earlier socialist parties) & 22 (Socialist Party in Wallonia (Belgium)) of 31. [11/21/08.)
[91] Brian Dolan, Wedgwood: The First Tycoon. Viking /Adult. ISBN 0-670-03346-4, cited as a Source at Wedgwood, Wikipedia, supra, at p. 3 of 4.
[92] Emma Darwin, Wikipedia, the free encyclopedia; http://en.wikipedia.org/wiki/Emma_Darwin, at p. 1 of 4. [2/14/09.]

Thus, Charles and Emma and the other Darwin ancestry fit in well with the scientific luminaries wanting to break away from these strongholds, especially the church. It is indeed curious that with the cornerstone of Darwinian macro being "natural selection," his own bulldog, Thomas Henry Huxley, was on the fence with "natural selection" as an explanation for macro (though it provided a good base to start with) and also did not adopt gradualism (uniformitarianism) very quickly.[93] One would think that if he wanted to rally 'round the flag, he'd be more attuned with that flag. This is further evidentiary of his looking for a poster child and that Darwin was the best he could come up with.

With all of his vigorous and sometimes aggressive advocacy for Darwin during debates and the written media, it is also interesting that the generally recognized premier anatomist of his time who was such a staunch Darwinian advocate never taught evolution in his classroom.[94] From this writer's perspective, that deserves kudos. It also raises a legitimate question, though, as to how much Huxley was convicted with Darwinism as opposed to anti-ecclesiastical dogma, with the former being a timely, expeditious means to an end, as opposed to a source of great conviction. His views toward natural selection and uniformitarianism give ammunition that the appeal was more anti-ecclesiastical than it was scientific. He certainly believed in macro itself (eventually anyway), being among the first to advocate for transmutation of dinosaurs to birds.[95]

Huxley himself was more opposed to religious extremism than he was religion itself, and what he protested was the dogmatism taught by organized religion (theology).[96] Part of his problem was that he saw no instructive basis for morality because it was defined partly by culture and partly by the individual. There were no firm guidelines. Certainly nature was not the paradigm: "Of moral purpose I see not a trace in nature. That is an article of exclusively human manufacture."[97]

---

93 Thomas Henry Huxley-Wikipedia, the free encyclopedia; http://en.wikipedia.org/wiki/ Thomas_Henry_Huxley, at p. 1 of 28. [4/4/09.]
94 The Huxley File, "@5. A Hidden Bond: Evolution," http://aleph0.clarku.edu/huxley/guide5.html, at p. 5of 9. [4/4/09.]; see also Michael Ruse, "Thomas Henry Huxley and the status of evolution as science" (1997), from Alan P. Barr, Thomas Henry Huxley's place in science and letters: centenary essays, Georgia: Athens, cited by Thomas Henry Huxley, Wikipedia, supra, at pp. 13, 14 of 28.
95 Thomas Henry Huxley, Wikipedia, id., at p.1 of 28.
96 Cyril Bibby, Scientist Extraordinary: the life and work of Thomas Henry Huxley 1825-1895 (1959), p. 155 & School Board Chronicle, vol. 2, p. 360, both cited by Thomas Henry Huxley, Wikipedia, supra, at p. 15 of 28.
97 Leonard Huxley, The Life and Letters of Thomas Henry Huxley (1900), 2 vols., 8vo, Thomas Huxley's Letter to W. Platt Ball, London: Macmillan.

His attitude toward organized religion puts him on the same footing as our Founding Fathers, especially Madison and Jefferson, wherein past Church abuses weighed heavily on their minds. I am unaware of the extent of Huxley's knowledge of the historical ecclesiastical basis for the framers' concern (which he may have had since he was deeply involved in education), but he clearly shared their desire for free discourse and exchange of ideas, and viewed ecclesiasticism as the antithesis of that aim. It is asserted that had they all known the Christ of the New Testament better, they would have found some communion with His attack on the Scribes and Pharisees. Christ was as against the traditions of men as they were, in the sense that they were an artifice for the expression of power rather than heart-felt religion.

We return now to Huxley's aforementioned animus against anatomist Richard Owen, who represented the scientific establishment that was linked so intimately with the Anglican church at the time.[98] Origin was the perfect opportunity not only for Huxley to throw in his unequivocal support for the general notion of macro, but for him to attack the provincial dogmatism as well and exercise his iconoclasm, which for him interfered with the pursuit of truth. In so doing, his early favorable reviews of Origin also attacked Owen,[99] who seemingly retaliated in April with his own attack on Darwin's friends and apparently was also condescending in dismissing Darwin's own ideas, which in turn angered Darwin.[100]

This is somewhat interesting and suggests hypocrisy on Darwin's part because it was Owen, whom Darwin had met through Henslow, who had helped explain the giant fossils that Darwin had returned home from the Beagle with, identifying them as gigantic extinct sloths, an unknown animal (Scelidotherium—near complete skeleton), a giant capybara-type rodent about the size of a hippopotamus (Toxodon—skull) and a giant armadillo (Glyptodon—armour fragments).[101] These

---

98 The Huxley File, supra, "@4. Darwin's Bulldog," http://aleph0.clarku.edu/huxley/guide4.html, at p. 1 of 7.
99 Adrian Desmond & James Moore, Darwin (1991), London: Michael Joseph, Penguin Group, ISBN 0-7181-3430-3, pp. 477-491.
100 Janet E. Browne, Aramont Professor of the History of Science, Harvard University, Charles Darwin: vol. 2, The Power of Place (2002) London: Jonathan Cape, ISBN 0-7126-6837-3, pp. 110-112, cited by "Charles Darwin," Wikipedia, supra, at p. 11; see also "Reaction to Darwin's theory," Wikipedia, supra, at p. 10.
101 Richard Owen, Fossil Mammalia Part 1. The zoology of the voyage of the H.M.S. Beagle, edited by C. R. Darwin, London: Smith, Elder and Co., pp. 16 (http://darwin-online.org.uk/content/frameset? viewtype=text&itemID =F9.1&pageseq=26), 73 (http://darwin-online.org.uk/content/frameset? viewtype=text&itemID= F9.1&pageseq=83) & 106 (http://darwin-online.org.uk/content/frameset? viewtype=text&itemID= F9.1&pageseq=83), cited by Charles Darwin, Wikipedia, supra, at p. 6.

fossil finds were closely ancestral to living species in South America.¹⁰² One would have thought that Huxley's swipe at Owen, which certainly in part fueled Owen's subsequent reaction, would have received some kind of gentle rebuke, or an attempt at peace-making by Darwin, which there is no record of whatsoever. Was it really surprising to Darwin that Owen may have retaliated in kind in some capacity?

Instead, to his discredit, Darwin actively encouraged Huxley's expressions of animosity toward Owen through the years (published weekly in the Athenaeum), the vitriol of the Huxley attacks bothering Lyell, who in turn was actually teased by Darwin for his reactions.¹⁰³ It is submitted that the Huxley-Owen dispute (which contributed to Huxley ultimately displacing Owen as the premier recognized anatomist of his time) shows one of the uglier sides of Darwin himself, who may well have been puppeteered in this regard by Huxley (psychologically, if in no other manner). It certainly fits into the main orchestrating of Darwin's theory by his friends and allies, and highlights one of the ways they were actually able to manipulate him into complacency when his so-called sense of decency and honor should have kicked in instead. Darwin appeared to have savored Owen's execution in a way uncharacteristic of an inherently decent-minded man, and one would have thought that Owen's initial role as Huxley's mentor would have also counted for something that Darwin would have reminded Huxley of. The manipulative thread is picked up below in the discussion of Darwin's health and other physical issues.

D. A MORE COMPLETE VIEW SHOWS THAT DARWIN WAS AN ATHEIST

At this point it seems necessary to address those who feel that language in Origin of Species suggests Darwin as actually being a Deist himself, which superficially is supportable, but under scrutiny becomes specious. There is indeed language in all six Origin editions, which date at 1859, 1860, 1861, 1866, 1869, 1872 and 1876 (additions and corrections to 6th edition and not considered a 7th), respectively, that are outwardly construable as such. From the second edition on, this same language appeared at the very end of all of the editions (as well as the 1876 6th edition revision): "Thus, from the war of nature,

---
102 Darwin, supra, pp. 201-205, & Janet E. Browne, Charles Darwin: vol 1 Voyaging (1995) London: Jonathan Cape, ISBN 1-84413-314-1, pp. 349-350, both cited by Charles Darwin, Wikipedia, ibid.
103 "Reaction to Darwin's theory," Wikipedia, supra, at p. 10.

from famine and death, the most exalted object which we are capable of conceiving, namely, the production of the higher animals, directly follows. There is grandeur in this view of life, with its several powers, <u>having been originally breathed by the Creator into a few forms or into one</u>; and that, whilst this planet has gone cycling on according to the fixed law of gravity, from so simple a beginning endless forms most beautiful and most wonderful have been, and are being evolved." (Emphasis added.) The 1859 first edition is worded exactly the same except "by the Creator" is omitted.

But any inclination to say that a supernatural power is being entertained by Darwin as an option for setting things in motion, similar to perhaps Aristotle's "Prime Mover" (discussed later), is illusory. There is enough evidence to show that Darwin's usage is nothing other than a convenient shorthand for first life and not a possible resolution for a problem he recognizes he cannot address, First Cause, because he is constantly seeking a natural explanation for which he has no idea of how to account for. This is apparent from the language of his letter to Joseph Hooker dated 3/29/1863 (after three <u>Origin</u> editions had already been published): "<u>But I have long regretted that I truckled to public opinion</u> & used Pentateuchal term of creation, by which I really meant "appeared" by some wholly unknown process.—<u>It is mere rubbish thinking, at present, of origin of life; one might as well think of origin of matter.</u>"[104] (Emphasis added.) Likewise, in a letter to the Athenaeum dated 4/18/1863, Darwin writes: "Your reviewer sneers with justice at my use of the "Pentateuchal terms," 'of one primordial form into which life was first breathed': in a purely scientific work I ought perhaps not to have used such terms; <u>but they well serve to confess that our ignorance is as profound on the origin of life as on the origin of force or matter.</u> ... Why certain whole classes, or certain numbers of a class, have advanced and others have not, we cannot even conjecture. <u>But as we do not know under what forms or how life originated in this world</u>, it would be rash to assert that even such lowly endowed animals as the Foraminifera, with their beautiful shells as figured by Dr. Carpenter, have not in any degree advanced in organization."[105](Emphasis added.)

---

[104] Darwin Correspondence Project, Letter no. 4065, at http://www.darwinproject.ac.uk/darwinletters/calendar/entry-4065.html, at p. 1 of 3.] [10/8/09.]

[105] Darwin Correspondence Project, supra, Letter no. 4108, http://www.darwinproject.ac.uk/darwinletters/calendar/entry-4108, at pp. 1, 3 & 4 of 4. [10/8/09.]

These cursory respective excerpts even by themselves reveal not a man willing to recognize perhaps a supernatural aspect to the creation of life only (what else can the words "Creator" and "breathed" used in conjunction with one another possibly connote?), but one who simply admits he cannot explain origins and uses words like creation and Creator for shorthand convenience, just like "natural selection" is used in that sense as we will be exploring later. There is no other rational way to collectively interpret his missives to both Hooker and the Athenaeum as above-referenced. While he did later on in his autobiography directed to his children describe himself as an agnostic (after Huxley coined the term, of course), his words, it is submitted, are more consistent with his being an outright atheist. Regardless, a Deist he definitely is not, and never was by the time he publicly expostulated on natural selection and evolution. His continuing to use "Creator" and "breathed" in ALL of his editions of Origin (save for Creator in the very first edition, but the allusion even there was the same) shows that in reality he "truckled" to the public throughout his entire life (I'd call it at the very least "game-played"), despite his expression of alleged regret in 1863 to Hooker at the truckling. It is highly arguable that even at best, Darwin was an "atheist" in agnostic clothing. He always lamented the failure to naturally explain life's origins, even contributing to some degree in driving away Sir Antony Flew from the atheistic ranks, as will be dealt with later in this work.

Still not convinced? Then how do we reconcile his struggles with life's origins and the famous (and scientifically inadequate) pond letter to Hooker in 1871 (this after publication of 5 editions of Origin) as explicated upon further below? He doesn't express satisfaction that a higher power kicked in an initial creative process but struggles with a speculation to "naturally" account for the first life, admitting, of course, the Herculean (and it is submitted, will later be shown to be the chemically "impossible") nature of the task.

I consider his above-referenced autobiography, written circa 1879, to be at best unreliable, and at worst disingenuous, when it comes to his own personal assessment of his status. A section therein is specifically titled "Religious Belief" but look at how he assails both the Old and New Testament. He writes: "But I had gradually come, by this time, to see that the Old Testament from its manifestly false history of the world, with the Tower of Babel, the rainbow as a sign, etc., etc., and from its attributing to God the feelings of a revengeful tyrant, was no more to be trusted than the sacred books of the Hindoos, or the beliefs of any barbarian."[106]

Darwin further records: "By further reflecting that the clearest evidence would be requisite to make any sane man believe in the miracles by which Christianity is supported,--<u>that the more we know of the fixed laws of nature the more incredible do miracles become</u>,--that they differ in many important details, far too important as it seemed to me to be admitted as the usual inaccuracies of eye-witnesses;--<u>by such reflections as these, which I do give not as having the least novelty or value, but as they influenced me, I gradually came to disbelieve in Christianity as a divine revelation</u>. The fact that many false religions have spread over large portions of the earth like wild-fire had some weight with me. Beautiful as is the morality of the New Testament, it can hardly be denied that its perfection depends in part on the interpretation which we now put on metaphors and allegories."[107] (Emphasis added.)

He also scribes: "Thus, disbelief crept over me at a very slow rate, but was at last complete. The rate was so slow that I felt no distress, and have never since doubted even for a single second that my conclusion was correct. <u>I can indeed hardly see how anyone ought to wish Christianity to be true; for if so the plain language of the text seems to show that the men who did not believe, and this would include my Father, Brother and almost all my best friends, will be everlastingly punished</u>. [New Para.] And this is a damnable doctrine. [New Para.] Although I did not think much about the existence of a personal God until a considerably later period of my life, I will here give the vague conclusions to which I have been driven. <u>The old argument of design in nature, as given by Paley, which formerly to me seemed so conclusive, fails, now that the law of natural selection has been discovered</u>. We can no longer argue that, for instance, the beautiful hinge of a bivalve shell must have been made by an intelligent being, like the hinge of a door by man. <u>There seems to be no more design in the variability of organic beings and in the action of natural selection, than in the course which

---

106 <u>The autobiography of Charles Darwin 1809-1882</u> (1958) Francis Darwin, ed., (1958), p. 85, http://darwin-online.org.uk/content/contentblock?hitpage=1&viewtype= 1&it..., at p. 1 of 9.
107 <u>The autobiography of Charles Darwin 1809-1882</u>, Id., at p. 86.

the wind blows. Everything in nature is the result of fixed laws."[108] (Emphasis added.)

Finally (for purposes of this presentation in following this thread), he asserts: "But passing over the endless beautiful adaptations which we everywhere meet with, it may be asked how can the generally beneficent arrangement of the world be accounted for? Some writers indeed are so much impressed with the amount of suffering in the world, that they doubt if we look to all sentient beings, whether there is more of misery or of happiness;-whether the world as a whole is a good or a bad one. According to my judgment happiness decidedly prevails, though this would be very difficult to prove. If the truth of this conclusion be granted, it harmonises well with the effects which we might expect from natural selection. If all the individuals of any species were habitually to suffer to an extreme degree they would neglect to propagate their kind; but we have no reason to believe that this has ever or at least often occurred. Some other considerations, moreover, lead to the belief that all sentient beings have been formed so as to enjoy, as a general rule, happiness."[109] (Emphasis added.)

To a convicted Christian, there are enough bullet holes in Darwin's above recitations to have independently sunk a pristine Titanic, although interestingly, the sheer randomness and yet fixity of natural selection as an immutable law from the Darwinian perspective, is vocalized perhaps more compellingly than anywhere in his actual public works (remember, this autobiography was for his kids). As a graduate seminary student, from the Christian perspective, he should have known better than to make the statements and examples that he did, and should have been aware of all the disputational counterpoints, but this kind of discussion is for a different time than I write in now.

I do not want to digress on this topic any further for now, but it is submitted that it simply is not objectively possible when the pertinent evidence is considered to say that Darwin, based on his actual known public writings and correspondences, even resembled a Deist, and it is strongly urged here that he was even an atheist, as opposed to being an alleged agnostic. Interestingly, in his autobiography, Darwin thinks he could be properly called a Theist, making the same mislabeling

---
108 Id., at p. 87.
109 Id., at p. 88.

that Flew does later on in this work, wherein, at best, he would have to be properly labeled a Deist. He writes (and with no small doubt as he concludes this passage): "Another source of conviction in the existence of God, connected with the reason and not with the feelings, impresses me as having much more weight. This follows from the extreme difficulty or rather impossibility of conceiving this immense and wonderful universe, including man with his capacity of looking far backwards and far into futurity, as the result of blind chance or necessity. When thus reflecting I feel compelled to look to a First Cause having an intelligent mind in some [New Para.] degree analogous to that of man; and I deserve to be called a Theist."

He uninterruptedly continues: "This conclusion was strong in my mind about the time [this is a new Para. in the actual text as well], as far as I can remember, when I wrote the Origin of Species; and it is since that time that it has very gradually with many fluctuations become weaker. But then arises the doubt—can the mind of man, which has, as I fully believe, developed from a mind as low as that possessed by the lowest animal, be trusted when it draws such conclusions?"[110] (Emphasis added.)

I consider Darwin's reflection that he had intelligent First Cause in mind when he wrote Origin of Species totally disingenuous when compared to the evidence above, but for our purposes, suffice it to say he totally misapplies the word Theist.

E. HOW UNIQUE WAS DARWIN'S THEORY?

Notions of macro were itself not unique, of course, and the Greek philosopher Anaximander between 610-546 B.C. theorized that all life forms originated from the sea and then became modified on land. Linnaeus, who in 1735 published the threshold book on taxonomy called Systema Naturae, later said that he thought that plants descended from a common ancestor.[111] Of course, Darwin's own grandfather Erasmus wrote his own contributions, including Zoonomia, concerning evolution. Lucretius, in the first century AD, perpetuated the naturalism taught by the "open society" of Epicurus in the third century BCE and the empirical inquiry methodology

---
110 Id., pp. 92 & 93.
111 Scientific American, January 2009, "Darwin's Living Legacy," pp. 38-43, at p. 40.

necessary for reaching and retaining it, even suggesting a "natural selection" in evolution.[112] So even from that historical lineage, there was nothing unique about the theory of evolution, of which Darwin himself always readily admitted.

In fact, Jean Baptiste de Lamarck tackled the issue in his <u>Zoological Philosophical Work</u> published in 1809, which was, ironically enough, the year of Darwin's birth. He felt that evolution was directly related to the environment, that needs resulted in reaction to it, that there was an inherent will among organisms to progress, and that once new characteristics in response thereto were developed, they were passed on to succeeding generations ("law of acquired characteristics").[113] The qualitative degree of difference between Lamarck and Darwin will be discussed a little later in this section. It is submitted that qualitatively the differences are much less than initially meets the eye or is argued by macros. This contributes to the "poster child" Darwin argument made in this book.

Before getting into Darwin's own form of macro, it must be pointed out that the prevailing ecclesiastical dogmatism up to him was that God created all life forms pristinely at the time of Creation and that once created, they were immutable. Thus, all variations within kinds were made at once and never changed. What you see now is the exact way it has always been. Adjustments were made to this view by Cuvier and his protégé, Agassiz, but they in essence involved subsequent creations. There were no changes internal to specific species or interspeciation from those events. There is, of course, no Scriptural support for either of those views whatsoever. It was simply an inference drawn by the ecclesiastics and scholars influenced by them, an assumption contrary to fact. There were already distinct, observable differences in mankind such as human races being white, yellow or black. Since Adam and Eve could not comport with all of these characteristics at once, something had to have happened since the Fall. The same dogmatic attitude exercised by the Scribes and Pharisees in Christ's day persisted then, as it does now in other ways.

---

112 Pat Duffy Hutcheon, "What Lucretius Wrought," third in a series of articles on the evolution humanism published in <u>Humanist in Canada</u> (Winter 1997/98), pp. 20-22, cited by http://humanists.net/pdhutcheon/ humanist%20 articles/lucritus.htm, at pp. 1 & 3 of 1-5. [8/8/09.]

113 <u>Lamarck, Darwin and Mendel</u>, Molwick Books, pp. 2 & 3 of 5; see also "Darwin, Mendel and History," at p. 1 of 1.

The introduction of Darwin's "natural selection," however, purportedly laid the foundational waters (validly or invalidly), and was hence revolutionary in that respect, despite much disagreement even among his supporters (especially bulldog Huxley) as to the validity of that part of the theory. Therefore, it is important to try to define the term as precisely, completely and fairly as possible. As stated in <u>Origin of Species</u> (again, a misnomer): "As many more individuals of each species are born than can possibly survive; and as, consequently, there is a frequently recurring struggle for existence, it follows that any being, if it vary however slightly in any manner profitable to itself, under the complex and sometimes varying conditions of life, will have a better chance of surviving, and thus be naturally selected. From the strong principle of inheritance, any selected variety will tend to propagate its new and modified form."[114]

This says very little other than when there is an advantage (trait) that better allows an organism to survive, it gets self-perpetuated and multiplies, thus becoming a variation, and thus continuing to carry on from generation to generation that same advantage. Frankly, that is as profound as saying that when a child has two tall parents, he very likely will end up tall himself. It is also nothing more than observational. That is not evidence that the phenomenon is an a priori scientific process with a mechanism all its own that is in essence a creative force and existed without benefit of an intelligence putting it there. It tells us nothing about how that process came into being or that it involves anything more than saying that beings with this trait and ability to reproduce it live on and others without it die off. That by itself is like saying that in a fight to the death, the healthy, full-grown tiger, all other things being equal, will more than likely beat the healthy, full-grown German Shepherd. It suffers from the same origin problem as the First Cause. In other words, it explains nothing about origins or the derivation of this tendency. As will be seen, this was a continuing concern of perhaps the most notorious atheist of the past 20th Century, Sir Antony Flew. This by itself did not cause his conversion to Deism, but he always recognized it as an argumentative thorn in the macro arsenal.

---

[114] Charles Darwin, <u>The Origin of Species</u> (1859) http://www.age-of-the-sage.org/evolution/ charles_darwin/origin_of_species.html at p. 3 of 5 (no page no. or chapter provided here or at other sources, but language appeared at many sources). [9/23/09.]

No modern-day, non-ecclesiastical Creationist worth his salt would deny natural selection, though it does not have a great deal of independent meaning. It is part of variation and adaptation, having no apparent connection to transmutation, and is simply a description and observation no more profound than saying that the sun rises in the day and sets at night. The process by which this happens, however, is of enormous interest and significance. Though in 2007 macro biologist Francisco J. Ayala of the University of California, Irvine, wrote that: "Darwin completed the Copernican Revolution [which, of course, was never initiated by Copernicus himself] by drawing out for biology the notion of nature as a lawful system of matter in motion that human reason can explain without recourse to supernatural agency,"[115] this "begs the question." The logical inference would be if there is a system operating in a "lawful" manner, some entity had to set the rules and put it in motion as a lawgiver. In other words, this phenomenon happens. How was it actuated? If natural, how? Most certainly the possibility of a supernatural agency, despite Ayala's conclusionary and unsubstantiated statement, still looms very large, indeed.

But let us deal with a more complete statement of this term. As stated in Britannica Concise Encyclopedia, natural selection is a: "Process that results in adaptation of an organism to its environment by means of selectively reproducing changes in its genotype. Variations that increase an organism's chances of survival and procreation are preserved and multiplied from generation to generation at the expense of less advantageous variations. As proposed by Charles Darwin, natural selection is the mechanism by which evolution occurs. It may arise from differences in survival, fertility, rate of development, mating success, or any other aspect of the life cycle. Mutation, gene flow, and genetic drift, all of which are random processes, also alter gene abundance. Natural selection moderates the effects of these processes because it multiplies the incidence of beneficial mutations over generations and eliminates harmful ones, since the organisms that carry them leave few or no descendants."[116]

As described in the opening remarks at answers.com, "natural selection is the process by which heritable traits that make it more likely for an

---

115 Scientific American, supra, at p. 40.
116 http://www.answers.com/topic/natural-selection, at p. 1 of 28. [9/23/09.]

organism to survive and successfully reproduce become more common in a population over successive generations."[117]

These definitions, of course, still tell us nothing about origins. It is therefore very bogus and premature to say that there is no need for a programmer or designer. We know of nothing in everyday life that performs a task that is inanimate without being given a conscious, planned direction by an intelligent inputter. The capacity for electricity has been there from the beginning, but was not harnessed until Edison and friends. It would still be unharnessed and useless to us without these enterprising people. Nobody is audacious enough to say that it was always there in its utilized by man form, simply there to be properly directed as we know it. But all natural phenomena, no matter what function it serves us, is, according to the macros, always there in the sense of being self-forming, without any assistance at all. Just as electricity did not gather itself on its own to serve us as it does, there is little rational reason to believe that anything natural did either. It's there so it always has been, all on its own. That contradicts common sense and experience, no question.

As far as integrating "natural selection" into his theory, Darwin factored in the Malthusian population principle (1798-"Essay on the Principle of Population"-the population will double every 25 years unless there is a limitation on food supply), so that the non sequitur of variation becoming transmutation could take place. This is a non sequitur because the evidence for transmutation was lacking and simply presumed under circumstances not meriting the presumption. It had to be because the alternative is highly unattractive. There should have been living transitionals, not just fossil record dead ones (which themselves are lacking), as transmutations should be ongoing. Darwin himself expected continuing macro. When considered with all of the other evidence, it is asserted that this "oversight" was deliberate. Unlike Lamarck, Darwin did not consider these changes caused by the environment. The nine different beak-sized and shaped Galapagos finch differences already existed. Inferred was that the finches flew to appropriate locations that best suited these characteristics, although further adaptation and variation presumably did develop from there. It is submitted that Darwin was never entirely clear as to this point.

---

117 Id., at p. 2 of 28.

As for Lamarck compared to Darwin, Darwin did factor in his verification of Lyell's uniformitarianism in concluding that since the South American continent had raised, it had to have taken a substantial period of time to do so, at least millions of years (ignoring a certain brand of catastrophism, of course). This permitted him to extrapolate that into a theory that small, progressive changes produced not only variation, but transmutation as well. But that should not have been such an easy leap for Darwin, who from his seminary training had to be aware that the flood resulted in large part from the opening of the fountains of the deep. Though tectonic plating was not known in his day, it is not hard to imagine a great upheaval as a consequence of even that Scriptural phenomenon. There should have been a discussion by him of how the Noahic flood could not accommodate his finding. He did not weigh the evidence but presumed Lyell's hypothesis to be correct. Strict uniformitarianism in terms of only pure gradual change, with no accommodation at all for catastrophism, of course, has not survived scientific scrutiny.

Even the assertion of environment not influencing these changes is a non sequitur, as a common progenitor would dictate environmental stimuli. Otherwise, where does the single-cell organism go from there, even provided it has developed an ability to reproduce by cell division? Any marine life, be it plant or animal, has to develop in response to the stimuli around it. How, then, can environment properly not be influential? It is inescapable that Lamarck correctly identified changes with environment, at least in that sense. Regardless of the variant sizes of the finch beaks, these birds grew beaks. That had to be in reaction to something they encountered or had anticipated. This is true whether or not it was coping with population growth or not, the immediate environment by necessity would have to be the coping target. If not, and adaptation was a sheer random event, the odds against any successful species would be astronomically high.

It can be well argued that the resistance acquired by over 200 insect and rodent species to DDT is adaptive, as well as bacterial strains overcoming antibiotics. It is highly unlikely for such a distinct adaptive process to have been acquired randomly. So even there, Lamarck was at least in part right. Even science tends to categorize in blacks and whites rather than greys, the Heisenberg principle of uncertainty notwithstanding.

Further, for all of the claims circulating about inheritance of acquired characteristics being debunked, it is hard to explain without it why warthogs, camels and ostriches inherit calluses on their knees with each succeeding generation that corresponds to exactly where they kneel.

The population thesis also has severe scientific hurdles to overcome to be a transmutation factor. Back in the 1950s, geneticist J.B.S. Haldane determined that only 1667 beneficial mutations could be substituted over a period of 10 million years, giving far too little time for many higher vertebrate species to develop. This has become known as <u>Haldane's Dilemma</u>.[118] Applied to the simian-like to man transmutation issue, 1667 beneficial mutations would comprise only about three ten-millionths of the human genome, rendering the "missing link" crusade an exercise in futility. Both sides of the issue have weighed in on the Internet, and macro George C. Williams himself asserted that he did not consider the dilemma to be solved.[119]

There are macros espousing the opposite view, of course, but since there is no unanimity on such an important hypothesis, this is exactly the kind of topic to get full point and counterpoint debate as our Founding Fathers intended for such issues to be. Only bias and prejudice would preclude a thorough examination of this issue. <u>Obviously, the younger and younger the earth can be demonstrated to be, the greater and greater becomes Haldane's Dilemma. This is another reason why these two hypotheses need to be mutually explored. As expressed thusly, this becomes a scientific pursuit for a secular purpose, not a religious one</u>.

Once a beneficial mutation occurs, inheritability is made difficult in that many traits are polygenous (derived from a combination of many genes) rather than monogenous (a single gene). Even in the latter case, a single gene often influences a wide range of traits. Applied, if a five-gene polygenous trait is to be inherited, it has a 1 in 32 chance of happening or only 3%. Since most females in higher vertebrate species

---

[118] Walter J. Remine, <u>The Biotic Message: Evolution versus message theory</u>, Saint Paul, MN: St. Paul Science, 1993, pp. 208-236.
[119] George C. Williams (1992) <u>Natural Selection: Domains, Levels and Challenges</u>, pp. 143-144. "Evolution versus Message Theory."

do not average 32 progeny each, the chances of the polygenous trait disappearing are quite high.

The synthesis of Mendelian genetics with Darwinian theory is the foundation for neo-Darwinism. But it is difficult to see how. All the Mendelian Law of Scission and the Law of Dominant Character say is that the recessive gene can and is repressed but reappears in succeeding generations, and heredity can be fairly mathematically expressed as a segregation ratio, utilizing statistics and mathematics in a manner well advanced for his time.[120] His theory has tremendous scientific utility and is rightly hailed in that community, but it does not give the "how." I have read contentions that Mendel was opposed to Darwinism (as an Augustine monk that would seem consistent) and that he wrote something to Darwin that the latter never opened, but I have not uncovered conclusive evidence to verify or deny this. I must therefore assume the "negative" until better evidence comes in.

Meanwhile, suffice it to say that arguably Mendel's principles do not require macro as its guide. As one Internet source stated: "The truly innovative and original idea in Darwin's work was the concept of population [I disagree. This was clearly taken from Malthus], from which the theory of natural selection proceeded. Heredity in Mendel's terms, however, far from producing evolutionary change, results in perfectly predictable segregation ratios."[121] This has not stopped the neo-Darwinists from deriving mutations from Mendel's hereditary principles to account for the changes that Darwinism predicts. While mutations can promote minor changes, it is hard to imagine the larger variety changes from that venue, and certainly not transmutation.

Speaking further of Mendel, it has been written that he was "rediscovered" in 1900 by Hugo de Vries and Carl Correns.[122] It has also been written that after Mendel had read his paper, Experiments on Plant Hybridization, at two meetings of the Natural History Society of Brunn in Moravia in 1865, it was published in 1866 in Proceedings of the Natural History Society of Brunn to very little fanfare, and was cited but three times over the next 35 years.[123] The

---

[120] General Theory: Conditional Evolution of Life, "Lamarck, Darwin and Mendel," Molwick Books, at pp. 3 & 4 of 5.
[121] Frank Eisenhaler & Alexander Schleiffer, "Gregor Mendel, The Beginning of Biomathematics," at p. 4 of 4, from IMP Bioinformatics Group.
[122] "Gregor Mendel"-Wikipedia, http://en.wikipedia.org/wiki/Gregor_Mendel, at p. 2 of 5. [7/4/09.]
[123] Ibid.

1900 rediscovery was also mentioned at two other Internet sources.[124] This alone is a "red flag," for as depicted above, Solomons in <u>1895</u> named a peak <u>Mt. Mendel</u> under the presumption that his work gave great glory to macro. That means that at least in inner circles (but now somewhat publicized by the mountain's designation, but still probably not observed by the general public), Mendel's theories must have received great recognition prior to this, yet this date alone <u>pre-dates</u> his purported <u>rediscovery</u> by at least five years.

So it seems that there is some game-playing going on here, and the reasons why could prove quite probing for anyone taking the time to explore such territory. It would appear that the macros were waiting for the right time to spring Mendel on the public and were surreptitiously holding back. One very prominent reason highly suspected by this writer could be that they wanted to wait until Mendel's death (which wound up being on 1/6/1884) before exploiting what they wanted out of his findings so he wouldn't be around to contradict them After all, look what they did to Copernicus! As aforementioned, there is no obvious reason why Mendel's theory need apply to macro at all, and being a man committed to God, it is highly likely the fur would have flown if they tried to manipulate his findings during his lifetime. Mendel's principles perfectly comport with DNA/RNA and no form of Darwinian or other macro theory is necessary for his principles to function.

So, again, how unique was Darwin's theory? When removed of its window dressing, not nearly as different from Lamarck's as first appearing. But England was ready for it, and it sold like hotcakes, selling out on the very first day it hit the stands on 11/24/1859, and there were six editions eventually printed by 1872.[125] In 1809, the time was not yet ripe and Lamarck did not receive the ticker tape parade that Darwin did. The Industrial Revolution was not far enough along yet. In fact, in the 1830s and 40s, there was a Christian fervor in England which could have had him labeled a seditionist and blasphemer, and perhaps criminally indicted.[126]

---

124 <u>Evolution Library</u>, "What Darwin Didn't Know: Gregor Mendel and the Mechanics of He , at p. 1 of 2 & "Early Theories of Evolution: Darwin and Natural Selection," at p. 6 of 8.
125 "Early Theories of Evolution: Darwin and Natural Selection," Ibid., at p. 5 of 8.
126 Ibid.

But 50 years can be a very long time for social and economic movements, and Erasmus Darwin was in between. Between the two and the social and economic climate discussed above, 1859 found a far more receptive audience. The scientists, economists and academics were by no means the only class that wanted change. So did the working man, who was also tiring of the Anglican Church's dogma. While certainly the expression "natural selection" was an effective gadget phrase, there was far more than the mere interjection of a viable macro mechanism involved in the acceptance of Darwin's work, which Huxley NEVER accepted. This lack of a more generally concrete scientific ground reveals more about the social milieu of the time than it does great scientific achievement.

The social phenomenon of the theory is strongly hinted at in considering that many serious scientific organizations remained unconvinced of its scientific merit. <u>In 1872, Darwin was denied membership into the Zoological section of the French Institute</u>. Listen to these words as the reason for rejection!: "What has closed the doors of the Academy to Mr. Darwin is that the science of those of his books which have made his chief title to fame-the 'Origin of Species,' and still more the 'Descent of Man,' <u>is not science, but a mass of assertions and absolutely gratuitous hypotheses, often evidently fallacious</u>. [New Para.] This kind of publication and these theories are a bad example, which a body that respects itself cannot encourage."[127] (Emphasis added.) Coming from the land of Louis Pasteur, where science was taken seriously as a discipline rather than a mere desperate, philosophical exercise, that was quite apropos. But this kind of scientific integrity didn't stop the rage, further indicative of an agenda and rally around the flag mentality rather than being based on serious science.

F. DARWIN COMPARED TO SCIENTIFIC GREATS

A strong case can be made for Darwin being overrated as either a naturalist or scientist. It took ornithologist John Gould to show him after his return from the Beagle that all of Galapagos bird species were different species of finches as opposed to some being wrens and blackbirds.[128] For all of his reputed organization and thoroughness, he required Fitzroy's and others' notes to connect specific species with

---

127 <u>Life and Letters of Charles Darwin</u>, D. Appleton and Co., London, 2:400, footnote, 1911.
128 Darwin, supra, at pp. 201-205 & Frank J. Sulloway, "Darwin and His Finches: The Evolution of a Legend," <u>Journal of the History of Biology</u> (1982) 15 (1):1-53, at pp. 20-23, cited by Charles Darwin, Wikipedia, at p. 6 of 31.

specific islands.[129] He was perhaps overly influenced by Charles Lyell's geological gradualism, seeing Lyell in every geological formation he beheld, as geologist Steve Austin will soon explain to us. As aforementioned, Richard Owen revealed the Megaltherium and Glyptodon fossils to be giant rodents and sloths from South America, not Africa as Darwin speculated.

Two queries result from these fossil finds: (1) When Darwin saw no catastrophic evidence in uncovering these fossils, did he really see no catastrophic evidence objectively or as surrogate eyes for his contemporary, Lyell?, and (2) Shouldn't it have occurred to Darwin that if the aforementioned fossils were of giant rodents and sloths as identified by Owen (and which he recognized anyway, he just had their origin misplaced), then maybe the much smaller rodents and sloths of the 19th Century were examples of diminution or devolution, rather than evolution or upgrading?

He also knew of mammoths and mastodons. Elephants of today, while the heaviest land animals and certainly impressive fellows in their own right, are small in comparison to certain types of these ancestors. While lions or tigers are not the kind of critters this unarmed writer would want to encounter in an open setting, they are much smaller than the Smilodon or Saber-toothed cat. These were known in Darwin's time, and, of course, he was privy to his own sloth and rodent fossils. Where's the progression that evolution is supposed to promulgate? It is submitted that this "oversight" was not accidental when Darwin's biographical information is fully assimilated.

But what of Darwin's speculations about life's origins? In a letter to botanist Joseph Hooker dated 1871, he scribed: "It is often said that all the conditions for the first production of a living organism are present, which could ever have been present. But if (and Oh! what a big if!) we could conceive, in some warm little pond, with all sorts of ammonia and phosphoric salts, light, heat, electricity, etc., present, that a protein compound was chemically formed ready to undergo still more complex changes, at the present day such matter would be instantly devoured or absorbed, which would not have been the case before living creatures were formed."[130]

---

129 "Darwin and His Finches," ibid., cited by Charles Darwin, Wikipedia, ibid.
130 "Post details: The story behind Darwin's warm little pond," http://www.arn.org/blogs/index.php/literature/209/11/06/the_story_behind_darwin_s_warm_little-po, at p. 1 of 5. [1/15/10.]

This betrays Darwin's ignorance of basic scientific principles such as the law of mass action, chirality, and other scientific principles named below. While, as we have seen in his letters, he dismissed origin issues of life as "rubbish" for those times, is it really not more likely that it was camouflage for the fact that he had no explanation of his own? Origin was already twelve years old by the time he penned the letter and the polemics were already hot and heavy. He could have theorized in far greater detail to friends in letters than he did, and that would have addressed objections even in his own time. Barnacle and wild orchid study led him to observe that homologous structures served different functions in different species. Why would that be surprising? He conjectured that stepped plains of Patagonian shingle and seashells were raised beaches, and that land was raising and had risen by observing and collecting seashells high in the Andes mountains. An earthquake he experienced in Chile raised the land. He theorized that sinking volcanic mountains are what formed coral atolls.

But with his theological training, were not these observations to be counterbalanced by the fact that the Noahic flood burst open "all the fountains of the great deep?" [Genesis 7:11.] Would not the violent upheaval of a global catastrophe account for lands having risen, if localized phenomena could produce like but smaller scale results? Although tectonic plating was not a topic of the day, Darwin was well aware that the Noahic flood was more than just torrential rainfall. He could have theorized through the hydraulic internal upheaval of the bursting of the fountains of the deep as depicted in Genesis, that land could rise from such activity. It should be clear that he didn't want to look. He didn't want to consider the truth, just speculative ways around it. Is there not a severe lack of basic observational skills involved here (unless deliberate, of course)? This seems to have extended to more than what I have just mentioned above. Institute for Creation Research (ICR) geologist Dr. Steve Austin (who will figure prominently in our later discussion of ICR's RATE project) recently visited Camp Darwin, a site where Darwin made observations concerning the Santa Cruz River in southern Argentina on his Beagle trip that were foundational to his adoption of Lyell's uniformitarianism. Darwin wrote in his journal dated 4/26/1834 of this river: "The river, though it has so little power in transporting even inconsiderable fragments, yet in the lapse of ages might produce by its gradual erosion an effect of which it is difficult to judge the amount." Austin simply wanted to witness the same things Darwin did to see how cogent it was for Darwin to conclude as he did toward uniformitarianism.

Austin wrote: "Darwin correctly observed that the modern river was moving just sand and pebbles. But he did not find a location where the river touches the basalt cliff. <u>Everywhere in the valley, cobbles and boulders on the floodplain separate the present river bank from the solid-rock cliffs.</u> [New Para.] <u>It is obvious that the minor power of the present river is *not* moving boulders, so the present river cannot be eroding the cliffs.</u> Only a big flood could sweep away the cobbles and boulders 50 feet deep below the river bed, and as wide as the valley, to erode the basalt. Darwin erred significantly in linking the modern river's process with the ancient erosion structure."[131] (Emphasis added, except for *not*).

According to Austin, Darwin's observations did not extend far enough. He notes: "Darwin described the narrow section of the valley of the Santa Cruz River as providing evidence that the basalt strata on <u>both</u> sides of the valley were united before somewhat less than 300 feet of erosion occurred, producing the two-mile-wide-gap. (Emphasis added.) I found the basalt stratum in the prominent cliff on the north side of the river. Darwin had correctly identified it. [New Para.] However, no basalt stratum occurs on the *south* side of the river. (Emphasis original.) The ridge on the south side of the valley is a gigantic depositional bar composed mostly of large redeposited basalt boulders and cobbles. Darwin misidentified the southern ridge as a volcanic stratum cooled *in situ* from a lava flow."[132] (Emphasis original.)

Austin goes on to argue: "Large boulders occur on top of the basalt cliff on the north side of the river. Darwin described one as being 15 feet in diameter. According to Darwin, flowing water could not move such big rocks. Water, according to Darwin, could not sweep a boulder 300 feet above the present level of the modern river to the top of a cliff. Therefore, Darwin assumed the big boulder was dropped from a melting iceberg when an ocean stood over the basalt. Again, Darwin was significantly in error. The cobbles and boulders overlying

---

131 Steven Austin, "Darwin's First Wrong Turn," Acts & Facts, ICR, February 2009, pp. 26 & 27.
132 Id., at p. 27.

the basalt at the cliff top are the spillover deposit accumulated rapidly when the flood exceeded the depth of the valley. Therefore, the colossal flood was likely 400 feet deep across the entire six-mile-wide valley!"[133]

From there, Austin inquires and postulates: "Why was Darwin so wrong concerning his interpretation of the river valley? First, he had expectations about what he would see at Camp Darwin before he arrived. His scientific judgment was tainted by preconceptions. Second, Darwin was reading the wrong book before his journey up the Santa Cruz River valley. He had been reading Charles Lyell's book Principles of Geology (1830) during his trans-Atlantic voyage on the *Beagle*. That book gave him the idea that the biggest boulders were deposited from melting icebergs. [New Para.] Third, Darwin was developing a new, woefully inadequate methodology for dealing with the world. He saw the structure of the present valley and understood it to have been formed by the continued slow action of the modern river during the lapse of great geologic ages."[134] Austin wonders that if Darwin had correctly surmised the river valley situation, being a geological macro before becoming a biological one, would he have extrapolated that to his theory concerning the finch beaks? While we will never technically know, it is submitted that based on his tendencies to ignore his previous training, he would have so extrapolated anyway.

Now let us establish some realities here. It is recognized immediately that ICR creates apologetics for young earth creationism, imbuing everything with a purely Creationist slant (although I do feel they give macro an adequate argumentative voice in the bulk of their work). But Austin nonetheless raises some powerful argumentative points. How does the river valley get that kind of erosion without dealing with the large basalt boulders that the river flow is clearly too weak to obviate? And what actual evidence did Darwin use to surmise the southern ridge as a volcanic stratum cooled in situ from a lava flow? And why did he unquestionably accept Lyell's hypothesis of the boulders being accounted for by the melting of icebergs? But the larger problem is this. Darwin was well aware of the big flood depiction in Genesis.

---

133 Ibid., Darwin's comment on the 15 foot diameter of one of the boulders was taken by Austin from (Darwin, C., 1842. "On the distribution of the erratic boulders and on the contemporaneous unstratified deposits of South America.") Transactions of the Geological Society of London.6:415-432—appearing as footnote 2 in his ICR article.
134 Ibid.

When all is factored in on its face, that event is the more immediately likely account for what he actually saw. Regardless, why was this factor completely ignored? Austin as a Creationist immediately resorts to this account and finds his observations totally consistent with the Genesis depiction, especially given the massiveness of the erosion observed. While this makes sense to me, obviously, what Austin concludes dictates nothing as to the validity of Darwin's conclusion other than that Darwin should have been acutely aware of how a Flood scenario would be consistent with what he observed. If macros scream that Austin has made some logical fallacy assumptions, Darwin's are argumentatively double his. While that makes neither conclusively correct, it illustrates the point argued herein. That is for the student to decide after having been presented both sides of the issue (as well as anything else reasonably credible). This presentation does further make Darwin's powers of observation open to serious question.

So how does Darwin stack up against some of the scientific immortals? What about compared to black American George Washington Carver (1864 or 65-1943), considered the father of modern agriculture? His restoration of soil nutrition from cotton farming through the growing of such crops as soybeans and peanuts was a major breakthrough in agriculture. His some 300 discovered uses for peanuts (medicines, food products, beverages, cosmetics, and dyes and paints) and more than 100 uses for the sweet potato demonstrated the vivid imagination and creativity that he invested into his work. He did all this without patenting any of his methods. He is quoted as saying: "One reason I never patent my products is that if I did it would take so much time, I would get nothing else done. But mainly I don't want my discoveries to benefit specific favored persons."[135] He credited his methodologies to a powerful Creator: "I never have to grope for methods. The method is revealed at the moment I am inspired to create something new. Without God to draw aside the curtain I would be helpless."[136]

Or how does Darwin fare against Frenchman Louis Pasteur (1822-1895), the father of modern microbiology? Comparing inorganic matter in sealed or filtered vessels to organic matter exposed to the air,

---

[135] Carver Quotes, Posed on the George Washington Carver National Monument website at www.mps.gov/gwca, quoted by Christine Dao, "Man of Science, Man of God, George Washington Carver, Acts & Facts, ICR, December 2008, p. 8.

[136] Federer, W.J. 1994. America's God and Country Encyclopedia of Quotations. Coppell, TX:FAME Publishing, 96, quoted from ibid.

Pasteur conclusively established that microorganisms growing from the air caused fermentation (the closed vessels revealed no activity), a triumph for biogenesis over spontaneous generation or abiogenesis, which was based on inorganic materials somehow combining to produce the organic. He pioneered Pasteurization and sterilization, and his meticulous, exacting scientific approach to experimentation (which was early criticized for its rigidity) led to the discovery of the rabies (hydrophobia) and anthrax vaccines, in the former case developing both a non-virulent and virulent vaccine. A devout Catholic, Pasteur left no doubt as to what the source of his inspiration was: "Are science and the passionate desire to understand anything else than the effect of that spur towards knowledge which the mystery of the universe has placed in our souls? Where are the true sources of human dignity, of liberty, of modern democracy, <u>unless they are contained in the idea of the infinite, before which all men are equal?</u>"[137] (Emphasis added.) And this is from a man who was a mascot for the scientific method.

Now let's compare Darwin to a fellow Brit, William Kirby (1759-1850, and born in Witnesham, Suffolk, England), considered the <u>father of entomology</u>. He and co-author, British entomologist William Spence, wrote the groundbreaking four-volume work, <u>An Introduction to Entomology: or Elements of the Natural History of Insects</u>. Was the enormous diversity of insect forms attributable to a purely natural process independent of supernatural agency? Not in Kirby's view. He wrote in 1835: "The infinite diversity of their forms and organs; the nice adaptation of these to their several functions; the beauty and elegance of a large number of them; the singularity of others; the variety of their motions; their geographical distribution; but, above all, their pre-eminent utility to mankind in every state and stage of life, render them objects of the deepest interest…<u>so that arguments in proof of these primary attributes of the Godhead, drawn from the habits, instincts, and other adjuncts of the animal creation, are likely to meet with more universal attention.</u>"[138] (Emphasis added.) For Kirby, diversity was one of the direct evidences of God as opposed to an undirected nature simply finding a way to get it done.

---

[137] Keim and Lumet, <u>Louis Pasteur</u>, 143, quoted by Christine Dao, "Man of Science, Man of God: Louis Pasteur," <u>Acts & Facts</u>, ICR, November 2008.

[138] Kirby, W. 1835. <u>The Seventh Bridgewater Treatise on the Power, Wisdom, and goodness of God as Manifested in the Creation: The History, Habits and Instinct of Animals</u>, Vol. 1. London: William Pickering, 1-2, quoted by Christine Dao, "Man of Science, Man of God: William Kirby," <u>Acts & Facts</u>, ICR, July 2008, p. 8.

Keeping it in the English family, let's look at Sir Isaac Newton (1643-1727, and born in Woolsthorpe, a hamlet of Lincolnshire, England), merely considered by some to be the most influential scientist of all time and, of course, the <u>father of universal gravitation</u>. His fame was such that on the epitaph of his grave (written by Alexander Pope) appears: "Nature and Nature's laws lay hid in night: God said, Let Newton be! and all was light." Now that's pretty impacting! How exacting was his scientific approach? He stated: "I frame no hypotheses; for whatever is not deduced from the phenomena is to be called an hypothesis; and hypotheses, whether metaphysical or physical, whether of occult qualities or mechanical, have no place in experimental philosophy." [Letter to Robert Hooke, February 5, 1675/1676.] It is either deducible from the evidence or not stated at all. There is no guesswork. In Newton's mind, diversity was also a testament to the Almighty: "<u>Blind metaphysical necessity, which is certainly the same always and every where, could produce no variety of things</u>. All that diversity of natural things which we find suited to different times and places could arise from nothing but the ideas and will of a Being, necessarily existing."[139] (Emphasis added.)

Newton recognized that consideration of the natural apart from the supernatural was irreconcilable, being a dichotomy that did not and could not exist. Again from his <u>Principia</u> we read: "Since every particle of space is *always*, and every indivisible moment of duration is *every where*, certainly the Maker and Lord of all things cannot be *never* and *no where*. ... God is the same God, always and every where. He is <u>omnipresent</u> not *virtually* only, but also *substantially*, for virtue cannot subsist without substance. ... It is allowed by all that the Supreme God exists necessarily; and by the same necessity he exists *always* and *every where*. ... <u>And thus much concerning God; to discourse of whom from the appearance of things, does certainly belong to Natural Philosophy</u>."[140] (Italicized emphasis original, underlined emphasis added.) And to leave no doubt on the subject of the influence of the <u>supernatural upon the natural</u>: "Gravity explains the motions of the planets, but it cannot explain who set the planets in motion. God

---

139 Newton, I. <u>General Scholium</u>. Translated by Motte, A. 1825. <u>Newton's Principia: The Mathematical Principles of Natural Philosophy. New York</u>; Daniel Adee, 506; quoted by Christine Dao, "Man of Science, Man of God: Isaac Newton," <u>Acts & Facts</u>, ICR, May 2008, p. 9 of pp. 8 & 9.
140 <u>Principia</u>, id., at pp. 505-506, quoted by Dao article, id.

governs all things and knows all that is or can be done."[141] For Newton, an obvious intellectual GIANT, it was inconceivable that nature, without a supernatural actuator, could have systematic properties all on its own, that it could possibly conceive and direct itself.

Still keeping ourselves within the United Kingdom, let's consider Darwin vs. Robert Boyle (1627-1691, born in Linsmore Castle, County Waterford, Ireland), regarded as the <u>father of modern chemistry</u>, and who also contributed mightily to physics. He expounded the atomic theory of matter in "The Sceptical Chymist," which established chemistry as a major science rather than being subordinate to medicine or alchemy. In turn, his Boyle's law (the volume of a gas is inversely proportional to the pressure of the gas) is one of the bulwarks of physics.

In 1681, he published <u>A Discourse of Things Above Reason</u>, for which he argued that reason alone cannot comprehend the majesty of God. Nature was a testimony to the supernatural, but inseverable from it. He also wrote: "When with bold telescopes I survey the old and newly discovered stars and planets; when with excellent microscopes I discern the unimitable subtility of nature's curious workmanship; and when, in a word, by the help of anatomical knives, and the light of chymical furnaces, I study the book of nature, I find myself oftentimes reduced to exclaim with the Psalmist, How manifold are Thy works, O Lord! In wisdom has Thou made them all!"[142] Boyle was indeed deeply involved with religion and authored numerous books and essays on the subject, and left in his will a series of lectures defending Christianity that even presently are read as lectures in London.[143]

Want a wider variety of fields? Let's turn to astronomy. The man considered to be the <u>father of physical astronomy</u> is German orthodox Lutheran Johann Kepler (1571-1630), credited with identifying the elliptical planetary rotation around the sun in addition to his three Kepler's Laws of planetary motion. Kepler defended Copernicus's heliocentric finding at a time when it was unpopular to do so, and reconciled it with Scripture. He also applied physics (then viewed

---

141 Tiner, J.H. 1975. <u>Isaac Newton: Inventor, Scientist and Teacher</u>. Milford, MI: Mott Media; quoted by Dao article, ibid.
142 Boyle, Robert. 1660. Seraphic Love; quoted by Christine Dao, "Man of Science, Man of God: Robert Boyle," Acts & Facts, ICR, April 2008, p. 8.
143 Dao article, ibid.

as a natural philosophy branch) to astronomy (then regarded as a mathematical branch), another unpopular move even with his mentor, Michael Maestlin.[144] He even stated at the beginning of one of his famous works: "I commence a sacred discourse, a most true hymn to God the Founder, and I judge it to be piety, not to sacrifice many hecatombs of bulls to Him and to burn incense of innumerable perfumes and cassia, but first to learn myself, and afterwards to teach others too, how great He is in wisdom, how great in power, and of what sort of goodness."[145] It would have been easy for Kepler to play the game and either be silent or outright criticize Copernicus, but he refused. He rocked the boat and established himself as one of the scientific greats despite opposition.

Let's now take a look at anatomy and surgery and the contributions of one Charles Bell (1774-1842, born in Edinburgh, Scotland), who in 1811, published that "Magna Carta of neurology," <u>Idea of a New Anatomy of the Brain</u>. His interest in neurology was extensive, and he and Francois Magendie formalized "Bell-Magendie's Law," which assigns exclusively sensory nerve fibers to the posterior (back) spinal nerve roots and only motor ones to the anterior (front) spinal nerve roots. His research into the nervous system produced such stalwart medical principles as Bell's Phenomenon, Bell's Palsy/Paralysis, Bell's Spasm and Bell's Nerve. He was a convicted Creationist, and in his 1837 publication wrote: "If we select any object from the whole extent of animated nature, and contemplate it fully and in all its bearing, we shall certainly come to this conclusion: that there is <u>Design in the mechanical construction</u>, Benevolence in the endowments of the living properties, and that Good on the whole is the result."[146] (Emphasis added.)

To Bell, the dependency of man upon <u>involuntary physical processes</u> for survival and functioning stood as testimony to the profound limitations of reason alone in man's controlling his own actions and destiny. He wrote: "Now, when a man sees that his vital operations could not be directed by reason—that they are constant, and far too important to be exposed to all the changes incident to his mind, and that they are

---

144 Christine Dao, "Man of Science, Man of God: Johann Kepler," <u>Acts & Facts</u>, ICR, March 2008, p. 8.
145 Kepler. J. 1619. "Proem." "Harmonies of the World," quoted by Dao article, ibid.
146 Bell, Sir Charles. 1852. <u>The Fourth Bridgewater Treatise on the Power, Wisdom, and Goodness of God as Manifested in the Creation: The Hand; Its Mechanism and Vital Endowments as Evincing Design</u>, 5thed. London: John Murray, 1, quoted by Christine Dao, "Man of Science, Man of God: Charles Bell," <u>Acts & Facts</u>, ICR, June 2008, p. 8.]

given up to the direction of other sources of motion than the will, he acquires a full sense of his dependence. ... [New Para.] <u>When man thus perceives, that in respect to all these vital operations, he is more helpless than the infant, and his boasted reason can neither give them order nor protection</u>, is not his insensibility to the Giver of these secret endowments worse than ingratitude?"[147] (Emphasis added.)

While, of course, unfamiliar with Darwin's particular theory, he was well aware of uniformitarianism, which he disfavored as being against the known scientific evidence: "We cannot resist these proofs of a beginning, or of a First Cause. <u>When we are bold enough to extend our inquiries into those great revolutions that have taken place, whether in the condition of the earth, or in the structure of the animals which have inhabited it, our notions of the 'uniformity' of the course of nature must suffer some modification.</u>"[148] (Emphasis added.)

The reader may have noticed in the cases of Kirby and Bell only that they contributed to what was known as the Bridgewater series. These works were requested in the will of the Reverend Francis Henry Egerton, Earl of Bridgewater (hence their title), who died in February of 1829, and directed specific topics to be addressed and for certain designated trustees of his estate to place eight thousand pounds sterling in the public treasury and appoint various scientists to write up the respective treatises, all devoted to proofs of God's basic power, wisdom and goodness. This directive was jointly implemented by the President of the Royal Society of London, the Bishop of London, the Archbishop of Canterbury, and a nobleman intimately connected with Egerton. <u>This aptly illustrates the nexus at that time between the ecclesiasts, scientists and the nobility.</u> The project cost too much and very little of the treatises, which were eight in number, were actually publicly distributed. The overall effect was a bust.

Thus, Bell and Kirby, as prevailing experts in the fields selected, were hired to contribute to the series. Both men were well entrenched at the time, Bell being 63 at publication and Kirby 76. These were not struggling scientists needing to score with the establishment. They

---

147 <u>Bridgewater Treatise</u>, id., at pp. 13-14, again quoted by Dao article, ibid.
148 <u>Bridgewater Treatise</u>, id., at p. 265, again quoted by Dao article, ibid.; see also, <u>Catholic Encyclopedia</u>: "Bridgewater Treatises;" http://www.newadvent.org/sathen/02783b.htm, at p. 1 of 2.] [7/22/09.], as well as <u>The Victorian Web</u>, "The Bridgewater Treatises on the Power, Wisdom and Goodness of God as Manifested in the Creation," added by John van Wyhe, Fellow, National University of Singapore; Researcher, History and Philosophy of Science, Cambridge University, http://www.victorianweb.org/ science/Bridgewater.html, p. 1 of 2. [7/22/09.]

were picked and accepted the assignments because they were highly qualified in these areas with seminal works under their belts as above-described. Bell's point in particular, about our reliance on our internal <u>involuntary</u> processes for survival, is very persuasive in terms of the futility of our controlling our own destiny. <u>We are hardly masters of our soul when we are, in fact, not even masters of our own body</u>. We do not will these functions, they just consistently occur, suggesting some outside force has a hand in our maintenance, and to some extent, our destiny. This is a compelling proposition regardless of the context under which it was generated. It challenges the humanist notion of man being his own ultimate arbiter and answerable only to himself.

The very desire of Egerton to have this series presented can be read to strongly suggest that intellectual revolutionary milieu was in the air that the church wanted to counteract. It was acting defensively. This is another indication of how Darwin fortuitously was in the right place at the right time in the right social context. Along with the Industrial Revolution, the church could feel its dogmatic grasp slipping away or at least substantially loosening. It felt threatened, and justifiably so. It deserved to be loosening.

Natural selection addresses none of the points made by that distinguished group of scientists as discussed. None of them would see it as a threat to a supernatural God who, to the extent they would agree that natural selection actually functions as Darwin contended, would simply have programmed the process to function as it does. There would be no chance in the world that they would perceive the phenomenon as unguided and self-actuating, but rather as a direct example of an intelligently pre-programmed mechanism.

These great men of science all saw an ingenious design in the universe as well as earthly organisms that they studied and specified what that was. Macro doesn't do that. It simply operates from the empty premise that nothing can be beyond nature, which obviously in terms of logical fallacies "begs the question." The ruse is that God is unknowable and beyond the realm of science, yet makes the assumption of abiogenesis and that man descended from a line of ape-like beings in the process. This is a non sequitur. If there factually are matters <u>beyond the realm</u> of science, how can they be per se eliminated from accounting for observable phenomena? How can assumptions be drawn in our limited known realm, when we publicly acknowledge there could be a great unknown out there? In this it deliberately breaks from the precepts of most organized religion (not per se a bad thing), but then tries to hide behind the separation of church and state veneer to indoctrinate public school students in education, and the general public through the press, with its own brand of dogmatism. That is where they come into fault.

Today's macro pseudo-science makes the preposterous assumption that since it is there, nature has always accounted for itself and is self-organizing, even though this process is accomplished in an arbitrary, undirected fashion. This insults the intelligence of any rational and reasonably informed person, but such is the stench of what is being presented in elementary and secondary schools today. This is not an offense against religion. It is an offense against common sense and logic. While we could run off a string of logical fallacies, the point is too obvious to need to resort to pedantry.

The struggle for the mind cannot be rightly manipulated by the religious-oriented or the economic, free enterprise-oriented; or, as history has shown, a combination of both. Its specific manifestation is not nearly as important as the reality that these are factious power plays that our Founding Fathers opposed in forming this country through the Constitution. Darwin was well connected, the Industrial Revolution was in full throttle, and natural selection as a mechanism with ascribed attributes beyond all rhyme or reason was the artifice needed to bring the macro pseudo-intellectual revolution to fruition. "Natural selection" as an artifice is here intended to mean that a very simple descriptive concept was overblown and artificially elevated to a pedestal it cannot satisfy, as being self-regulatory, which Wallace clearly saw it was not but was rather the end result of a process he couldn't explain.

All of the great scientists above simply took the evidence where it logically led them, whether popular or unpopular, and considered all of the evidence before them, and concluded that nature cannot act on its own without a prime director. But the religious skeptic might say, "Wait a minute! These guys were still influenced by the religious dominance of their respective eras. Even if contrarian, they still based arguments on consistency with religious doctrine, even though different than previously pre-supposed. There was still a bias, and perhaps undue influence, behind all of this." I have two comments concerning that. First, regardless of initial bias (presuming that to be true), they still drew conclusions based from purely scientific observations. They did not contrive evidence or make a priori assumptions simply to fit the theory. Second, even if this were true, how is that atmosphere any different from today's atmosphere for scientists who disagree with macro? With such education curriculum bias drilled into their heads, plus the reaction when mavericks such as Guillermo Gonzalez state their opinions and are denied tenure for it, how can they not at least be as pre-disposed toward macro as the earlier scientists the macros accuse of bias were toward religion? This is simply all the more reason for having a third party arbiter of the meaning of the facts where no worldview is being prioritized over another. This only further legitimizes my proposed pedagogy.

But if one wishes to hunt for an acknowledged scientific pioneer of 20th Century vintage, he need look no further than to Ernst Boris Chain (1906-1979), a biochemist and physiologist whose work in antibiotics is credited with saving millions of lives. His specific work in isolating and purifying penicillin won him the Paul Ehrlich Centenary Prize, the Pasteur Medal, the Bezelius Medal, and a knighthood,[149] as well as a designation as a fellow of the Royal Society.[150] He also was the first to produce lysergic acid by the deep fermentation process, which was once considered to be an impossible task.[151] None of his honors was more notorious than sharing the 1945 Nobel Prize for Physiology or Medicine with colleague Howard Florey and Sir Alexander Fleming for his research that revealed penicillin's structure and allowed for its practical application through isolation by freeze-drying the mold broth.[152] He was also a religious man who disapproved of the stature of Darwinian macro, both on scientific and moral grounds. As far as he was concerned, Macro did not even qualify as a theory.[153]

---

149 Lax, The Mold in Dr. Florey's Coat, p. 253, cited by Dr. Jerry Bergman, "Ernst Chain: Antibiotics Pioneer," Acts & Facts, ICR, April 2008, at p. 11 of 10-12.
150 Curtis, R. 1993. Great Lives: Medicine, New York: Scribner, pp. 77-90, cited by Bergman, ibid.
151 Barton, D. 1977. "Introductory Remarks," in Herns, D.A. (ed.). Biologically Active Substances—Exploration and Exploitation, Chichester, NY: John Wiley and Sons, xviii., cited by Berman, ibid.
152 McMurray, E. 1995. Notable Twentieth-Century Scientists, Detroit, MI:Gale Research, Inc., 334, cited by Berman, ibid.
153 Clark, R.W. 1985. The Life of Ernst Chain: Penicillin and Beyond, New York: St. Martin's Press, 147, cited by Bergman, ibid. Author Bergman is a Professor of Biology at Northwest State College in Ohio. The references that follow below for Chain are all endnotes from his article.

Chain wrote of macro: "This mechanistic concept of the phenomena of life in its infinite varieties of manifestations which purports to ascribe the origin and development of all living species, animals, plants and micro-organisms, to the haphazard blind interplay of the forces of nature in the pursuance of one aim only, namely, that for the living systems to survive, is a typical product of the naïve 19th century euphoric attitude to the potentialities of science which spread the belief that there were no secrets of nature which could not be solved by the scientific approach given only sufficient time."[154] (Emphasis added.) Yes, Chain called the macro theory naïve.

Chain also wrote that the genetic code transmission of information was at odds with Darwin's theory,[155] a statement of Intelligent Design well before the movement as we know it took foot. He also wrote that macro "willfully neglects the principle of teleological purpose which stares the biologist in the face wherever he looks, whether he be engaged in the study of different organs in one organism, or even of different subcellular compartments in relation to each other in a single cell, or whether he studies the interrelation and interactions of various species."[156] (Emphasis added.) For him, the hypothesis that biological adaptation and survival "was entirely a consequence of chance mutations" was a "hypothesis based on no evidence, and irreconcilable with the facts."[157] (Emphasis added.) While Chain recognized a role in mutations for adaptation and therefore variety, transmutation was out of the question. As can be seen, this great biochemist and physiologist (it's hard to dispute that adjective in his case) considered nature acting on its own ordinance in such a sophisticated and refined way as its systems do (such as the genetic code) to be a preposterous notion.

Returning to the evidentiary point made above, can the same weighing of the actual evidence be said of Darwin? The bottom line is that there was extant data to cause Darwin to question his "natural selection" hypothesis specifically and macro theory generally in the sense of upgrading and transmutation of species. He had direct fossil evidence of devolution. Why didn't he ponder more deeply? Does the logical fallacy of "selection and elimination" leer its ugly head here? Selection

---

[154] Chain, E. 1970. Social Responsibility and the Scientist in Modern Western Society. London: The Council of Christians and Jews, pp. 24-25, quoted by Bergman, ibid.
[155] Id., at pp. 25-26, cited by Bergman, ibid.
[156] Id., at p. 25, cited by Bergman, ibid.
[157] Ibid, cited by Bergman, ibid.

and elimination is a form of "special pleading," which only uses data that in isolation supports a predetermined conclusion and ignores the rest that contradictorily does not.[158] It is also submitted here that this is just as much a matter of "Begging the Question," which "selection and elimination" also appears to be a subspecies of. At any rate, let's look at some external motivations for Darwin's approach.

G. THE QUESTION OF DARWIN'S HEALTH AND OTHER PHYSICAL PROBLEMS

Starting in 1837, Darwin suffered from trembling, vomiting, severe boils, heart palpitations and other symptoms, particularly at meetings or when dealing with controversies over his <u>Origin</u> book.[159] Speculation for these health issues (among the more serious candidates, that is) runs from Chagas disease caused by insect bites during his South American Beagle adventures[160] to Crohn's disease of the upper small intestine[161] to psychobiological issues modernly referred to as panic disorder, such as social phobia (fear of social contact) and agoraphobia (fear of social gatherings or visitors outside a defined space such victims consider themselves to be in control of).[162] A more complete itemization of adult symptoms is: "<u>For over forty years</u> Darwin suffered intermittently from various combinations of symptoms such as malaise, vertigo, intestinal gas, muscle spasms and tremors, vomiting, cramps and colics, bloating and nocturnal intestinal gas, headaches, alterations of vision, severe tiredness/nervous exhaustion, dyspnea, skin problems such as blisters all over the scalp and eczema, crying, anxiety, sensation of impending death and loss of consciousness, fainting, tachycardia, insomnia, tinnitus, and depression."[163] (Emphasis added.)

There are possible links to psychological problems stemming initially from Darwin's loss of his mother when he was age 8.[164] Darwin basically denounced God after the death of young daughter Annie on 4/22/1851, aged ten, and thereafter no longer attended church.[165] Mary

---
158 James H. Fetzer, Princeton Professor Emeritus of Philosophy, "Reclaiming History: A Closed Mind Perpetrating a Fraud on the Public," <u>Assassination Research</u>, Vol. 5 No. 1, 5 June 2007, at p. 10 of 11. [9/5/09.]
159 <u>Darwin</u>, supra, pp. 252, 476, 531, cited by "Charles Darwin," Wikipedia, supra, at p. 7 of 31. [3/28/09.]
160 "Charles Darwin's illness"-Wikipedia, the free encyclopedia; http://en.wikipedia.org/wiki/Charles_Darwin's_illness, at p. 8 of 14, which lists 8 reasons why this is unlikely. [9/6/09.]
161 <u>The Royal Society-Notes & Records</u>, "Darwin's illness: a final diagnosis," by Fernando Orrego and Carlos Quintana (2006); http://rsnr.royalsocietypublishing.org/content/61/1/23.full, pp. 1-9. [9/6/09.]
162 Charles Darwin's illness, supra, at p. 5.
163 Id., at p. 2.
164 <u>Darwin</u>, supra, pp. 12-15, cited by "Charles Darwin," Wikipedia, supra, at p. 3.
165 Id., at pp. 9, 14&15.

Darwin died much earlier, on 10/16/1842, at less than a month old.[166] In essence, Darwin lost three women in his life at vulnerable stages. He also lost a male child at about age 1 ½, Charles Waring Darwin, but that was on 6/28/1858, well after his renunciation of a loving Old Testament God.[167] Even as a youth, Darwin had 'episodes of abdominal distress, especially in distressful situation' and 'premorbid vulnerability' based on 'sensitivity to stress of criticism in his youth.'[168]

While I have read entries where Darwin was basically an invalid from age 33, there are other accounts which show significant interruptions of that condition, where one may honestly challenge whether he truly was as unavailable for personal appearances (i.e., if he chose to so indulge) as some texts suggest. E.g., it has been written in the Journal of the Royal Society of Medicine (which speculates about but draws no definitive conclusion regarding Chagas disease): "Darwin, in his 1851-55 health diary – a daily record of his symptoms (Bernstein, 1982) – does not note the taking of any medication. Periodicity of symptoms occurred, with reported episodes of some severity noted for 1840-41, 1848-52 and 1863-65. But in his prolific writing years (1866-82), Darwin enjoyed reasonable, even good health."[169]

Further aspects of his demeanor would suggest that his "stage presence" as a speaker, if you please, was not a very compelling one. Let's take a look at a synopsis of Darwin's physical attributes as described by his family: "Most of Darwin's physical characteristics are known from his later years as described by his children. <u>Charles Darwin had no natural grace of movement and was awkward with his hands. He walked with a swinging action, striking his cane loudly on the ground as he went. Indoors his step was slow and labored</u>. He became excited when engaged in conversation and was very animated and bright eyed, even when he was in ill health. He often used hand gestures when talking, perhaps as an aid to himself, rather than to the listener. In old age Darwin stooped a great deal. He had a hearty laugh, often raising his hands or bringing them down with a slap on his thighs. <u>It is known that Darwin sometimes spoke with a stutter. Apparently, when puzzled</u>

---

166 Id., at p. 14.
167 Id., at p. 10.
168 Charles Darwin's illness, supra, at p. 2.
169 Ralph E. Bernstein MB FRCPath, Department of Pharmacology, Medical School, University of the Witwatersrand, 2193 Johannesburg, South Africa, "Darwin's illness: Chagas' disease resurgens," JRSoc.Med. 1984 July; 77(7):608-609, at p. 609, accessible by downloading from http://www.pubmedcentral.nih.gov/ articlerender.fcgi?artid=1439957. [9/7/09.]

<u>during a conversation he pronounced the first word of a sentence with a slight stammer, mainly words starting with the letter "W". Another interesting attribute is that unless a topic of conversation was related to his current research, Darwin was very slow at forming the wording of an argument. The flow of his conversation with others must have been difficult to follow, for he would often go off on a tangent this way, then another tangent that way, in whatever topic he was discussing."</u>[170] (Emphasis added.)

The above does not suggest Darwin was either a distinguished or imposing public speaker. One could see why he needed bulldog Huxley to make public appearances for him, as he had all the dynamic qualities Darwin lacked. In contrast, at pp. 382, 384 and 390 of his book, The Heretic in Darwin's court: The Life of Alfred Russel Wallace, Columbia University Press, Ross A. Slotten depicts Wallace as having had a commendable, though not commanding, public speaking style and physical appearance, suggesting again that Darwin's prominence over the younger Wallace as evolutionary mascot was primarily for his manipulability.

Darwin had an aversion to surgery, which outwardly seems contradictory since he loved to hunt. However, putting a fatal bullet into quarry from a distance and literally cutting them up from a position of being up close and personal are two distinctly different endeavors. Plus, doing such to humans rather than animals is also a factor. It is also seminal that these were the pre-anesthesia days. Many who might otherwise tolerate the act of surgery under sedate conditions could understandably be turned off in those times. Hearing patient shrieks had to surely be highly discomforting even to the hardest of hearts.[171]

I have read in some circles that Darwin loved to torture animals as a child. I have not pursued this because I cannot substantiate that, his unlikelihood to have done that or felt that way being equally enunciated in various other articles throughout the Internet. It is, on its face, hard to imagine a love of torturing animals when surgery so repulsed him, though one might argue the surgery reaction suppression due to

---

170 David Leff (self-described as: "I am an amateur scholar of the History of Science, with a focus on scientific developments during the Victorian era (around 1835 to 1900)," "What were some of his other physical attributes?" AboutDarwin.com: Dedicated to the Life and Times of Charles Darwin, (started on 2/12/00), http://www.aboutdarwin.com/Darwin/ WhoWas.html, at p. 2 of 13. [9/24/09.]

171 "He Was a Poor Student and Liked a Drink, but Darwin turned out OK," 2/12/09, Times Higher Education, http://www.timeshighereducation.co.uk/story.asp?storyCode=405365&sectioncode=26. [7/28/09.]

remorse over his childhood habits. Such is all highly conjectural, so for purposes of this work, that assertion will be presumed to be inaccurate. In like manner, though I have read Creationist accounts of Darwin's racism, I have not been able to properly substantiate that either, as I have seen a number of Internet accounts to the contrary. While there are certain quotations from his works that would suggest racism that I have seen in Creationist treatments, these could well have been taken out of context (I would suspect inadvertently, but nonetheless taken out of context—What is more maligned than the Bible in this regard, both maliciously and innocently?). Interestingly, perhaps my favorite converter away from atheism to at least Deism has actually defended Darwin when it came to accusations of racism. According to Sir Antony Flew, "… there seem to be absolutely no grounds for pillorying Darwin as a racist. On the contrary … he shared … principled hatred for Negro slavery."[172] Again, for purposes of this work, that assertion will also be presumed to be inaccurate. Furthermore, neither assertion is necessary for my ultimate assessment.

This personal individual and family history, as well as obvious youth health problems, combined with his revulsion over the reversion of the young missionaries to violence and of the slavery he saw during his Beagle adventures, were great motivations to concoct reasons to denounce God in the most extreme way possible, by making a process so abhorrent to common equation with a just God that the logical alternative is no God at all (despite his being a self-proclaimed agnostic). Given the religious climate of England at the time, it was the safer way to go.

Darwin's conjecture about life emanating from a pond exposed his lack of basic scientific knowledge. He projected that the necessary ingredients for life would be molested today but that since those molesting elements did not exist in the primordial world, they would nonetheless have a chance for survival. The scientific realities that this lame effort ignores are discussed later below.

---

[172] Antony Flew, <u>Darwinian Evolution</u> (2d ed.) (1997) Piscataway, NJ: Transaction. ISBN 1-56000-948-9, quoted at Darwin, Wikipedia, supra, at p. 15 of 31. [9/25/09.]

H. DARWIN MARRIED HIS FIRST COUSIN

The marriage to Emma Wedgwood took place on 1/29/1839. Darwin himself pondered whether this produced health issues that plagued his ten children, three of whom died early, and many of the survivors left with serious health problems.[173] The perceived inadvisability of such lineage mixing was known even then. So when daughter Annie died on 4/22/1851 and Darwin allegedly gave up all notions of a just and beneficent God, did he really have a personal foundation to draw such a conclusion when he entered into the matrimonial union itself with such doubts? Is God logically to blame if one plays biological Russian roulette and guesses wrong while spinning the chamber and pulling the trigger?

But it is the cumulative circumstances that are the most condemnatory in this case, rather than one isolated factor. Even more fundamentally, Darwin's physical symptoms had developed starting in 1837. How could such a combination of his own dubious health (regardless of its true origin) and questionable lineage mixing NOT affect progeny (though some of the survivors did have distinguished careers)? And how could Darwin conscionably go through with such a marriage when symptoms were already manifesting themselves with him personally? Only a miracle (a concept which he never acknowledged) could have prevented serious repercussions. Does one walk into a viper's pit and still feel justified in condemning the serpent when he bites, when such behavior reflects it simply being itself when both concerns over lineage and his own physical health combine to threaten the health of prospective offspring?

The actual danger from marrying a first cousin, it might be argued, has historically been exaggerated. There are even Internet sites stating that the offspring risk difference is nominal: children of related couples having a 4 to 6% chance of adverse effects compared to 2 to 3% for non-related couples; and further that the National Society of Genetic Counselors has determined that the increased risk for first cousins is from 1.7 to 2.8% greater, the rough equivalent of the risk that a mother over the age of 40 takes.[174] But such argument (I do not render an opinion on its accuracy here) is irrelevant. It was a concern of

---

173 Charles Darwin, Wikipedia, id., at p. 14.
174 See, e.g., "Facts About Cousin Marriage," http://www.cousincouples.com/?page=facts, pp. 1 & 2 of 2. [10/16/09.]

Darwin's that is reflected even in his autobiography that is discussed in other terms later in this work, and a number of his offspring did have distinct physical problems, even early death. It is how he handled his own perceived predicament that is the main issue, and his own physical complaints most certainly would predictably have a compounding risk effect under any circumstances.

This latter consideration perhaps most distinguishes Darwin from other famous persons who married in the family; among them, my own oft-referenced and quoted Thomas Jefferson, who, besides becoming the third President of the United States, married his third cousin, Martha Wayles Skelton Jefferson, in 1772, had six children with her, and never remarried after her death on 9/6/1782. No less than perhaps the most recognized intellectual giant in history, Albert Einstein, married his second cousin, Elsa, in 1919, and never remarried either after her death in 1936. While by no means exhaustive, other famous people in this category include Morse code inventor Samuel F.B. Morse, who married his first cousin once removed, Sarah Elizabeth Griswold, and had four children with her, and Franklin D. Roosevelt (who I also quote in this work) and his wife Eleanor were also cousins.[175]

Darwin's failure to properly rationalize the facts before him extends to his Beagle observations. He had actually graduated from seminary college. If he was aware of the theological basis for the Fall of Man (and how could he NOT be?), why did the reversion of the three Tierra del Fuego missionaries back to savagery and the slavery he saw in his South American travels (as well as cannibalism) alienate him from his religious orientation? It is suggested here that he did not analyze his data very objectively, nor did he feel motivated to try to constructively deal with these realities, which someone with his religious background should have considered. This is quite consistent with his flawed geological observations concerning uniformitarianism as exposed by Austin.

Darwin, it is submitted, struck back at God in the only manner he knew how consistent with his pre-disposed attitudes—pseudo-intellectually. He was a bitter man (at least in part arguably of his own doing) who felt a compulsion to lash back with the pen since he

---

[175] "Famous People Who Married Their Cousin," Quazen, http://quazen.com/reference/biography/famous-people-who-married-their-cousin/, at pp. 1 & 2 of 3. [10/16/09.]

was powerless to do anything else. Also at work is that he was limited intellectually (compared to the true giants of science discussed above) and physically. He could not be impacting at all unless controversial and part of a revolution that was already taking place on other fronts and which simply needed him as the watering agent interacting with the incipient seed to germinate. Darwin could fairly be summed up in the day to day, in the trenches-type advocacy of his adherents, to be a <u>follower</u> rather than a leader, and his delicate physical condition (regardless of the extent to which it was real or imagined) made him conveniently manipulable by Huxley and others, who wanted to ride his gravy train and use it for their own purposes. He was the perfect foil for this activity.

I. AN UNJUST GOD IS NOT PROOF OF THE ABSENCE OF ONE

An oft-mentioned criticism of the notion of there being a God is that a beneficent God would not allow the obvious suffering that has occurred in the past and continues now, such as even the church atrocities we have referenced let alone the disease, aging and other forms of natural causes we experience, and which will undoubtedly continue to go on as long as we have a planet. Granted, it is difficult not to be visceral when considering this fact. It can only be suggested that Scripture be consulted as to all of its explanations for the good-evil dynamic, its raison-d'être, if you will, both Old and New Testament, before uncategorically making that assertion. The Fall of Man scenario and redemption plan must be considered.

Argumentatively, however, it must be mentioned that even if the reader concluded after doing all his homework and appropriate contemplation that God simply is not a nice guy, or is perhaps even malevolent, that does not logically go to His existence but rather to His character, which is a far different question. This would be no different than concluding that macro is meritless SOLELY because of the circumstances under which it arose without otherwise testing it. The one means of elimination is no more valid than the other. One feeling that way, in fact, could be drawn into thinking of a different form of intelligent agency for origins, etc., than the Scriptural God. That would remain a valid intellectual possibility. Likewise, in terms of logical fallacies, to deny God's existence because He does not intervene in a positive way for man as perceived that He should is to commit the logical fallacy of "Appeal to Consequences of a Belief."[176] While such evidence (assuming its accuracy for purposes of this discussion) might direct itself to the character of God, it does not go to His existence.

Further, your atheistic conclusion would be drawn based on a totally religious and philosophical basis rather than secular consideration of the evidence, totally ignoring the evidence for design that could suggest an existence of some supernatural intervention if you gave yourself a chance to even have it presented to you. This would be just as extreme an example of "Begging the Question" as if you said you believed in God because that's what your parents and grandparents believe (also, of course, there would be authority fallacies). Remember, we are looking for where the evidence leads, not any preconceptions, even your own.

---

176 http://www.nizkor.org/features/fallacies/appeal-to-consequences.html. [7/14/09.]

CHAPTER THREE

Macro's Biased Foundation

A. ELIMINATING THE SUPERNATURAL AS AN EXPLANATION AB INITIO IS NEITHER GOOD SCIENCE NOR GOOD LOGIC

If science is unwilling to consider all alternatives, it is engaging in "selection and elimination" and intellectual dishonesty. Since none of us saw Creation, there are no eyewitnesses, and we simply are only speculating as to what happened if we try to reconstruct matters exclusively based on what we know, see and have observed in our direct experiences. We have tried to surmise macro from extremely incomplete and unreliable evidence simply to eliminate a Creator. There is no need for such. Why not simply remain silent on the matter? That macros would indulge in needless speculation itself exposes an agenda and is not science. Science is based on the observable and falsifiable, and macro enjoys neither attribute, certainly not in terms of origins or transmutation. And adaptation or variation under micro-evolutionary application has its own problems to be discussed later.

In the automatic elimination of the supernatural, we get into the realm of logical fallacies. For this task I will primarily refer to the Internet source of the Nizkor Project, a compilation of fallacies by Dr. Michael C. Labossiere, who developed the Fallacy Tutorial Pro 3.0 MacIntosh tutorial, which has already been cited throughout this work. As defined by Labossiere, a logical fallacy is where an argumentative conclusion is derived from operative premises that do not supply the evidence necessary to reach that conclusion. Or as he specifically puts it: "... a fallacy is an "argument" in which the premises given for the conclusion do not provide the needed degree of support."[177]

Let us be clear that committing logical fallacies does not pre-determine the ultimate truth or falsity of a statement. A statement of fact could be true no matter how recklessly it was arrived at. But the threat and likelihood of it being false is far higher when it violates the rules of critical thinking, which is the avoidance of logical fallacies. By avoiding them and committing to factual conclusions based upon sound reasoning, we are providing an argumentative environment wherein the conclusion is based on actual evidence rather than speculation, bias or prejudice, or at least comes closest to assuring ourselves of that. It better insures the reliability of such a conclusion, and if we are to teach our schoolchildren valid scientific principles, we must give these conclusions the highest probability or likelihood we can of being accurate, at least to the extent our available data allows.

As applied herein, the automatic elimination of the supernatural is subject to two logical fallacies, that of (1) begging the question (already mentioned but explained now more fully) and (2) setting up a false dilemma. "Begging the question" is also known as circular reasoning, reasoning in a circle, Petitio Principii, or also, a tautology (a term not included in Labossiere's Internet text). I will quote the first example he uses: "Bill: God must exist. Jill: How do you know? Bill: Because the Bible says so. Jill: Why should I believe the Bible? Bill: Because the Bible was written by God."[178] Two assumptions are self-contained within the syllogism, that God exists because the Bible says so and that God wrote the Bible. A conclusion is therefore erroneously drawn based on factual allegations within the syllogism that are not based upon evidence, so that the one allegation is improperly used to support the other. Whether the conclusion in the real world ends up fortuitously being literally true or false is entirely irrelevant. What is important here is that it is based entirely on assumptions lacking supporting evidence, so that while we may or may not have made an ultimate error in fact, we definitely have committed an error in reasoning.

---

177 Introduction to Nizkor Project, http://www.nizkor.org/features/fallacies, at p. 2 of 3. [1/30/10.]
178 Nizkor Project; http://www.nizkor.org/features/fallacies/begging-the-question.html, at p. 1 of 2. [1/30/10.]

The second fallacy of "false dilemma" (also called black & white thinking) involves a statement that assumes that if one of two premises is false, then the other must be true, even though, in fact, both could be false. Here, let's use Labossiere's second example under his "Examples of False Dilemma," from the Nizkor Project. "Bill: Jill and I both support having prayer in public schools. Jill: Hey, I never said that. Bill: You're not an atheist, are you Jill?"[179] This is fallacious as a matter of reasoning, e.g., because even Christians might oppose prayer in public schools on Establishment Clause grounds. Jill could have at least one reason for opposing public school prayer other than being an atheist, if in fact she actually does oppose it. She could also simply be offended that somebody is speaking for her without consulting her, even if she in fact does support prayer in public schools. Or, she could be an agnostic rather than an atheist and oppose such prayer due to its presumptuousness and/or compulsoriness. Applied, by confining Intelligent Design to the supernatural, other possible sources for the intelligence (advanced extraterrestrial beings, e.g.) are erroneously eliminated, so that if the supernatural is eliminated, then that assumes that nature is self-actuating and perpetuating, which in fact still might not be the case. Instead of two alternatives, there could be a number more.

In truth, there is no evidence macro can produce to show that supernatural agency (or any other form of third party interventional agency) is not or has not been involved in establishing our natural principles. In fact, no scientist worth his salt would say that observing nature by itself reveals to us its fundamental essence. As Niels Bohr (1885-1962), noted physicist who won the Nobel Prize for Physics in 1922 and was renowned for his work in quantum physics and atomic structure, and who also worked on the Manhattan Project, stated: "In our description of nature the purpose is not to disclose the real essence of the phenomena but only to track down, so far as it is possible, relations between the manifold aspects of our experience."[180] (Emphasis added.)

We cannot know the "how" and "why" but can only utilize the manifestation by studying its behavior and determine and utilize its characteristics and optimize its application to our needs. Nonetheless,

---

179 Nizkor Project; http://www.nizkor.org/features/fallacies/false-dilemma.html, at p. 1 of 2. [1/30/10.]
180 Niels Bohr, Atomic Theory and the Description of Nature (1934).

macros argumentatively assume the "how" and "why" and then erroneously draw conclusions from there based upon that edifice or false front. It does not follow from their own thread (if they are being honest) that because the supernatural cannot be included for Establishment Clause purposes or that God is unknowable and beyond the realm of science that they can then logically arrive at the conclusions that they do. E.g., one cannot properly say (though they do it anyway) that, despite the dearth of fossil record confirmation, macro must have occurred because we can't factor in a God to have done anything. The more intellectually honest statement (from their thread only) is: "More complex organisms appear abruptly in the fossil record and we currently do not know their derivation." True objectivity, when burdens of proof are considered as discussed immediately below, would more completely cause the statement to read: "More complex organisms appear abruptly in the fossil record and under our current state of knowledge, it would appear that design is involved in some unknown capacity. As always, this position is subject to change as we learn more and more about the natural world around us." However, even the first, less complete statement is far better than what we have now.

B. INTELLECTUAL HONESTY DEMANDS AN EVIDENTIARILY REBUTTABLE PRESUMPTION OF DESIGN, MAYBE EVEN RES IPSA LOQUITUR, AND DESIGN INCLUSION WOULD HAVE BEEN FAVORED BY OUR FOUNDING FATHERS

When somebody sees a person who appears to the naked eye to be an African-American black person, the normal presumption is he was born that way. We do not assume a special operation was given him, that black tar was poured over him, that special makeup has been applied, etc., we presume he was born that way. Unless there is evidence presented to the contrary, we continue to think that way. When a pedestrian is hit by a speeding locomotive, we presume serious injury or death. Unless there is evidence presented to the contrary, we continue to think that way. If we get familiar-looking envelopes from public service providers that are associated with bills, we presume that such looking envelopes are once again bills from recognizable specific providers until we open it up and, to our surprise (and relief), it is something else instead.

Our life experiences tell us that certain sets of conditions or circumstances yield predictable and expected results, and only evidence to the contrary will change our minds. Indeed, this is only practicable because we could barely function in life if we did not make these presumptions, as we would always be hesitant and unsure of whether serious repercussions would follow our most innocent-thinking acts.

Accordingly, if we see an animal that looks, walks and quacks like a duck, we are entitled to think it is a duck until shown otherwise. We make deductions of fact called inferences that it is so, that indeed, the animal is a duck. We mentally assume the inference to be the case until, again, shown otherwise.

In this regard, law both pre-trial and during trial acts the same way. We are entitled to make certain presumptions in determining a legal matter that arise from certain sets of facts. Since I practice civil law in California, I will use its state evidence code in making up this argument. With little to no deviation, it is representative of all of the states in this country and certainly so within its usage here. Please feel free to revisit this area after your first reading as many times as needed to feel comfortable with it. This can get confusing to the non-acclimated. Also, since most states model their evidentiary codes after the Federal Rules of Evidence, there is little to no deviation from that standard either. The California Evidence Code ("EC") at Section 600, subdivision (a) states that: "A presumption is an assumption of fact that the law requires to be made from another fact or group of facts found or otherwise established in the action. A presumption is not evidence." (Emphasis added.) At subdivision (b), the Section states: "An inference is a deduction of fact that may logically and reasonably be drawn from another fact or group of facts found or otherwise established in the action."

Presumptions are either conclusive or rebuttable. If conclusive, it is the final word on the subject and no evidence against it is even entertained. If rebuttable (and that is the status of most evidence), then it is only the final word if the party it is being used against does not come up with evidence to show otherwise. In legal terms, a rebuttable presumption dictates who must go forward to produce evidence (i.e., who has the burden or responsibility to do it) to try to persuade the fact-finder (judge or jury) that the presumption is false in support of a particular inference after evidence to the contrary has been shown or presumed, OR, who has to present initial proof for their position to start with, known as the burden of proof.

As stated in California EC Section 604 as to producing evidence: "The effect of a presumption affecting the burden of producing evidence is to require the trier of fact to assume the existence of the presumed fact <u>unless and until evidence is introduced, which would support a finding of its nonexistence</u>, in which case the trier of fact shall determine the existence or nonexistence of the presumed fact from the evidence and without regard to the presumption. <u>Nothing in this section shall be construed to prevent the drawing of any inference that may be appropriate</u>." (Emphasis added.)

For the burden of proof as to who has the responsibility to establish the case or proposition to start with, EC Section 606 says: "The effect of a presumption affecting the burden of proof is to impose <u>upon the party against whom it operates</u> the burden of proof as to the nonexistence of the presumed fact." (Emphasis added.)

Applied as to the above, if some one claims that that animal that otherwise appears to be a duck through all facts observed in common experience is not a duck, it is up to him (i.e., he has the burden of proof) to show that it is not. If and after he has presented satisfactory evidence to show it is not, then the burden of presenting evidence to support the original inference that it is a duck goes to the other party.

In law generally, considering civil actions of two persons or entities against another, the party complaining that he has been wronged (usually called the "Plaintiff") has the initial "burden of proof" to show that he has been wronged <u>by the party he is suing</u> (usually called the "Defendant"). In other words, the Plaintiff has the burden of showing that he not only has been legally wronged but that the Defendant he is suing is the person legally responsible for it. The Defendant does not start off having to show or prove his innocence, that he did not do it so to speak; <u>the Plaintiff has to affirmatively show the Defendant's guilt, that he did do it</u>. If the Defendant makes an appropriate pre-trial motion and the Plaintiff produces no initial evidence that the defendant did it, his case is usually dismissed by a judge on the grounds that he failed to carry his burden of proof before it ever gets to a jury (called "Summary Judgment"). If it gets to a jury and the jury is not convinced with the evidence presented by the Plaintiff, it will find for the Defendant. The burden of proof lies with the Plaintiff at all times from start to finish of the case. He has to prove his side at all times, the Defendant never has to disprove it.

To get a feel for instances depicting who has to initiate matters under California Evidence Code law, the following are among the presumptions affecting the burden of proof: (1) Section 662: "The owner of the legal title to property is presumed to be the owner of the full beneficial title. This presumption may be rebutted only by clear and convincing proof;" (2) Section 663: "A ceremonial marriage is presumed to be valid;" (3) Section 664: "It is presumed that official duty has been regularly performed. This presumption may be rebutted only by clear and convincing proof;" (4) Section 665: "A person is presumed to intend the ordinary consequences of his voluntary act. This presumption is inapplicable in a criminal action to establish the specific intent of the defendant where specific intent is an element of the crime charged;" (5) Section 666: "Any court of this state or the United States, or any court of general jurisdiction in any other state or nation, or any judge of such court, acting as such, is presumed to have acted in the lawful exercise of its jurisdiction. This presumption applies only when the act of the court or judge is under collateral attack;" (6) Section 667: "A person not heard from in five years is presumed to be dead," and (7) Section 668: "An unlawful intent is presumed from the doing of an unlawful act. This presumption is inapplicable in a criminal action to establish the specific intent of the defendant where specific intent is an element of the crime charged."

Applied, taking no. (6), e.g., if a person is not heard from in five years, then he is presumed to be dead under the law and anyone claiming otherwise has the burden of instituting legal action or whatever other appropriate procedure and is the one who must prove that that person is actually alive for whatever purposes they want to accomplish. The burden of proof refers to who has to act to get something done, to make a claim, to have something work on their behalf, to have a particular status recognized to be the case, etc. That missing person is dead under the eyes of the law and public authority until it is convincingly shown otherwise by the holder of the contrary position. If the person holding otherwise does nothing, that status continues unabated.

Under California EC law, among the following are considered to be presumptions affecting the burden of producing evidence (coming forward with it): (1) Section 631: "Money delivered by one to another is presumed to have been due to the latter;" (2) Section 632: "A thing delivered by one to another is presumed to have been due to the latter;" (3) Section 633: "An obligation delivered up to the debtor is presumed to have been paid;" (4) Section 634: "A person in possession of an order on himself for the payment of money, or delivery of a thing, is presumed to have paid the money or delivered the thing accordingly;" (5) Section 635: "An obligation possessed by the creditor is presumed not to have been paid;" (6) Section 636: "The payment of earlier rent or installments is presumed from a receipt for later rent or installments;"

(7) Section 637: "The things which a person possesses are presumed to be owned by him;" (8) Section 638: "A person who exercises acts of ownership over property is presumed to be the owner of it;" (9) Section 640: "A writing is presumed to have been truly dated;" (10) Section 641: "A letter correctly addressed and properly mailed is presumed to have been received in the ordinary course of mail;" (11) Section 642: "A trustee or other person, whose duty it was to convey real property to a particular person, is presumed to have actually conveyed to him when such presumption is necessary to perfect title of such person or his successor in interest;" (12) Section 644: "A book, purporting to be printed or published by public authority, is presumed to have been so printed or published," and (13) Section 645.1: "Printed materials, purporting to be a particular newspaper or periodical, are presumed to be that newspaper or periodical if regularly issued at average intervals not exceeding three months."

In the above instances, in a court of law, when a party has presented what he purports to be the subject-matter of the above sections, the other party has the burden of presenting evidence that that is not so, in order to "rebut" that presumption in an attempt to show that it is not so. These are procedural rules governing the order of presentation of evidence necessary among the legal parties as well as an assigning of who has to produce what. Referencing no. (9), e.g., once a writing is produced showing a date, assuming the authenticity of the document itself, the validity of that date need not be proven by the one using the document as evidence. The party opposing the validity of the date must come forth with evidence attacking its veracity.

Applied, it is expected in common experience that if no affirmative action is taken, nothing constructive happens. Without someone laying the foundation, nailing in the wood, hanging up the shingles, and other appurtenances, the house doesn't get built at all, let alone be in livable condition. Without someone designing and constructing a properly functioning printing press, that newspaper doesn't get printed. It is absolutely assumed that some form of intelligence was involved in accomplishing these tasks. The burden of proof would be on someone holding the contrary position that that was not the case.

Even an alleged simple cell has DNA assigning and RNA messengers carrying out specific tasks so that proteins are manufactured and other operations are performed. There is a double-helix structure to DNA. A single cell is not the blob that Darwin thought it was. Human physiology and anatomy is enormously complex and sophisticated and without proper timing in performing its functions, death would ensue, be it in a single-cell or higher organism.

The bottom line is experience shows that where construction is necessary to have anything coherent and operable, somebody or something has to make it that way. It doesn't just happen by itself. Never has and never will. Not only does the second law of thermodynamics not allow it in scientific circles, common sense doesn't either. For this reason, we are logically, legally and practically compelled to adopt that premise.

Applying legal standards to the Creation v. macro issue, there can be no such allowable adage as "giving the appearance of design without being design" (Ayala) without the proof to substantiate it, which is severely lacking and regardless, must be presented because the <u>burden is on the macros</u>. If it admittedly gives the appearance of design, the presumption and inference must be of design until shown otherwise. That is the starting premise that is the burden of the macros to overcome.

This is consonant with the legal concept of "res ipsa loquitur" (Latin for "the thing speaks for itself"). Therein, prima-facie negligence, e.g., can be established by the following taken in pertinent part from

CACI no. 417 [Judicial Council of California Civil Jury Instructions book, 2006 ed.]: "1. That [name of plaintiff]'s harm ordinarily would not have happened unless someone was negligent; (2) That the harm was caused by something that only [name of defendant] controlled; and (3) That [name of plaintiff]'s voluntary actions did not cause or contribute to the event[s] that harmed [him/her]."

The point herein is that "res ipsa loquitur" is basically a circumstantial evidence rule to be applied when the situation is such that a logical mind is INITIALLY permitted to reach conclusions based on the general facts before it without elaborate detail and otherwise point-by-point exactness and testing. Or, as California courts themselves have described it (taken from "Sources and Authority" within CACI No. 417), "The doctrine of res ipsa loquitur is fundamentally a doctrine predicated upon inference deducible from circumstantial evidence." [Hale v. Venuto (1982) 137 Cal.App.3d 910, 918.] The doctrine "is based on a theory of 'probability' where there is no direct evidence of defendant's conduct, permitting a common sense inference of negligence from the happening of the accident." [Gicking v. Kimberlin (1985) 170 Cal.App.3d 73, 75.] (Emphasis added.) Earlier case law described it as: "All of the cases hold, in effect, that it must appear, either as a matter of common experience or from evidence in the case, that the accident is of a type which probably would not happen unless someone was negligent." [Zentz v. Coca Cola Bottling Co. of Fresno (1952) 39 Cal.2d 436, 442-443.] (Emphasis added.)

The First Cause principle is somewhat analogous to this. There had to be a beginning for life and macro cannot explain it. Darwin couldn't come close, and it is submitted not because he did not want to bother with it but because he knew he absolutely had no answers. His pond example is replete with scientific error, as discussed below. If it looks like design, then the evidence per se points in that direction and the jury (all of us considering the issue) has the right to say there is an intelligence that caused it. If still one is not convinced, there is still the right to decline it, just as with res ipsa, which affords the civil jury the right to find for negligence against the Defendant and that such negligence was a substantial factor in causing [name of plaintiff]'s harm, or both or not to find for either at all, as CACI no. 417 further explains.

The point herein is that the jury may consider that evidence as substantial enough to make such findings as a matter of law, though it is not compelled to. The jury on one of the greatest questions presented by life itself is entitled to take Intelligent Design seriously, or not, at its own individual discretion. That is as fair, open, legal and logical as it can get, with bias and prejudice toward none.

In sum, based on burden of proof and of presenting evidence principles (he who has the burden of proof must start first), the <u>initial</u> burden in both instances is on macro to show a cosmological naturalness as a basis for origins (of everything, but herein for this discussion, of life).

The practical ramifications of this are quite telling. If the true starting inference is of design (and logically and legally it MUST be), educational curriculum textbooks cannot be allowed to presume macro and must be even-handed in presenting the "challenges" to macro instead of just exclusively its own propositions. The evidence for Intelligent Design must also be presented, but within the context of how it differs from macro, and that it is presented for consideration rather than presumed priority. Whether Intelligent Design rebuts macro or the other way around is for the student to decide.

The First Amendment separation of church and state is irrelevant to this issue. If Intelligent Design is a backdoor attempt at Creationism, then macro is a backdoor attempt at atheism. The burden of <u>proof</u> (and not bald statements without evidentiary support) is on macro and not the other way around, and it is intellectually dishonest to state otherwise.

The Founding Fathers would not disagree with the above at all. They would even be flipping in their graves if they realized how much the courts have perverted the issue. What they opposed is subjugation of minorities by the church in light of the abuses discussed earlier, and wanted to establish a legal paradigm through the Constitutional mechanism of the First Amendment that would nip that possibility at the bud, so that the focus of government is upon secular governance and in no way ecclesiastical. The two had to be separated from one another for the benefit of both, so that both may flourish. Neither is to trespass upon the other's turf. In this regard, we are reminded that originally this stricture applied only to the Federal government.

The states were not so directed until the Fourteenth Amendment in 1868, about 77 years after the 12/15/1791 adoption of the First and remaining Bill of Rights.

The pertinent First Amendment language is: "Congress shall make no law respecting an establishment of religion, or prohibiting the free exercise thereof ..." (Emphasis added.) But that does not permit the suppression of ideas, so long as they are balanced so that no one religion is favored over the other and, for that matter, religion itself is not being highlighted by itself. At most, ID shows not just a designer, but a programmer. Who or what that programmer is remains to be seen. Just simply let the evidence lead where it may. If it is inconclusive to the inquiring mind, then educational goals are accomplished, which is to present the unbiased picture so that where reasonable minds can differ, they have at least the same knowledge base to differ upon. This is much like where a legal jury can hear the same evidence and differ as to whether liability or guilt either civilly or criminally has been shown.

In his notes for a 1779 speech in support of the 1786-passed "Bill for Establishing Religious Freedom in Virginia," Mr. Declaration of Independence himself, Thomas Jefferson (1743-1826), probingly wrote: "Well aware that the opinions and belief of men depend not on their own will, but follow involuntarily the evidence proposed to their minds; that Almighty God hath created the mind free, and manifested his supreme will that free it shall remain by making it altogether insusceptible to restraint; that all attempts to influence it by temporal punishments, or burthens, or by civil incapacitations, tend only to beget habits of hypocrisy and meanness, and are a departure from the plan of the holy author of our religion, who being lord of both mind and body, yet chose not to propagate it by coercions on either, as was his Almighty power to do, but to extend it by its influence on reason alone ... ."[181] (Emphasis added.)

Did the post-Constitutional Jefferson change his mind about this posture? Not in the least. He wrote for his own epitaph: "Here was buried Thomas Jefferson, Author of the Declaration of American Independence, of the Statute of Virginia for Religious Freedom, and Father of the University of Virginia." (Emphasis added.) Note no

---

[181] A Documentary History of Religion in America, Vol. I (To the Civil War), Edwin S. Gaustad, ed., Grand Rapids: William B. Eerdmans Publishing Company, 1982, pp. 259-261.

reference to his service as governor of Virginia or Third President of the United States or involvement with the Louisiana Purchase. Note prominence given to his role in the Virginia religious freedom statute. Likewise, note his accentuation of being founder (he expresses it as "Father") of the University of Virginia. To him, freedom and liberty (in part through education) even trumped his Presidency and any other form of formal government service or office.

This is well consistent with his opinion of freedom of the press and newspapers and their priority even over government, and the link between free discourse of information and the ability to read and understand it (education): "The basis of our governments being the opinion of the people, the very first object should be to keep that right; and <u>were it left to me to decide whether we should have a government without newspapers or newspapers without a government, I should not hesitate a moment to prefer the latter. But I should mean that every man should receive those papers and be capable of reading them</u>."[182] (Emphasis added.)

As to the preparation for his 1779 speech, note at the top his implied urging for education being broad in scope by presenting to the student a panoply of ideas for proper consideration and evaluation, since their opinions are necessarily only based on the information provided them ("<u>the opinions and belief of men depend not on their own will, but follow involuntarily the evidence proposed to their minds</u>"). Ultimately, you can only evaluate based upon your factual exposure. Besides being implicit in the speech itself, his epitaph shows that that always remained prominent in his mind throughout his life. It follows *a fortiori* from this that only an open discourse of all facts and theories so that the question of origins can receive its proper evaluation is fully endorsed in his notes to his speech. Otherwise, we would have a coercion of the mind through the deliberate omission of vital information to properly form an opinion, which would have been abhorrent to Jefferson. He wrote: "Subject opinion to coercion: whom will make your inquisitors? Fallible men; men governed by bad passions, by private as well as public reasons. And why subject it to coercion? <u>To produce uniformity. But is

---

182 Letter from Thomas Jefferson to Edward Carrington, 1787, University of Virginia Library, electronic text center, "Jefferson on Politics & Government: Freedom of the Press," ME 6:57; http://etext.virginia.edu/jefferson/quotations/jeff1600.htm. Thomas Jefferson Digital Archive, edited by Eyler Robert Coates, Sr., editor (1995-2001 compilation). [9/15/09.]

uniformity of opinion desirable? No more than of face and stature."[183] (Emphasis added.)

The conclusions reached by the students are irrelevant to Jefferson (as they are to this writer): "The legitimate powers of government extend to such acts only as are injurious to others. But it does me no injury for my neighbor to say there are twenty gods, or no God. It neither picks my pocket nor breaks my leg."[184]

Applied to education, this passage from Jefferson concerning a free press is apropos to an open, informative, disclosive education: "The most effectual engines for [pacifying a nation] are the public papers... [A despotic] government always [keeps] a kind of standing army of newswriters who, without any regard for the truth or to what should be like truth, [invent] and put into the papers whatever might serve the ministers. This suffices with the mass of the people who have no means of distinguishing the false from the true paragraphs of a newspaper."[185] The bracketed information was put in by the website, not this author. Applied, we are educated only to the extent of our input, and that input must be filled with information that permits us to best understand the facts as they truly exist. It is submitted that our current educational system controls curriculum content in much the same way that Jefferson's despotic government would, and which will be shown below.

In correspondence with his nephew, Jefferson favored the notion of putting God to the test like all other precepts: "Do not be frightened from this enquiry by an fear of it's [sic] consequences. If it ends in belief that there is no god, you will find incitements to virtue in the comfort and pleasantness you feel in it's [sic] exercise, and the love of others which it will procure you. If you find reason to believe there is a god, a consciousness that you are acting under his eye, and that he approves you, will be a vast additional incitement. ... In fine, I repeat that you must lay aside all prejudice on both sides, and neither believe nor reject any thing because any other person, or description of persons have rejected or believed it. Your own reason is the only oracle

---

[183] Notes of Virginia, 1782; from George Seldes, ed., The Great Quotations, Secaucus, New Jersey: Citadel Press, 1983, p. 263.
[184] Jefferson notes on the State of Virginia; Faith of Our Fathers: Religion and the New Nation, San Francisco: Harper & Row, 1987, pp. 42-43.
[185] Thomas Jefferson letter to G.K. van Hagendorp, Oct. 13, 1785. ME 5:181, Papers 8:632, Jefferson Digital Archive, supra.

given you by heaven, and <u>you are answerable not for the rightness but for the uprightness of the decision</u>. ..."[186] (Emphasis added.) Clearly, for Jefferson, the important part of the ratiocinative, learning process was not the conclusion (the rightness) itself, but procedurally how it was arrived at (the uprightness). We are not to believe anything of weight simply because others do or do not. It must pass our own individual test.

Jefferson always recognized the difference between Christ's doctrines and those who claim to be His followers: "But a short time elapsed after the death of the great reformer [Jesus] of the Jewish religion, before his principles were departed from by those who professed to be his special servants, and perverted into an engine for enslaving mankind, and aggrandizing their oppressors in Church and State."[187] He also wrote: "In every country and every age, <u>the priest has been hostile to liberty. He is always in alliance with the despot</u>, abetting his abuses in return for protection to his own. <u>It is easier to acquire wealth and power by this combination than by deserving them</u>, and to effect this, <u>they have perverted the purest religion ever preached to man into mystery and jargon, unintelligible to mankind, and therefore the safer for their purposes</u>."[188] It is apparent that Jefferson alleges a <u>conspiracy between church and state</u>, all the greater reason for their separation. But his message clearly states that Christ and his doctrine are not to blame, but how man has perverted it through the unholy alliance of church and state.

As is evident, the educational curriculum issue presented herein is unrelated to establishment of religion concerns. No specific God is being advocated but rather the goal is in presenting the facts and allowing, from there, the <u>possibility</u> of a conclusion that something other than mere nature acting by itself in a random manner was involved in <u>establishing the laws of nature</u>; arrived at not by suppressing evidence of macro but rather, by allowing it to stand in the light of day against conflicting evidence and theories. Thus the dichotomy between Creator (whatever or whoever that might be) and Creation (the universe and the natural laws within) is explored, but only by

---

[186] Thomas Jefferson, letter to his young nephew Peter Carr, August 10, 1787. From Adrienne Koch, ed., <u>The American Enlightenment: The Shaping of the American Experiment and a Free Society</u>, New York: George Braziller, 1965, pp. 320-321.
[187] Thomas Jefferson, in a letter to Samuel Kerceval, 1810; from <u>The Great Quotations</u>, supra, p. 370.
[188] Thomas Jefferson, in a letter to Horatio Spofford, 1814; from George Seldes, ed., <u>The Great Quotations</u>, Secaucus, New Jersey: Citadel Press, 1983, p. 371.

inference based on the facts than by direct effort of persuasion, with no purposeful red flags being waved.

Argumentatively for the Creationist, the universe and natural law under which it operates is too precise, too intricate, too finely-tuned in the sense of intricately described divisions of labor requiring strict synchronicity to PRESUME otherwise (again, without the presentation of evidence contradicting it). This does not narrow matters to any God such as Christian, Buddhist, Muslim, whatever, but that some form of outside agency not even necessarily supernatural (people could even believe in extraterrestrial cosmology) could well have established our natural laws. The only inquiry is, "In what direction does the evidence lead?" The answer is purely up to the student, the individual trier of fact, and an answer entirely different from either a macro or ID conclusion is perfectly permissible provided it is backed up with accurate factual data.

This point and counterpoint approach leads to the free discourse of ideas that Jefferson embraced in establishing the University of Virginia. "This institution will be based on the illimitable freedom of the human mind. For here we are not afraid to follow truth wherever it may lead, nor to tolerate error so long as reason is free to combat it."[189] (Emphasis added.) Jefferson surely was not speaking of direct religious instruction, not by a long shot. He was the first to point out, "A professorship of Theology should have no place in our institution [the University of Virginia]."[190] Religion had a valid place, but only in the sense of its moral contributions. "What is really significant in religion, its moral content, would be taught in the University of Virginia, but in philosophy, not divinity."[191]

And even that can be rejected. If the student, after the presentation of all of the applicable evidence, including all that macro wants to counter with, still wants to believe in macro, then so be it. As Jefferson once put it: "If M. de Becourt's book be false in its facts, disprove them; if false in its reasoning, refute it. But, for God's sake, let us freely

---

[189] Thomas Jefferson, to prospective teachers, University of Virginia; id., at p. 364.
[190] Thomas Jefferson, letter to Thomas Cooper, October 7, 1814. From Gorton Carruth and Eugene Ehrlich, eds., The Harper Book of Quotations, New York: Harper & Row, 1988, p. 492.
[191] Ed and Michael Buckner, "Quotations that Support the Separation of State and Church" (1993), citing E.S. Gaustad, "Religion," in Merrill D. Peterson, ed., Thomas Jefferson: A Reference Biography, New York: Charles Scribner's Sons, 1986, pp. 282-283 in support of their statement.

hear both sides, if we choose."¹⁹² (Emphasis added.) Nor is religious pluralism frustrated in any way. This would do nothing to destroy the notion of religious freedom in any way whatsoever. "Freedom of choice" is unimpinged here no matter how the phrase is spun.

One of the biggest clues as to why Jefferson would not have tolerated exclusively macro taught in the schools as it has been is for the very reasons why he saw no place for religion in the public classroom nor in his University. As the Buckners wrote: "It was what he did not like in religion that gave impetus to Jefferson's activity in that troublesome and often bloody arena. He did not like dogmatism, obscurantism, blind obedience, or any interference with the free exercise of the mind."¹⁹³ (Emphasis added.) In other words, he intensely disliked the very qualities that the approach to macro is currently given in our public school system.

Madison (1751-1836), deemed by many to be the "Father of the Constitution" for his influence on it, felt at least equally as strongly as did Jefferson on the separation of church and state. But undoubtedly the dominance of one idea to the exclusion of another would have abhorred him as well. No good purpose is served, and because the education system is an organ of state government, teaching only the macro view in the public schools is a form of state action that he would not have approved of. This is implicit in his letter to the Rev. Jasper Adams, Spring, 1832: "I must admit moreover that it may not be easy, in every possible case, to trace the *line of separation between the rights of religion and the civil authority* (emphasis original) with such distinctness as to avoid collisions and doubts on unessential points. The tendency to a usurpation on one side or the other or to a corrupting coalition or alliance between them will be best guarded against by entire abstinence of the government from interference in any way whatever, beyond the necessity of preserving public order and protecting each sect against trespasses on its legal rights by others."¹⁹⁴ (Emphasis added.)

Madison did not disagree with the virtues of a proper education giving the student the free-flow dissemination of ideas: "I congratulate you

---

[192] Thomas Jefferson, in a letter to N.G. Dufief, Philadelphia bookseller, 1814, on the occasion of prosecution for selling De Becourt's "Sur le Creation du Monde, un Systeme d'Organisation Primitive"; from The Great Quotations, supra, p. 371.
[193] Religion, supra, at p. 279.
[194] Madison letter to Jasper Adams, Spring, 1832; http://candst.tripod.com/tnppagejasper.htm, at 3 of 3. [1/26/10.]

on the foundation thus laid for a general System of Education, and hope it presages a superstructure, worthy of the patriotic forecast which has commenced the work. <u>The best service that can be rendered to a Country, next to that of giving it liberty, is in diffusing the mental improvement equally essential to the preservation, and the enjoyment of that blessing.</u>"[195] (Emphasis added.)

Madison also wrote: "No feature in the aspect of our Country is more gratifying, <u>than the increase and variety of Institutions for educating the several ages and classes of the rising generation</u>, and the meritorious patriotism which improving on their most improved forms extends the benefit of them to the sex heretofore, sharing too little of it. <u>Considered as at once the fruits of our free System of Government, and the true means of sustaining and recommending it, such establishments are entitled to the best praise that can be offered.</u>"[196] (Emphasis added.)

To place these remarks in their proper context, the free discourse of information was for Madison the monument of a free government, a necessary ingredient for liberty in all of its dimensions. He had earlier written: "A popular Government, <u>without popular information, or the means of acquiring it</u>, is but a Prologue to a Farce or a Tragedy; or, perhaps both. <u>Knowledge will forever govern ignorance: and a people who mean to be their own Governors, must arm themselves with the power which knowledge brings</u>."[197] (Emphasis added.) Obviously, Madison considered the education system for this information to be one of those <u>means of acquiring it</u> (a free press would, of course, be another). And implicit within the use of the word "knowledge" is that it is true information. That is very much at issue in our present day.

The equivalence of information with freedom is the same calculus that Jefferson used: "If a nation expects to be ignorant and free, in a state of civilization, it expects what never was and never will be."[198] Jefferson also wrote: "<u>Enlighten the people generally</u>, and tyranny and <u>oppressions of mind and body</u> will vanish like evil spirits at the dawn of day."[199] (Emphasis added.)

---

195 Madison letter to Littleton Dennis Teackle, 3/29/1826; from the Madison Papers at the University of Virginia.
196 Madison letter to Gulian C. Verplanck, 2/14/1828; from the Madison Papers at the University of Virginia.
197 Madison letter to WT Barry, 8/4/1822.
198 Jefferson letter to Colonel Charles Yancey, 1/6/1816; Bartlett's Familiar Quotations, Sixteenth Edition, 1992, Little, Brown and Company (Inc.), p. 344, no. 18.
199 Jefferson letter to Du Pont de Nemours, 4/24/1816, quoted by Bartlett's, ibid., no 19.

JFK (1917-1963) recognized the mutually dependent aspect of liberty and learning. As he put it, "Liberty without learning is always in peril and learning without liberty is always in vain."[200] As expressed by FDR (1882-1945), "The only sure bulwark of continuing liberty is a government strong enough to protect the interests of the people, and a people strong enough <u>and well informed enough to maintain its sovereign control over its government.</u>"[201] (Emphasis added.) Note the recognition by FDR of the power of the people and accountability of the government to the people, the latter being the masters of the former.

Public school curriculum is a form of state action and to the extent that dissemination of information is complete, the public controls its government as was intended. To the extent it is not, the government controls the public, which is against all of the parameters of a democratic republic. While stated in the context of World War II, substituting a war over the minds of our schoolchildren through their textbooks in the public education forum can be aptly inserted within another FDR quote: "Books cannot be killed by fire. People die, but books never die. No man and no force can abolish memory. ... In this war, we know, books are weapons."[202] Or, as successor Harry Truman (1884-1972) once said, "Secrecy [in this instance, censorship] and a free, democratic government don't mix."[203]

In the broader spectrum, this entire issue of what should be taught in our public schools is really a question of whether the basic rights of the governed as common men and humanity are to be preserved, or, whether those who wish to control them acting under an authority akin to independent authorization through a sense of superiority (be it economically, artistically, or otherwise) should be prioritized. Abraham Lincoln (1809-1865) expressed it thusly: "That is the issue that will continue in this country when these poor tongues of Judge Douglas and myself shall be silent. It is the eternal struggle between these two principles—right and wrong—throughout the world. <u>They are the two principles that have stood face to face from the beginning of time; and will ever continue to struggle. The one is the common</u>

---

200 Remarks on the ninetieth anniversary of Vanderbilt University (3/18/1963), quoted by <u>Bartlett's</u>, id., at p. 741, no. 17.
201 Fireside Chat (4/14/1938), quoted by <u>Bartlett's</u>, id., p. 649, no. 11.
202 Message to the American Booksellers Association (4/23/1942), quoted by <u>Bartlett's</u>, ibid., no. 21.
203 From Merle Miller, <u>Plain Speaking: An Oral Biography of Harry S. Truman</u>, quoted by <u>Bartlett's</u>, id., p. 655, no. 22.

right of humanity, and the other the divine right of kings. It is the same principle in whatever shape it develops itself."[204] (Emphasis added.)

The macros, while denying the supernatural, take it upon themselves to censor facts necessary to the ascertainment of truth as if they have some inherent authority or entitlement to do so. They are acting under the same principle as the divine right of kings, whether they dispute divinity or not. This is the very attitude that leads to subjugation of the mind and body that our Constitutional framers and succeeding leaders have all cautioned against in the very strongest of terms, but yet is what is being practiced today in our public school systems across this nation.

One might protest, "Wait a minute here pal. This is all well and good, but we are not in a formal courtroom, so you know what you can do with your burden of proof. Our courtroom is a far less formal one and much more vast in scale, known as the court of public opinion. We do things differently than that here. This isn't a 12 person jury, it's millions." My response is: no, you don't PROPERLY do anything differently here. Firstly, this is a federal Constitutional issue, so legal standards apply across the board to everybody in this country. Second, and even more importantly, the principle of burden of proof is not confined to strict legal situations but rather, to all manners of disputation and critical thinking in life—not just the courtroom, but to any public controversy. A misplaced burden of proof is a logical fallacy applying to all forms of dispute and the ramifications of it are seminal.

Let's hear what Labossiere has to say about it: "Burden of proof is a fallacy in which the burden of proof is placed on the wrong side. Another version occurs when a lack of evidence for side A is taken to be evidence for side B in cases in which the burden of proof actually rests on side B. A common name for this is an Appeal to Ignorance."[205] (Emphasis added.) It is for this reason that so much time has been taken to set up who should rightly bear the burden. Macros have appealed to ignorance as well as defied burden of proof principles generally, which is critical to not only who should be the one to have to produce evidence, but also as to how it is treated and analyzed. They have made it appear that the burden should be on the ID advocates

---

204 Reply, seventh and last joint debate, Alton, Illinois (10/15/1858), quoted by Bartlett's, id., at p. 448, no. 11.
205 http://nizkor.org/features/fallacies/burden-of-proof.html, at p. 1 of 2.

because macros practice "science" (which in reality is pseudo-science) and ID deals with abstractions and the strictly religious realm by being backdoor Creationism, when nothing could be further from the truth. This will become clearer and clearer as you read on and you see how the evidence has been manipulated and censored even above and beyond what has already been discussed.

C. THE EVIDENCE IS REPLETE WITH SUPPRESSION OF BOTH HUMAN ORIGINS AND SIZE BECAUSE IT DOESN'T FIT MACRO'S THEORY

Suppressed evidence of human origins that remotely challenges the pre-conception of ape-like lineage for humans has long been the name of the game for the macros. In their 900-page, 1993 work, Forbidden Archaeology: The Hidden History of the Human Race, Michael A. Cremo and Richard L. Thompson report: "These discoveries are not well known, having been forgotten by science over the course of many decades or in many cases eliminated by a biased process of knowledge filtration. The result is that modern students of paleoanthropology are not in possession of the complete range of scientific evidence concerning human origins and antiquity. Rather most people, including professional scientists, are exposed to only a carefully edited selection of evidence supporting the currently accepted theory that protohuman hominids evolved from apelike predecessors in Africa during the Late Pliocene and Early Pleistocene, and that modern humans subsequently evolved from the protohuman hominids in the Late Pleistocene, in Africa or elsewhere."[206] In other words, macros typically "beg the question" rather than properly formulate and address it, and exercise censorship over anything threatening their sacred macro cow.

Forbidden Archaeology describes evidence uncovered showing a human presence during the Pliocene, Miocene and Tertiary Periods. Much of the evidence came not long after the first Origin of Species in 1859. A great deal of the fossils and artifacts were discovered prior to the Java Man discovery by Dubois in 1891/92. Among them were incised and broken bones and shells considered to cover the Pliocene,

---

[206] Michael A. Cremo and Richard L. Thompson, Forbidden Archaeology: The Hidden History of the Human Race, San Diego, CA; Bhaktivedanta Institute, 1993; p. 150, quoted by David Pratt, "Suppressed evidence of human antiquity," Human Origins: the ape-ancestry myth, February 2004, Part 2 of 3, http://david pratt.info/ape2.htm, at pp. 1&2 of 32, taken from David Pratt, "Exploring Theosophy: The Synthesis of Science, Religion and Philosophy, http://davidpratt.info/.

Miocene and even before. While appearing initially in professional journals and debated at scientific congresses, they have been modernly suppressed. The "politically correct" modern view is that they could not be stone tools because the hominids of these respective periods were very primitive australopithecines considered to have been incapable of making stone tools.[207] Discovered in 1881, eventually ignored was a crudely carved human face on the outer surface of a shell from the Late Pliocene Red Cray formation in England. Rudimentary stone tools (eoliths) were found by geologist J. Reid Moir in the early 20th Century along with more advanced stone tools (palaeoliths) in and beneath that same formation, with estimates between 2 to 55 ma (million years ago). Even eolith critic Henri Breuil was impressed with the finds, and in 1923, they were pronounced to be genuine by an international scientist committee that traveled to England to investigate them.

Stone implements were found between 1912 and 1914 by Carlos Ameghino such as signs of fireplaces and bolas (throwing balls) in Late Pliocene strata 2 to 3 ma at Miramar on the Argentine coast, as well as a stone arrowhead embedded in a Toxodon's femur (an extinct Plioscene species). Lorenzo Parodi, Ameghino's co-worker, discovered a bola stone in a Pliocene cliff at Miramar. While having witnesses to his extracting that stone, second and third stones were found at the same site within 200 metres of one another. Parodi later found a human jaw fragment in the same formation at Miramar in 1921. These findings have been suppressed today because the conventional wisdom is that humans did not inhabit the Americas until within 25,000 years ago.[208]

Other finds include 19th and early 20th Century human skeletal remains of modern-looking humans at Ipswich, Moulin Quignon, Galley Hill, Clichy and La Denise in Europe, all in Middle Pleistocene formations. Despite strong evidence to the contrary, since it was predetermined that Homo sapiens could not be older than 200,000 years, it has been concluded that they HAD to have been buried recently. This, despite anthropologist Sir Arthur Keith insisting that the Galley Hill discovery near London in 1888, having been found in undisturbed

---
207 Human Origins, supra, at p. 3 of 32.
208 Forbidden Archaeology, supra, pp. 313-334 & 438-439, cited by Human Origins, supra, at p. 5 of 32. [9/9/09.]

strata, was impossible to deny the authenticity of "without doing an injury to truth."[209]

A glowing example of the hypocrisy of the scientific establishment is presented in J. Boucher de Perthes (1788-1868), a customs officer in northern France who enjoyed archaeology as a hobby. In 1838, he had tried to publish finds from the Somme River gravel deposits linking stone tool artifacts found with the bones of extinct animals to prehistoric man. At the time, these finds were scoffed at by scientists and scientific journals and written off as being "lightning stones" (byproducts of lightning bolts). By 1858, however, they were becoming more widely accepted by the scientific community and became largely accepted by the publication of Origin in 1859.[210] This is further evidence of the theme that England was ripe for a change and that Darwin's presence conveniently allowed for the final piece in the mosaic. Again, the need for a poster child was "in the air."

However, when other finds by de Perthes did not fit the catalogued and preconceived time line, they were rejected. In 1863, he also found an anatomically modern jaw in the Moulin Quignon gravel pit in Abbeville, France. But these finds would have placed the implements in a time frame of some 400,000 years ago, which did not fit the presumed time line, and would have been too early for modern man to have developed. While a commission of French and British archaeologists and geologists initially found the jaw authentic, two British dissidents persuaded them otherwise. Under further strict controls and trained scientific observers, de Perthes's further finds of modern human bones, bone fragments and teeth were suppressed.[211] Historically, the jury is still out as to the authenticity of the Moulin Quignon jaw, which met with resistance from those advocating the now rejected theory that Neanderthals were Homo sapiens' immediate ancestors. There was also other evidence suggesting that the jaw's coloring was suspect and could be scrubbed off, invalidating the find, which Keith did not concur with.[212] But whatever the jaw's fate may ultimately be, the final adjudication of the issue is for these purposes irrelevant. The very verdict of forgery or authentic is made under a

---

[209] Arthur Keith, The Antiquity of Man, London: Williams and Norgate, 1925, p. 256, cited and quoted by Human Origins, supra, ibid.
[210] "Early Theories of Evolution: Darwin and Natural Selection," http://anthro.palomaredu/evolve/ evolve_2.htm.at p. 7 of 8. [9/27/09.]
[211] Forbidden Archaeology, supra, pp. 402-404, cited by Human Origins, supra, at p. 5 of 32. [9/9/09.]
[212] Id., at p. 403.

biased climate of convenience—where it fits the macro scenario, it is officially unchallenged. As Cremo and Thompson point out (and as we have already seen), Piltdown Man went about 40 years before the fraud was exposed.[213]

The finds of geologist Giuseppe Ragazzoni in 1880 met a similar fate. At Castenedolo in northern Italy, he found a woman's, man's and 2 children's bones from a Middle Pliocene formation (3 or 4 ma). The woman's cranium was measured at 1340cc, comfortably within modern range, and the condition of overlaying sediment was undisturbed. His findings were even verified and confirmed by anatomist Giuseppe Sergi in 1883. But these did not conform to the pre-conceived guidelines, either, being much too old (even further off than de Perthes's finds), and were hence rejected over Sergi's protests of scientific prejudice.[214]

Sergi was not alone in his evaluation of these specimens. Armand de Quatrefages, a member of the French Academy of Science and professor at the Museum of Natural History in Paris, also commented: 'The deposit was removed in successive horizontal layers, and not the least trace was found of the beds having been mixed or disturbed.'[215] De Quatrefages also wrote: '… there exists no serious reason for doubting the discovery of M. Ragazzoni, and … if made in a Quaternary deposit no one would have thought of contesting its accuracy. Nothing, therefore, can be opposed to it but theoretical *a priori* objections, similar to those which so long repelled the existence of Quaternary man.'[216] (Emphasis original.) The bottom line was that there was no evidence whatsoever of any mixing of the contents from the separate strata beds, ruling out intrusive ceremonial human burial of any kind.

Further, the actual excavations of all four specimens were separate events on different days, and Ragazzoni, who was well familiar with the stratigraphy of the area (he was a geologist and teacher at the Technical Institute of Brescia, which was only about six miles from the discovery site at the Colle de Vento approximately 25 meter (82 foot) low hill formation near Castenedolo),[217] had four separate

---
213 Id., at pp. 403 & 404.
214 Forbidden Archaeology, id., at pp. 422-432, cited by Human Origins, at pp. 5&6 of 32.
215 Quoted by S. Laing, Human Origins (1894) London, Chapman and Hall, p. 371 (not to be confused, of course, with Pratt's Human Origins website section of much later date), in turn quoted by Forbidden Archaeology, id., at p. 429.
216 Quoted by S. Laing, Problems of the Future (1893) London, Chapman and Hall, p. 119, in turn quoted by Forbidden Archaeology, id., pp. 429, 430.
217 Forbidden Archaeology, id., p. 423.

opportunities to observe the unearthings, but in no instance were indications of burial evident.[218] It would have been an easy call because succeeding stratigraphic layers contained yellow and red clay (ferretto) going from bottom to top, respectively. The specimens themselves were found in blue clay.[219]

Incidentally, a singular human specimen had been discovered by Ragazzoni in 1860 (top of cranium, portions of thorax and limbs), some 20 years earlier in this same strata, among marine shells and coral, which he had surmised indicated the bones were transported along with the shells by ocean waves. He had thrown the bones away after they had been superficially discredited as being recent by geologists A. Stoppani and G. Curioni, a move he later regretted.[220] The later 1880 finds were under attack by Professor R.A.S. Macalister in his book Textbook of European Archaelology (1921) for lacking marine shell and coral incrustations, but this was also erroneous. Both Ragazzoni and Sergi had reported that the human specimens were so incrusted, along with the blue clay wherein they were found.[221]

Hypocritically, Macalister, while acknowledging both the competence of Ragazzoni as a geologist and Sergi as an anatomist, and even pronouncing that the Castenedolo finds, 'whatever we may think of them, have to be taken seriously,' stubbornly refused to accept these finds. He wrote of the anatomically modern bones: 'Now, if they really belonged to the stratum in which they were found, this would imply an extraordinarily long standstill for evolution. It is much more likely that there is something amiss with the observations. ... the acceptance of a Pliocene date for the Castenedolo skeletons would create so many insoluble problems that we can hardly hesitate in choosing the alternatives of adopting or rejecting their authenticity.' [222] I.e., if it doesn't fit preconceptions, throw it out!

Macalister even further argued that accepting Tertiary man with Tertiary stone tools that were also discovered for that period produced the logical incompatibility of having modern man intellectual capacities despite crude, rudimentary implements. But Cremo and Thompson

---

218 Id., at p. 427.
219 Id., p. 422, Fig. 6.3, and pp. 425 & 426.
220 Id., p. 423.
221 Id., at p. 431.
222 R.A.S. Macalister, Textbook of European Archaeology (1921), pp. 184 & 185, quoted by Forbidden Archaeology, supra, pp. 430 & 431.

were up to that task, noting: "There is, however, no fundamental incompatibility between advanced intellectual capabilities and the manufacture of crude stone tools—even today tribal people in various parts of the world, with the same brain capacity as modern city dwellers, make such implements. Also, there is no reason why anatomically modern humans could not have co-existed with more apelike creatures in the Tertiary, just as humans today coexist with gorillas, chimpanzees, and gibbons."[223]

Another objection aptly fielded by Ragazzoni himself was the possibility that streams had stripped away the blue clay layers, partially penetrating the blue clay itself, so that the human skeletal remains could have washed into hollows that were subsequently filled in with new material, concealing the fact of actual human burial. To this he responded: 'The fossil remains discovered on January 2 and January 25 lay at a depth of approximately 2 meters. The bones were situated at the boundary between the bank of shells and coral and the overlying blue clay. They were dispersed, as if scattered by the waves of the sea among the shells. The way they were situated allows one to entirely exclude any later mixing or disturbance of the strata.'[224]

Also of note is Sergi's assessment that the Castenedolo remains were likely from a family shipwrecked along a Pliocene coastline.[225] To be shipwrecked indicates a point of origin from a civilization advanced enough to construct ships for transport, be it commercial, private or both. So this family's orientation, arguably, is from a far higher level of what would otherwise be classified as hominid development. The fossils themselves, of course, were indisputably of modern man, though co-habitation with hominids and other ape-like ancestors would not be out of the question for reasons similar to those exposited by Cremo and Thompson above in terms of handling an objection to the finds. Therefore, it can be argued that even the presence of these specimens at levels associated with cruder tools does not necessarily mean their point of origin contemporary inhabitants also used these implements, although as the Forbidden Archaeology authors have noted, that would not disqualify the finds.

---

[223] Forbidden Archaeology, supra, p. 431.
[224] Giusseppe Ragazzoni, "La collina di Castenedolo, solto il rapporto antropologico, geologico ed agronomico." Commentari dell' Ateneo di Brescia, April 4 (1880), p. 126, quoted by Forbidden Archaeology, supra, p. 425.
[225] Forbidden Archaeology, supra, at p. 427.

Prejudicially calibrated dating methods were also used in the succeeding 20th Century to disingenuously challenge Ragazzoni, Sergi and de Quatrefages's 19th Century conclusions. In 1965, nitrogen content was purportedly measured to be at a level comporting with the Late Pleistocene and Holocene. I say "purportedly" because it is known that the nitrogen preservation amount can depend on the host environment, and clay retains nitrogen well, so that a higher amount of nitrogen would be remaining under that kind of host than under others, and a false reading of youthfulness would thus be observed. Disregarded were the high fluorine and uranium contents that were also tested for that were consistent with great age and that would verify Middle Pliocene placement. Contrarily, Radiocarbon testing measured at 958 years, and possible contamination betraying an overly high radiocarbon content resulting from 90 years of being in a museum display was conveniently overlooked to portray a very overly young age.[226] All future Human Origins references are to be considered to be from Pratt rather than Laing unless otherwise indicated. Of note is that bias and prejudice not only reigned contemporarily with the Castenedolo specimens, but persists even today.

This entire biased treatment by the general "scientific" community to Ragazzoni's finds prompted Cremo and Thompson to close their Castenedolo discussion with this admonition: "The account of human origins now dominant in the scientific community is the product of attitudes like Macalister's. For the last century, the idea of progressive evolution of the human type from more apelike ancestors has guided the acceptance and rejection of evidence. Evidence that contradicts the idea of human evolution is carefully screened out. Therefore, when one reads textbooks about human evolution, one may think, 'Well, the idea of human evolution must be true because all the evidence supports it.' But such textbook presentations are misleading, for it is the unquestioned belief that humans did in fact evolve from apelike ancestors that has determined what evidence should be included and how it should be arranged and interpreted."[227] (Emphasis added.) In other words, folks, there is big-time censorship going on of the "selection and elimination" logical fallacy variety, deliberately selecting the favorable evidence (if only so favorable in many cases because it in

---

226 Forbidden Archaeology, supra, at pp. 432, 755 (755 was referenced to ascertain the 1965 date for nitrogen testing), p. 432 was cited by Pratt's Human Origins, supra, at p. 6 of 32. [9/9/09.]
227 Forbidden Archaeology, supra, at p. 432.

being taken out of context, though not always so, wherein it is only a small part of the factual landscape that you are being informed of) and discarding or eliminating the unfavorable.

Even J.D. Whitney (1819-1896), Mt. Whitney's namesake and California's appointed state geologist in 1860, had his finds suppressed when he published a review in 1880 describing advanced stone tools from California gold mines uncovered during the gold rush. They didn't fit in with the conventional scenario, either. He attributed ages of 9 to 55 million years to stone mortars, spear points and pestles deep in mine shafts found beneath thick, undisturbed lava layers, insisting that the implements could not have entered from other levels. This prompted W. H. Holmes of the Smithsonian Institution to say: "Perhaps if Professor Whitney had fully appreciated the story of human evolution as it is understood today, he would have hesitated to announce the conclusions formulated, notwithstanding the imposing array of testimony with which he was confronted."[228] (Emphasis added.) In other words, forget the actual facts and just censor them or squeeze diluted or even false ones into the extant theory. That altar of worship must not be frustrated by the facts.

Calaveras County finds met the same fate. In another part of the Sierra Mountain range where Whitney reported his findings, a fossilized human skull was found in 1866 in a pre-Pilocene layer of gravel circa 40 meters below the surface. Additional human skeletal remains were found in the same region, again comporting with a range between 9 and 55 million years old, which Sir Arthur Keith insisted could not be disregarded. They were anyway.[229]

Many of the depicted discoveries above were made in situ, in well-defined strata under conditions superior to those of acknowledged discoveries (at least at the time). E.g., the famous Lucy (Australopithecus afarensis), an alleged African hominid fossil, was a surface find wherein the age was assumed from loosely associated exposed strata. Most of the Java man discoveries, including Dubois's, were dated 800,000 or more years on the assumption that they were eroded bones from Middle Pleistocene formations. The Java Man discoveries were made by paid, unsupervised native collectors who either sent or brought

---

[228] Forbidden Archaeology, supra, pp. 368-393, cited by Human Origins, ibid.
[229] Forbidden Archaeology, supra, pp. 439-452, cited by Human Origins, id., at p. 7 of 32.

them to scientists for study. Yet they prevail or prevailed over many of the above instances that were uncovered under more tightly controlled conditions, and seemingly more inherently reliable.[230]

As far as Lucy and Java Man are concerned, the scientific community is not nearly as convinced of their authenticity as macros would like you to think. Luminaries such as Ernst Mayr, Lord Solly Zuckerman, Greg Kirby and C Loring Brace have expressed their dissatisfaction with the legitimacy of the 1974 Lucy discovery.[231] At best, the 1892 discovery of Java Man (Pithecanthropus) by Eugene Dubois appears to be an amalgam. From talkorigins, a decidedly macro website, comes the admission: "Creationists are right about one thing. Most modern scientists agree that the femur is more recent than the skullcap, belonging to a modern human. Some of the teeth found nearby are now thought to be from an orangutan, rather than Homo erectus."[232]

While the website does not conclude that Java Man is inauthentic, Lucy's pedigree really does have to be open to substantial doubt. W.E. LeGros Clark also stated: "The Java skull cap shows ape-like characters in its general flattened shape, its enormous eye-brow prominence, the complete absence of what is usually called a forehead, and the small size of the brain-case."[233] There are other criticisms of the finding. As the Darwin Papers also noted: "The thigh bone and the partial skull cap were found fifty feet apart in separate digs."[234]

There are Creationist websites contending that ["for"] the 1922 discovered Nebraska Man (Hesperopithecus [ape of the western world] haroldcookii) ["a"] pig's tooth (Prosthennops) was used as evidence ["for his existence"] in the Scopes Monkey Trial, as does Wikipedia as of the date of review on 6/19/09. This is denied at the talksorigin website and an article in the answersingenesis website (obviously Creationist) confirms that it was in fact not used, so the better answer appears to be that it was not used. This is not to say, however, that the

---

230 Human Origins, ibid. [9/9/09].
231 http://thedarwinpapers.com/oldsite/number9/Darwin.htm, at pp. 31&32 of 41, taken from James M. Foard, The Nebulous Hypothesis: A Study of the Social and Historical Implications of Darwinian Theory (1996). [6/19/09.]
232 "Creationist Arguments: Java Man," Talk Origins.org, http://www.talkorigins.org/faqs/ homs/a_java.html, at p. 1 of 4.
233 W.E. LeGros Clark, History of the primates: An introduction to the study of fossil man, Fifth ed. p. 82, 1966, University of Chicago Press, quoted by The Darwin papers, supra, at p. 8 of 41.
234 [Ibid.] For a more complete analysis, see those same Darwin papers at pp. 7-9 of 41.

macros deserve exoneration. It was not actually declared a pig's tooth until 1927, when its simianship was denied in the journal Science.²³⁵

The Scopes trial itself was held during July of 1925 and was manufactured by the ACLU, who openly advertised that they would defend anyone accused of teaching evolution in the classroom (which was prohibited by the Butler Act, a Tennessee state statute). Scopes, a substitute teacher for the Principal in the school science class who was regularly Clark County High School's football coach, was urged by George Rappleyea, the manager of several local mines, to teach evolution (was Rappleyea hoping for future fossil finds of his own?). Despite the statute, a state required text, Civic Biology (1914) by George Hunter, openly endorsed evolution. Scopes admitted to covering the evolution chart and chapter in class, whose date was assigned as 4/7/25. He was never actually jailed, though formally arrested. Paul Patterson, who owned the Baltimore Sun newspaper, posted his $500 bail. H. L. Mencken was a reporter for the Sun then and covered the trial. Scopes even encouraged students to testify against him.²³⁶

As is typical of Hollywood, the trial was grossly misrepresented in the film Inherit the Wind, starring Spencer Tracy and Frederick March. March was made up to physically appear remarkably like Bryan (under the fictitious name of Matthew Harrison Brady) and Tracy portrayed Darrow (under the fictitious name of Henry Drummond). In the actual trial, since many defense witnesses were precluded from testifying (that part was depicted in the film, the total accuracy of which I am not sure), Darrow did not even ask the jury to return a "Not Guilty" verdict nor did he even make a final closing argument. Under Tennessee law, with the defense waiving final argument, the prosecution was prevented from doing so also. Basically, the case was set up for an appeal. On appeal, to the defense's surprise, The Butler Act was upheld as constitutional by the Tennessee Supreme Court, but the conviction was overturned anyway in that the judge, in establishing a $100 fine, had usurped the jury's function, and it also exceeded the

---

235 W.K. Gregory, "Hesperopithecus apparently not an ape nor a man," (1927) Science 66: 579-581. doi:10.1126. science.66.1720.579 (http://dx.doi.org/10.1126/science.66.1720.579). PMID 17810385 (http://www.ncbi.nlm. nih.gov/pubmed/17810385), cited by "Nebraska Man"-Wikipedia, the free encyclopedia, http://en.wikipedia. org/wiki/Nebraska_Man, at p. 1 of 2. [10/9/09.]

236 Douglas Linder, "An introduction to the John Scopes (Monkey) Trial," UMKC Law, http://www.law.umkc.edu/ faculty/projects/ftrials/scopes, evolut.htm; James Presley & John T. Scopes, Center of the Storm (1967) p. 60, New York: Holt, Rinehart and Winston, all cited by "Scopes Trial"-Wikipedia, the free encyclopedia; http:// en.wikipedia.org/wiki/Scopes_Trial, pp. 2&3 of 16. [6/21/09.]

state mandatory fine legally imposable by judges of $50. The Butler Act was not actually repealed until 1967. In the interim, the ACLU could not find another voluntary test case.[237] [Note: the court's opinion as of this writing is online at http://www.law.umkcedu/ faculty/projects/ ftrials/ scopes/statcase.htm.] [9/27/09.]

It appears to date that only one book has been written to refute Cremo and Thompson's claims, Michael Brass's The Antiquity of Man: Artifactual, Fossil and Gene Records Explored (2002) Publish America, and that only about a handful of the cases were attacked. Among other things, Cremo and Thompson point out the dishonest practice of morphological dating, and bring the case to focus with the Gombore humerus (attributed age of 1.5 ma, found in Ethiopia in 1977 and first likened to Australopithecus boisei and then Homo ergaster), an ER 813 talus (ankle bone) (1.5 to 1.9 ma, likened to Homo ergaster) and 2 femurs from Kenya (ER 1481 & 1472 and likened to Homo rudolfensis) (2 ma). All of these specimens were described as very much like either a modern bushman or other modern humans.[238] This morphodating in total disregard to a complete discussion and point and counterpoint is exactly what Jefferson and Madison would find abhorrent, and yet what is done all too routinely by the macros. As early as 1884, anthropologist Armand de Quatrefuges commented: "The objections made to the existence of man in the Pliocene and Moncene seem to habitually be more related to theoretical considerations than direct observation."[239] (Emphasis added.) In plain English, the macro community goes out of its way to "fudge" finds linking man's lineage to ape-like ancestors.

A rather harsh review of Brass's Antiquity of Man was written on 9/9/01 by Richard Milton, a British journalist and avowed secularist who has authored Shattering the Myths of Darwinism (1997) Park Street Press. He attacks Brass's criticism of Forbidden Archaeology as follows: "I've read Cremo and Thompson's book. I didn't find any religious propaganda or creationist messages, but I did find a mountain of carefully compiled scientific observations and reports that uniformly tend to undermine the conventional view that people like Brass hold so tightly and are unwilling even to debate openly and honestly.

---

237 Id., at pp. 6-8.
238 Forbidden Archaeology, supra, pp. 686-687, 691-693 & The Antiquity of Man, supra, p. 56, cited by Human Origins, supra, at p.8 of 32.
239 Human Origins, supra, at p. 2 of 32, quoted by Michael Cremo, Human Devolution (2003), p. 19.

Certainly there are a few geological and palaeontological observations in Forbidden Archaeology that I found weak or questionable. That is hardly surprising since the book is 1000 pages long and contains thousands of references. (new Para.) What a book like Forbidden Archaeology shows, in my view, is that if even a half (or even a tenth) of the objections raised by its authors are valid scientific objections, then Darwinism is a theory that is in deep, irremediable trouble. And the best that Brass can do in the way of rebuttal is to question a handful of their cases as unproven or badly chosen. His preferred method of rebuttal in almost all cases is that described earlier: he simply recites again, more loudly, the accepted Darwinist view."[240] (Emphasis added.)

To their credit, the book review website in an Update hyperlinked Brass's response, "A critique of Richard Milton's review," which is five-pages when downloaded and printed[241] and then included below that the Update notice, Milton's "Ten Challenges to Michael Brass," dated 10/29/02, a reply to Brass's response, occupying about eight printed pages when downloaded.

While there was vitriol from the macro community at large for Forbidden Archaeology (though not in terms of actual books written against), David Heppell of the Department of Natural History of the Royal Museum of Scotland, was complimentary, describing it as: "A very comprehensive and scholarly compilation. ... Whether one accepts the evidence presented or not, it certainly looks as if there will no longer be any excuse for ignoring it."[242] But ignore and censor it is exactly what the macro community has done. Again, it is clear that the scientific community as a whole has not resolved man's descent issue. Such a critical issue needs full exposition of the evidence and what it means from both macro's pros and cons, and in terms of factual comparisons, not opinions. Reiterating Jefferson, it is not the rightness that is to be diligently pursued, but the "uprightness."

It should not have escaped the reader's attention that both Cremo (Drutakarma Dasa—his religion is more specifically designated as Gid Gaudiya Vaishnavism) and Thompson (1947-2008—Sriman

---

[240] Book Review by Richard Milton dated 9/9/01; http://www.grahamhancock.com/library/review001_brass.php, at p. 3 of 14. [6/27/09.]
[241] http://www.antiquityofman.com/book_miltonreview.html
[242] Michael A. Cremo, Forbidden Archaeology's Impact, Los Angeles, p. 257, CA: Bhaktivedanta Book Publishing, 1998, cited by Human Origins, supra, at p. 2 of 32.

Sadaputa dasa Adhikari) are Hindus (both American-born from upstate New York) and members of the Bhiktivedanta Institute and the International Society for Krishna Consciousness (ISKCON—Hare Krishnas). Both have described themselves as Vedic Creationists. Cremo even believes that man has existed on this planet for at least many millions of years, hardly compatible with my young earth beliefs, and he also believes that man devolved from spirit and that he personally has lived multiple lives through reincarnation. As I have said, far from all Creationists are Christian Creationists, but I see this "melting pot" aspect as a virtue rather than a detriment. One does not have to be stuck in any particular religious orientation to oppose the common sense and evidentiary failings of Darwinian evolution.

The ISKCONs as a whole oppose at least Darwinian evolution, though not necessarily evolution in its entirety. It is the evidence they have uncovered that is relevant herein, not their creed (for those who may be uncomfortable with Hinduism, which this Christian Creationist writer is not. He just respectfully disagrees with them). To approach it otherwise would be committing the logical fallacy of "poisoning the well" due to their different religious beliefs,[243] just as I would be "poisoning the well" if I discounted evolution solely because of my Christian beliefs. These men are (or in Thompson's case, was) highly intellectual. Cremo had a scholarship to study International Affairs at George Washington University, for which he did extensive traveling and became well acquainted with Eastern religion, and his associations also include membership in the History of Science Society, World Archaeological Congress, Philosophy of Science Association and the European Association of Science. However, Cremo developed an early interest in Eastern religion and culture well before this, and traveled extensively because his father was an Air Force Intelligence Officer stationed in Europe. Thompson earned a Ph.D. in mathematics from Cornell University and specialized in probability theory and statistical mechanics. He also extensively researched quantum physics and mathematical biology both in American universities and at Cambridge. He was eminently well credentialed.

But origins itself merely in terms of time frames is not the only issue. The physical size of ancient man (more akin to the giants of Scriptural

---

[243] http://www.nizkor.org/features/fallacies/poisoning-the-well.html.

reference) is ripe for dispute. Just as there are suppressed findings relating to ages where human remains are concerned, there is also suppression when it comes to the size of many fossils that have been uncovered. While there have been hoaxes such as the Cardiff giant in New York in 1869, discovered within three months of the dig (why not years like some other British "fossils" we know of?),[244] there have been many other findings not so easily dismissed. While dismissed as <u>isolated</u> cases of giantism among Indians, during the 19th and early 20th Century exploration of North American mounds, bones of giants from 7 and up to 10 feet were found. However, it was determined that some of them were of an extinct, non-Indian race, and Indian legends describe giants in their land. Some Smithsonian scientists were involved in these finds, but no giant bones have ever been displayed.[245]

Off the California coast on Santa Rosa Island, a giant man's remains were excavated. He sported double rows of teeth, a not uncommon feature found among such giants.[246] Another not uncommon feature is six toes, which were discovered with scores of footprints near Brayton, on Tennessee River headwaters, impressed upon solid rock. One such track measured 16 inches long (40 cm) and 13 inches (33 cm) across the toes. Apparently there were horses' prints also, those measuring 20 by 25 cm.[247]

Yet another suppressed story was of a fossilized Irish giant allegedly 12 feet, two inches tall and weighing two tons, and excavated while its discoverer was digging for iron ore in Ireland's County Antrim. This story was in Strand Magazine, the December 1895 issue. Following a legal battle over ownership, nothing was heard about the specimen since.[248] If curious, consult this last footnote to see where on the Internet a picture of the giant appears. In 1929, a Mexican government scientist and Dean Byron Cummings discovered the skeletons of 2 men and a

---

244 Stephen J. Gould, <u>Bully for Brontosaurus</u>, London: Penguin, 1991, pp. 42-45, found at http://www.empiremuseum.com/cardiff.htm, cited by <u>Human Origins</u>, supra, at p. 15 of 32.
245 Ross Hamilton, "Holocaust of the giants: the great Smithsonian cover-up," greatserpentmound.org/ articles/giants3.html; H.P. Blavatsky, <u>Isis Unveiled</u>, TUP, 1972 (1877), 1:303-5; <u>The Secret Doctrine</u>, 2:293; William R. Corliss (comp.), <u>Biological Anomalies: Humans III</u>, Glen Arm, MD: Sourcebook Project, 1994, pp. 44-45, cited by <u>Human Origins</u>, supra, at p. 14 of 32.
246 Frank Edwards, <u>Stranger Than Science</u>, New York: Lyle Stuart, 1959, pp. 113-114, cited by <u>Human Origins</u>, supra, at p. 15 of 32.
247 <u>Stranger than Science</u>, id., pp. 112-114; "Fossilized human footprints," www.subversieveelement.com, cited by <u>Human Origins</u>, ibid.
248 W.G. Wood-Martin, <u>Traces of the Elder Faiths of Ireland</u>, London: Longmans, Green, and Co., 1902, 1:57-58, cited by <u>Human Origins</u>, ibid., at p. 16 of 32.] An actual picture of the specimen can be found at <u>Human Origins</u>, id.

woman at least 2.4 meters tall and of children 1.8 meters tall. There was interference from local Yaqis, who destroyed some of the pieces.[249]

In the late 1950s, road construction workers uncovered giant human remains (14 to 16 feet tall) in southeastern Turkey.[250] Even a finding by the renowned Louis Leakey in 1958 got suppressed. He reported finding a giant human molar from Middle Pleistocene living floors in Tanzania at Olduvai, in the company of two giant pigs with teeth like normal elephant tusks and the specimens being the size of a hippopotamus.[251] Huge stone artifacts such as pounders, knives, chisels, adzes, clubs and hand-axes, weighing between 3.6 and 11.3 kg, and scattered over a wide area, were uncovered in old Pleistocene river gravels near Bathurst, New South Wales (Australia) by amateur scientist Rex Gilroy. He estimates that some of these finds go back 240,000 years, and that the humans making and using them were over 3 meters in height (10 feet or more). He has also uncovered fossilized footprints and teeth from the Pliocene that point to even larger giant hominids.[252]

The reader may have also noticed as a source, David Pratt, who has written much about Theosophy. For convenience, let us settle on this definition of theosophy: "a system of belief based on mystical insight into the nature of God and the soul."[253] Obviously, we are dealing with the opposite of a materialistic approach to nature. Again, however, it is not the philosophy of these writers that is at issue, but rather, the nature of the fossil finds they have researched and reported about, a preponderance of which are from very reputable scientists and often under conditions indicating far more inherent reliability than those that are made famous by the macros. In fact, while there are maverick scientists from the more grounded, materialistic school who buck Darwinian evolution (we have already run into a number of those), discovering these suppressed finds to begin with would not surprisingly come from those who feel no allegiance to the traditional

---

249 Harold T. Wilkins, "Secret Cities of Old South America," Kempton, IL: <u>Adventures Unlimited</u>, 1998 (1952), pp. 44-47 www.wisdomworld.org/additional/ScienceAndThe Secret Doctrine/Series/Number99-of-103.html, cited by <u>Human Origins</u>, supra, at p. 17 of 32.
250 <u>Human Origins</u>, id., citing "Discoveries of giant human bones," http://www.returnofthenephilim.com/GiantBonesDiscoveries.html.
251 "The country of the giants," New Scientist, 24 April 1958, p. 11, cited by Human Origins, at pp. 17 & 18 of 32.
252 Rex Gilroy, "Giants of the Dream Time, 1999, www.internetezy.com.au/Australasian_Ufologist2.html; Rex Gilroy, "And there were giants", 1976, www.internetezy.com.au/~mj129/strangephenomenonb.html., <u>Human Origins</u>, supra, at p. 18 of 32.
253 wordnetweb.Princeton.edu/perl/webwn. You must enter "theosophy" (no quotes) in the Search window. [1/30/10.]

systems to start with. The fossil finds themselves are what they are, and let the interpretive spins issue where they may, but they must be dealt with regardless. The hard data is there to be grappled with, not suppressed or censored.

Clearly, in the macro world of twisted, force-fed science, when the facts don't fit, you must acquit. The slogan should read, when the facts depict, you must convict, but the "scientific" community could not bear any intrusions of fact. When de Perthes, Whitney, and Leakey conform to expectations, they are warmly embraced. When they don't, they are anathema, the same applying to Dean Kenyon. And when macro doctrine is directly challenged by a perceived to be hostile Intelligent Designer like the very scholarly Guillermo Gonzalez, tenure is denied. Idealogy and other agendas clearly prevail over objectivity and fundamental fairness. But stick around—it gets even worse. Let's look at other information that gets suppressed because the macros don't want you to hear it.

D. THERE IS NO COMPLETE STRATIGRAPHIC COLUMN ANYWHERE ON EARTH

By complete is meant "nowhere on earth is the geologic column complete in the sense of having the <u>maximum thickness of sedimentary rock attributed to each geologic period</u>."[254] (Emphasis added.) So how thick of a column is expected and how close to an expected thickness do any of the discovered columns come? According to Woodmorappe, 100 to 200 miles comprising of 10 geologic ages or Phanerozoic systems is the expectation, and the average actual thickness found is one mile and the thickest to date has been 16 miles.[255]

As far as all ten periods, systems or ages being present at any one location are concerned, there are at most 50 such locations known (only 10 to 20 conclusively confirmed), which represents 1% of the earth's surface provided ocean basins are not counted. If they are (and not one features more than a few of these systems), then the percentage reduces to 0.4%. Erosion would appear to be a very weak explanation for both this rarity and the huge discrepancy between the expected thickness

---

[254] John Woodmorappe, "The Geologic Column: Does It Exist?", <u>Creation Ex Nihilo Technical Journal</u> 13(2):77-82, 1999, cited by <u>The True.Origin Archive: Exposing the Myth of Evolution</u>, http://www.trueorigin.org/geocolumn.asp., p. 2 of 10. [1/30/10.]
[255] Ibid.

and that found in nature. Referring to erosion, R.A Watson wrote: "Is it circular to think of a process that would remove some rock, and then to use the absence of the rocks to argue that the process was in operation in the past? No, not if the argument is coupled with further evidence that the rocks were in fact once there."[256] Head spinning over that one? It should be. Caveat: multiple readings don't cure its irrationality any, when the huge disparity between expectation and reality is considered. To deem it "inconclusive" even is being generous.

The $64,000 question appears to be then, are there sufficient geological explanations to account for such huge discrepancies? To average one mile thick, to be at most 16 miles in the real world as opposed to an expected 100 to 200, is a gross disparity. On the surface, no, there are no viable explanations. Arguments such as erosion, reworking, angular unconformities, and non-deposition seem to fail miserably to account for them. Under that microscope, it certainly appears that the burden of proof to establish the validity of the geologic or stratigraphic column falls squarely on the macros. The inference would favor a global catastrophic event, a sudden compression during a short period of time, as opposed to over a slow, accumulated, graduated time that is nowhere near the thickness to be expected.

This also makes sense in that for layers to be formed at all representing even a few geologic periods, local floods and similar disasters would seem unable to account for what is formed. Besides, there are too few events of large enough scale to cause the compaction necessary for fossilization. While it is not submitted that the Noahic flood caused all of the fossilization that has occurred, it IS submitted that it formed most of it.

E. FOSSILS AT CONTRADICTORY STRATIGRAPHIC LEVELS ARE ARBITRARILY EXPLAINED AWAY, AND DATING IS DETERMINED BY CIRCULAR REASONING (LOGICAL FALLACY)

Revisiting circular reasoning, a particular premise is basically used to verify itself rather than evidence. In the case of the stratigraphic columns, the fossils are dated through expectations and predictions of

---

256 Watson, R.A., "Absence as evidence in geology," Journal of Geological Education 30:300-301, 1982, quoted by trueorigin.org, ibid., at p. 10 of 10.

how they would "evolve," which is a presupposition. It is based on a conclusionary premise untested by empirical data to essentially make the finding a self-fulfilling prophecy. Consider this quote from Steven Stanley: "In about 1830, Charles Lyell, Paul Deshayes, and Heinrich George Bronn independently developed a biostratigraphic technique [geologic column] for dating Cenozoic deposits based on relative proportions of living and extinct species of fossil mollusks ... Strangely, little effort has been made to test this assumption. This failure leaves the method vulnerable to circularity."[257] Is there not a little of the cart before the horse happening here? Yes, Mr. Stanley, that failure leaves the method MOST vulnerable to circularity.

Niles Eldridge proclaimed: "Paleontologists cannot operate this way. There is no way simply to look at a fossil and say how old it is unless you know the age of the rocks it comes from. ... And this poses something of a problem: If we date the rocks by the fossils, how can we then turn around and talk about the pattern of evolutionary change through time in the fossil record?"[258] Intellectually, you cannot. Eldridge, a convicted macro, at least earns a merit badge for being upfront about it.

Incredibly, geologist and paleontologist O. H. Schindewolf (1891-1971) asserts: "The sedimentary rocks, by themselves, however, do not yield any specific time marks, setting aside the old law of superposition, which can provide relative age indication only in a restricted manner, and which is unfit for age correlations. Moreover, it may be misleading in some cases: the beds in a section may be overturned or, owing to a hidden thrust plane, older beds may overlie younger ones. The only chronometric scale applicable in geologic history for the stratigraphic classification of rocks and for dating geologic events exactly is furnished by the fossils. Owing to the irreversibility of evolution, they offer an unambiguous timescale for relative age determinations and for world-wide correlations of rocks."[259] Unambiguous, eh? Schindewolf could not have attended too many logic classes, or instead only applied them when they conveniently fit his hypothesis.

---

[257] Stanley, Steven M., Warron O. Addicott, and Kuyotaha Chinzei, "Lyellian Curves in Paleontology: Possibilities and Limitations," Geology, Vol. 8, 1980, p. 422.
[258] Eldridge, Niles, Time Frames, 1985, p. 52.
[259] Schindewolf, O.H., "Comments on Some Stratigraphic Terms," American Journal of Science, vol. 255, 1957, pp. 394-395.

The veracity problems for lithology are self-evident. Both the time scales re the rock strata and the fossils are interdependent upon one another and presume long ages. As can be seen below, when younger ages are factored in based on discrepancies with the old age presumption and the residual evidence of trace elements that are either too plentiful or shouldn't be there at all, young ages are derived. Both results are predictably biased, so that the continuing viability of using these biased methods is open to serious question in either direction.

F. RADIOISOTOPE DATING METHODS ARE UNRELIABLE

Skeptics may respond to the stratigraphy issue by saying that even if there is circular reasoning or a tautology involved, despite this logical fallacy, empirical data arrived at by concrete radiographic dating methods have confirmed these assumptions, adopted prematurely or not, to be nonetheless ultimately correct. The operation may not have been a success, they argue, but the patient lived. Not so. Radiographic dating has not proved reliable and has also garnered markedly different results when various methods have been used on the same resource material.

A case in point occurred with the RATE (Radioisotopes and the Age of the Earth) project initiated in 1997 by a seven-man Ph.D. ICR team, consisting of two geologists (Steven Austin [of So. Argentina river valley fame] & Andrew Snelling), a geophysicist (John Baumgardner), three physicists (Eugene Chaffin, Don DeYoung & D. Russell Humphreys), and a meteorologist (Larry Vardiman, RATE chairman). As part of this project, rock samples were taken from two different sites: the Beartooth Mountains of northwest Wyoming near Yellowstone National Park, and a diabase sill located at Bass Rapids in the central portion of Arizona's Grand Canyon. Diabase is igneous rock with basalt that has visible mineral crystals. A sill is created when volcanic lava (magma) seeps through previous existing rock strata layers and cools off. At Beartooth, amphibolite rock samples were taken at a 10,200-foot elevation after being exposed during highway excavation. Previous studies from other geologists had already been made there, as they also were for the Bass Rapids location. So that they could be used for mineral isochron testing, the minerals biotite, quartz, plagioclase, hornblende, titanite (sphene), and magnetite were extracted from the Beartooth rock. Four isotope pairs were tested: lead-lead (Pb-Pb), potassium-argon (K-Ar), rubidium-strontium (Rb-Sr) and samarium-neodynium (Sm-Nd).

The readings themselves were contracted out by RATE to commercial labs in Massachusetts, Colorado and Ontario, Canada. The data was compiled on isochron graphs and statistically analyzed by using the widely accepted Isoplot computer software program. Both the minerals within each rock and separate whole rock samples themselves tested markedly different within each test method as well as between each. These differences are referred to as being discordant (when the results agree, they are concordant). The results for Beartooth were discordant, with sometimes the mineral averages being older than the rock samples they were extracted from, and vice-versa. Austin particularly noted that the K-Ar mineral ages were from 1520 to 2620 million years and when subjected to the Rb-Sr measure recorded between 2,515 plus or minus 110 million years, and for Sm-Nd, 2886 plus or minus 190 million years (the latter two representing a difference of 371 million years).

The Bass Rapids results were also discordant. The generally accepted age for the formation tested was 1070 million years (Elston & McKee, 1982). These were hardly the results here, with discordance shown for all types of comparisons as discussed for Beartooth. Austin points out the most dramatic difference, that of the whole rock sample, which yielded for K-Ar a range from 841.5 plus or minus 164 million years compared to an Sm-Nd reading of 1,379 plus or minus 140 million years, representing a sizeable difference of 537.5 million years.

For both locations, the alignment of data would have suggested concordance, but yet dramatic discordance was found. Austin noted three other different studies at three different locations to illustrate that discordant findings are not unusual in this line of work, citing the Great Dike formation in Zimbabwe, Africa, the Stuart Dike swarm in south-central Australia, and a dike swarm in Uruguay, South America location discrepancies. Despite all three studies, as at Beartooth and Bass Rapids, showing isochron plots giving straight lines with very consistent data, for which would be expected concordant results, discordances were actually found.

Austin's discussion for the possible accounting of his results leads to a dramatic factor not considered much in the geologic field. While certainly the discordance between the various dating methods themselves is itself noteworthy, the most probable explanation for it could be that nuclear decay was accelerated in the past but by unequal factors for the various isotopes. While the isochron slope is determined by the total amount of decay rather than the decay rate itself, if the past accelerations were different for each isotope, the discordances found could be accounted for.[260]

In his study, Austin also pointed out two data trends. Presuming past accelerated decay, alpha decay was greater than beta. He also described the second trend as being tentative, that isotopes with a longer half-life yield greater ages for rocks, which could be related to their atomic weights. Heavier radioisotopes like samarium and uranium tend to yield older ages. He also found these trends to be characteristic of the Zimbabwe, Australia and Uruguay studies as well, which he suggested might aid in eventually identifying the actual mechanism causing the decay alterations in the past. Various other aspects of the radioisotope decay theory are discussed in the two succeeding chapters of the book, Ch. 8, "Radioisotope Dating Case Studies" by Andrew Snelling and "Theories of Accelerated Nuclear Decay" by Eugene Chaffin.

Another study not mentioned by Austin was that done on the five historic andesite lava flows from New Zealand's Mount Nguaruhoe. The dates from these flows range from less than 0.27 to 3.5 million years ago, suspect indeed, since one of these flows happened in 1949, three more in 1954 and one in 1975.[261] The macro explanation for this is excess argon in the rocks found from below the earth's crust in the upper mantle. The very nature of the industry always begs for explanations to cover up embarrassing discrepancies. It also "begs the question": Just how many other "discrepancies" lie out there to have tainted other hitherto considered reliable readings for rocks of unknown time origin? Perhaps even more problematic for the macros is that the argon not having escaped by now is more consistent with a young earth hypothesis than an old one.

---

260 Steven Austin, "Discordant Radiosotope Dates," pp. 109-121, Ch. 7, Thousands, Not Billions: Challenging an Icon of Evolution, Questioning the Age of the Earth, 2005, edited by Dr. Don DeYoung.
261 A.A. Snelling, "The Cause of Anomalous Potassium-argon 'Ages' for Recent Andesite Flows at Mt. Nguaruhoe, New Zealand, and the Implications for Potassium-argon 'Dating'," Proc. 4th ICC, 1998, pp. 503-525.

There are other radiodating examples, one of which was when Sidney P. Clementson, a British engineer, who in studying volcanic rocks KNOWN TO BE between 200 to 300 years old, found that Soviet uranium-lead tests registered many millions of years old. In fact, depending upon the exact radiodating methods, samples and corrections, these outrageous dates ranged from 50 ma to 14.6 billion years, with emphasis on the latter.[262] Generically speaking, there are consistently problems with either the Uranium or Thorium to lead measurements, and going back for some time, from at least the middle of the 20th Century. As stated by L.T. Aldrich: "The two uranium-lead ages often differ from each other markedly, and the thorium-lead age on the same mineral is almost always drastically lower than either of the others."[263] Henry Faul also noted: "Most of the ages obtained by the lead-thorium method disagree with the ages of the same minerals computed by other lead methods. The reasons for this disagreement are largely unknown."[264]

Potassium-argon radiodating also has the same historical problems: "The two principle problems have been the uncertainties in the radioactive decay constants of potassium and in the inability of minerals to retain the argon produced by this decay."[265] Since argon is a gas, this leakage is hardly to be unexpected. Of course, only those dates within the accepted range of pre-determined age are counted. Nothing can be more "unscientific" than that closed, biased approach.

The means of changing decay rates was illustrated by radiation physicist H.C. Dudley, wherein he altered 14 radioisotope rates via stress in monomolecular layers, temperature, pressure, and electric and magnetic fields.[266] Any methodology that fragile should be viewed under very strict scrutiny, but the macros do not exercise a trace of that standard.

The RATE project also introduced some additional hypotheses that offer evidence of a young age for the earth, as the book's title directs.

---

262 "Critical Examination of Radioactive Dating of Rocks," Creation Research Society Quarterly, December 1970, cited by http:evolution-facts.org/Ev-V1/1evlch07a.htm, "Chapter 7 – "Dating Methods Part 1," p. 13 of 18. [6/15/09.]
263 L.T. Aldrich, "Measurement of Radioactive Ages of Rocks," Science, May 18, 1956, p. 872, quoted by "Dating Methods," ibid.
264 Henry Faul, Nuclear Geology (1954), p. 295, quoted by "Dating Methods," ibid.
265 G.W. Wetherill, "Radioactivity of Potassium and Geologic Time," in Science, September 20, 1957, p. 545, quoted by "Dating Methods," id., at p. 14 of 18.
266 H.C. Dudley, "Radioactivity Re-Examined," Chemical and Engineering News, April 7, 1975, p. 2, cited by "Dating Methods," ibid., at p. 17 of 18.

Experimentation by Dr. Russell Humphreys revealed <u>less helium escape in Zircon crystals</u> than could support an older earth presumption, and Dr. John Baumgardner detected <u>more carbon in diamonds than would be expected</u> unless the earth was only thousands rather than billions of years old, to name two other findings.

Baumgardner discussed his findings and concluded that, if there were a great Flood, it would be a large factor in the results obtained because the large biomass caused by the event would have diluted the C-14 that existed beforehand. "The RATE team concludes that a key assumption used in obtaining these carbon-14 ages is not correct because the ratio of carbon-14 to total carbon was almost certainly less during pre-Flood times than it is today. We know this from the great reservoir of fossil fuels which were buried during the Flood. This large [vegetative] biomass would have diluted the C-14 in the pre-Flood world to give a very low ratio of C-14/C-12 compared with the present world."[267] Also factored in is that the geomagnetic field was much stronger pre-Flood. "This early earth magnetism would deflect cosmic rays away from the earth more efficiently than today and would diminish the historical production of carbon-14."[268] Combining the effects of the two phenomena, he wrote: "Together, these factors can easily decrease the calculated carbon-14 dates of coal and diamond samples tenfold, from 50,000 to just 5,000 years, a value consistent with Flood history."[269]

But that would tend to simply reduce C-14 and make it even less likely to be present now. How does the other RATE claim of accelerated decay fit in? Baumgardner explores that as well: "It was shown earlier … that the decay of heavy isotopes is incapable of producing the observed amounts of carbon-14, but this is only true at today's rates of disintegration. If nuclear decay was greatly accelerated in the past then substantial carbon-14 might have formed as a result. Alpha particles produced by uranium decay, for example, can interact with common elements in rocks such as oxygen, silicon, aluminum, and magnesium. As a result, neutrons are produced. These neutrons, in turn, can interact with underground nitrogen-14 and carbon-13 atoms to produce carbon-14. This could occur in both organic and mineral samples. The

---

267 <u>Thousands, Not Billions</u>, ibid., at p.59.
268 Ibid.
269 Ibid.

unexpected carbon-14 findings may be an indication of accelerated decay events in the past. <u>The RATE team defines accelerated decay as millions of years' worth of nuclear decay, at present rates, taking place very quickly, perhaps in just a few days. Another way of describing accelerated decay is a temporary, extreme reduction in nuclear half-lives.</u>"[270] (Emphasis added.)

This is consistent with their aforementioned empirical finding of C-14 both being present in their diamond samples and in different quantities. The variation in the diamond samples that unexpectedly had C-14 in them have a viable explanation if accelerated decay is true, and is consonant with their premise that the Noahic flood (or a similar global deluge) actually did happen to cause it. Baumgardner argued: "The carbon-14 content of the placer diamonds shows considerable variation (Table 3-3). One placer sample in particular has a percent modern carbon value of 0.31, higher than the other diamond samples measured. <u>This suggests that some placer diamonds may have experienced intense nuclear reactions which produced their internal carbon-14 atoms</u>. Perhaps the geological setting of these surface diamonds may have exposed them to the full effects of accelerated nuclear decay."[271] (Emphasis added.)

It is submitted that Baumgardner's discussions are very highly plausible and based on the empirically proven premise that diamond samples did show unexpected but notable C-14 in them. They should not contain any C-14 at all if the older earth hypothesis were true. All three scenarios contribute to the situation in differing degrees. The reduction of the C14-C12 ratio from pre-flood days means that the original amount of C-14 in the environment was greater and was reduced by the biomass. The greater pre-flood electromagnetic field, on the other hand, would have inhibited C-14 formation by the greater deflection of the cosmic rays, but as the progression of time has weakened the strength of the field, causing less deflection of the cosmic rays, then C-14 production has been increasing accordingly. On the other hand, the accelerated decay would infuse more C-14 than expected. While

---

270 [94] Id., at p. 60.
271 [95] Id., at pp. 60, 61.

there has been some fluctuation, an overall decreasing electromagnetic field is an established fact.[272]

Regardless of the confluence of the above three conditions, we are still left with the incompatibility of C-14 content in diamonds (whose hardness one would think would even prevent penetration of C-14, so that we are dealing with how much C-14 escaped the diamond that was in the coal before compression, rather than what entered post-formation), which should be unsustainable if the earth was of great geological age. This is a serious challenge to the old age of the earth macro belief and the uniformitarian presumption upon which it is based.

Aside from the RATE project, radioisotope inconsistencies were also found when C-14 was used to date the muscle and hair on a frozen Alaskan musk ox carcass. The muscle measured 24,000 years as opposed to 17,000 years for the hair.[273] When author Brown re-calibrated dates of 35,000 to 40,000 years to correlate with the calculated Biblical date for the Noahic flood (circa 2700 B.C., or again, like event), the findings corresponded to within the ox's approximate life span.[274]

Instead of carbon-14 having been a constant on this planet, other factors decreasing its presence would be pollution from the Industrial Age (and now, of course, for that matter. This is known as the Seuss Effect) and nuclear testing. If there were a Noahic flood, expected post-flood volcanism would also decrease its presence. <u>The presence of Carbon-14 in coal for no matter what specimen man has inspected does not bode well for the old age of the earth macros.</u>

There are other notable examples of grossly inaccurate C-14 dating. Newly killed seals were dated at 1,300 years and 4,600 years were recorded for seals that died no more than 30 years ago.[275] Likewise, the shells of snails and other living mollusks were subjected to C-14 dating and were found to have died about 2,300 years ago.[276]

---

272 K.L. McDonald and R.H. Gunst, "An Analysis of the Earth's Magnetic Field from 1835 to 1965," <u>ESSA Technical Report IER 46-IES</u>, 1965, U. S. Government Printing Office, Washington, D.C., p. 14.
273 R.H. Brown, "Correlation of C-14 Age with Real Time," 1992, <u>Creation Research Quarterly</u>, 29:45-47.
274 Dr. Robert Bennett, "Radio Dating: Special Creation vs. Specious Creativity" endnote 7—http://kolbecenter.org/Bennett.radiodating.htm. [6/15/09.]
275 W. Dort, "Mummified Seals of Southern Victoria Land," <u>Antarctic Journal of the U.S.</u>, June 1971, p. 210, cited by Chapter 7-"Dating Methods" Part II, http://evolution-facts.org/Ev-V1/levlch07b.htm, at pp. 11 & 12 of 21. [6/15/09.]
276 M Keith and G. Anderson, "Radiocarbon Dating: Fictitious Results with Mollusk Shells," <u>Science</u>, 141, 1963, p. 634, cited by "Dating Methods," id., at p. 12 of 21.

Another lithological problem for macros is the presence of fossils that traverse vertically through several rock layers (called polystrate fossils). It is quite problematic how these could have maintained their verticality for long stretches of geologic time while they were slowly getting buried. In fact, sediment deposit experiments by geologist Guy Berthault strongly detract from the notion that the stratigraphic record should be used for dating calibration.[277]

The limitations of isochron reliability are well-known even to macros. Some as articulated by recognized scientists make an objective observer wonder why the inconsistencies are even tolerated by the scientific community, and why greater demand is not raised for more control and perhaps entirely different methodologies. Harvard pharmacologist Y.F. Zheng noted: "Some of the basis assumptions of the conventional Rb-Sr [rubidium-strontium] isochron method have to be modified and an observed isochron does not certainly define valid age information for a geological system, even if a goodness of fit of the experimental results is obtained in plotting Strontium-87/Strontium-86. This problem cannot be overlooked, especially in evaluating the numerical time scale. Similar questions can also arise in applying Sm-Nd [samarium-neodymium] and U-Pb [uranium-lead] isochron methods."[278]

Similar problems are presented with the uranium-lead Concordia method, which combines the two uranium-lead decay series into one diagram. Despite this, zircon results are discordant. Again, there are explanations posed, but despite their validity or invalidity, once again track-covering has to be performed, and even if those particular trails eventually get "resolved," one can legitimately ask, given the ambiguity of the field, as to what other tracks have thus far been unidentified?

Another indicator of macros relying on calibrated dating bias is Mitochondrial DNA (mtDNA), which is only inherited from the mother. All mtDNA changes come from non-functional neutral mutations over time happening over a constant rate, exceeding nuclear DNA. This theoretically allows biologists to establish a "molecular clock" whereby macros could determine the divergence of species

---

277 Guy Berthault, "Geological Time Scale Questioned," cited by Robert Bennett, "Special Creation vs. Specious Creativity", taken from http://www.kolbecenter.org/bennett/radiodating.htm at p. 16 of 17, quoting from http://www.cs.unc.edu/~plaisted/ce/mitochondria.html (1997). [6/15/09.]
278 Y.F. Zheng, "Influence of the Nature of Initial Rb-Sr System on Isochron Validity," Chemical Geology, 1989, 80:1-16 (p. 14).

through the number of mutant genes between them. Using this technique based on the assumptions engendered into the fossil record leaves a "Mitochondrial Eve" of circa 200,000 years. The problem is that when the mtDNA rate of change was observed with modern humans by macro scientists, the result was a rate 20 times faster than that taken from the fossil record. Wrote experimenter Parsons: "…Using our empirical rate to calibrate the mtDNA molecular clock would result in only ~6,500 y.a., clearly incompatible with the known age of humans. … it remains implausible to explain the known geographic distribution of mtDNA sequence variation by human migration that occurred only in the last ~6,500 years."[279]

Applied to the topic of this chapter, how the dating methods are calibrated rests on pre-conceived conceptions of the results sought, just as is the case for the stratigraphic columns. The C-14 musk ox original study gave absurd results and puts a severe damper on the reliability of even that methodology. An adjustment on a Biblical scale puts the musk ox age right where it would be expected in the young earth hypothesis. The same can be said for the New Zealand study reported by Snelling, wherein known entities were tested and the measured ages grossly discordant with reality. Carbon dating not only presumes facts not in evidence, but which also contradict the assumption that the carbon leakage rate has been constant throughout time. Even discounting a great flood, the electromagnetic field intensity difference is a powerful influence. And regardless of operative assumptions for radiosotope testing from either camp, it is highly problematic for macros that helium remains in zircons, carbon-14 in diamonds, and that no coal sample has been found yet lacking carbon-14. These definitely tip the scale toward the young earth hypothesis. These phenomena are not reliant upon calibrator bias depending on which camp is making the assumptions, and so would appear to have particularly strong probative value.

So there you have it. We have talked about macro's dubious and postured beginning in terms of Darwinism, the doubts among its contemporary proponents as to its postulates, the suppressed fossil findings concerning man's origins and original size, the incomplete stratigraphic columns, the lack of fossil evidence therein, and the

---

279 Bennett, "Special Creation," supra, at p. 3 of 17. Bennett notes that no further dating research using mtDNA has been conducted since.

specious authenticity of radioisotope dating methods, and independent evidences for a young earth other than false dating methods. Why is this part of macro history and scientific discovery antithetical to it virtually unknown to the general public and its children of public school age? We are about to dig deeper into that very question now.

G. THE MODERN SUPPRESSORS OF TRUTH, WHO THEY ARE, AND WHY THEY WOULD FAIL WITH A PROPERLY PRESENTED CASE TO THE U.S. SUPREME COURT, CONSISTENT WITH EDWARDS V. AGUILLARD

Modernly, the undue influence of Executive Director Eugenie Scott (since 1987) and the NCSE (again, National Center for Science Education) upon our education system (a government organ), plus another accomplice to be named shortly, is an example of the very corrupting coalition or alliance that Madison warned against earlier. The free flow of information and discourse of ideas that is supposed to hallmark our education system has been defiled by a powerful, factious oligarchy.

This is against the very pluralism that Madison promulgated throughout his political life for the proper control of factions as perhaps best articulated (and certainly most famously so) in his No. 10 contribution to the Federalist Papers, "Factions: Their Cause and Control." He wrote: "By a faction, I understand a number of citizens, whether amounting to a majority or minority of the whole, who are united and actuated by some common impulse of passion, or of interest, adverse to the rights of other citizens, or to the permanent and aggregate interests of the community."[280] This is part of human nature: "As long as the connection subsists between his reason and his self-love, his opinions [of the factious person—author's note] and his passions will have a reciprocal influence on each other; and the former will be objects to which the latter will attach themselves."[281] He further declared: "If the impulse and the opportunity be suffered to coincide, we well know, that neither moral nor religious motives can be relied on

---

[280] James Madison, "Factions: Their Cause and Control," Alexander Hamilton, John Jay and James Madison, The Federalist Papers, Andrew Hacker, ed., 3d printing (1968), Washington Square Press, p. 17.
[281] Ibid.

as an adequate control."[282] We now know the backdrop under which Madison made that statement.

It is generally acknowledged that the NCSE was initially formed as a response to the Creationist movement, the latter of which Scott adamantly opposes. Their control, therefore, over educational public school content cannot possibly be an unbiased one, and most certainly for the above-described reasons has not played out that way. They are even most adamantly a response against Creationist "bulldog" Duane Gish, recognized as perhaps the most accomplished Creationist debater of his time. Scott is noted for detesting his use of a debating technique that she refers to as the "Gish gallop." Her group and its leadership are hardly an example of objectivity and restraint, and when one looks into the accusation that Gish hopelessly and predictably spiels forth error after error within his initial 40 or 45 minute address that cannot possibly be all retorted against in one session by any macro (something which has been "known" about him for a considerable time), one eventually gets the impression that it is not the style but rather the Gish substance that almost inevitably victimizes the macros. If his facts were flawed substantively, should they not have solved that problem of getting in their shots years ago, knowing of his alleged "galloping" and what he'll be galloping about? This objection does not ring true.

But while the NCSE seems to be the most vociferous, the largest organization advocating evolution in the schools, while trying to beat back Creationism or Intelligent Design at every turn, is the AIBS (again, American Institute of Biological Sciences), founded in 1958 as part of the effort for American education to keep pace with the Soviets. The AIBS has worked hand in hand with the NCSE on numerous occasions in their mutual fight against Creationism (with ID being the backdoor variety). They even coordinate with them by providing an AIBS/NCSE State Evolution List Serve Network so that those wishing to support macro efforts are kept up to date on the progress and struggles presented in the field.

It must be made clear that these two organizations are the most publicly participatory, vocal and visible. There are most certainly other groups committed to macro, such as the NAS (again, National

---
[282] Id., at p. 20.

Academy of Sciences), the National Science Teachers Association and the National Science Foundation, just to name a few. In fact, the NAS will be discussed more thoroughly later on in this book.

The issue is not a religious one but rather the scientific question: "Does the evidence show that change and development by blind chance and perhaps necessity without planning is responsible for what we observe in nature, as well as the origins for phenomena that we observe, or are there other theories that better explain the total evidence available for which origins is a part of the inquiry?" I would allow that phrasing even though I feel that an inference toward design stating it with Intelligent Design in the lead would be the more appropriate way to phrase it. Adaptation is easily linkable to the genetic code (I know I have Chain on my side), which in no way supports macro and is probably the most brilliant piece of engineering yet known to man, as well as being far beyond his own capacity to replicate.

Maybe this goal could best be accomplished by offering a specific Scientific Foundational Theory class, and separating that from the other formal classes of Chemistry, Biology, Physics, Geology, etc., so that it is an additional, independent subject in the syllabus. A decision could then be made by the respective school boards as to whether it should be a required class, or offered as an elective. Textbooks in the specific disciplines would still have to be re-formatted so that neither macro nor Intelligent Design is directly referenced. There would be no right or wrong answers in the Theory classroom as to which persuasion is preferred. That is up to the student. The student simply should have to know the arguments in each direction and then state why he prefers a particular set in defense of his preference. He must be aware of the arguments supporting his position and accurately regurgitate them back, and show why he thinks these arguments superior to the others, which must also be recited and discussed. Nothing more can be morally or ethically demanded than that.

The above is totally consonant with the U.S. Supreme Court case of Edwards v. Aguillard (1987) 482 U.S. 578, 107 S.Ct. 2573, 96 L.Ed.2d 510, 1987 U.S. Lexis 2729, 55 USLW 4860. Though in some aspects the majority opinion is deeply flawed (in part pointed out by the Scalia dissent; also, Antony Flew is right about that, as discussed below, though he is gracious to macro in only pointing out what he does), the court did make one thing clear that is consistent with the principles espoused by Jefferson, Madison and, if he was a man of his word, even Darwin bulldog Thomas Huxley himself re the free dissemination of ideas and avoidance of dogmatism (again, he did not even teach macro in his classroom): "We do not imply that a legislature could never require that scientific critiques of prevailing scientific theories be taught. ... <u>Teaching a variety of scientific theories about origins of humankind to schoolchildren might be validly done with the clear secular intent of enhancing the effectiveness of science instruction</u>. But because the primary purpose of the Creationism Act is to endorse a particular religious doctrine, the Act furthers religion in violation of the Establishment Clause." [<u>Edwards v. Aguillard</u> (1987) 482 U.S. 578, 593.] (Emphasis added.)

It is significant that Powell's concurring opinion notes that, "A religious purpose is not enough to invalidate an act of a state legislature. <u>The religious purpose must predominate</u>." [Id., at p. 599.] (Emphasis added.) He further adds: "A decision respecting the subject-matter to be taught in public schools <u>does not violate the Establishment Clause simply because the material to be taught 'happens to coincide or harmonize with the tenets of some or all religions</u>.' [Cita. omitted by me.]" [Id., at p. 605.] (Emphasis added.) In sum, the majority, in its otherwise poorly reasoned decision on other grounds, nonetheless shows that the mere touching upon of religious aspects in legislation, where the intent is not to endorse a religion, but rather to present the more total facts addressing an issue so that decisions as to their merits can be properly made (i.e., fulfilling the secular purpose of giving schoolchildren a more complete informational database to draw from), does not violate the First Amendment. This is so even if the end result is ultimately and coincidentally found to be compatible with religious doctrine.

A very important point was also raised by the Scalia dissent (joined by Chief Justice Rehnquist) as far as the courts sometimes even allowing certain decidedly religious-oriented activities under State aegis to take place: "... since we have consistently described the Establishment Clause as forbidding not only <u>state action</u> (emphasis added) motivated by the desire to *advance* (emphasis original) religion, but also that intended to "disapprove," "inhibit," or evince hostility toward religion, [cita. omitted by me]; and since we have said that government "neutrality" (emphasis original) toward religion is the preeminent goal of the First Amendment, [cita. omitted by me]; a State which discovers that its employees are <u>inhibiting</u> (emphasis added) religion must take steps to prevent them from doing so, even though its purpose would clearly be to advance religion." [Id., at p. 616.] Thus, neutrality in religion cuts both ways—neither can a state inhibit religion. Neither endorsement nor inhibition is acceptable, and steps can be taken by a state to neutralize its position even though such purpose "would clearly be to advance religion."

This squares with my contention herein that the disingenuous and undue influence of the AIBS and NCSE is being unconstitutionally exercised to "prohibit the free exercise thereof [of religion]" by sabotaging the true state of the facts, such as the non-supporting reality of the fossil record concerning macro, the fraud concerning recapitulation, the misrepresentation of the horse series, etc., to make it appear that it is uncontradicted by empirical data that man came from other life forms in an unguided transitional manner, when nothing could be further from the truth. Obvious conflicts concerning the arrival of man upon the scene ex nihilo as opposed to transitionally, as well as a relatively young age for our planet earth (perhaps even 6000 to 10000 years old), just to name two, exist between Creationism (which here however becomes subordinated to the rubric of Intelligent Design) and macro, wherein students need to hear the EMPIRICAL DATA for BOTH postures.

Students as a matter of entitlement on a secular level (origins is surely important on that level, too, or macro would not hypocritically try to jam their theory down students' throats, and <u>Aguillard</u> has acknowledged that anyway) are entitled to being given full disclosure of all competing evidence concerning these issues, as opposed to the watered-down, inaccurate, <u>censored</u> version of the facts that they are now being handed. And should some of these students be religious-oriented, the contradictions presented them without a means of comparing the merits of both views through direct State sabotage could well work to show State "disapproval," "inhibition" or "hostility" toward their treasured beliefs that Powell admonished about. In fact, it would be hard under that scenario to reasonably conclude otherwise.

The bottom line here is not that I feel that under my proposal religion is being advanced because I do not think it is being. The fact that the true evidence is supportive of religious postures is submitted to be coincidental. But rather, even if the proposal were construed to be a religious advancement, the judicial milieu is there for exemption from Establishment Clause stricture to counteract the deliberate censorship by the macros of the evidence that seriously challenges macro positions. This is a vital part of my argument (even though auxiliary to my main theme), and covers many of the objections otherwise posed by opponents.

Scalia also made the salient point that even if a creator is inferred from the evidence, it need not be the Genesis creator. That is not an inevitable conclusion at all. He wrote: "We have no basis on the record to conclude that creation science need be anything other than a collection of scientific data supporting the theory that life abruptly appeared on earth. ... Creation science, its proponents insist, no more must explain *whence* (emphasis original) life came than evolution must explain whence came the inanimate materials from which it says life evolved. But even if it were not so, to posit a past creator is not to posit the eternal and personal God who is the object of religious veneration. Indeed, it is not even to posit the "unmoved mover" hypothesized by Aristotle and other notably non-fundamentalist philosophers. Senator Keith [who proposed the bill—author's note] suggested this when he referred to 'a creator, *however you define a creator.*'" [Id., at pp. 629 & 630.] (Last emphasis original.)

While I disagree that macro need not come up for an origin for its inanimate matter it relies on so heavily because of the CHEMICAL IMPOSSIBILITY of creating a living organism outside of a closed system as postulated by macro, I heartily agree that the identity of the Creator is anybody's guess (again, even though my own spiritual leanings are quite obvious.) In fact, I do not even approach this as a supernatural source, though I suspect that is what it is. It is empirically unknown what the intervening agent is. I am approaching this from an Intelligent Design standpoint and nothing else.

Of course, the majority's language of enhancing the "effectiveness of science instruction" is a tautology because since macro operates under the a priori exclusion of supernatural agencies, it starts off with "Special

Pleading" as its very artificial (and dishonest) edifice. This is especially so because not only does macro NOT have any current explanation for life origins, but it faces the chemical impossibility of life happening by accident hurdle discussed below. The burden of proof should be on it and not the other way around. Until it can legitimately negotiate that highly problematic area (a summit this writer submits it will never reach), it has no rightful claim to make in discussing human origins. It most certainly should not be making claims of scientific fact that it inherently knows are either erroneous or premature to make. It is follies like that that our Highest Court should be attacking. It should publicly call a spade a spade and expose the fraud for exactly what it is. Again, though Intelligent Design is not fairly subsumed as backdoor Creationism, it is clear that if that is argued, it must inexorably be admitted that macro is backdoor atheism. Chapter 9 deals with this issue.

Nonetheless, science and education are still very much promoted (and an all-around unbiased public education should be the goal of all this, and not a bias shown to warring factions because one has leverage and the other does not) so long as students are addressing the question as phrased above (or the functional equivalent thereof). Of course, since macro can only guess at origins, it by definition does not explain everything and is incapable of reaching any conclusions about origins, be they extraterrestrial, terrestrial or human. It is all guesswork (fully acknowledged by Darwin, as we have seen), and no matter how educated and learned a guess it is, it is nothing but that, and the "discipline" (graciously put) should have the integrity to admit it, an integrity that is outrageously lacking to date.

It is further submitted that not only is such an approach permissible, but if the intent of the Framers is considered in construing the First Amendment provision, as it arguably must be since legislative intent is used to interpret any statute when any ambiguity exists (and it is phrased with ambiguity as Jefferson admonished), then it must be deemed unconstitutional NOT to teach both theories in the classroom. With the language in <u>Aguillard</u>, it is by no means a stretch to reach such a ruling if the U.S. Supreme Court were approached in a case with the facts and issues referenced in this work. That religion through Intelligent Design type factual presentation is being promoted is a concoction of the macros that simply does not hold up under reasonable, probing, clinical analysis. In fact, it could be strongly argued that a properly drafted statute reflecting such a compelling state interest in giving students a balanced rather than biased education would be subjected to relatively loose scrutiny because of the objective sought.

The fraudulent aspects of this deception being put aside, the macros have committed "special pleading" in their advocacy of macro in the public schools. If special pleading were considered in the espionage context rather than the educational, it would be labeled "disinformation."

The words of Alexander Hamilton in Federalist Paper no. 1 ("Defects of the Articles of Confederation") come glaringly to mind in describing how right-minded people (assuming that status for the sake of argument) nonetheless have as much bias and prejudice as wrong-sided ones: "And a further reason for caution, in this respect, might be drawn from the reflection, that we are not always sure that those who advocate the truth are actuated by purer principles than their antagonists. Ambition, avarice, personal animosity, party opposition, and many other motives, not more laudable than these, are apt to operate as well upon those who support, as upon those who oppose, the right side of a question."[283] (Emphasis added.) It is this articulation of the potential for abuse that must be harnessed, that even the proverbial "right side of the fence" can be motivated by highly subjective factors that must be guarded against. The target of the AIBS and NCSE is to beat down the Creationists and Intelligent Designers, and the manner in which they done this, by cutting off all issues concerning the conclusions and facts evinced by the macros, is against the teachings of Hamilton as well as Jefferson and Madison.

Applied, this reiterates the very point made above that this censorship violates the latter part of the First Amendment admonition concerning religion, "prohibiting the free exercise thereof." By denying students the facts, they want to steer them against a possible conclusion of even a Deistic presence of God, and by invertly poisoning their minds in one direction as Jefferson so aptly pointed out in his aforementioned words, the opinions and belief of men depend not on their own will, but follow involuntarily the evidence proposed to their minds, as well as, For here we are not afraid to follow truth wherever it may lead,

---

283 Alexander Hamilton, "Defects of the Articles of Confederation," The Federalist Papers, supra, at pp. 2 & 3.

nor to tolerate error so long as reason is free to combat it. The unduly influential AIBS and NCSE do not trust the student populace (or the general public, for that matter) to independently make decisions based on the "allegedly" right way, their macro way, the only way. The students are not being allowed to exercise even their religion freely while being given only information geared to sway their opinions in favor of macro and its inevitable atheistic tendencies.

Of particular importance is that the AIBS tactics are specifically opposed to and contradict their own Ethics Statement (Revised 22 March 2002) as expressed on the Internet, which specifically states: "Preamble: AIBS believes that a code of ethics is basic to the conduct of science and essential to the maintenance of an honorable profession. Members of AIBS shall conduct their professional lives in accordance with the ethics standards stated below. ... [bullet one] Conduct research and teaching in a manner that is consistent with accepted scientific and teaching methods, maintaining the highest standards of honesty and integrity in all professional endeavors ... [bullet three] Expose scientific fraud and other forms of professional misconduct whenever it is found ... [bullet five] Be constructive and professional in evaluating the work of colleagues, students, and employees [and]... [bullet seven] Promote the free and open exchange of information, not withholding information to substantiate a personal or scientific point of view."[284] (Emphasis added.)

It is quite apparent that the deliberate suppression of ID arguments and other challenges to macro violate the very tenets the AIBS professes to follow. Elsewhere at their website, they point with pride to their Public Policy, wherein they state: "The AIBS Public Policy Office provides services in support and defense of biology, including analyses, representation, and advocacy ... Recent activities have ... blocked creationist attacks on evolution education ..."[285] (Emphasis added.) Note how the total commitment to teaching evolution is undiluted and unchallenged. So much for the free and open exchange of information and non-withholding of information they otherwise advertise to substantiate a personal or scientific point of view. One does not have to strain the imagination to picture the reaction that Jefferson, Madison and even Hamilton would have had to that assertion.

---

284 http://www.aibs.org/about-aibs/ethics_statement.html, at p. 1 of 2. [6/22/09.]
285 http://www.aibs.org/organization-membership/, at p. 3 of 7. [6/22/09.]

Back in our imaginary courtroom, the reader as a juror would have the right to consider any suppressed evidence as going against the cause of the suppressor. CACI no. 204 provides: "<u>Willful Suppression of Evidence</u>. You may consider whether one party <u>intentionally concealed</u> or destroyed evidence. <u>If you decide that a party did so, you may decide that the evidence would have been unfavorable to that party</u>." (Emphasis added.) As a corollary, Evidence Code section 413 holds: "In determining what inferences to draw from the evidence or facts in the case against a party, the trier of fact may consider, among other things, ... the party's ... willful suppression of evidence relating thereto, if such be the case." (Emphasis added.) There can be no doubt that as a reader (juror), you are entitled to consider suppressed evidence that is drawn to your attention to have adverse inferences to the suppressing party and hold that evidence directly against it.

So it is quite evident that what is needed is a greater presentation of relevant evidence to be weighed by the jury (both public school students and the general public) on this issue of origins and other related issues. <u>Our jury here must be necessarily narrowed to the public school issue. Further dissemination of information from the press and other means of publication for the general welfare of the general public are vital, of course, but beyond the scope of this work.</u>

A good starting point in the pursuit of a balanced education is to have formal, televised public debate with panels of established and highly credentialed scientific authorities engaging in point and counterpoint argumentation, so that the grain (clinical, untampered, unbiased empirical evidence) is sifted from the chaff (fabricated, biased, incomplete and disinformation evidence). We owe that much to the education of our young people (and some older folks might benefit, too).

It is imperative that the federal government come forward with legislation (just as it did with the National Defense Act of 1958) in this crucial area, to set up at least curriculum guidelines for the states, who cannot be trusted to be totally autonomous in this area but overall subject to the undue influences of the AIBS and NCES. Likewise, it has been demonstrated that the states cannot take the lead in this endeavor, and the few states that have tried objectivity and balance have statutes struck down that at least attempt at balance.

<u>Just as the Articles of Confederation had to consensually give way to the Constitution of the United States for purposes of installing a strong central government, similar leadership on the national front is needed now.</u>

Another error frequently made in this polemic is that intelligent minds conclude either macro or Creation and never the twain shall meet. In other words, that there are intellectually only two alternatives. Hence, a "false dilemma." While that is my own ultimate reasoned position after my personal weighing of the evidence, it is nonetheless a logical fallacy to closed-mindedly begin the intellectual journey with that bias or predisposition because we have Morris and Gingerich going the way of Theistic Evolution. For them, rather than disjunctive, it's conjunctive. The fact that two men of such impressive station both lean that way does not make it right or wrong, but does clearly show that intellectual paths can opt that way (and they are, of course, not alone). This is important for the secular purpose of studying origins. There are a number of different intellectual paths the student can ultimately take, among them (without being exhaustive): Atheism with a macro leaning, Atheism without a macro leaning, Theism, Deism, Theistic macro, or, despite a properly presented curriculum of scientific fact addressing key issues, Undecided, with no emphasis on any of these paths being placed. It truly boils down to where the evidence leads (or possibly does not lead, to leave the jury still out on origins and other key scientific issues).

That there are evidentiary problems with a strictly macro approach has led luminaries such as Gingerich and Morris to challenge the panoramic sweep given it by conventional scientists. Its dogmatism and presumptuousness simply do not commend it. In an interview conducted prior to a Cambridge address on Galileo's embroilment with the Vatican, Gingerich stated his Theistic macro position this way: " 'Dare a scientist believe in design? In an intelligent designer of the universe? ... [New Para.] It seems to me, <u>yes</u> ... But this is a complex question, however ... Intelligent design has become a code word for something that is very controversial. I hope my position on this topic is nuanced in a way that is different from the code word. Thus, I wouldn't consider myself part of the intelligent design movement, <u>even though I believe there is a God as a designer, who happens to be using the</u>

evolutionary process to achieve larger goals – which are, as far as we human beings can see, [the development of] self-consciousness and conscience.'"[286] (Emphasis added.) Are we not hearing the resonance of Alfred Russel Wallace in these words?

In an approach to science similar to Neils Bohr in terms of science becoming a viewpoint rather than an actuating force, Gingerich further commented: " 'The idea of design is contrasted to the kind of randomness of classical Darwinian evolution – non-directed, without a goal, without a purpose. Now, that is *a* way of looking at the scientific record. But I am offended by some of the evolutionists who not only use this as a working relation, but declare that this [is] how the universe *is*, that evolution teaches us the *nature* of the universe. And I say, No – it is just a working rule for one way of going about making an explanation.'"[287] (Emphasis original.) Implicit in Gingerich's words is that macro is not self-actuating but is an expression of what is going on in the universe, an observation, so that it helps to put a perspective on the universe so we can begin to comprehend it. It is part of a much larger mosaic picture in which the macro process is but a parcel. While I totally disagree with Gingerich, his is still a reasoned perspective logically arrivable by other reasonable minds. That is why, in my view, the syllabus has to be presented as I have outlined.

Gingerich is not alone in his perception or his philosophy. Wikipedia lists other current Theistic macros and I am not offering this up as exhaustive but simply illustrative of the company he and Simon Conway Morris contemporarily keep. That list includes: John M. Page, author of The Genesis Code; Paleontologist Robert T. Bakker; R.J. Berry, Professor of Genetics at University College London; Microbiologist Richard G. Colling of Olivet Nazarene University, author of Random Designer: Created from Chaos to Connect with Creator; Geneticist Francis Collins, whom we will deal with below; Biologist Darrel Falk of Point Loma Nazarene University, author of Coming to Peace with Science; Biologist Denis Lamoureux of St. Joseph's College, University of Alberta, Canada who has co-authored with evolution critic Phillip E. Johnson Darwinism Defeated? The Johnson-Lamoureux Debate on Biological Origins (Regent College,

---

[286] "Science & Spirit, Eyes Wide Open: An Interview with Owen Gingerich," by Chris Floyd, http://www.science-spirit.org/article_detail.php?article_id=144, at pp. 1 & 2 of 5. [7/27/09.]
[287] Id., at p. 2 of 5.

1999); Evangelical Christian and geologist Keith B. Miller of Kansas State University, who compiled an anthology Perspectives on an Evolving Creation (Eerdmans, 2003); Kenneth R. Miller, professor of biology at Brown University, author of Finding Darwin's God (Cliff Street Books, 1999), in which he states his belief in God and argues that "evolution is the key to understanding God" (Dr. Miller has also called himself "an orthodox Catholic and an orthodox Darwinist" in the 2001 PBS special "Evolution"); Biologist Joan Roughgarden at Stanford University is author of various books including Evolution and Christian Faith: Reflections of an Evolutionary Biologist and Biologist Richard T. Wright, emeritus professor of biology at Gordon College, Wenham, MA, author of Biology Through the Eyes of Faith, Rev. Ed. (San Francisco: HarperSanFrancisco, ©2003.[288]

Morris was listed as well but not Gingerich, though I presume that to have been an oversight. These people do keep some considerable company. I am confining my remarks in this context to scientific academia. The website does also list the degrees of concurrence to theistic macro expressed by the Anglican, United Methodist, Eastern Orthodox and Roman Catholic Churches, as well as the Church of the Nazarene.

An illustration of just how open the scientific field is to the interpretive expanse of Deistic or Theistic macro is provided by Michael J. Behe, Biological Science professor at Lehigh University in Pennsylvania. His controversial book Darwin's Black Box (1996) Free Press introduced the concept of "irreducible complexity," that there is a bare-bones level of configuration and function to molecular machinery that simply cannot be accounted for by any application of Darwininan natural selection. I.e., there had to be an intelligence behind the design of it. His follow-up to that work is The Edge of Evolution: The Search for the Limits of Darwinism (2007) Free Press, which uses irreducible complexity as a basis for application of statistic data that allows for a more precise approach to the issue of the limitations to Darwin's theory. As Behe himself explains it: "... the more quantitative approach to The Edge of Evolution actually builds on the concept of irreducible complexity, and allows us to put numbers on the likelihood of random processes

---

[288] Wikipedia, http://en.wikipedia.org/wiki/Theistic_evolution, at pp. 8 & 9 of 14. [7/28/09.

building a coherent structure. It can show us that design reaches much deeper into life than we otherwise would have thought."[289]

He summarizes his thesis to the work as follows: "... the gist is to find reasonable estimates for the limits of what Darwin's theory—natural selection acting on random mutations—can actually accomplish. <u>Clearly Darwin's process can account for some small changes in biological systems, such as antibiotic resistance</u>. But can it account for more complex systems, such as the intricate molecular machinery that science has discovered in the cell? Up until recently that question was impossible to answer because the molecular mutations underlying biological changes were unknown, and also because we couldn't examine really vast numbers of organisms. But in the past ten years all that has changed. As I detail in the book, the molecular changes underlying resistance to malaria by humans, resistance to antibiotics by malarial parasite, and other well-studied systems show that random mutation is incoherent—<u>that is, a series of mutations usually has little to do with each other, and doesn't add up to a new molecular machine</u>."[290] (Emphasis added.)

As he also added in response to Dawkins's criticism that his approach is incompatible with the variation in dogs (admittedly enhanced from breeding), Behe said as to the content of <u>Edge of Evolution</u>: "I would suggest that Richard Dawkins re-read my book. In it I clearly state that random evolution works well up to the species level, perhaps to the genus and family level too. But at the level of vertebrate classes (birds, fish, etc.), the molecular developmental programs needed would be beyond the edge of evolution. Darwinian evolution works well when a single small change in an organism's DNA produces a notable effect. That's what happens to give the various breeds of dogs. <u>But when multiple, coordinated changes are needed for an effect, chance mutation loses its power</u>."[291] (Emphasis added.)

As to his personal education in private schooling, he asserts: "I'm a Roman Catholic; <u>I never was taught a literal interpretation of the Bible. In fact, I was taught Darwin's theory of evolution in parochial school</u>. As far as I'm concerned, the universe and earth are as old as

---

[289] Interview:Michael Behe Intelligent Design, <u>The Edge of Evolution</u>, http://calitreview.com/260, at p. 4 of 146 (interview itself is only four pages, and responses follow from there). [7/31/09.]
[290] Id., at p 1.
[291] Ibid.

most physicists say they are, and life developed over immense ages. <u>My main point of disagreement with the standard scientific story is that I think most of the development of the universe and life was set up; little was left to chance.</u>"[292] (Emphasis added.) So how much of a role does Behe think God played in the overall scheme of this planet? He states in answer to a like phrased question: "Well, as a Christian I think God has intervened in human history. But in order to set up the general universe—including the design apparent in cells—I think God could have done that in a single instant, which unfolded over time."[293]

Behe's remarks should help put the kibosh to the notion of Intelligent Design being a mere backdoor Creationist approach. His notion of ID is at great odds with strict Creationists, who do take the Bible literally in terms of the Creation scenario and believe in a young age to the earth, again, depending on the advocate, usually between 6,000 to 50,000 years. He is a God who daily reacts to prayers and is highly active in each person's life who has a relationship with Him. It would pose no threat to Establishment Clause fears of any one religion becoming endorsed by the state because too many conclusions can be reached on too many different issues, even though the most seminal point, of course, is that no specific target is being emphasized anyway, which is the beauty of the point-counterpoint approach. How can a particular religion be emphasized when conclusions reached by the student can run the gamut as has been observed in the varying postures of the scientists we have discussed?

No single religion or even philosophy is being sought here. Stating the contrary facts and counter-arguments to macro postulates is the only given. Where that leads the individual student per capita we can only guess, but it is clear that there are a number of prospective routes to take. The student chooses which, and we cannot (and MUST NOT) do that for him.

I am, of course, well aware of the decision in <u>Kitzmiller v. Dover Area School District</u>, 400 F.Supp.2d 707 (M.D. Pa. 2005), wherein Judge John E. Jones III concluded that ID was a religion and violated the Establishment Clause. It is not discussed here because <u>Kitzmiller</u> in no way controls <u>Aguillard</u> and the U.S. Supreme Court will continue

---
292 Ibid.
293 Id., at p. 3.

to abide by it own rationale therein rather than Kitzmiller. I find it difficult to believe that any rational judge could conclude ID is a religion when presented with all of the facts concerning ID and its argumentation as discussed in this work, and I have no evidence that Jones was provided with such facts. Since there is prejudice against it in "conventional" science right now, there would certainly be nothing evidentiary of its being religion simply by not being published in peer-reviewed journals, and it is error to say that ID proponents have not engaged in research and testing, which I know did appear in the body of the opinion. Likewise, Scalia's comments as to the Establishment Clause in Aguillard nonetheless permitting religious-oriented enactments to counter State sanctioned activities that disapprove, inhibit or evince hostility toward religion, presented an opportunity for a different ruling entirely even on that basis, though there is no indication that the context of this case afforded Jones an opportunity to consider that.

Finally, even the status of religion (which, again, I do not think ID qualifies as) would be irrelevant to the presentation posed here, even though ironically, macro is also a religion. Kitzmiller would be inapplicable on that ground alone. With such apples and oranges in mind, I have intentionally declined to analyze the case further because it would be a totally different ballgame in a different court arena, including, of course, the Supreme Court itself. While winnable anyway, I am not at all convinced that that body would call ID a "religion" in terms of being window-dressed Creationism. Besides, the material facts that Jones decided upon were far different than what a jurist would face in this situation. He was presented with a disclaimer in a macro text that in no way resembled the syllabus recommended herein. I am quite confident as well that Jones was not aware of the fraud perpetrated by the macros both in the past and now.

One last point is important to make in this thread. The introduction of the alternative theories for interpreting science phenomena brings into play analysis from all disciplines in order to address the issue. In answering that question for themselves, the student must know more about mathematics, geology, astronomy, chemistry, physics, genetics, even history, etc., than would likely ever be within his ambit of interest in any other setting. In my personal exploration of the empirical merits involved in the Creation v. macro controversy, I have learned more about each of the above, and have wanted to learn more, than in any of my years of formal education. This examination and adventure that the student would be taken on is a far more stimulating educational environment than our public school system could otherwise provide. The student would far more often acquire a desire and sometimes a hunger to learn more, which, of course, could also potentially spread into other learning arenas. It could even greatly influence what he chooses to make his living at. Is that not what the educational experience should be all about? The revered Thomas Jefferson most certainly thought so.

Behe is a good case in point for this argument. Is he even aware of the various controversies over the fossil record as to the dating of fossils re radiodating, suppression of evidence pointing toward both the antiquity of man and his earlier physical stature, etc., the viability of the astronomical postures for the universe that could support a younger earth than he thinks, etc. His statements at least sound like he isn't, and his parochial schooling re the Darwinist slant certainly did not address those issues. I heartily applaud his contributions to the overall ID scenario through his molecular work, and they have been substantial, but he seems pretty well confined in his information database to that arena. Exposure to this in his own secondary school days could have given him a broader perspective. Would he still think the earth old if he had been so exposed? Maybe, maybe not. He simply should have been exposed to it. His conclusions from there would have been his own.

This conveys yet another reason why this methodology is so important in the public school system. Even the future professionals that come out of it will have been given a far more balanced treatment as to what all of science represents and would not have pre-conceived notions formulated only because of lack of information. <u>We are not looking for any set opinion but merely an informed one</u>. Another perk of this procedure is that with a heightened, more deeply defined database, even wiser decisions can be made by students as to what they want to vocationally pursue because they have a better perception and conception of all that there is to offer out there. This is an invaluable contribution to him that transcends whatever conclusions he draws on origins and anything else scientific for that matter. This is yet another purely secular result of this methodology, which is intended to address secular concerns first and religious ones only incidentally.

CHAPTER FOUR

IT IS A PHYSICAL AND CHEMICAL IMPOSSIBILITY FOR LIFE TO ORIGINATE WITHOUT A PRE-PROGRAMMED, CLOSED SYSTEM, WHICH COULD NOT HAPPEN BY ACCIDENT

The lack of a First Cause explanation for macro has more than just philosophical implications. It poses a very real scientific roadblock to the possibility of macro having existed in an accidental manner. In fact, there are at least eight barriers to chemically creating life out of non-life through accidental means: (1) Unreactivity; (2) Ionization; (3) Mass Action; (4) Reactivity; (5) Selectivity; (6) Solubility; (7) Sugar and (8) Chirality.

As to the first barrier, water is an unreactive medium for all chemicals in nature. For proteins and DNA/RNA formation, a polymer must be formed by a combination of amino acids and nucleotides. They cannot combine at all in a water medium. For a laboratory reaction to be induced to form a polymer, the chemical components have to be activated and postured in a reactive, completely devoid of water environment, eliminating a primordial soup scenario right at the bud. As to the second barrier, ionization, proteins are dependent upon amine bonding, which is the by-product of hundreds of reactions between an amine group of one amino acid with the acid group of another amino acid. The very nature of an acid and base (amine group) combination creates an instant ionization in water, making the necessary components for protein formation absent in any necessary reactive form.

The third barrier of mass action is also compelling. Any necessary component of a polymer-forming reaction reacting with another produces a water by-product. The Law of Mass Action (based on Le Chatelier's Principle) provides that all reactions proceed in a direction from highest to lowest concentration, which creates the practical dilemma that any water-producing reaction cannot itself take place in water, an oxymoron in a "watery" soup forum. <u>If condensation did take place, it would be instantly hydrolyzed in its watery medium</u>. With the fourth barrier of Reactivity, all the components for the polymer (amino acids and nucleotides) have different chemical structures and hence all have different rates, creating a severe timing issue for the macros. <u>The polymer chain sequence residing in natural proteins and DNA/RNA does not correlate with the individual components reaction rates</u>. The polymeric sequence that would be hypothetically created in the primordial soup would not and could not match the actual, precise sequence observed in our bodies.

Fifthly, there is the selectivity barrier. A random mixture of amino acids would create multitudinous undesired isomers as they randomly add to both ends of the polymer chain. Natural selection in the sense of opting for the correct sequence is not in evidence because there would need to be <u>billions</u> of excess DNA/RNA (from nucleotides) and proteins (from amino acids) found in the human body, and they are simply not there. <u>Sixth, as the size of the polymer chain increases as more and more components are added,</u> its <u>solubility in water decreases,</u> and it would reach a saturation point in length wherein it would no longer be soluble in water and production would stop. <u>The required sum total work effort to build the whole chain we find in the human body could never be made</u>. For the seventh barrier, the reducing sugar needed to form nucleotides for DNA and RNA synthesis would cause the formation of undesired reaction products and eliminate necessary components to the reaction, and even if this reaction survives the unsurvivable, <u>these same reducing sugars would react with the amino acids needed to form proteins, and they would consequently annihilate each other</u>.

Finally, the barrier of chirality relates to the precise configuration of the amino acid-nucleotide bond, which requires an exact fitting of the respective molecules. Chirality refers to the "handedness" of each molecule. All protein amino acid molecules are "left-handed" and all nucleotide DNA/RNA molecules are "right-handed." These fittings must form the exact three-dimensional structure to properly configure, and if they don't, there is no life.

It is seminal that the failure to hurdle any one of these barriers (which is why the name was chosen over obstacles) would be fatal to a life-creating process, and the combination of all eight of them in an uncontrolled setting could never be randomly negotiated. The odds against it would be so astronomical as to render chance meaningless, and we can come up with only one conclusion: IMPOSSIBLE. And to think, we are only dealing with a "simple" single-cell organism.[294]

Despite the high percentage of water in our bodies, that very liquid would make the formation of the very micro-world structures it hosts impossible to form to start with. <u>So we are led to the inevitable conclusion that life had to have originated within a self-contained, closed system instantaneously complete</u>. It could not have been constructed gradually but must have been a completed whole ab initio. Macro loses before it starts.

Chirality, especially, is considered by many (including McCombs) to be the most insuperable barrier of them all. It has much more significance than simply being an irreplaceable component of life origination, however. It is also pivotal in everyday biological life sustenance and maintenance. As one text describes it: "Except for inorganic salts and a few low-molecular-weight organic substances, the majority of molecules in living systems- both plant and animal- are chiral."[295]

Among other things, this has great implications for analytical chemistry. As one of a plethora of examples, enzymes are considered the most glaring demonstration of biological molecular chirality. Interestingly, using Chymotrypsin as illustrative, which is a catalyst for protein digestion in animal intestines, there are a massive number of what are called stereoisomers available from a base of 251 stereocenters for the enzyme to utilize to accomplish its catalyzation, about 2 to the 251st place of zeros, yet biological economy, in an amazing display

---

[294] Charles McCombs, Ph.D., Associate Professor of the ICR Graduate School, and Assistant Director of the National Creation Science Foundation, "Chemistry by Chance: A Formula for Non-Life," ICR, Acts & Facts, Vol. 38, No. 2, February, 2009, 30 & 31.
[295] Frederick A. Bettelheim, William H. Campbell, Shawn O. Farrell, <u>Introduction to General, Organic and Biochemistry</u> (2009) Brooks/Cole CENGAGE Learning, Belmont, CA, p. 130.

of efficiency and proficiency, is such that the organism employs only one of the stereoisomers to accomplish its mission.[296] Also, about 50% of medications given to the public employ chirality principles based on what are called enantiomers, which the vast majority of organic isomers display.[297] Thus, chirality plays a continuing major role in how we live our lives, and tremendous pre-programming exists to choose between so many vast alternatives.

It is submitted that the above chemistry factors eliminate any form of accidental creation. This appears to be an insuperable barrier to all but any form of Deistic or Theistic macro. Some form of intelligent origin causation seems to be inescapable.

---

296 Ibid.
297 Id., at p. 115.

CHAPTER FIVE

THE GENETIC CODE SPEAKS AGAINST STRICT MACRO, NOT FOR IT, AND HAS DEEP PHILOSOPHICAL IMPLICATIONS (THE FLIGHT OF SIR ANTONY FLEW), ESPECIALLY WHEN COMBINED WITH REPRODUCTIVE FIRST CAUSE

Purely naturalistic macros may be screaming that despite the chemical First Cause argument just discussed, that collective barrier had to have been overcome because look at the huge 98% to 99% similarity between the human and chimp genomes (others argue for 96%). They are too much alike from that perspective for First Causation not to have occurred, which they argue would be accidentally. Really? Let's look at the evidence. The chimp genome is 10% to 12% larger than the human and has not been as nearly completed as has the human. Yet, when large regions between the two are compared, a number of key chromosomes reveal much dissimilarity, including great dissimilarity between the entire male (Y) chromosomes. When these are factored, the actual similarity reduces to as low as 86% or less. <u>Even more compellingly, research has shown that the priority must be placed upon gene function and regulation as opposed to DNA sequencing</u>. So even the concept of DNA sequencing is an exercise in misdirection, a red herring if you will.

Macros deliberately concentrated on limited sequence comparisons to select what they wanted and eliminate what they did not. Those sequences containing the crucial <u>information</u> transcribed into RNA (the when, why, how much and how often) are routinely omitted from the comparisons.²⁹⁸ The messages contained by the messengers would seemingly be somewhat important, would they not?

Finally, it is important to realize that even using an alleged 99% chimp-human correlation (which, of course, is disputed here by all the dilution factors just discussed) does not bring the semblance of parity that superficially appears on the surface between the two primates. The difference in information and concomitant unlikelihood for sufficient mutation to ultimately result from any chimpanzee-like ancestor is still astronomically huge and in reality would be an insuperable gap to close. The human genome was first published in Science and Nature magazines in February of 2001, and that of the chimp in August of 2005. There are about 35 million base pairs that are different between human and chimp, with 45 million base pairs in humans that are absent from chimps, and an equal number in chimps absent from humans. In fact, "the amount of information in the three billion base pairs [of nucleotides] in the DNA of every human cell has been estimated to be equivalent to that in 1000 books of encyclopedia size. If humans were 'only' 1% different this still amounts to 30 million base pairs, equal to approximately 3 million words, or 10 large books of information. This is surely an impossible barrier for mutation (random changes) to cross."²⁹⁹

As can be seen, when the pivotal factors for similarity are introduced and the "false front" ones are put in proper perspective, the alleged genome similarities are far more apparent than real. Reality emphasizes the differences in the genome sequence when the essential aspects of it are considered, not the similarities, and commonality looks more and more the end product of a common design.

Homeotic genes (genes relating to like function in different life forms) seem to fall within this category of common design. E.g., Pax-6 (a gene for eye development) is similar in humans and other mammals as well as flies (now there's diversity for you) and some of the gene is also featured in squids and worms. As Jonathan Wells so aptly put it: "If the same gene can 'determine' structures as radically different as ... an insect's eyes and the eyes of humans and squids then that gene is not

---

298 Jeffrey Tomkins, Ph.D., Research Associate at the Institute for Creation Research, "Human-Chimp Similarities: Common Ancestry or Flawed Research," Acts & Facts, ICR, Volume 38, No. 6, June, 2009.
299 Darren Gordon of the Pennsylvania State University Origins Club, compiler, Creation Science FAQ Version 3.5.0, http://mysite.verizon.net/vzeph10d/, at p. 25 of 36. [9/7/09.]

determining much of anything. ... Except for telling us how an embryo directs its cells into one of several built-in developmental pathways, homeotic genes tell us nothing about how biological structures are formed."[300] So DNA not only does not complement macro, it does not even begin to tell the story of how our anatomy becomes our anatomy. Macro cannot even begin to explain this.

In fact, DNA structure presents macro with a quagmire similar to First Cause considerations regarding an organism being fully formed within a closed system being required to overcome the laws of chemistry. With a somewhat different slant, the same principle holds true for the DNA/RNA/protein triage. While DNA encrypts for proteins and RNA executes the information transfer and commands given it, the encryption process itself and DNA's replication to daughter cells itself requires protein. So in a variation of the chicken and the egg, the issue becomes, which came first? The DNA and RNA, or the protein? Or did it come complete in itself as a closed system with the initial interdependent parts all provided as a whole? The integration with the protein introduces a tremendous stumbling block in explaining the presence and integration of the protein into the system.[301]

The double helix structure of the DNA and its coordination with RNA through well-developed complex machinery is an engineering marvel. But the human genome in the process is also a marvelous study about marvelous programming. It is antithetical to everything that macro stands for, however, and is anything but related in any way to random, undirected action. There is simply too much organization, too much synchronization of multiple factors that must happen for any major change to take place even for adaptation. And this problem is compounded for transmutation. The transmutational macro hurdle was very well stated by I.L. Cohen to be: " 'Survival of the Fittest' and 'natural selection'. No matter what phraseology one generates, the basic fact remains the same: any physical change of any size, shape or form is strictly the result of purposeful alignment of billions of nucleotides (in the DNA). [New Para.] Nature or species do not have the capacity to rearrange them. Consequently no leap (saltation) can occur from one species to another. [New Para.] The only way we know

---
300 Michael A. Cremo, Human Devolution: A Vedic alternative to Darwin's theory, Los Angeles, CA: Bhaktivedanta Book Publishing, 2003, p. 69, quoted by David Pratt, Evolution and Design, May 2004, Part 1 of 3, http://davidpratt.info/evod1.htm, at p. 18 of 25. [9/7/09.]
301 Evolution and Design, supra, at p. 4 of 25. [6/19/09.]

for a DNA to be altered is through a meaningful intervention from an outside source of intelligence – one who know[s] what it is doing, such as our genetic engineers are now performing in the laboratories."[302] (Emphasis added.)

This is a compelling aspect of any purported natural mechanisms for change—it must occur within a remarkably complex, <u>programmed</u> setting where often billions of entities, in this case, nucleotides, must be orchestrated in a specific direction in order to even effectuate adaptation and variety, let alone transmutation. This occurring by random chance is totally illogical and natural selection is totally incapable as a blind device to organize this anatomically and physiologically to allow this to happen if it had had infinite time within which to do it, and that has been far from the case.

In fact, natural selection produces its effects by subtraction or elimination, not addition or supplementation. It does not have a creative capacity, but would be better thought of as a body manager which distributes attributes within its existing pool of resources, being unable to bring anything additional or new into its overall armamentarium. Microbial geneticist and microbiologist Kevin Anderson is the director of the Creation Research Society's Van Andel Creation Research Center. In a radio interview with Jan Mikelson (J) during November of 2003, Anderson (K) revealed how the role of mutation either alters or eliminates but does not add: "J-There's no known mutation that adds information that's useful. <u>K</u>-There's no mutation that gives them [Macros] what is necessary for common descent with modification. There are all kinds of mutations that eliminate proteins. They may eliminate transport protein, an enzyme, the action of an enzyme, or regulatory systems. J-Okay. There are mutations that take away information, but there are none that add information. … <u>K</u>-Correct! They're not making new transport proteins! They're not making new regulatory systems! Antibiotic resistance is an excellent example of that. … [New Para.] When we look at the … genetic mechanisms of what's going on, the antibiotic resistance is the result of loss of a protein, loss of the binding capacity of a protein, or the loss of a

---

302 I.L. Cohen, Officer of the Archaeological Institute of America, Member New York Academy of Sciences. "Darwin Was Wrong – A Study in Probabilities" <u>New Research Publications, Inc.</u>, p. 209, quoted by http://www.evolutionisdead.com/quotes.php?QID=409. [8/8/09.]

transporting system ... Yes, it's beneficial to the organism, to the microbe, if it's trying to survive the onslaught of the antibiotic."

Anderson reiterated that natural selection doesn't build. He said to Mikelson: "K-No. In fact, natural selection does just the opposite. J-It removes information? K-Exactly. If you have a natural selection process going on where you are selecting for shorter animals, you are not creating genes for shortness; rather, you are taking away the genes for tallness. Miniature horses, for example, are the result of a lot of inbreeding of regular horses; and they keep getting smaller and smaller and smaller. So, what you have actually done, you have removed the genes that give you the taller horses, so most of what you have left are the genes for the shorter horses."[303]

Thus, the chain of custody between micro gradually leading to macro has been broken by the fact that even micro changes for adaptation or variation through mutation do not add information to the genome matrix, but rather, subtract from it. Therefore, the necessary mechanism is missing to promote transmutational change in kinds.

Thus, on a larger scale, human genome study reveals nothing about the diversity of life on earth and portrays no mechanism to accomplish it. Christopher Booker, English journalist and author, has commented in regard to the human genome explaining how diversity arrived on this planet: "To believe that genetics have solved the riddle relies as much on a leap of faith as that Biblical 'Creationism' which causes the more fanatical Darwinians to foam at the mouth."[304] (Emphasis added.)

And as majestic an arrangement as the genetic code with its double helix structure and coordination with RNA as its messenger service is, its limitations also belie randomness in that it is yet but a small part of a much larger functioning puzzle. It is not the roadmap that most think it is. All DNA does is sequence the amino acids that produce the proteins (but which initially depend, of course, on protein to be able to do that). It does no more of the planning for the functioning of the organism than that, even though with RNA it sends the information. Consider this by theosopher David Pratt: "The role of genes is vastly overrated by mechanistic biologists. The genetic code in the DNA molecules

---

[303] "Radio Interview with Dr. Kevin Anderson," Part 1, p. 3 of 4, Creation Matters, Vol. 9, No. 4, July/August 2004.
[304] Christopher Booker, "Why do People think Creationism is a Perfect Creation," Telegraph.co.uk, http://www.telegraph.co.uk/comment/columnists/christopherbooker/ 4623686/Why-do-people... . [3/28/09.]

determines the sequence of amino acids in proteins; <u>it does not specify the way the proteins are arranged in cells, cells in tissues, tissues in organs, and organs in organisms</u>. As biochemist Rupert Sheldrake remarks: 'Given the right genes and hence the right proteins, and the right systems by which protein synthesis is controlled, the organism is somehow supposed to assemble itself automatically. This is rather like delivering the right materials to a building site at the right times and expecting a house to grow spontaneously.'"[305] (Emphasis added.)

So as astounding and sophisticated a system as the composing and relay system that DNA/RNA comprises is, <u>it is for the very narrow and specific function of manufacturing and instructing proteins, which ironically, the process itself would be impossible without the initial presence of protein</u>. The rest of the integrative process with the organism even in terms of just the arrival of our structural anatomy itself remains a mystery.

And when these compound factors are aggregated against strict naturalistic macro, its elimination as a viable scientific theory in terms of random action <u>is</u> a question of logic. As mathematical physicist Frank Tipler wrote: "When I began my career as a cosmologist some twenty years ago, I was a convinced atheist. [New Para.] I never in my wildest dreams imagined that one day I would be writing a book purporting to show that the central claims of Judeo-Christian theology are in fact true, that these claims are straightforward deductions of the laws of physics as we now understand them. [New Para.] <u>I have been forced into these conclusions by the inexorable logic of my own special branch of physics</u>."[306] (Emphasis added.)

Let's begin by exploring how, in part, the First Cause/genetic code combination is responsible for converting the former world's foremost modern atheist to Deism. In truth, there have been conversions in both camps, from Creationist to macro and macro to Creationist, although it is suspected here that there is substantially more of the latter when all of the operative facts have been examined. In this writer's humble opinion, most Creationist-macro proselytes were already ripe for the

---

[305] Rupert Sheldrake, <u>The Rebirth of Nature: The greening of science and God</u>, New York: Bantam Books, 1991, p. 107, quoted by <u>Evolution and Design</u>, supra, at p. 15 of 25. [6/19/09.]
[306] Frank Tipler, (Professor of Mathematical Physics):Tipler, F.J. 1994. <u>The Physics of Immortality</u>, New York, Doubleday, Preface, cited again by evolution is dead at http://www.evolutionisdead.com/ quotes.php?QID=101. [8/8/09.]

plucking, disillusioned in life by its ups and downs (as was Darwin himself) but not thinking out how poor an alternative macro is. So it is more traceable to a lack of proper foundational underpinning to begin with, which is avoidable when Creationism and macro are both treated objectively and observed and contemplated clinically.

Regardless, one of the more interesting macro to Creationist converters (or Intelligent Design to be more precise, and definitely not Christian [not yet anyway]) is Professor Sir Antony Flew, a long-time former champion advocate of atheistic naturalism. He wrote the classic volume <u>God and Philosophy</u> with updates, as well as <u>Theology and Falsification</u> and <u>Darwinian Evolution</u>. In fact, "Theology and Falsification," was an address Flew gave in 1950 to the Socratic Club (chaired by C.S. Lewis no less) and was considered the paradigm for modern atheism.[307]

His works targeted toward miracles and their impossibility include, as listed in the interview below at endnote 3: "Miracles and Methodology," in <u>Hume's Philosophy of Belief: A Study of His First Inquiry</u> (London: Routledge and Kegan Paul, 1961); "The Credentials of Revelation: Miracle and History," in <u>God and Philosophy</u> (New York, Dell, 1966); "Miracles," in <u>Encyclopedia of Philosophy</u>, ed. Paul Edwards (New York: Macmillan, 1967); "The Impossibility of the Miraculous," in <u>Hume's Philosophy of Religion</u>, (Winston-Salem, N.C.: Wake Forest University Press, 1985); introduction to <u>Of Miracles</u>, by David Hume (La Salle, IL: Open Court, 1985); "Neo-Humean Arguments about the Miraculous" in <u>In Defence of Miracles: A Comprehensive Case for God's Action in History</u>, ed. R. Douglas Geivett and Gary R. Habermas (Downers Grove, IL: Inter Varsity Press, 1997.)

So how unlikely was this Apostasy in public terms? It prompted Cliff Kinkaid, editor of the AIM Report, in his 12/21/04 newspaper article "Former Atheist Says God Exists," from <u>Insight On the News</u>, to write *"This is comparable to High Hefner announcing that he is becoming a celibate."* (Emphasis original.) Basically because of the genetic code (discussed below) and other convincing I.D. fine-tuning arguments, Flew flew to Deism (sorry, couldn't resist it). One post-conversion interview was with Dr. Gary R. Habermas, Professor of

---

307 Roy Abraham Varghese, "Academics viewing the universe through a narrow scope should rethink assumptions," Dallas Morning News. [12/15/04.]

Philosophy and Theology, for the Winter 2005 edition of <u>Philosophia Christi, the Journal of the Evangelical Philosophical Society</u> (www.biola.edu/philchristi), in a treatment titled, "My Pilgrimage from Atheism to Theism."[308] Habermas served on the <u>Philosophia Christi</u> editorial board.

The Theism is actually a mislabel, as Deism is the better fit, although Flew did consent to the title of the interview for reasons not understood by this writer.[309] After all, Theism lays direct and continuing responsibility for natural law upon God and his imminence therein, while Deism is more of an intellectual reasoning based on the order of things that someone or something put natural law into place but no longer participates in any of its dynamics. As already shown, Darwin himself made that same error in his autobiography.

As a Deist, Flew subscribes to an Intelligent Design God, but only an impersonal and not a revelation one ("But it seems to me that the case for an Aristotelian God who has the characteristics of power and also intelligence, is now much stronger than it ever was before.")[310] Interestingly, the book is not entirely closed for Flew due to physicist Gerald Schroeder's Genesis 1 comments.[311] As Flew described it, "That this biblical account might be scientifically accurate raises the possibility that it is revelation."[312] One of these days, it might dawn on Flew that the books of Daniel (OT) and <u>Revelation</u> (NT) might also be revelation. If he ever ends up concluding Genesis is accurate, he has to let Daniel and Revelation have their day after serious consideration of their content, which he has apparently hitherto paid little attention to. Prophecy, of course, is contained in other books, but we are distinguishing here between the divine inspiration of the Scriptural writers generally, and the visionary-type revelation as featured in those two books.

Of course, Flew had always admitted that macro (again, naturalism) could never quite come up with "a plausible conjecture as to how any of these complex molecules might have evolved from simple

---

[308] For the specific interview, go to http://www.biola.edu/antonyflew/index.cfm (accessed December 12, 2004).
[309] Id., at endnote 8.
[310] Id., at p. 3.
[311] Gerald Schoeder, <u>The Science of God: The Convergence of Scientific and Biblical Wisdom</u> (New York: Broadway Books, 1998.)
[312] Habermas-Flew interview, supra, at p. 3.

entities."[313] He could have added, "Firstly, how can such simple single-celled organisms end up being not all that simple at all, and capable of generating on their own enough power to light up all of New York City on an otherwise very dark night?"

But the main selling point for Flew's conversion was overall Intelligent Design and the aforementioned genetic code whose connection is established a little later below. ["Habermas: So you like arguments such as those that proceed from big bang cosmology and fine tuning arguments? Flew: Yes."][314] In this writer's continuing effort to be as objective and clinical as possible, Flew remains unconvinced on moral grounds (which, on the other hand, this writer antithetically finds compelling): "Habermas: You also recently told me that you do not find the moral argument to be very persuasive. Is that right? Flew: That's correct. It seems to me that for a strong moral argument, you've got to have God as the justification of morality. To do this makes doing the morally good a purely prudential matter rather than, as the moral philosophers of my youth used to call it, a good in itself."[315] While this writer could not agree less, that is still Flew's position.

He does expose a profound foundational weakness in macro theory, however, in that Darwin started out with a reproductive being already intact without then or EVER being able to account for it (i.e., First Cause in the sense of a complete reproductive system intact rather than a total consideration of the other chemical issues re origin of life). In Flew's own words: "It seems to me that Richard Dawkins constantly overlooks the fact that Darwin himself, in the fourteenth chapter of The Origin of Species, pointed out that his whole argument began with a being which already possessed reproductive powers. This is the creature the evolution of which a truly comprehensive theory of evolution must give some account. Darwin himself was well aware that he had not produced such an account. It now seems to me that the findings of more than fifty years of DNA research have provided materials for a new and enormously powerful argument to design."[316] (Emphasis added.)

---

313 Id., at endnote 12, from Flew's "God and the Big Bang" (lecture 2000), 5-6; "this is a lecture commemorating the 140th anniversary of the British association meeting regarding Charles Darwin's *The Origin of the Species*."
314 Id., at p. 4.
315 Ibid.
316 Id., at p. 5.

Flew noticed what I noticed, and doubtless what a large number of Theistic or Deistic macros have also. Comprehensive macro theory must account for the origin of life, which even Darwin acknowledged he did not do. The DNA comment is also not unique to this interview, either. Flew was quoted by Ray Varghese of the Associated Press as saying: " 'What I think the DNA material has done is show that intelligence must have been involved in getting these extraordinarily diverse elements together,' he said. " 'The enormous complexity by which the results were achieved look to me like the work of intelligence.' "[317] (Emphasis added.)

Flew could have added what Varghese himself added in that same article: "Many people assume that the intelligence in the universe somehow evolved out of nonintelligence, given chance and enough time, and in the case of living beings, through natural selection and random mutation. But even under the most hardheadedly materialistic scenario, intelligence and intelligence systems come fully formed from day one. [New Para.] Matter came with all its ingenious, mathematically precise laws from the time it first appeared. Life came fully formed with the incredibly intelligent symbol processing of DNA, the astonishing phenomenon of protein-folding and the marvel of replication from its first appearance. Language, the incarnation of conceptual thought with its inexplicable structure of syntax, symbols and semantics, appeared out of the blue, again with its essential infrastructure as is from day one. [New Para.] The evidence we have shows unmistakably that there was no progressive, gradual evolution of nonintelligence into intelligence in any of the fundamental categories of energy, life or mind. Each one of the three had intrinsically intelligent structures from the time it first appeared. Each, it would seem, proceeds from an infinitely intelligent mind in a precise sequence." (Emphasis added.) Varghese has stated his case with elegance and profundity. It is small wonder that this man from Garland, TX is the author of The Wonder of the World: A Journey from Modern Science to the Mind of God (Tyr Publishing) and yet helped organize presentations by Flew in his atheistic days on two occasions. His contact is tyrpublishing.com.

Flew also made a statement in the Habermas interview to which this writer completely subscribes in describing the importance of Flew's

---

317   Roy Abraham Varghese, "Academics viewing the universe through a narrow scope should rethink assumptions," Dallas Morning News, 12/15/04.

moral education urging in public schools, both in the UK and US: "To the US because the Supreme Court has utterly misinterpreted the clause in the Constitution about not establishing a religion: misunderstanding it as imposing a ban on all official reference to religion." Jefferson and Madison and probably also Hamilton could not have agreed more with him, as do I.[318] I never said that I agreed with Aguillard. I simply said that its strictures can be accommodated in the introduction of ID and other theories based on established facts by methodologies such the one that I propose in this book.

Flew also has made the mistake of most philosophers in saying: "I suppose that the moment when, as a schoolboy of fifteen years, it first appeared to me that the thesis that the universe was created and is sustained by a Being of infinite power and goodness is flatly incompatible with the occurrence of massive undeniable and undenied evils in that universe, was the first step towards my future career as a philosopher! It was, of course, very much later that I learned of the philosophical identification of goodness with existence."[319] His mistake is in not discussing the implications of the Garden of Eden. IF that actually happened, it must be evaluated as a reason for the trials of man, past and present, along with redemption (as well as the Second Advent also being analyzed re Christian Creationism).

It is amazing how much philosophers indulge in judiciously selecting certain aspects of Scripture without considering the relationship to the whole. Logical fallacy "selection and elimination" fits here. This glaring weakness is revealed in his response to the following: "Habermas: In your view, then, God hasn't done anything about evil. Flew: No, not at all, other than producing a lot of it."[320] Deeper into the interview, there is this discourse: "Habermas: ... Given your great respect for Christianity, do you think that there is any chance that you might in the end move from theism to Christianity? Flew: I think it's very unlikely, due to the problem of evil."[321]

Again, there is no consideration of the Garden of Eden and biblical explanation of sin and its consequences. Likewise, there is no consideration for the role of redemption in restoring man to his

---

318 Habermas-Flew interview, supra, at p. 7.
319 Ibid.
320 Ibid.
321 Id., at p. 15.

original state of Paradise. One must consider one part of Scriptural doctrine in its relationship to the whole. Considering the sorrow and woe of this planet in total disregard of its root cause of sin and then the plan for redemption is incomplete. Confront it and dispose of it as you will, as Jefferson was fond of saying, but do deal with it.

Whether Flew is being just Scripturally ignorant or intellectually dishonest is hard to ascertain here. From the Christian Creationist standpoint at least, ignorance certainly seems to be part of it in his statement: "I think that those who want to speak about an afterlife have got to meet the difficulty of formulating a concept of an incorporeal person." This is incompatible with the Second Coming of the NT, where Christ's elect, both living and dead, meet with Him corporeally in the air. It is equally baffling, however, that he would have such ignorance where his household was doubtlessly subjected to religious exposure as he grew up. In his Habermas interview, he expressed an admiration for John and Charles Wesley in their establishment of the moral values of Methodism among the working class in England, which he credits as preventing the Communist Party from ever getting a substantial foothold there. This he linked to his father's own Methodist ministry, who was the first non-Anglican to earn a doctorate in theology from Oxford University. One would have thought this would have at least inculcated him with a personal desire to read Scripture thoroughly and completely.[322]

In summing up his conversion, in a phone conversation that he had with Habermas on 9/5/04, Flew said that he, taking the lead from Socrates, "had to go where the evidence leads."[323] That is this writer's invitation to every reader herein as well: go to where the clinical, empirical and inferential evidence leads. Don't let the veneer of "expertise" command your thoughts but simply introduce the data. Let them describe the seas you navigate but make sure your own faculties are doing the steering.

In 2007, Flew and Varghese co-authored, There Is a God: How the World's Most Notorious Atheist Changed His Mind, Harper One, hardcover. It has received favorable Internet reviews and while no small controversy was sparked by it, with many atheists barking foul

---

[322] Id., at p. 14.
[323] Id., endnote 7, at p. 2.

play and undue influence over the 84-year old Flew by Varghese, this is to be expected given the notoriety of the convert, and philosophic circles have also attacked the critical atheists like Oppenheimer.

It is important to note that the deeper thinkers much better dichotomize the differences between mechanistic change and its inner dynamics than do the naturalistic macros. While Flew appears to be a Deist, there are other highly scientific minds that have turned elements of the subtleties of life, its higher capacities, such as reason, emotion, etc., into reasons for adopting Theistic macro, as well as having an independent actuating force to put all of nature in motion, as is discussed above. For them, the chemical impossibility for life's origin should give them further reason to contemplate an intelligent intervention that they refer to as God.

The purpose of this, of course, is not to craft Theistic or Deistic macros, either. It is just to introduce the subtleties involved in even a strictly scientific approach to the physical phenomena that science studies to further enhance the informational database of the public school student.

CHAPTER SIX

MACRO THEORY BEGS FOR ASEXUAL REPRODUCTION OVER SEXUAL, SIMPLICITY OVER COMPLEXITY, AND UNIFORMITY IN LIFE, NOT DIVERSITY, AND FACES THE FURTHER PROBLEM OF MULTIPLE CREATIONS

While it seems that it is argumentatively over in terms of the physical evidence of our natural world for the actual origin of life (the First Cause) to have been brought about accidentally, naturalistic macro would have an uphill logical battle even if the first problem (which has been fatally resolved against it) could be surmounted.

The first logical hurdle for macro is simply that once there is a one-celled organism, there is no obvious reason for replication and reproduction. What impels an organism to reproduce to begin with? The sub-atomic machinery that we observe for all living organisms, no matter how relatively simplistic (though we know there is no such thing as a simple cell, even in the case of a single cell organism) could logically try to sustain itself, but what is the motive for reproduction without a consciousness for it? How could such consciousness possibly be acquired without being planted by a planner? There is nothing logically automatic for this to happen.

Second, even if there is an inherent, a priori instinct for survival (one even wonders how that could exist without being devised and planted by a designer) and a means for reproduction, why transcend simple division of cells and the basic single cell organism. Why progress to anything beyond, say, bacteria? Why progress beyond anything microscopic? Not only is there an organizational problem for complexity (here, programming), there is no apparent reason for it. By extension, asexual reproduction has no apparent reason to progress to anything beyond that. In other words, once there is survival, why grow from there? Instead of an inquiry into what came first, the chicken or the egg, why have either? It is not necessary for basic survival of the simplest organism. <u>The simplest organisms, once there, do not need to expand to anything else. There is nothing further to adapt to. What is there to cope with that that becomes a necessary function? If not necessary, then why be done at all</u>? It is a non sequitur to advance further when the main object, <u>survival</u>, is already achieved. If this is an overall plan, advancement is logical. If just random, it is not.

That is one of the profound weaknesses of naturalism generally, that there is no true impetus to be natural to begin with beyond a single-cell organism. There is no environmental motivation to progress beyond that. It is not necessary for survival. Survival at a single-cell organism state of being should be all that there is. Fauna should not depend on plants and there should be no issue of survival being based on a supply and demand dynamic because there shouldn't be fauna as we know it and there shouldn't be plants. Not without a planner to plan it that way, that is.

And asexual reproduction (even granting reproduction by any means) is simply more efficient. George Williams, a population biologist at the State University of New York at Stony Brook, is quoted by Howard Peth as saying: "At first glance, and second, and third, it appears that sex shouldn't have evolved."[324] Dr. Graham Bell, a geneticist at Montreal's McGill University, has expressed similar sentiments: "Nobody's gotten very far with the problem of how sex began."[325] Why a problem? Because sex is logically not needed for reproduction of successful life forms, as long as the simplest organisms can propagate through asexual reproduction. The ones that are already successful need not advance any further, not under macro theory, nor under simply pure logic if things are undirected.

---

[324] Maranto & Brownlee, "Why Sex?" <u>Discover</u>, Vol.5, No. 2 (Feb., 1984), p. 24, quoted by <u>Blind Faith: Evolution Exposed</u>, by Howard Peth, (1990), Amazing Facts, Inc., at p. 86. (Blind Faith was excerpted and adapted by permission from Peth's book, <u>Seven Mysteries ... Solved</u> (1988).)

[325] <u>Discover</u>, ibid., quoted by Peth, ibid.

Further, the concept of First Causation is at odds with macro not just because of the inevitable Creator implications for its lineage (supernatural or otherwise), but because there is an inherent illogicality to the notion of an initial common progenitor "branching" out into what we see today or what the fossil record reveals from the past. Any intellectually honest inquisitor must ask, if there is a common progenitor, how can there be different enough responses to common environmental stimuli to cause anything but minimal variety among like organisms so that even speciation is restricted and transmutation non-existent? There is no reason for vertical (transmutational) direction at all, simply horizontal (adaptation and intra-species variety). If speciation is expanded within kinds, then there could be that, but nothing beyond. Nor is there a motivation or plausible explanation for independently creating other traits outside of immediate environmental considerations and then seeking out other environments (which may or may not exist) where these qualities are best accommodated.

Even if that hurdle could be overcome (despite no logical reason for that happening), further, if organisms coming from a common progenitor are exposed to like conditions in any given environment, how can like stimuli produce anything other than like changes, so that adaptation again simply goes in a consistent, horizontal direction? Speaking now strictly in terms of all fauna, either there are all carnivores or all herbivores. There may be differences in size and strength, general physical health, and passiveness and aggressiveness, but that is it. Dogs would always be dogs or cats always cats. There would be sameness, not diversity. There is no rationale or scientific formula for the conflicting dynamic of predator and prey. All would have the same predilection. But even if not, it would still be among the same grouping, with one breed of dog attacking another, etc. Transmutation would still be an impossibility, and there would be no natural motivation or impetus for it.

If, indeed, increased population among advanced organisms caused competition, which in turn promoted changes, <u>there is too little time for formerly herbivorous forms to become carnivorous. They would starve and become extinct before they could compete</u>. There is the concomitant problem of deciding which species go carnivorous and which don't. What realistic guidelines could there be? On the flip side, adaptive changes by prey to confuse or avoid predators would take too long to be effective. If extermination was threatened, no species would have even hundreds of years to adapt. They would be a footnote in history (if ever discovered) before the critical changes could occur for survival. And is it simply coincidental that the smaller animals reproduce more rapidly than the larger? Does it not actually stretch credulity that predators reproduce at lesser rates than prey simply to effectuate balancing? Are we to truly believe that this "balance" just happens by accident? If planned, it is highly logical. If random, it is not.

As the saying in sports goes, when you're in a slump, get back to basics. In this line of study, it has to be going back to the very beginning, when allegedly the first organism and our common progenitor appeared. There is insufficient cause for there being two distinct lines that its asexual initial means of reproduction goes in, fauna and flora (I am well aware that there are organisms with characteristics of both, even those that generationally alternate between asexual and sexual reproduction, but they are far too minimal to reorient this discussion). If separate creation acts, then a similar accident happens at least twice. But then there has to be at least a third, because it cannot rationally be expected for vegetation to progress from the sea to land. There had to therefore be a land creation. The vegetation itself is unlikely to have crawled. As suggested below, there seem to be problems with proper lineage for worms, insects, arachnids and snakes.

More specifically, "natural selection" could only act in terms of intraspecies, not interspecies, activity, because no meaningful speciation would be possible. In terms of colors, you would have various shades of gray, but never other distinct colors.

We have already seen that the reality of DNA does not aid the macro cause. But nevertheless, DNA is highly sophisticated, programmed information with a precise division of labor and complex configuration of the resulting protein molecule. This is so in even the most pristine, one-celled organism. For information gathering and storage and translation into instructions that in turn are disseminated throughout the cellular body and executed upon by literal microscopic machinery to occur, the organizational structure required (and present) is staggering! Not only is the origin of the information a mystery, but its processing into executed acts perhaps even a greater one. An obvious (and compelling) Intelligent Design spin could be woven from here, but that is not the point of this immediate discourse.

What IS the point is that no matter how the DNA is structured in the single cell organism, it would be reacting to the same stimuli and never have a scientific reason to deviate into different genomes for different species or perhaps families or however the concept of different "kinds" is articulated. The ultimate instructions to react to the same environment could never vary enough for such a radical transformation to occur, gradually or otherwise.

The bottom line is that there is no mechanism allowing for differentiation amounting to transmutation to occur. There is no "bits and pieces" approach possible for meaningful differentiation when origin of life is truly beheld from the necessary starting point. All of the variances amount to a "distinction without a difference" because there is no scientific opportunity for them to be otherwise.

Perhaps even more fundamentally, logically there should be no need to progress beyond the simplest life form that can survive and multiply, be it the single-celled organism or something as pedestrian as the worm, certainly one of the earliest invertebrate life forms. Since it can reproduce and multiply and has found a successful survival mode, why "progress" at all? There is no need. <u>And the flip side, of course, is that if progressing, why stop? If unplanned, this makes no sense, and is illogical. If planned, it is consistent with a design, and is logical</u>.

Of necessity, macro thinking has to get past that sticking point to even justify its own posturing. But how does it get "past" it in practice? By the only way it can—it IGNORES it and hopes proponents and critics alike don't notice. Obviously, we have an example of the logical fallacy of "begging the question," which appears to recur for this controversy more than any other single fallacy.

I have read in various literature that Darwin did not really expect constant improvement and upgrading (which, of course, ignores the language of the First Edition referenced above). In fact, it has been written following this thread, "Ecosystems are "systems" precisely because they involve <u>elaborate interaction among organisms that have co-evolved in adaptive relation to one another</u>, as predator, prey, parasite and symbiont."³²⁶ (Emphasis added.) This, of course, describes a radial branching (which the tree of life allegedly depicts) as opposed to linear development as proposed by Lamarck. But even ignoring the language of the First Edition, even radial branching requires an upgrading. Predators presumably get more efficient at killing and prey at escape and survival.

There would not be a reason not to. Even with geographical distribution causing different varieties that eventually become entirely different species in yet another environment, there is still a given wildlife and floral arrangement in a particular locality, and upgrading as described would still be required consistent with the theory. The contrary would require a degree of nomadic nature in animals beyond what has been observed in the real world. Otherwise, there should not have been progression beyond the worm as discussed before. And the stop of progression still has to be explained to make sense. The process should be unlimited in the sense of beneficial changes continuing to be made and being readily observable rather than obscure and only subtle (though there will be those as well). This purported limitation aspect definitely requires further explanation, which has never been given. Devolution still is perilously unaccounted for by Darwinian or any other macro theory.

---

326 Charles Darwin and Joseph Carroll, On The Origin of Species By Means of Natural Selection (2003) Joseph Carroll, ed., Broadview Press Ltd., Canada, p. 59.

CHAPTER SEVEN

UNDIRECTED, NATURE PROCEEDS FROM GREATER PROGRAMMING TO LESSER, AND THE SECOND LAW OF THERMODYNAMICS MILITATES AGAINST MACRO

Much ink has been spilt in both camps over whether the Second Law of Thermodynamics does or does not militate against macro, so let's hear from both. According to electrical engineer and intelligent designer Mark Duck (a graduate of Louisiana Tech University and not to be confused with macro's Wayne Duck): "This law states that energy, unconstrained or naturally, always flows in a direction that will result in its dissipation (but not its destruction). Alternatively, it states that processes, systems and stuff in general naturally change from a state of more order to a state of less order."[327] Duck describes energy as the "ability to do work"[328] and, in that context, also refers to the First Law of Thermodynamics, which states that energy cannot be created or destroyed or, in his words, "Stated another way, the amount of energy in the universe is always exactly the same."[329]

The clear import of Duck's remarks is that energy, in its dissipation after being applied in some manner, breaks down in terms of usefulness and ability to be constructive, and without maintenance and direction, its generating source becomes less and less efficient until it no longer functions at all. Even with maintenance and direction, the source exhausts itself and must ultimately be replaced. As it executes its energy task, the energy it utilizes is not recaptured into anything else useful

---
[327] Mark Duck, "Evolution and the Second Law of Thermodynamics—Detecting Truth," http://www.detectingtruth.com/?p=19, at p. 1 of 7. [7/29/09.] [authored on 5/18/08.]
[328] Ibid.
[329] Ibid.

(i.e., performing meaningful work), without intelligent intervention that is. This resulting condition Duck refers to as being disordered, and a scientific synonym for disorder is <u>entropy</u> (which he defines as the "amount of energy NOT available to perform work").[330] (Emphasis original.)

Duck cites the example (he uses several) of snow melting from a mountaintop and flowing down into a valley. When the resulting stream of water is vigorous enough, the force created causes a paddlewheel connected to a generator but to produce electricity. As the snow source exhausts and becomes less available for melting, its entropy increases. Whereas before, the snow when converted into water served as an electricity-generating mechanism, when the water ceases either being produced or rendered of insufficient force (becomes "dissipated" because the snow source becomes "dissipated") to turn the paddlewheel and produce further electricity, there is naturally no alternative action that takes place to perform useful work and reduce entropy.[331] As Duck explains it, "By naturally, I mean without outside interference by man or other means (i.e., letting nature take its course)."[332] In his own bold letters he states: **"Things just naturally move from a state of more order to a state of less order when left unattended."**[333]

So do origins and theological implications arise from this principle? They do. The stars and any and all other energy sources in the universe are exhausting without being replaced, which means they must have had a beginning of some sort (origins) as well as an impending end. From this Duck concludes: "Since natural processes have never been observed creating something from nothing, the only explanation for the existence of the universe is an **un-natural** or **super-natural creation**."[334] (Emphasis original.) He loops into this summation: "So, consider how life could come into being. Whether you consider a bacteria or a human being, life represents a state of very high order and complexity that operates and performs according to the known laws of nature. Is it conceivable that non-organic matter (atoms, molecules, etc.) could arrange themselves into ever increasing sets of complexity over time that ultimately led to the first single cell organism? If this

---
330 Id., at p. 2.
331 Id., at pp. 1&2.
332 Id., at p. 1.
333 Id., at p. 2.
334 Ibid.

did occur, it would represent a contradiction with the Second Law of Thermodynamics and would be the only natural process that has resulted in continuously INCREASING order over time rather than decreasing in order over time."[335]

Duck is not oblivious to macro counter-arguments and tries to address some, such as that the second law does not apply because it is based on a closed system and the earth is in an open one. Ergo, the Second law is successfully countered by the continual natural injection of supplemental energy. While he agrees that, "an investment of energy does temporarily decrease entropy of a system," [Ibid.] he states that the argument is flawed because the energy must be in a specific form (QUALITY) for any particular application and it must be directed in a deliberately purposeful way (PLAN). He integrates this by examining photosynthesis: "For sunlight to be used by a plant, there must exist an amazingly complex set of processes (the plan) in each cell to use the sunlight to produce food for the plant. Additionally, the plant requires energy in the form of (or have the quality of) sunlight. If you put plants in a dark room and add heat energy instead, the plant will eventually die (in spite of the continuous investment of "heat" energy)."[336]

Duck analogizes the situation to his own line of work: "Consider any other investment of energy that you can think of. Isn't there a particular quality of energy required and a plan for the use of that energy[?] I'm a project manager and use energy in the form of human manpower to increase order around me at work. I spend a lot of time making a plan on how to use the manpower made available to me to achieve specific objectives of the project. Petroleum based energy (diesel) is used by earth moving equipment to prepare lands for a new building. The list goes on."[337]

Frank L. Lambert, Professor Emeritus at Occidental College, wrote an Internet article called, "The Second Law of Thermodynamics and Evolution." He appears to have written independently of Duck's specific article but in defense of macro generally and puts a macro spin on photosynthesis in this way: "Of course, the most complex substances that we know of are produced by organisms. The photosynthetic example often cited by creationists is as follows: Trees make sugars and

---

[335] Id., at p. 3.
[336] Ibid.
[337] Ibid.

cellulose as well as the green chlorophyll and other colored chemicals that we see in Fall leaves, among hundreds of other compounds. They use energy from sunlight by means of intricate chemical processes to synthesize the complex higher energy content substance just mentioned from lesser energy compounds like carbon dioxide and water. <u>But the second law says that the opposite process – of higher energy compounds changing into less-energy substances – is what tends to happen by itself, spontaneously, without outside aid from any energy source. Therefore, photosynthesis is a thermodynamically non-spontaneous process</u>."[338] (Emphasis added.)

Lambert contends that Creationists commonly assert two errors: (1) it is impossible for more complex substances to be spontaneously formed from simpler matter and (2) a non-spontaneous process like photosynthesis requires the presence of an organism, such as a plant.[339] As to the first error, he writes: "There are millions of compounds that have less energy in them than the elements of which they are composed. That sentence is a quiet bombshell. It means that the second law FAVORS – yes, predicts firmly – <u>the spontaneous formation of complex, geometrically ordered molecules from utterly simple atoms of elements</u>. Popular statements such as 'the second law says that all systems fundamentally tend toward disorder and randomness' are wrong when they refer to chemistry, and chemistry precisely deals with the structure and behavior of all types of matter."[340] (Emphasis original.) He also states boldly in his own article: "**Energetically, the second law of thermodynamics favors the formation of the majority of all known complex and ordered chemical compounds directly from their simpler elements. Thus, contrary to popular belief, the second law does not dictate the <u>decrease</u> of ordered structure by its predictions. It only demands a "spreading out" of energy when such ordered compounds are formed spontaneously.**"[341]

He further issues this caveat: "Also, to repeat a caution: The foregoing <u>only</u> describes <u>energetic</u> relationships involving the second law. It does <u>not</u> mean that most complex substances can be readily synthesized just by mixing elements and treating them in some way. <u>The second law has</u>

---

338 Frank L. Lambert, "The Second Law of Thermodynamics and Evolution," http://www.2ndlaw.com/evolution.html, at p. 4 of 7. [7/29/09.]
339 Ibid.
340 Id., at p. 2.
341 Id., at p. 3.

nothing to do with pathways or procedures of synthesis."[342] (Emphasis original, except for last sentence, which is added.] He further reminds us that "... the second law is a **tendency**, not an instantly effected edict. Its predictions might not come true for millions or billions of years. These kinds of delay are due to the second law being **obstructed** and hindered by what chemists call 'activation energies.' All the biochemicals in our bodies except inorganic substances are protected and kept from oxidation or other disastrous reaction by activation energies. Almost all the materials from which our orderly prized artifacts are made are similarly kept from rapid oxidation in air. The second law is a powerful generality, but it is often blocked (to our human advantage) in chemical substances, chemical reactions, and physical events in everyday life."[343] (Emphasis original.)

As to the second point concerning non-spontaneous photosynthesis, the formation of patterned molecules is inherent in the nature of atoms combining with one another without the aid of an external template or organism. "Non-spontaneous," he explains, "simply means the addition of energy to a system of elements during the process of forming a new compound."[344] He notes that chlorophyll has been lab produced in glass vessels absent any organisms, although admittedly over many years, and that the "process was extremely difficult," with many humans cooperatively working on the project.[345] He comments: "The non-spontaneous syntheses of greater-energy, complex substances from lesser-energy simple molecules without the aid of organisms is not prevented by the second law. It is just not favored. Over the past two centuries, millions of complex substances – admittedly less so than chlorophyll – have been made similar in laboratory glassware without the need for organisms."[346]

I do not find the macro arguments persuasive here. First, I think the word complex is being used in different senses by the two camps. Complex in Creationist or even Intelligent Design circles necessarily involves some kind of programming targeted for being useful for work. The combination of hydrogen and oxygen to form water is not in that sense complex under this form of reasoning. They do not target by

---
342 Ibid.
343 Id., at pp. 3 &4.
344 Id., at p. 4.
345 Ibid.
346 Id., at p. 5.

themselves life-sustaining functions or are directed for life-sustaining purposes. They are not part of a systematic process promoting life or working toward that end. Water without more, e.g., would not be a conducive host to originate life, and it has already been shown that no living organism could have formed with water as its host in an open system. By complexity in the context used by Creationists is meant "programming" toward that of useful work.

However, despite the context for complexity, this is not to say that chemical bonding by itself is not programmed. Lambert argues that it is an internal mechanism requiring no external template. But that commits the logical fallacy of "begging the question." More parochially, it puts the "cart before the horse." It presumes that this internal mechanism was there a priori without a stitch of proof that that was the case, it being ASSUMED because macros want nothing but natural agencies involved and considered no matter what. If such a bonding process was planned in any way, it either needed a "designer entity" (the phrase need get no more specific than that) or was self-actuating. Here is where the student is left with a choice as to what the evidence shows (or does not show). But to bald-face say that it randomly occurred with nothing more is intellectually dishonest.

Further, and perhaps more tellingly, Lambert seems to argumentatively shoot himself in the foot by explaining how the complex system of photosynthesis, though admitting the arduousness of the task and the protracted length of time it took to accomplish it, has been reproduced in the laboratory (along with millions of other complex substances but lesser examples than chlorophyll). How is not the injection of such an obviously controlled (and usually quite elaborate) environment <u>not</u> the functional equivalent of both QUALITY and PLAN as Duck would describe it and, as Lambert would describe it, how does it not serve as an external template (though previously used in the spontaneous reaction context) as well as an organism (or, as I would put it, the "designing entity"), the considerable <u>human guidance</u> serving that function? To say that non-spontaneous syntheses to higher energy and complexity from lower and lesser is not favored does not even address the issue and is a straw man: The issue is, how does the equivalence of QUALITY and PLAN come into being? Lambert makes this sound like a random act, that it can happen no matter how "unfavored" it is, and it is submitted here it cannot argumentatively happen without redefining probability in a way that would make the snowball's chance in hell look promising and EXPECTED in comparison.

It is in these meaningful processes such as life origin, photosynthesis, and all the higher aspects that define "life" as we know it, that macros ignore these factors as if irrelevant. The observable facts are that no forces do any work on their own without imposed agency direction, no more than electricity provides light without the required wiring or circuitry and designed pattern through which it flips on the light bulb (lightning doesn't count, wise-guy). Entropy is a recognized aspect of the second Law of Thermodynamics discussed in numerous technical works. None of the elements and compounds derived there from function in any way to either originate or sustain life without an imposed set of circumstances that is not presented in nature itself.

Despite the remarks of Duck, Lambert or even me, however (what we think per say dictates nothing and is at best persuasive), there is a definite scientific controversy afoot, and these and other facts and arguments must be posed to the student for their ultimate determination, including an "I don't know" if that's how they feel as long as they present cogent reasons for the uncertainty based on the database provided them or the logical inferences they themselves draw therefrom.

A major point, however, with thermodynamics not being involved with or addressing mechanisms is the major contradiction that I see in macro scientific arguments generally. They use ALL of their alleged principles as if they address AND ESTABLISH "mechanisms" rather than being manifestations of mechanisms, which is what they really are and doubtlessly as Bohr would have agreed. While natural selection is a greatly exaggerated term imputed with meaning far above any argumentative justification (hopefully already shown), the fact that it functions at all is imputed by macros to mean that it was always there fully functioning without any apparent source for it. If it is claimed that it "evolved" as a functioning device (which, of course, necessarily means it wasn't always there), then that random accident itself must be explained. Everything simply arranges itself in an order with no directedness involved, which is absurd on its face because there is nothing else that is sophisticated in nature (programmed) that remotely behaves that way.

It is interesting in his article that Duck references the textbook Fundamentals of Classical Thermodynamics (2d ed.), by Dr. Gordon J. Van Wylen & Dr. Richard E. Sonntag as having been part of his electrical engineering La. Tech matriculation. Van Wylen is a Christian who got a doctorate at MIT in 1951. He was President of Hope College from 1972-1987. Sonntagg taught Mechanical Engineering and Applied Mechanics at the University of Pennsylvania in Philadelphia for over 35 years (1963-1998) and has co-authored three other textbooks: Fundamentals of Statistical Thermodynamics, Introduction to Thermodynamics, and Thermodynamic and Transport Properties. Duck notes that his textbook is now in its 7th edition and is the leading textbook in its field.[347] These men (at least in the 2d ed.) wrote at the end of their chapter on the Second Law that: "The final point to be made is that the Second Law of Thermodynamics and the principle of the increase of entropy have philosophical implications. {skipped text [Author's note: so notated within the work]} The authors see the Second Law of Thermodynamics as man's description of the prior and continuing work of the creator, who is also the answer to the future destiny of man and the universe."[348] (Emphasis added.)

It is significant that modern-day authors of the leading textbook in electrical engineering conclude as they do, just to show how reasonable minds may differ with macros and for no other reason. Under our point and counterpoint presentation, that statement would not appear in the curriculum. (I don't know if the 7th ed. still has that statement.) It could arguably be includable as a separate chapter in a general treatment as to how scientists view scientific phenomena from the philosophical perspective, but only as part of a much larger integrated topic where ALL viewpoints are expressed and totally separated from the factual point and counterpoint that is the meat of the presentation.

That, of course, is up to the school boards under carefully measured criteria hopefully guided by federal legislation. They would ultimately decide whether to include or exclude such a treatment.

---

347 "Detecting Truth," supra, at p.1.
348 Ibid.

CHAPTER EIGHT

INTELLIGENT DESIGN AND CREATION SCIENCE HAVE NOTABLE DISTINCTIONS, AND INTELLIGENT DESIGN IS A SCIENCE

I will not spend a great deal of time on this issue because for purposes of this book, it is a red herring. With the pedagogy involved with the proposed syllabus, featuring a factual and observational point and counterpoint starting with the macro perspective, the similarities and differences between ID and Creation Science are superfluous. But these two approaches are nonetheless quite different, with the only real thing in common is that under ID, it would be possible (but by no means necessary) to end up with crediting a Christian God with having caused the phenomena observed. As applied, Creation Science is actually narrowed to Christian Creationism because its advocates try to support the doctrines of the Holy Bible. Strictly speaking, one could also be a Jewish Creationist or a Buddhist Creationist or Hindu Creationist, etc., where Christ is either subordinated or a non-factor. So for purposes of the controversy involved that we are dealing with, Creation Science in practice is a narrow form of Christian Creationism.

Regardless, the tenets of Creation Science or Scientific Creationism and ID are pretty well capsulized in Intelligent Design 101: Leading Experts Explain the Key Issues, 2008, edited by H. Wayne House, Kregel Publications. At p. 270 therein, at endnote 182, he describes the Scientific Creationism blueprint: "1. There was a sudden creation of the universe, energy and life from nothing; 2. Mutations and natural selection are insufficient to bring about the development of all living kinds from a single organism; 3. Changes of the original created kinds of plants and animals occur only within fixed limits; 4. There is separate ancestry for humans and apes; 5. The earth's geology can be explained via catastrophism, primarily by the occurrence of a world-wide flood, and, 6. The earth and living kinds had a relatively recent inception."

At p. 271 of endnote 182, ID's tenets are described as: "1. High information content (or specified complexity) and irreducible complexity constitute strong indicators or hallmarks of past intelligent design; 2. Biological systems have a high information content (or specified complexity), and utilize subsystems that manifest irreducible complexity; 3. Naturalistic mechanisms or undirected causes are not sufficient to explain the origin of information (specified complexity) or irreducible complexity, and 4. Therefore, ID constitutes the best explanation for the origin of information and irreducible complexity in biological systems."

As noted, these are quite dramatically different precepts in scope and target. ID certainly leaves wide open just who or what is responsible for the information dynamic and the student is left to decide for himself what that might be (even in terms of a non-deity), provided he goes that way to begin with. He is still free to go the macro way or a Theistic or Deistic macro route, among other things. As having read or viewed through videos both positions from the respective camps for a number of years now, I think the above are fair statements concerning the two.

Certainly Creationist concepts could be submitted within the rubric of point and counterpoint as a challenge to macro's assertions. It would be perfectly valid, e.g., to submit a variation of "3. Changes of the original created kinds of plants and animals occur only within fixed limits," by submitting something to the effect of: "The breeding of animals under highly controlled conditions has failed to produce anything other than limited variation," and give examples of such studies. "Nothing close to transmutation has ever been produced or approached." Another example would be: "The fossil record is devoid of transitional fossils," and argue from there, without imputing a Creator into the argumentation. This would be a simple exploration of scientific fact that hints at origins but leaves the student to decide whether macro passes muster or what might be viable alternative explanations. Instead of "4, There is separate ancestry for humans and apes," it can simply be pointed out that "no "missing links" between humans and apes have withstood scientific scrutiny and been established when serious analysis has been undertaken," and get into Lucy (Australopithecus afarensis) and other failed examples by citing comments by noted scientists, etc.

Intelligent Design is a science because it takes what is observable in physical data and/or behavior, such as molecular machinery, and draws logical inferences or conclusions from that. The DNA/RNA grandeur of engineering is observable under the microscope, and its timing and scale of synchronicity validly can lead one to a design inference. It is hypocritical (and unconstitutional) to permit speculation as to dark matter or dark energy or expansion concerning cosmology of the universe, and then not allow for other possible scientific explanations other than macro based on where the evidence leads.

Let us not forget that ID has added "fine-tuning" in convincing enough fashion for Sir Antony Flew to switch to Deism, despite his otherwise being aware of design arguments dating back to at least Plato (c. 427-c. 347 BCE) and Aristotle (c. 384-322 BCE), his pupil, the latter referring to a "Prime Mover" in his work <u>Metaphysics</u>. But this is far from a disguised, desperate Creationist spin as macros contend, and simply incorporates the advances of science to show how science complements design, rather than being contrary to it. That is the abundant theme of <u>Privileged Planet</u>. The study of design in nature and ascertaining purposes for existence is known as teleology, which as has been shown, has very old (and distinguished) roots. But the notion of design itself being demolished by science is a total falsehood and part of a vicious deception by the macros to try to link design and Christian Creationism as being mutually inclusive, which is an irresponsible and intellectually dishonest disputation. Design does call for some form of higher intelligence as an agency, no question; but this book has hopefully conclusively shown that that is not interdependent upon a Christian God. Scalia in <u>Aguillard</u> even went so far as to say that a Creationist God is not necessarily a Genesis God, but we need not go that far, even though I agree with that assessment.

I pointed out in the Prologue that statistics can be misleading and quoted Andrew Lang in that capacity. While this is certainly so, it is important to identify a non sequitur argument that gets misapplied in considering the statistical likelihood or unlikelihood of our universe originating from chance. Macros often cite isolated events to show that the odds of such events occurring are astronomically high against them, and yet they routinely occur. In this vein, John Allen Paulos is often quoted as writing: "... rarity by itself shouldn't necessarily be evidence of anything. When one is dealt a bridge hand of thirteen cards, the probability of being dealt that particular hand is less than one in 600 billion. Still, it would be absurd for someone to be dealt a hand, examine it carefully, calculate that the probability of getting it is less than one in 600 billion, and then conclude that he must not have been dealt that very hand because it is so very improbable."[349]

True enough, but applying this fact to cosmological probabilities is mixing apples and oranges. Paulos has applied this himself so between this, his book Irreligion: A Mathematician Explains Why The Arguments for God Just Don't Add Up. (2008) Wang Hill, and his 2006 article for ABC News, "What's Wrong with Creationist Probability," there is no doubt he uses this logic for precisely that application, which again, mixes apples and oranges. For one, there is the obvious problem that neither the concept of the playing cards nor their manufacture undirectedly "evolved" in any way. A definite intelligence "created" the game. I doubt he would consider this a "concession" of a planned Creation, but the argument can be made for it. Sure, the hand must be dealt and something result, no matter how improbable the precise sequence is, but that begs the question. The very deck being dealt was the end product of an intelligent agent. So the source of this probability game is itself an example of ID and how it is played as well.

But let's approach this question from an even more pragmatic slant. To be meaningful, probability in this way has to be coupled with predictability. Every single bridge hand ever dealt has its own unique characteristics, and the odds of that precise hand being dealt in isolation are extremely low. While there are other mathematical problems with such isolation, for our purposes, the odds against any specific hand only count if you are trying to predict in advance the exact hand that will be dealt to you or you are trying, as a gambler, to calculate what your next play should be using probability based on what others have thrown already in a card game and what you have

---

[349] John Allen Paulos, Innumeracy: Mathematical Illiteracy and its Consequences (1989) Wang Hill.

in your own hand, and how many cards are left to be dealt. In other words, outside of that scenario, this particular mathematics is being misapplied for a purpose outside of any practical value, or anything germane to the discussion of design. The only thing that would truly defy chance in this instance would be for someone to be able to predict in advance each and every time what exact cards are to be dealt to him with his each successive turn, so that his continuing ability to <u>honestly</u> predict that exact arrangement in advance over and over again would be truly astonishing, even more so if a fresh deck of 52 cards (after being shuffled to break up the pre-manufactured sequence) was being dealt from on each occasion!

But cosmological odds do not resemble that singular event of what specific 13 cards will be dealt on any given occasion at all. It is the continuing ability to originate and then sustain life when, without intervention, such could not have eventuated at all to begin with, and could not have developed the necessary properties for continued sustenance, that is being calculated. Billions and trillions of coordinated interactions, from microscopic to macroscopic, must be accounted for over countless operations to arrive at what we have now that we call earthly life and its surrounding solar system, let alone universe. What specific thirteen cards are dealt with from a 52-card deck is mere <u>static</u> chickenfeed with far less combinations of factors compared to the dynamics we are considering here. All card games factor in are the disposition of the cards in play. Cosmology encompasses how life could randomly be accounted for with the dynamics of gases, liquids and molecules and the interplay of competing scientific principles that would defeat life's formulation to start with, as we have seen with the chemical impossibility of the First Cause to begin with. Parlor games with a deck of cards are not worthy of mention in comparison to cosmological issues. Multiple laws of science from numerous disciplines are being defied by attributing creation to chance, along with other aspects of mathematical probabilities. Only limited laws of mathematics are involved with playing cards. Without human intelligence, the deck of cards that was the invention of the human mind and manufactured, mass produced and mass distributed by humans, could not even be used as an example. The macros can surely do better than insult our intelligence with arguments like that.

An equally unpalatable argument against design in nature is presented by George H. Smith, who writes: "Consider the idea that nature itself is the product of design. How could this be demonstrated? Nature, as we have seen, provides the basis of comparison by which we distinguish between designed objects and natural objects. We are able to infer the presence of design only to the extent that the characteristics of an object differ from natural characteristics. Therefore, to claim that nature as a whole was designed is to destroy the basis by which we differentiate between artifacts and natural objects. Evidences of design are those characteristics *not* found in nature, so it is impossible to produce evidence of design *within* the context of nature itself. Only if we first step beyond nature, and establish the existence of a supernatural designer, can we conclude that nature is the result of conscious planning."[350] (Emphasis original.)

Smith's argument is a non sequitur. Distinguishing artifacts from natural objects based on design is to apply an intelligence other than nature as the object's author. That does not mean that nature itself can't be analyzed for design. Certain literary authors have unique styles that distinguish them from other authors. All authors apply intelligence to their works nonetheless. Being able to tell one from another is no different than distinguishing artifacts from natural objects. Besides, it is the scientific principles behind the natural objects that are under consideration, the existing forces that must work in conjunction with one another to form an object to begin with that are at issue, not the object itself. By saying we have to step outside nature and independently discover a designer to ascribe design to it is like saying the only way to solve a crime is to be there during its commission, so that the perpetrator and means of perpetration can be clearly identified. We would not be able to use forensic evidence under this approach because it is within the aftermath of the crime and thus can't be used to evaluate.

Unlike Smith's statement, evidence of design is not determined just by what is not in nature, but also by what IS. Its intricate mesh of molecular forces in both animate and inanimate objects can logically allow us to make a call on design or not. Under Smith's approach, we should almost never be able to convict a perpetrator of a crime because

---

[350] George H. Smith, Atheism: The Case Against God (1980), Prometheus Books, p. 268.

usually we were not there to actually witness the perpetrator do it and the means by which he accomplished it.

There are, of course, many other points and counterpoints to this issue, but therein lies the crux of this proposed process. There are viable points and counterpoints to consider, which herein seem to lie more in a philosophy class than in a science one. Nonetheless, it is that database for the student's consideration that our forefathers would emphasize. As can be seen, ID is not mere Creationism in different clothing, but an extension that science has provided for teleological consideration that is first traceable to antiquity itself, and highly secular antiquity at that, well outside of religious inquiry.

CHAPTER NINE

MACRO AS RELIGION

If religion is characterized by dogmatism and faith, then macro is part of that brotherhood. As stated by Paul Ehrlich and L.C. Birch, Professors of Biology at Stanford University: "Our theory of evolution ... is thus 'outside of empirical science.' No one can think of ways in which to test it. Ideas, either without basis or based on a few laboratory experiments carried out in extremely simplified systems have attained currency far beyond their validity. They have become part of an evolutionary dogma accepted by most of us as part of our training."[351] (Emphasis added.) In other words, they are accepted on blind faith because not testable. In fact, they are largely premised purely on philosophical attitude because if there is macro, that must be how it works, and we, of course, must insist that there is macro without any empirical evidence of it. Is this any different than a religious posture? Are we not dealing with circular reasoning and a tautology? This is FAITH at its zenith!

But then again, maybe the reader considers these men rogues and mavericks, and not really true to macro's themes. Then tackle this remark by none other than Darwin Bulldog Thomas Henry Huxley himself: "To say, therefore, in the admitted absence of evidence, that I have any belief as to the mode in which the existing forms of life have originated would be using words in a wrong sense ... I have no right to call my opinion anything but an act of philosophical faith."[352]

---

[351] Paul R. Ehrlich & L.C. Birch, "Evolutionary History and Population Biology," Nature, Vol. 214 (April 22, 1967), at p. 352, quoted by Peth, Blind Faith: Evolution Exposed, supra, at p. 14.
[352] Thomas Henry Huxley, Discourses: Biological and Geological (1896 ed.), at pp. 256, 257, quoted by Blind Faith, id., at p. 15.

(Emphasis added.) The origin of life without a supernatural agency, as admitted by Huxley, is an act of faith, as much blind and DOGMATIC as any religious zealot could be.

Skeptics have often said that man invented God. That may or may not prove to be the case (I insist heavily upon the latter), but macros definitely INVENTED MACRO. They didn't like the duties imposed upon them by a Supreme lawgiver, so they decided to make their own laws. The only way that could be intellectually legitimized was to deny the existence of God. Take Him away, and they are free to legislate their own moral and ethical guidelines, if any. This is surely the point behind the three Humanist Manifestos promulgated by the American Humanist Association in 1933, 1973 and 2003, respectively, the obvious result of macro brainwashing to be discussed shortly below.

So are there motives for adopting macro? There are, such as perceived liberation, if Aldous Huxley is to be believed when he said: "I had motives for not wanting the world to have meaning; consequently assumed that it had none, and was able without any difficulty to find satisfying reasons for this assumption. ... For myself, as, no doubt, for most of my contemporaries, the philosophy of meaninglessness was essentially an instrument of liberation. The liberation we desired was ... liberation from a certain system of morality. We objected to the morality because it interfered with our sexual freedom."[353] (Emphasis added.) Whether all would concur with sexual freedom being the major macro concern is problematic, but certainly Thomas Huxley would concur with at least his perception of the freedom to think (distorted in this writer's view) being threatened.

Now it is not being submitted that simply because one has motives for a particular belief system, that that in and of itself disqualifies that system. That would be a form of "genetic fallacy."[354] Many turn to God out of desperation in their lives as well. That by itself neither confirms nor denies evidence of God's existence. An extension of whether or not man invented God is the corollary that man would have invented Him regardless of His independent existence. There is likely much truth to that statement, just like Aldous Huxley and others have invented macro. But that is why both systems need to be put to the proof, to

---

[353] Aldous Huxley, "Confessions of a Professed Atheist: Aldous Huxley," Report (June, 1966), p. 19, quoted by Blind Faith, id., at p. 146.
[354] http://www.nizkor.org/features/fallacies/genetic-fallacy.html.

determine what is grain and what is chaff, which it is submitted that macro has failed badly to do. In the context of this Chapter, a major point herein is that it is a mistake to presume that macro arose simply out of a pristine, cool, clinical mind that just wanted to know the truth for the altruistic sake of the truth alone. That is one of the reasons (though not the only one) why the historical and social contexts have been treated here, to show that there was a yearning for an alternative. In that context, we are as much dealing with a "necessity is the mother of invention" scenario as we are at any attempts at scientific and philosophic objectivity and truism.

Macros, with Piltdown Man, Nebraska Man, and Haeckel's fraudulent drawings and wood carvings, with circular-reasoned methods for dating chronological ages, with obviously perverted notions of separation of church and state as pushed through by the oligarchic NCSE and AIBS, with the subjected status of Wallace in the macro picture under seemingly biased circumstances depicting avoidance of macro hot spots rather than objective disqualification, etc., have promoted an agenda that violates true Science and the mere search for truth in a damaging and vicious, pre-meditated way, with the minds of our young people and the public targeted victims. This is unforgivable and inexcusable and must be remedied now, before other methods of persuasion are used (not necessarily violent, though that's possible, but certainly exercising undue influence) to convince the public of a system, which, in this case, is actually demonstrably wrong. As Bogie's Sam Spade said in the <u>Maltese Falcon</u> as he was about to send Mary Astor's character up the river for, among other things, killing his partner and not being able to trust her, you may or may not agree with some of these reasons, but look at the number of them. Even if macro is not demonstrably wrong (certainly not conceded by this writer), the ends of its promotion do not justify the means.

Public religion is based on faith and a priori assumptions in the sense of an allegedly directly unprovable God, but macro operates on an unprovable First Cause without intervention in any form, be it divine or extraterrestrial, or anything else devisable within our imagination. That is faith (and asserted here, the BLIND AS A BAT variety) if ever it existed. As Peth put it at p. 83 of <u>Blind Faith</u>: "Believing evolutionary theory requires faith—not in scientific fact, but in <u>mathematical impossibility</u>."

In <u>The Myths We Live By</u> (2003) by Mary Midgley, an English moral philosopher, she points out at p. 40: "It turns out that the evils which have infested religion are not confined to it, <u>but are ones that can accompany any successful human institution</u>."[355] (Emphasis added.) Does this not remind us of Madison's comments on corporations, both religious and secular, that acquire too much property and money and therefore power? In like manner, men rely too much on scientism (i.e., applying scientific method inappropriately) rather than confining science to science.[356] She also wrote: "In exposing these rhetorical attempts to turn science into a comprehensive ideology, I am not attacking science but defending it against dangerous misconstructions."[357] A frequent subject of her attacks is Richard Dawkins, wherein in <u>Philosophy</u>, Vol. 4 (1979), "Gene-Juggling," she criticized his book <u>The Selfish Gene</u>, as an exercise in psychological egoism. While she later apologized for her vitriol, she did not apologize for her criticisms, and to this day appears to maintain them.

While raised a Christian, Midgley does not believe in God, though she sees a utility in religion. She wrote <u>Evolution as a Religion: Strange Hopes and Stranger Fears</u> (1985) and <u>Science as Salvation</u> (1992) as a check to the undue use of science to try to promote social positions. In her 2002 introduction to the reprint of <u>Evolution as a Religion</u>, she wrote that the purpose of the two books was to counter the "quasi-scientific speculation" engendered by evolutionary biologists like Dawkins in Religion, and physicists and artificial intelligence researchers in <u>Salvation</u>.[358] She concluded that: "These schemes still seem to me to be just displacement activities proposed in order to avoid facing our real difficulties."[359] In other words, a fiction is created so that reality need not be dealt with. Like Lambert asserted (but failed to prove in this writer's opinion re the Second Law of Thermodynamics), this statement is also a "quiet bombshell" (for opposite reasons, of course).

---

355 http://en.wikipedia.org/wiki/Mary_Midgley, endnote 7, at p. 10 of 11. [6/18/19.]
356 "The Guardian Profile: Mary Midgley / Books / The Guardian: Mary, Mary, Quite Contrary," http://www.guardian.co.uk/books/2001/jan/13/philosophy, p. 6 of 10, quoting John Cornwell, the writer and director of the science and religion project at Jesus College Cambridge. [6/18/09.]
357 Id., <u>Myths</u>, p. 21, Wikipedia, supra, at p. 4 of 12.
358 Id., at p. 4 of 12.
359 Id., p. x of Religion update intro.

While this writer could not disagree more with Midgley as far as the actual authenticity of Darwinian macro, the point she raises about using science as an agenda rather than for its true value is profoundly accurate, and is a practice used not only now, but in Darwin's time. In a 2005 letter to The Guardian, Midgley advanced: "[There is] widespread discontent with the neo-Darwinist – or Dawkinsist – orthodoxy that claims something which Darwin himself denied, namely that natural selection is the sole and exclusive cause of evolution, making the world therefore, in some important sense, entirely random. This is itself a strange faith which ought not to be taken for granted as part of science."[360] (Emphasis added.) She also submitted in a 9/07 interview: "The ideology Dawkins is selling is the worship of competition. It is projecting a Thatcherite take on economics on to evolution. It's not an impartial scientific view; it's a political drama."[361] (Emphasis added.) How little has changed from the mid 19th Century on.

Where Midgley and I differ is that it is submitted herein that men with their own agendas extrapolated observations from Darwin (as he did himself), which transcended the boundaries of science into unwarranted cosmological implications that have no connection with the observations made, and clearly abused them, and even misrepresented them along the way. Conclusions were made to remove higher intelligence agency so that their own biases could be promoted, to replace one form of tyranny, if you will, with another—namely, their own. Though couched in terms of the tyranny of dogmatism, one dogmatic form was replaced by an equally insidious other. The statements of the two Huxleys confirm this. So what she calls legitimate Darwinian science is false doctrine impersonating as science, probably caused by her misunderstanding Darwin's misapplication of his own observations (submitted on this end as being deliberate, but misapplications regardless). Dogmatic religious extremism was being escaped, though it is asserted here in dishonest fashion. While the issue was not quite that of a church-state like in the case of the Vatican, the political and social influence of the Anglican Church was indisputably very powerful.

---

[360] "Designs on Darwinism," The Guardian at http://www.guardian.co.uk/letters/story/0,,1563242,00.html, 6 September 2005. [6/18/09.]
[361] Jackson, Nick. "Against the Grain: There are Questions that Science Cannot Answer,"-http://www.independent.co.uk/incoming/article2977701.ece), The Independent, January 3, 2008. [1/30/10.]

The free flow of ideas is not only endorsed by the Founding Fathers, but by honest philosophical pursuit. As Bertrand Russell wrote in his History of Western Philosophy (1946): "To teach how to live without certainty, and yet without being paralyzed by hesitation, is perhaps the chief thing that philosophy, in our age, can still do for those who study it."[362] I applaud that remark, as does Midgley. It is the essence of conviction, knowing that a position is solidly premised, but lacks absolute proof in the sense of not removing at least some form of lingering metaphysical doubt. It is, in sum, the very essence of faith, which in practice to varying degrees, we all have to adopt regardless of philosophy.

Making propositions like transmutation, without the proper evidence to back it up, is the calling card of macro, based purely on faith and dogmatism. Yet it purports to address origins, one of the calling cards of Creationism, which Intelligent Design is improperly labeled as being a vehicle for. This has the same characteristics of any organized religion, and must be deemed to be equally as much of a religion.

Besides the similarity of characteristics of macro and any organized formal religion that has already been noted, we have a categorization by the U.S. Supreme Court itself that secular humanism is a religion. [Torcaso v. Watkins, 367 U.S. 488, 495, n. 11 (1961).] This was even admitted by dissenting Justice Scalia (again, Chief Justice Rehnquist concurred) in Aguillard as referenced above at 482 U.S. 578, 635, n. 6 (1987). The link between humanism and macro is inescapable, as shown by the three Humanist Manifestos. The operative one would have been the very first in 1933. Looking at that document, it by extension would have to be found that macro itself is a religion. The first Paragraph of the Preamble, last sentence, even specifically identifies humanism as a religion: "In every field of human activity, the vital movement is now in the direction of a candid and explicit humanism. In order that religious humanism may be better understood we, the undersigned, desire to make certain affirmations which we believe the facts of our contemporary life demonstrate."[363] (Emphasis added.)

The linkage between humanism and macro is inescapable when these "theses" are considered: "First: Religious humanists regard the universe

---

362 http://www.goodreads.com/quotes/show/15051. [1/30/10.]
363 "Who We Are," Humanist Manifesto, Who_Are/About_Humanism/Humanist_Manifesto_I, at p. 1 of 5. [7/17/09.]

as <u>self-existing</u> and <u>not created</u>. Second: Humanism believes that man is a part of nature and that <u>he has emerged as a result of a continuous process</u>. ... Fifth: Humanism asserts that the nature of the universe <u>depicted by modern science makes unacceptable any supernatural</u> or cosmic guarantee of human value. ... Sixth: We are convinced that the time has passed for theism, deism, modernism, and the several varieties of "new thought". Seventh: Religion consists of those actions, purposes, and experiences which are humanly significant. ... <u>The distinction between the sacred and the secular can no longer be maintained</u>. ... Tenth: It follows that there will be no uniquely religious emotions and attitudes of the kind hitherto associated with belief in the supernatural."[364] (Emphasis added.)

For the humanist, despite the altruism and utilitarianism expressed, there is no room for God in any capacity. He is an outmoded token who must be dispensed with. But at least this expression is more honest than the ABIS, NCSE and NAS have been, with their garbage of the supernatural being beyond the province of science, which it does not purport to address, and that there is no reason for conflict with religion. For the humanist, God and man are incompatible. The macro <u>brainwash</u> as far as it being an established science, however, was in full evidence even back in 1933.

So it comes off as Promethean hypocrisy to find people such as Eugenie Scott, NCSE's head, as a signatory to Humanist Manifesto III, "Humanism and Its Aspirations," which is self-described as "a successor to the Humanist Manifesto of 1933."[365] Macro, as a basic thesis of humanism (**"Humans are an integral part of nature, the result of unguided evolutionary change."**)[366] (bold emphasis original), and as a source of the "knowledge of the world" through established science, demonstrates how nature is <u>self-existing</u>, which by implication includes being <u>self-actuating</u> and <u>self-perpetuating</u>.

Incidentally, a further credo at Manifesto III is: "Progressive cultures have worked to free humanity from the brutalities of mere survival and to reduce suffering, improve society, and develop global community.

---

364 Id., at pp. 2&3 of 5. [7/17/09.]
365 http://www.americanhumanist.org/Who_We_Are/AboutHumanism/Humanist_Manifesto_III, at p. 1 of 3 & http://www.americanhumanist.org/Who_We_Are/About Humanism/Humanist_Manifesto_II..., at p. 3 of 5. [7/17/09.]
366 <u>Manifesto III</u>, supra, at p. 2 of 3.

We seek to minimize the inequities of circumstance and ability, and we support a just distribution of nature's resources and the fruits of human effort so that as many as possible can enjoy a good life."[367] (Emphasis added.) This language is unlikely to thrill many capitalists. This also seems at odds with Dawkins' belligerent attitude through the New Atheist movement and his form of Social Darwinism. Yet, hypocritically, Dawkins is himself a signatory to Manifesto III.[368]

It should be made clear here that even the Manifestos themselves admit that the signatories join in the spirit of the document as a whole, and that individually they might phrase things differently if they were to author them themselves. However, the overall expression of all of the Manifestos toward both the preclusion of the supernatural from consideration of any kind because through modern science it has been shown to be non-existent, and the working together to cure the social imbalances and inequities so that as many as possible can enjoy a good life, is inimical to the positions vocalized by Scott as to the first part, and by Dawkins as to the second. Their words simply do not square with their actions.

Macros have known for some time that they were proposing atheism as opposed to any form of compatibility with a supernatural presence, no matter how categorized. Modern-day arguments for a basic lack of conflict between the two as suggested by the NAS because of the supernatural being, e.g., beyond the realm of science, are all smoke and mirrors, rhetoric to disguise an attempt to impose atheism upon schoolchildren through censorship. Historically, efforts under the guise of science were undertaken to establish this connection.

They even went to an unsuccessful extreme (again, mostly censored today) to try to experimentally show macro's validity so that atheism would be proven. In the middle of the 1920s, noted Russian biologist Ilya Ivanov (1870-1932), renowned for his artificial inseminations in horses and other animals (he once fertilized 500 mares with a single stallion's semen), undertook with Soviet funding, experiments to hybridize humans and apes through artificial insemination. The British government also expressed interest and pledged financial support, and American science patrons also expressed an interest. Further, noted

---

367 Id., at p. 2 of 3.
368 Manifesto II..., supra, at p. 2 of 5.

biologists Professor Hermann Klaatsch and Dr. F.G. Crookshank supported it.

In one phase of the project, attempts were made to use ape males and human females for hybridization, but they were stopped when at least five of the women died. The American Association for the Advancement of Atheism gave vocal support for the project (I don't know if they were aware of the human life consequence at the time or not) based on its potential for establishing "proof of human evolution and therefore of atheism."[369] (Emphasis added.) So let us make no mistake about it, <u>macro is backdoor atheism</u>, plain and simple, and devious organizations such as the <u>AIBS, NCSE and NAS want to jam that down the throats of our schoolchildren through veiled censorship under the ruse or sham of science</u>. THIS MAKES SCALIA'S POINT IN <u>AGUILLARD</u>, ABOUT THE GOVERNMENT PERMITTING RELIGIOUS ADVANCEMENT WHEN STATE EFFORTS TO SHOW DISAPPROVAL OR TO INHIBIT OR TO EVINCE HOSTILITY TOWARD RELIGION ARE BEING PUBLICLY DEMONSTRATED, ALL THE MORE PROMINENT. Again, I do not feel my proposal is even advancing religion, but this counter-argument supporting it in any form of polemic nonetheless exists.

ICR's Jerry Bergman, an Adjunct Associate Professor at the University of Toledo Medical School in Ohio, the source for the last footnoted reference, concludes by explaining how scientifically such ill-advised experiments could never be successful: "In the end, the research failed and has not been attempted again, at least publicly. Today we know it will not be successful for many reasons, and Professor Ivanov's attempts are, for this reason, a major embarrassment to science. <u>One problem is humans have 46 chromosomes—apes 48—and for this reason the chromosomes will not pair up properly even if a zygote is formed. Another problem is a conservatively estimated *40 million base pair differences exist between humans and our putative closest evolutionary relatives, the chimps*</u>. These experiments are the result of evolutionary thinking and they failed because their basic premise is faulty."[370] (Emphasis added.) Other sources to read about these

---

369 Etkind, A. 2008. "Beyond Eugenics: The Forgotten Scandal of Hybridizing Humans and Apes." <u>Studies in History and Philosophy of Biological and Biomedical Sciences</u>. 39 (2):205 & 209, cited by Jerry Bergman, "Human-Ape Hybridization: A Failed Attempt to Prove Darwinism," ICR, <u>Acts & Facts</u>, May 2009, pp. 12 & 13.

370 Richards, M. 2008. "Artificial Insemination and Eugenics: Celibate Motherhood, Eutelegenesis and Germinal Choice." <u>Studies in History and Philosophy of Biological and Biomedical Sciences</u>. 39 (2):211-221, cited by Bergman, id. at p. 13.

experiments are Kirill Rossiianov (Institute for the History of Science & Technology of the Academy of Science, Moscow), "Beyond Species: Ilya Ivanov and His Experiments on Cross-Breeding Humans with Anthropoid Apes," <u>Science in Context</u> (2002), pp. 277-316, as well as "Humanzees: Ultimate Soviet experiment," April 15, 2008, <u>DNA: Read the world</u>.[371]

So do we have a wash, with two religions being espoused and therefore neither teachable in our public schools under the First Amendment Constitutional "establishment of religion" clause? Not at all. As long as the <u>empirical observations</u> of macro are taught alongside the <u>empirical observations</u> of Intelligent Design, with no salesmanship being exercised toward either, both evidentiary postulates as well as alternatives can be taught to allow students to arrive at their own conclusions concerning origins. The U.S. Supreme Court strongly suggested this could be done so long as the focus is not to establish a religion but to promote the <u>secular, educational goal</u> as intended by our forefathers of more thoroughly examining through the available evidence the truth about origins. It is about time, however, that the Supreme Court not duck the issue and DIRECTLY acknowledge that macro is every bit as much a religion as is Creation Science, or their misinterpretation of the nature of Intelligent Design, which is not backdoor creationism. Perhaps the class we have been referencing could be called, "The Evidence Concerning Origins." That way neither "religion" is being approached as one or being "endorsed" or "inhibited" in any Constitutionally impermissible way.

It is important to note that I do not personally consider Creation Science a religion at all, but rather nothing but a true "science," because it responds to the evidence discovered that under unbiased review just happens to support a Creation hypothesis. It, as part of a movement, does serve as an apologetic toward Creationism, but that is just based on an honest, objective, clinical interpretation of the empirical data presented, which they submit to be foundationally supportive toward those believing in Creationism. Whenever the data presents some other "issues" or "problem areas" that need to be addressed because the evidence remains incomplete, I have found the extensive Creationist literature I have received from ICR to be open and honest about it,

---

[371] http://www.dnaindia.com/scitech/report_humanzees-ultimate-soviet-experiment_1159879. [9/25/09 for both.]

as well as are their tapes and seminars. ICR openly admits that the existence of God cannot be conclusively empirically proven, but that there is evidence that is highly consistent with all of the tenets of Creationism, leaving a rational foundation for all believers to take comfort and stability in. Thus, they assert, creationism is not simply just an exercise in wishful thinking for frightened or neurotic people to desperately cling to. It is not just a bus stop for those who feel, "Well, we can't win in this life, so let's grab the next." The fact that there are so many highly intelligent advocates for Theistic macro should remove that concern, be they right or wrong in their conclusions. The point is, there is a sufficient scientific and philosophical underpinning for Theism, which is all that can be realistically striven for.

The character of the pure macros, however, is clear. They are atheists, not even agnostics, and should lay their "zero tolerance" of opposing viewpoints right on the table. Their censorship merely confirms that attitude, contriving such a constrictive, narrow perception of "science" that nothing but their atheistic principles are allowed entry. More scientific minds than Newton, Kirby, Pasteur, Bell and Chain never existed. If they perceived science as they espoused, that was their right. Are the macros so audacious as to say these beacons of truth were not scientists? They may not say it vocally, but their actions say "yes." Their acts of censorship are incompatible with the practices of those scientists named.

CHAPTER TEN

THE MODELS COMPARED

Of course, one of macro's biggest obstacles is always having to depend on the presence of something else that is, itself, unaccounted for, to even be discussed. There already has to be a planet fully formed with a watery medium and shaped sufficiently to entertain terrestrial life, and in the exact chemical and gas proportions needed to qualify the various organisms, plants and animals for survival. That planet has to be in sufficient balance with the forces of nature to be compatible with its own solar system, the solar system with its galaxy, and each galaxy to other galaxies, until we arrive at a total universe. Everything has to be "just right" for all to occur, which <u>purportedly</u> given millions or billions of years, can happen. Saying that elemental things combine <u>on their own</u> (that could also be programmed), such as hydrogen and oxygen atoms to form water, is not only an assumption, but is irrelevant even if true. Elements by themselves do not per se form or support life or do useful work any more than unhammered nails build a house.

There have to be, of their own accord, elements that combine and recombine to form physical phenomena such as water and dirt for fundamental starters, and that would have even a proclivity to do so. Basically, there has to be machinery already there that performs functions so that life and the proper environment for compatibility is present. To a reasoned mind, it should seem preposterous on its face that this enterprise received no outside agency assistance in order to happen, either to provide the beginning resources, or to see to it that once there, the proper mix was achieved. This writer feels macro has already been reduced to absurdity on that precept alone, but we are here to explore avenues of absurdity given something functioning on its own without any actuating help. So as tempting as it is, for our purposes, the discussion cannot end here.

The biggest test that macro fails is one of my own coinage, the "integration" principle. It's the failure to relate all of the aspects of a discipline under discussion to the whole various, relevant disciplines that normally are relevant to a fair treatment of that topic, and which also make complete all of the relationships listed above. While isolation of a discipline for discussion itself is convenient and necessary for meaningful, informational gain, this is not so when it ignores the sea of evidence out there that militates against the conclusions arrived at, and essentially debunks them. It then becomes a matter of "selection and elimination," a form, as I have already argued, of both "Special Pleading" and "Begging the Question."

In other words, discussions and conclusions concerning biology are all well and good, but only when they are not in obvious conflict with chemistry, physics, geology and the other disciplines. It would be the same as saying one can take a sea bass, throw him in the hot Sahara Desert sand, and have his gills perform the same process for survival with the sand granules that they can in water, so that he lives thrivingly thrashing about in the hot desert sand. No matter what mumbo-jumbo is asserted trying to pass under the guise of science for this position, we know that it simply ain't so. It can't happen. Macro is guilty of this same crime.

As we have already seen, the use of "natural selection" is perverted ab initio. To say that a process exists called "natural selection," that determines which traits stay and which go to allow for survival and replication and reproduction is one thing, but to ascribe to it the machine-like precision which the DNA and RNA processes require (the programming without the programmer), is a quantum leap that is anything but scientific. Bohr would have doubtless agreed with that statement. When Creationists are accused of similar manipulations, it is called faith (and as a corollary, bad science). That is exactly what macros are doing here (making it a religion, of course), but blindly. If it looks, walks and sounds like a duck, without studied rebuttal, that's exactly what it is. Macros take what is nothing more than an <u>observation</u>, and through tortuous (torturous would actually fit here as well) logic/tautology/circular reasoning, ascribe <u>programming</u> functions to something that by Darwinian definition has not been programmed. Under their "religion," atoms and molecules just orient themselves in response to some imaginary survival mode with an organization that they are demonstrably incapable of. We return to "burden of proof" issues and even res ipsa loquitur. One doesn't prove assumptions with more assumptions, and programming must be presumed until otherwise empirically and evidentiarily rebutted.

Now let's expand this theme to the current discussion. What the integration principle does is prohibit isolated explanations for the individual discipline, and forces a unified test. I.e., the micro-world discussion must be compared to the macro-world to see whether it holds up under macro-world scrutiny. To pose a legal analogy, this is sort of like the states not passing laws under their own legislation or even drafting their own constitutions contradicting the U.S. Constitution. When done, they are thrown out as unconstitutional once presented in the proper forum for testing. In like manner, the micro-world scientific conclusion must be subjected to scrutiny to see that it does not <u>violate and contradict</u> the macro-world, because there is an interdependency of the micro-world upon the macro-world. What satisfies the chemist might not be enough for the physicist, geologist and botanist, and vice-versa.

Applied, it is not enough to, in isolation, take an extant set of circumstances, wherein life and different forms of it and varieties within it are already there, and expostulate from there, through an unwarranted assumption presupposing origins for life itself, that man descended from a common progenitor (and most closely through simian-like lineage). We then have to explore how this planet permits life and continual survival at all. The first life has to be totally understood by asking the appropriate questions. How does it happen chemically that a closed system comes into being totally by accident? Because of the chemical and physical characteristics of life, it is impossible; and regardless of how the earth has the proper chemical balances to sustain life, we must explain <u>how</u> that is so. We must also show <u>how</u> Earth integrates, as mentioned above, with its own solar system, solar systems coordinate within their galaxies, and ultimately, coordination of galaxies within the universe.

In other words, we don't just need a proper history for ourselves on this host planet, but that same host and history has to be able to coordinate with its own further external surroundings. Still further, besides a first life, we have to consider how and why it is that replication is available for reproduction, body sustenance, etc.; that there are higher intelligence levels among kinds of fauna when we all, under this theory, started from the same source and surrounding. We must account for how and why emotions occur, and how and why we can communicate in an understandable way (be it verbally, written or visually). Is the fact that life is sustainable both in marine and dry land form simply by accident? Human sexuality is necessary for the propagation of the species, <u>but is it also pleasurable entirely by accident</u>? We need food and drink to survive, but are doing these things also pleasurable entirely by accident? Is predation necessary for the fauna-flora balance to be properly maintained, as well as for the proper proportion of species populations, or is something else involved? Thought and critical thinking, emotion, senses of humor, etc., were they really very likely formed via an undirected process? Mere survival is accomplishable without emotion or feeling, yet these characteristics are inescapably and undeniably present.

Origins generally (planets, solar system, galaxy, universe) must be included and coordinated with man's own origin. Macro cannot presently explain human origins (again, the lightning in the pond simply doesn't cut it) because there is no scientific (naturalistic) accounting for the first life, let alone the arising of any living organism that can claim the common progenitor crown. If Darwin had said, "The <u>Observation</u> of the Species," he would have at least been far more grammatically correct and intellectually honest. When one knows he does not know true, <u>initial</u> origins, the Granddaddy of them all, the title should reflect that. Darwin did not deal much with true origins not because it is irrelevant but rather, for one salient reason—he was simply <u>incompetent</u> to do so. He lacked the chemical knowledge to discuss it intelligently. He could not explain what no one else can explain either, how natural laws arise without supernatural or other form of intelligent imposition.

Further, under macro, the process should conceptually be continuing and nonstop, and there should be <u>living intermediate forms</u>, which, of course, are unobservable in nature. DNA/RNA should be undergoing constant change and upgrading. There is absolutely no evidence that there are any informational or structural additions to the DNA/RNA polymeric system. Even alleged mutations happen within the volumes of data that are already there. Nothing is added. Not only refinement (adaptation or variation), but also the means of refinement (the genomes for the respective species), should be constantly upgrading. Those species that have already survived should be getting bigger, stronger, faster and living longer. They simply do not. Macro has stopped cold turkey with no satisfactory, systemic reason for it. The species' genomes are warehouses of power and have capacities to stimulate themselves, but don't. To the degree that hybridization improves the species, both flora and fauna, the natural process itself should be doing it. Hybridization shows that improvements can be made (with limitations, of course. No speciation is possible under that methodology, either, however). But such intervention should not be necessary.

Rodents and felines of today are smaller and weaker, not bigger and stronger, nor in any way better equipped than before. The fossil record already shows that. If Chapter 13 is accurate, then human life spans have reduced dramatically throughout history, and presumably, animals as well (and since dinosaurs, particularly). All of these changes should unconsciously be building toward a greater and greater survival rate, even if the changes between predator and prey do not result in a net gain for either. The hunter should be changing and building toward more efficiency and deadliness and the hunted toward being more elusive and difficult in other ways to bag. Darwin, though not aware in his time of DNA/RNA, double helixes, and the awesome capacities of even the single cell, himself expected constant change with no end in sight: "Slow though the process of selection may be … I can see no limit to the amount of change."[372] He also, as covered earlier, saw upgrading as continuing in his ultimate paragraph to all of the Origin editions. Though Darwin allowed for even regression among the lower life forms such as worms, etc., for the higher life forms he did not.

Darwin was speaking of upgrading, and in so doing, was defying the facts that he already had before him. This is doubtless a form of

---

372 Charles Darwin, On the Origin of Species: A Facsimile of the First Edition.

"special pleading," another logical fallacy we have already touched upon in other contexts. Approaching it now a little more thoroughly, this occurs when someone exempts himself (or others with whom he has a special interest) from the same critical standards he applies to others, with no logical justification for doing so. One of the Nizkor Project examples is: "1. Barbara accepts that all murderers should be punished for their crimes. 2. Although she murdered Bill, Barbara claims she is an exception because she would really not like going to prison. 3. Therefore, the standard of punishing murderers should not be applied to her."[373] In Darwin's case, he had already seen devolution for himself in the fossils he uncovered and yet announced no limit to constructive change, which he had to have meant because natural selection always, from his perspective, selects for improvement and upgrading. For some reason, however, he feels that that same history should not now apply because it does not fit into Darwinian theory.

So far, the discussion has concerned inter-disciplinary "integration," i.e., macro as compared to chemistry, physics, geology, etc. Let's now turn to intra-disciplinary discussion, whereas macro has to be treated as a whole within itself. In order to be that, there has to be a logical sequence for all forms of life that we are totally familiar with but for which John Q. Public is totally left hanging. In other words, we need to be shown more than bacteria-metazoa-fish-amphibian-reptile (dinosaur to bird has been referenced)-mammal (and simian-like line to man) lineage, but rather, just how some familiar fauna arrived in our lives by means that are very far from obvious. And separate from that, we need to know how that other living kingdom, plants (the flora), came about (both aquatic and terrestrial). The conventional high school textbook does not touch upon these aspects at all.

This can get truly complicated. The fauna for this discussion are worms, insects, arachnids and snakes. None is readily obvious, but the hardest of the group to reconcile is how worms participate at all in the macro cycle.

Insects (crawling or flying) and arachnids (here, specifically spiders) present a problem as well in determining how they result, if they do, from the familiar Tree of Life and common macro literature. If not, then is there not a second origin to account for? Where would they

---

373 Nizkor Project, http://www.nizkor.org/features/fallacies/special-pleading.html, supra, at p. 1 of 3. [1/30/10.]

come from, independently from the sea? That would seem hardly likely. But unless something like that is traceable, we are left with either amphibians or reptiles as their ancestors, or an entirely separate event for the natural creation of a single cell organism taking place on dry land rather than water. Is it not hard to imagine an ant, fly, bee, cockroach, beetle and spider coming from that lineage? Yet development of a single cell organism on its face in an open-air environment has seemingly more chemical obstacles than the first conception in the sea. The structural and morphological differences between these, and either amphibians or reptiles, is extremely stark. Nor is there published discussion <u>from the fossil record</u> concerning these events in terms of transitionals. Either we are dealing with transmutation that demands special attention or there was at least a second creation of a single-celled organism that took place on dry land. These events seem so inherently illogical that the gauntlet is being formally thrown now for the macros to explain them.

It is not that macros have not addressed the issue at all. They reason that the phyla containing insects (Unirama) and spiders (Chelicerata), e.g., developed separately from primitive softed-bodied segmented annelid ancestors (worms such as the Velvet worm).[374] This seems to stretch credulity. Velvet worms are carnivorous and live in the decaying leaves on the forest floor, feeding on plant and animal tissues. While they are covered by a chitinous cuticle that sheds for continuous growth (chitin is a hard, outer protective integument that is especially found on insects and crustaceans), the story needs much more development to be plausible. There are common characteristics to many animals that still don't connect to form a viable lineage. This cannot be differentiated from common design and, for now, is much more likely to be simply homeotic. Other Unirama include centipedes, millipedes, pauropods, onychophora, and symphylans. The Chelicerata phylum also includes mites, ticks, scorpions, sea spiders, and horseshoe crabs.[375]

Of course, transitionals are lacking, as is the case with all the lineages macros try to portray. We have seen that all candidates for transition ultimately fail to fulfill that function when greater scrutiny and further evidence is accounted for.

---

[374] "The First Arthropods," Evolution and Diversity –page 2, http://www.cals.ncsu.edu/course/ent425/ text02/ arthropods.html, at p. 4 of 7. [1/30/10.]
[375] Ibid.

While at least the structural and anatomical relationship between snakes and other reptiles is more closely visible, it is not at all clear how or why any other types of reptiles would lose their legs for any kind of perceived advantage. What on the surface would it be? Certainly snakes are not inherently swifter than most legged forms. They are not known to run down prey per se. They usually use concealment as a way of hunting. There are certainly other kinds of animals that are venomous, so that form is not necessary for that attribute. While the great constrictor snakes have the great strength from the compound effect of their coils, they are, again, very slow hunters, a distinct disadvantage. Further, their necks are very vulnerable. They do not have claws or hands or any other means to rip and slash or hold off other animals.

Snakes are excellent swimmers. But there is no revealed record of snakes coming first from the sea, and no transitionals to account for that development. The bottom line is that there is no obvious reason for either adaptation or transmutation resulting in this life form, actually for neither sea nor land, but especially for land.

Of course, even with the standard lineage, it is very difficult to conceive of how animals that originated from the sea would even seek out the land, nor how adaptive organs would come about. What would be the environmental reason to even attempt it? How could that be done? Would it be with sea life popping up its head for oxygen and seeing how long they can last each time, and allowing genomes to kick in gradually so they can become amphibians? If there were a sea population problem, wouldn't the process take too long to resolve the problem, and, if prepared in advance, where would the marine life acquire the sense to do that? Is that not a matter of foresight and planning? There is most certainly no way it can be argued that it is a matter of conscious conversion. If to escape from predation or to transform as a predator to expand or alter its scope of prey, it would take much too long to occur. The problem driving them would consume them in the meantime.

Why there would be as a matter of course plants at all is a distinct mystery. Functioning as food for fauna and to convert carbon dioxide into oxygen for terrestrial purposes are legitimate functions and are all well and good, but this relationship between fauna and flora is all too convenient. Does not this balance sound like planning? Where would mindless molecules find the prescience to achieve a balance or even operate with such a target in mind? Is that not a demonstration of intelligence that brainless organisms should not have and belongs to the cranial creatures, especially man? Also, even if sea plants performed the invaluable function of providing life for marine fauna, is there not the problem of their separate macro development? If they pre-existed, how did that occur? Was it a separate single-organism event like Darwin's pond speculation? There have to surely be at least two different creation events on that basis alone, confounding the mathematical probabilities even more greatly than already operative! Plant life at both the marine and land levels is a tremendous problem for macros.

This does not comport well at all with Darwin's explanation of natural selection emanating from competition among fauna and flora as populations began to swell. He wrote: "What a struggle between the several kinds of trees must there have gone on during long centuries, each annually scattering its seeds by the thousand; what war between insect and insect – between insects, snails, and other animals with birds and beasts of prey – all striving to increase …"[376]

Striving to increase is not an automatic logical corollary to a survival instinct. It is doubtful mice calculate to reproduce to just enough population to account for the net effect of cats and other hazards, or otherwise act in such a conscious manner for their overall survival as a species. If their internal organs end up working that way, that requires a planner outside themselves, so that a balance of nature results. Bell's point about involuntary physical processes is on point here. When we cannot will our involuntary functions as humans, reminding us of how dependent we really are, how can our rodent friends be any less dependent, nor can they control their destiny in a coordinated way without an outside agency calling the shots?

Darwin assiduously ignored this problem by his broad definition of "natural selection," which for him is an amalgamation of laws that operate for a given result. But by taking it as a given rather than explaining it, he sidesteps the entire controversy. Here are his own

---

[376] Charles Darwin, The Origin of Species, Ch. 3., as appears at http://www.readprint.com/chapter-2210/The-Origin-of Species Charles Darwin, (the chapter is reprinted in its entirety, as are all 15 of them at the website), at p. 10 of 14. [9/25/09.]

words in a later <u>Origin</u> edition: "It has been said that I speak of natural selection as an active power or Deity; but who objects to an author speaking of the attraction of gravity as ruling the movement of the planets? Everyone knows what is meant and is implied by such metaphorical expressions; and they are almost necessary for brevity. So again it is difficult to avoid personifying the word Nature; <u>but I mean by nature, only the aggregate action and product of many natural laws, and by laws the sequence of events as ascertained by us</u>. With a little familiarity such superficial objections will be forgotten."[377] (Emphasis added.)

But by the operation of various laws integrating together to give us an ultimate process, how can Darwin possibly not see an intelligent agency behind such integration? He instead takes it for granted as being without planning, where there is no rhyme or reason for it. He claims he uses nature as such for brevity, but this interplay has to be explained as to how it can possibly be undirected. The more working parts for which greater and greater coordination is required, the more design would be expected and inferred. It is a non sequitur to presume randomness rather than planning under such circumstances, as this is the proverbial looks, walks and quacks like a duck. As Darwin uses "natural selection" throughout his works, his critics are right. He does deify it.

The burdens of proof and going forward are both imposed on Darwin, and he completely drops the ball. He is guilty of a tautology and "selection and elimination" at its zenith. Select the reality of knowing it is a complex coordination of many natural phenomena, but eliminate the necessity of accounting for it. Take the phenomenon as a given and go from there. It is not that each and every phenomenon must be individually dissected ad infinitum, but there has to be an explanation for the coordination without a formal coordinator. It is like taking a timed sprinkling system, seeing it operate, and then assigning to it random activity when obviously someone set the timer. Having a buzzword for convenience of expression is one thing, but assigning a functionality to that buzzword without explaining and considering how that can possibly be is quite another, and procedurally, substantively, and argumentatively improper.

---

[377] Charles Darwin, Ch. 4, "Natural Selection—Or the Survival of the Fittest," <u>Origins</u>, supra, at p. 2 of 42. [9/26/09.]

This is entirely unforgivable. Darwin in one breath recognizes he is integrating, and in the next chooses to ignore it and presume it just is, undirected and entirely on its own. He acknowledges that critics in essence say he is deifying "natural selection" (and again, they are absolutely right in that criticism), and the best he can come up with is that it is a shorthand expression for an observed process he does not care to specify and account for. An objective observer expects far more than such obvious avoidance. It is submitted that when the observations he did make concerning the fossils he discovered on the Beagle journey are weighed with the Scriptural considerations he was fully aware of but did not even broach, this avoidance is made for far more than convenience in proceeding forward. He knew he had no answers for them. This is not my bias as a Christian Creationist talking, but rather my role as a cold, clinical, objective analyst looking at what Darwin knew was in glaring opposition to his postulates, and deliberately failing to address them, as though they were non-existent.

For Darwin, altruism in any form (individual or group) is simply a reflection of concealed selfishness that has nonetheless evolved because what may be even detrimental to the individual is beneficial to the group, so that group survival is best assured under such qualities, and thus altruism hallmarks and is an expected corollary of "natural selection."[378] Mothers supposedly care for their children in an effort to ensure gene continuity, not because there is any intrinsic, genuine maternal affection. Try selling that to an adoring Homo sapiens mother or even other lower forms of mammal such as lions, wolves, domestic dogs and cats. When there was the publicity years ago about a 20 foot killer whale attacking and killing a 10 foot great white shark in defense of its young, was that with a calculation of extending the overall species, or was there an independent defensive posture of concern for the well-being of its children (a maternal or paternal love) that motivated the killer whale? While there was a size mismatch there, doubtless the killer whale would have combated the shark under even more equitable circumstances for the shark.

When human parents suffer grief over the loss of a child, is it a genuine loss felt through deprivation of their beloved in what we would call love, or is it just because there is one less organism to perpetuate the

---

[378] "Biological Altruism," Biological Altruism (Stanford Encyclopedia of Philosophy), http://plato.stanford.edu/entries/altruism-biological/, at p. 3 of 20. [9/25/09.]

species or the family name? And what of the reverse? When one loses an elderly parent (upon whom a literal dependence has long since passed), is the resulting grief because they can't reproduce anymore, or is there a deeper-seated love having nothing to do with the propagation of the race or family name?

Even much lower levels of animal demonstrate capacities of even sacrificing themselves for the welfare of the group or otherwise helping others within their group, like a vampire bat regurgitating its own blood conquest to share with a disabled group inhabitant, or monkeys in a group warning of an approaching predator, even though they might place themselves in greater danger by doing so. But the only rational explanation for even the possible sacrifice of the individual specimen would be if there was a built-in programming mechanism for it that imbues the specimen with a sense of community that transcends even its own immediate survival instinct. It is irrational to suppose that natural selection could blindly lead into such an arena. There is not a good reason for the individual to worry about survival beyond its own immediate orbit, for its own individual self-preservation. Acting for the good of the rest of the species is a <u>selfless</u> (not selfish) act that imputes a consciousness and brotherhood (even an ethical aspect) that blind forces could not possibly concoct. Again, Wallace realized that, which is another reason why he expressed the limitations on natural selection that he did. What this smells of is design, plain and simple, and is far more compelling evidence of it than the blind enactment that Darwin assigns to natural selection and heredity.

Am I overstating or contorting Darwin's position? Judge that for yourself. He himself wrote: "Turning now to the social and moral faculties. In order that primeval men, or the apelike progenitors of man, should become social, they must have acquired the same instinctive feelings, which impel other animals to live in a body; and they no doubt exhibited the same general disposition. They would have felt uneasy when separated from their comrades, for whom they would have felt some degree of love; they would have warned each other of danger, and have given mutual aid in attack or defence. <u>All this implies some degree of sympathy, some degree of fidelity, and courage. Such social qualities, the paramount importance of which to the lower animals is disputed by no one</u>, were no doubt acquired by the progenitors of man in a similar manner, namely, through natural selection, aided by inherited habit."[379] (Emphasis added.)

Clearly, Darwin ascribes natural selection and inherited habit as being responsible for all altruistic qualities. It is submitted that the derivation for this habit is far more susceptible to a "pre-programmed" ability than having coincidentally become an option for the "natural selection" process that just happens to fit a social purpose, which again, is clueless as to how. This is another example of an academic choice whose option must be provided the reader.

The plant conveniently being present for the betterment of fauna (both for conversion of carbon dioxide to oxygen as well as food, etc.), which itself seems to reek of design, is not Darwin's only problem with that kingdom, however. He argued in his "On the Various Contrivances by Which British and Foreign Orchids are Fertilised by Insects" (1862) that the shape of orchid flowers and pollinia was influenced by natural selection for the further inducement of insects to cross-fertilise different plants.[380]

Does this not call for a planning and orchestration that infers an intelligence that plants simply can't otherwise have? This is not a matter of self-coping defensive devices like horns, claws, pincers, sharp teeth, etc., a direct, internal response to an outside environment, but of orchestrating a mechanism by which perpetuation can be achieved by appealing to outside sources, a cooperation between flora and fauna (even if unconscious on the fauna's part) that calls for planning, an elaborate symbiosis beyond their capacity to self-orchestrate. And this is all allegedly done in a blind fashion. Under Darwinian theory, there would be no natural selective design targeting fish for the evolution of appendages for eventual terrestrial use as amphibians. No more so than when Hunt in her horse treatment acknowledged there was no specific target for the horse series to play out as it did (which is not at all, when subjected to the scrutiny we gave it earlier).

This symbiotic pollination scheme is not based on just a series of direct interactions between the organism and its immediate environment.

---

[379] Charles Darwin, The Descent of Man (1871), Chapter 5 (whole chapter provided, as well as the rest of the twenty-one chapters and Supplemental Note), http://www.infidels.org/ library/ historical/ charles_darwin/ descent_of_man/chapter_05.html, at p. 3 of 15 (Darwin's pagination not provided). [1/30/10.]
[380] http://www.christs.cam.ac.uk/darwin200/ pages/ index.php?page_id+c2, "Charles Darwin & Evolution," at p. 3 of 8. [3/22/09.]

It is somewhat analogous to independently figuring out that one is supposed to put mail in the mailbox so as to properly utilize the postal service, except that this flora-fauna interaction is far more sophisticated than that. But there is no evolutionary explanation that can allow randomness to result in such a symbiotic enterprise. Darwin <u>observed</u> it but offered no cogent means to explain it. How "natural selection" influences this is totally unexplained. <u>Planning</u> is avoided in an illogical manner. But the burden of disproving design as explained earlier is there and yet entirely lacking.

The inference of an intelligence behind this unquestionably elaborate scheme is compelling, so much so that to return to a previous theme, the burden of proof is clearly thrown to the macros to produce evidence showing that it is not. Again, a creature that looks, walks, quacks and otherwise acts like a duck is inferred (and for practical purposes, assumed) to be a duck unless proven otherwise.

So expressed as models, how do Scriptural Creationism and macro stack up against one another? The Bible speaks of giants among men, so the suppressed archaeological findings of this phenomenon revealed earlier are consistent with such a hypothesis. Devolution would be consistent with the consequence of sin and the fall of man, both among fauna and, it seems by the possible evidence, man himself, and that is what the fossil record shows for fauna. Devolution is against the macro model. The abrupt appearance of life forms fully formed is also consistent with Scripture, and against macro. A brain with emotions is fully consistent with Scripture and a direct component of the evil vs. good controversy. Macro has to dubiously struggle in trying to explain it, which is a principle basis for departure by people such as Wallace, Simon Conway Morris (sometimes fully named to distinguish him from staunch Creationist, ICR's John Morris) and Gingerich, among others of the theistic macro persuasion. Deists such as Flew point out the inadequacy of macro for providing a First Cause. On the other hand, Scripture well addresses that issue.

The Scriptural fall of man, it is posited here, gives the better explanation for why there is so much bad or evil in the world and so much suffering. Greed itself is very hard to account for under macro, but is an expected corollary under Scripture. Predation is explained as part of the struggle between population v. limited food supply under macro, but even if that were true (which is contested here), greed itself does not necessarily logically follow. Greed and the survival instinct are not obvious corollaries.

The macros have another daunting logical hurdle. If man did stop evolving under their thread some 100,000 years ago as Creationists maintain that macros assert, he necessarily had the intelligence to develop historical writing very shortly thereafter (perhaps during). Counter-arguments of continuing evolution inevitably reference micro-type changes rather than hominid transition to modern man. E.g., TalkOrigins references brain size continually evolving during the last 37,000 and 5800 years, but that would yield contradictory results with historical fact. Both Neanderthal Man and Cro-Magnon enjoyed larger brain sizes than modern man (1450 cc. for Neanderthal—some 100 cc. larger than the modern average),[381] yet progress in writing is not indicated through them, though creative wall drawings and precise toolmaking are credited to Cro-Magnon.[382] Other changes discuss lactose tolerance and sickle-cell resistance (simple adaptation, a clear micro commodity) and dispersal of humans from Africa to develop agriculture. But that latter cognitive dispersal event should have led to quicker writing development.[383]

Yet, there is no historical presence of written communication until proto-writing (the basic use of symbols for communication) arose about 30,000 years ago (the accuracy of this date is presumed only for sake of argument). The earliest known authors whose compositions are generally recognized to constitute literature are Ptahhotep and Enheduanna, traced to 24th and 23rd centuries BCE. This stunted progress toward coherent text, indicated to be circa 3200 to 2600 BCE,[384] does not seem realistically possible, unless, of course, that's much closer to how old man actually is, and he had such abilities far sooner than generally credited.

Quoting from Wikipedia text: "*True* writing, or phonetic writing, records were developed independently in four different civilizations

---

381 Roger Lewin, Human evolution: an illustrated introduction (1999) Blackwell Publishing Ltd.-Neanderthal, and 1600 cm. for Cro-Magnon—"Fossil Hominids: Cro-Magnon Man," http://www.talkorigins.org/faqs/homs/cromagnon.html, at p. 1 of 2. [both on 9/5/09.]
382 Ibid.
383 http:www.talkorigins.org/indexcc/CB/ CB928_2.html, at p. 1 of 2. [9/5/09.]
384 "History of writing – Wikipedia, the free encyclopedia; http//en.wikipedia.org/wiki/History_of –writing, at p. 4 of 13. [9/5/09.]

in the world. Writing systems developed from neolithic writing in the Early Bronze Age (4th millennium BC) [an endnote excepts Mesoamerican writing systems from this statement]. The invention of the phonetic system is roughly contemporary with the beginning of the Bronze Age in the late Neolithic of the late 4th millennium BC, with earliest coherent texts from about 2600 BC. The Chinese and Mesopotamian Phonetic systems have especially been influential in the development of the systems of writing in use in the world today."[385] These facts comport far more readily with young-earth Creationism than it does macro, especially in terms of man's comparable accomplishments architecturally and mathematically. It is submitted that written communication had to be refined far more acutely than popularly represented to communicate the principles demonstrated by those other disciplines, or to even devise them for that matter. The required symbolism and abstractions for both disciplines do not seem conceivable without the concomitant growth of communicative writing, which also utilizes those skills. Again, ALL sides need to be heard from on this issue.

Curiously, Steven Novella, M.D., academic clinical neurologist at the Yale University School of Medicine, states that Stephen Gould and other macros argued for non-progressive evolution, species merely adapting to their local and immediate conditions, progress itself being described as an accidental "epiphenomenon."[386] If true, this would inexorably lead to the point earlier that there was no real reason for macro to progress beyond the worm, which seems ideally adapted to its environment.

An afterlife conditioned upon salvation is one of the great hopes that Christianity offers. As the Humanist Manifestos make abundantly clear, the macro future is the irredeemable grave. It cannot be emphasized strongly enough that this by itself is NOT proof of Christianity (or any other form of Creation or even Intelligent Design) and by itself does NOT falsify macro. Indeed, to use an argument based on favorable or unfavorable effects to either verify Christianity or falsify macro would be committing the logical fallacy of "Appeal to Consequences of a Belief,"[387] and is clearly improper polemic. But

---
385 Ibid.
386 Steven Novella, M.D., NeuroLogica Blog-"Neanderthal Intelligence," http://www.theness.com/neurologicablog/?p=364, at p. 1 of 14. [9/5/09.]
387 http://www.nizkor.org/features/fallacies/appeal-to-consequences.html. [1/30/10.]

it does make one wonder why the macros try to push so aggressively for a posture that does not have long-term benefits for them. It is submitted that the comments of the NOW freedom as expressed by the generations of Huxleys is the probable reason, which fits for instant gratification, but is not of much use for the long haul on either a personal or social level. Macros could argue that with one life to live, go for the gusto and feel fulfilled in a liberated way that having a God to satisfy cannot deliver. As a convicted Christian Creationist, I want to live and be enriched too, with the unmatched fulfillment that alone comes through Christian fellowship, and which necessarily involves interaction with others in ALL ways.

On a personal level, theism might be well worth looking into by the agnostics on their own time. There is, of course, no place for this inquiry in the public school system, at least not in terms of a science application that is being submitted here. The only role religion plays in this scenario is that it provides a source of postulates for testing (e.g., is there programming?), which it is submitted has to a great extent already been done, and it is that empirical evidence that must be presented in a challenge to macro postulates. It must be made clear that what offends Creationists (or other forms of Intelligent Designers) is not a contrary conclusion to their beliefs, but that contrary conclusions not based on proper supporting evidence are presented as foregone conclusions and uncontested statements of fact to our public school children. While that annoyance or anger (the degree depends on the individual) may provide a motivation for involvement in the controversy, it is not the end goal and ethically cannot be, as otherwise it would be an alternative form of brainwashing. We have the legal construct of the Establishment Clause to deal with and, of course, it must be dealt with. But it should be apparent by now that there would have to be moral and ethical restraints upon the imposition of religion in the public school curriculum whether the Establishment Clause existed or not. The long train of church-state abuses is historical fact (Establishment Clause or no) and has to be prevented from repeating.

The true issue is not Creationism v. macro, though the macros sweat and strain to try to make it that (curious since theirs is a religion as well), but whether nature functions as macro purports. If the evidence shows it is blind, that is one thing. But if it shows that it is in any way directed, that is a horse of a different color (hear that, Eohippus?). That is the task of the scientific public school curriculum, to address that question, and that question only, and it encompasses a tremendous panoramic scope of scientific phenomena and data to properly address that question. The best way to do that is to take Macro's postulates and then present opposing evidence. The opposing evidence may attach an Intelligent Design inference with it, but that is simply allowing the evidence to lead wherever it may, which Socrates and our Founding Fathers would applaud. That is not unconstitutional.

CHAPTER ELEVEN

FROM THE MOUTHS OF HYPOCRITES

We now know enough about the basic philosophical and evidentiary controversies between Creationism v. macro to examine how the macros' words compare to their actions. From the prestigious NAS came the book Science, Evolution and Creationism (2008). We will now consider the import and ramifications of the following quotes from this work and other references along the way in terms of language vs. deeds (and it will soon be seen that they talk the talk but definitely DO NOT walk the walk):

"Definition of Science—The use of evidence to construct testable explanations and predictions of natural phenomena, as well as the knowledge generated thru this process."[388] In terms of macro, what evidence do they offer that comports with that definition? The non-existent transitional forms from the fossil record? From the horse series? From Archaeopteryx? From Lucy? From Piltdown Man? From Nebraska Man? We all know the "quality" of that tainted evidence. We have seen stark confessions from ardent macros that macro cannot be tested.

"Any scientific explanation has to be *testable*—there must be possible observational consequences that could support the idea *but also ones that could refute it.* Unless a proposed explanation is framed in a way that some observational evidence could potentially count against it, that explanation cannot be subjected to scientific testing."[389] (Emphasis

---
[388] Science, Evolution and Creationism, http://books.nap.edu/openbook.php?record_id=11876& page=10, at p. 2 of 2. [7/8/09.]
[389] Id., at p. 1 of 2.

original.) In other words, to be testable, a hypothesis MUST be BOTH verifiable and falsifiable. These are mutually <u>inclusive</u> terms. <u>So how is falsifiability accomplished when all the competing facts from other theories are suppressed</u>? Representative of this suppression is the section on the AIBS website it calls, "State News on Teaching Evolution." Therein, for an entry for Missouri dated 5/27/08, it states: " 'Teacher academic freedom' act dies at end of session," and the following pertinent language appears: "In Missouri, HB 2554, an act 'relating to teacher academic freedom to teach scientific evidence regarding evolution,' died on 16 May 2008 when the Missouri legislative session ended. Passed by the House Committee on Elementary and Secondary Education, the legislation was full of <u>similar and suspicious</u> <u>rhetoric</u> used in the other 'academic freedom' bills-including an emphasis on the <u>critical analysis of the strengths and weaknesses of evolution</u>."[390] (Emphasis added.)

So how does language emphasizing the <u>critical analysis of the strengths and weaknesses of evolution</u> constitute <u>suspicious rhetoric</u>? Does it not instead sound like the hallmark of clinical and objective thinking? Aren't the strengths and weaknesses of "any" system or theory the EXACT kind of educational data that Jefferson and Madison envisioned students getting consistent with an informed public? Macros construe this objective as an "attack" upon macro? What it really is, of course, is an attack upon their ability to fraudulently conceal the truth, a roadblock to their exercise in intellectual dishonesty. For some reason, macro is pre-deemed to be above challenge.

Nonetheless, to remove the disingenuous inference of favoring religion through semantic gamesmanship, the matter need not even be expressed in terms of "strengths and weaknesses" at all, though that seems balanced enough to me, since both good and bad points are given equal attention. It can, again, be expressed in terms of hypotheses posed by macro and then counterpoints expressing a different view. Whether a given hypothesis is a "strength" or "weakness" is entirely up to the reader after reading the facts upon which a "point" and "counterpoint" are based. This would not be an attempt under <u>Aguillard</u> to emphasize religion or any scientific theory for that matter. Nor should the "strengths" and "weaknesses" of the legislation under attack be if

---

[390] <u>AIBS State News</u>, http://www.aibs.org/public-policy/evolution_state_news.html, at p. 35 of 67. [6/22/09.]

properly presented, but suggesting emphasis of the opposing hypothesis by labeling its information an exposure of the "weakness" of macro could be speciously construed as being leading and overly suggestive and, regardless, is totally unnecessary. Under this methodology, the conveyance of the information does not even emphasize a scientific theory. The only "priority" would be macro's position being expressed first, since that is the prevailing theory in what is nowadays loosely referred to as science, which is really an expression of a worldview as opposed to an honest analysis of scientific data.

Still, what is described as happening there in Missouri is clearly wrong, but Missouri is not an isolated instance. This same form of suppression or attempts thereof have been evidenced in New Mexico, Ohio, Florida, Kansas, Michigan, Minnesota and Tennessee, to name a few, and show no signs of slowing down.[391] Case Western Reserve University physicist Lawrence Kraus has been quoted as saying: "The question of whether there is a divine intelligence behind creation of the universe is not a question that science can address."[392] Well, actually it can, in the sense of the data leading one to make that inquiry, without requiring a pre-disposed answer for it for the inquirer. But taking Kraus's statement at face value, then neither is random chance a conclusion that "science" can address (reach), it being nothing but speculation. There has been no evidence that addresses that aspect whatsoever, but is rather a desperate conclusion force-fed by individuals who do not want to objectively consider the possibility of a supernatural source of origination for the natural laws we observe and study; or even in simpler terms, do not want to entertain the notion that nature as observed cannot explain everything. Such stalwarts as Thomas and Aldous Huxley have already shown us why that is the case. It is merely a disguised way to eliminate God and accountability to a higher authority, even though denied in writing.

Let's examine other excerpts from Science, Evolution and Creationism: "Science is not the only way of knowing and understanding. *But science is a way of knowing that differs from other ways in its dependence on empirical evidence and testable explanations.*" (Emphasis original.) Again, from the Macro perspective, dependence on empirical evidence from where?—from the non-existent transitional forms from the

---
[391] Id., at pp. 38, 39, 11, 19&20, 30, 32, 53 of 67.
[392] Id., at p. 42 of 67.

fossil record? From the horse series? From Archaeopteryx? From Lucy? From Piltdown Man? From Nebraska Man? From radioisotope dating? We again all know the "quality" of that tainted evidence.

Continuing: "In science, explanations *must* [emphasis original] be based <u>on evidence drawn from examining the natural world</u> [emphasis added]. Scientifically based observations or experiments that conflict with an explanation eventually *lead* [emphasis original] <u>to modification or even abandonment of that explanation</u>"[393] [emphasis added]. Macros decidedly have not abided by that criterion at all. They still insist on a discredited application of the stratigraphic record, and still utilize textbooks based on known lies such as Haeckel's drawings and woodcarvings, and Archaeopteryx's perfect placement in the fossil record to constitute the ancestral bird. It is hard to get more hypocritical than they already are. The biggest problem is that the "explanations" are based on a pre-conceived worldview of the evidence and, more importantly, the true evidence is not even presented (censored), and what is presented is false or not adequately proven to justify it being asserted in any conclusory fashion.

"<u>Because they are not a part of nature</u>, supernatural entities cannot be investigated by science. In this sense, science and religion are separate and address aspects of human understanding in different ways. Attempts to pit science and religion against each other <u>create controversy where none needs to exist</u>."[394] (Emphasis added.) It is hard not to chuckle at the senselessness of these statements. Since when are supernatural entities, if they indeed created natural law, not part of nature? Uncovering the laws of nature help reveal the supernatural sense of order and character. Again, no seeker of truth with a rational and open mind simply says, "God did it," and then abruptly moves on without investigating and exploring the how and why. He wants to know to the degree knowable how these phenomena operate so as to better understand and utilize what nature has to teach, and by extension, what God has to teach. There is no Creation scientist of any sincerity whatsoever who would do any less. But by saying that everything is explicable by natural law and that it acts randomly and undirected, that through evidence that is contrived and exaggerated, transmutation has occurred when Darwinism is emphasized, Macro

---

[393] Id., at p. 2 of 2.
[394] Ibid.

deliberately creates controversy because it is expressed in conclusionary terms with no opposing viewpoints based on hard empirical data being allowed to be stated. Their behavior INVITES controversy, even BEGS for it.

Further re controversy, how can the Genesis account not contradict Darwinian pseudo-science on either a common progenitor or descent from common ancestry for apes and man platform? Compatibility is simply not possible. Why not? Well, not because deep time from one day to the next would not accommodate such a process (though it is submitted that that is a profound misreading of Scripture), but because that process would still be directed by God (or another "designing entity"), and hence be a by-product of Intelligent Design. So that we are clear, showing examples that purportedly support Intelligent Design does not inexorably lead one to a Theistic account of origins based on Scripture per se. One can always disagree with the identity of the intelligent agency, or can even take a Deistic or limited Theistic approach, which is also contrary to Scripture. But there is no way that the Scriptural God is not one of creation by Intelligent Design. Therefore, that kind of controversy necessarily does exist. To call it a random process is a definite conflict. That kind of Creation is <u>necessarily</u> directed.

How can the NAS say that God is beyond the province of science when the conclusionary statements referenced above have caused churches to take positions on macro being taught in the public schools? Worse yet, since they have been fed illogical, factually unsupported conclusions based on assumptions, outright lies, half-truths and censored contrary evidence, they have conceded aspects of their faith to these falsehoods.

So just how well has their suppression of information (again, scientific disinformation) scheme succeeded? Listen to this incredible statement signed by over 10,000 "Christian" clergymen: "We, the undersigned, Christian clergymen from many different traditions, believe that the timeless truths of the Bible and the discoveries of modern science may comfortably coexist. <u>We believe that the theory of evolution is a foundational scientific truth, one that has stood up to rigorous scrutiny and upon which much of human knowledge and achievement rests</u>. To reject this truth or to treat it as 'one theory among others' is to deliberately embrace scientific ignorance and transmit such ignorance to our children. <u>We believe that God's good gifts are human minds capable of critical thought and that the failure to fully employ this gift is a rejection of the will of the Creator</u>.... We urge school board members to preserve the integrity of the science curriculum by affirming the teaching of the theory of evolution as a core component of human knowledge. We ask that science remain science and religion remain religion, two very different, but complementary, forms of truth."[395] (Emphasis added.)

How could a statement like this possibly emanate from some 10,000 clergymen without a <u>suppression of facts</u> by the macros such as the true evidence in the horse series (one-toed and three-toed contemporaries, Eohippus probably being a rock hare and definitely not the "dawn horse," reverse order of alleged evolution depending on whether stratigraphy in North or South America, failure to include an obvious horse-like fossil because it wasn't placed right, etc.), the true nature of the stratigraphic column (almost never in order predicted, not nearly as thick as should be, polystrate fossils, etc.), the true status of Archaeopteryx (more birdlike than anything else, not in proper stratigraphic order, with at least one or more ancient birds at lower levels, more of a mosaic, etc.), the finding of more ancient human fossils than publicized (including those of possible human giants and of persons possibly coexisting with dinosaurs, etc.), Piltdown Man, Nebraska Man, and Haeckel's fraudulent drawings and wood carvings, the inherent unreliability of radioisotopic dating methods (known ages greatly distorted upward, grossly inconsistent readings for the various methods measuring the same sample, different parts of a fauna body measuring large differences between them, etc.) and the strengths and weaknesses of the cosmological Big Bang along with the same for Humphreys' and Hartnett's theories (explained below at Ch. 13), etc.? It cannot.

Apparently, unbeknownst to these clergymen, the macros have deliberately deprived them of the proper exercise of their <u>God-given</u> gift of critical thought by denying them the data with which to be critical. The Discovery Institute has the curriculum theme of "teach the controversy." While I do not know the precise spin they put on the phrase and hence cannot comment on its efficacy per their

---

[395] <u>Science, Evolution and Creationism</u>, supra, http://books.nap.edu/openbook.php?record_id= 11876&page=14, at p. 1 of 1. [1/30/10.]

own usage, as I have not examined their actual texts personally with regard to this phrase, it is a conceptually good pedagogical tool in the sense of teaching point and counterpoint for all scientific hypotheses, and certainly emblematic of how Jefferson, Madison and probably Hamilton projected the goal of a proper education to be. Perhaps another way of phrasing it could be, "teach the competing evidentiary facts and supporting arguments." Socrates surely meant going where the evidence leads under the presumption of all the relevant evidence being presented for consideration.

Notably, there is a notation under "State News on Teaching Evolution" entitled "8/20/07 Science Education Advocates Urged to Avoid Complacency" that describes a Discovery Institute endorsed text that on its face displays promise, however.[396] The textbook is, Explore Evolution: The Arguments For and Against New-Darwinism. This appears to be the foundational basis for the "teach the controversy" theme. As reported in this write-up (which is macro-slanted, of course): "Rather than blatantly endorsing creationism or intelligent design, the Discovery Institute encourages science educators to 'teach the controversy,' emphasizing the process of critical inquiry when teaching evolution. According to promotional materials, the textbook examines fossil succession, anatomical homology, embryology, natural selection, and mutation, and then, for each of these areas, 'explains the evidence and arguments that lead some scientists to question the adequacy of Darwinian explanation.'" At least on its face, that is precisely how science, in its truest sense, should be taught. Notice that macros get defensive to any form of Darwinian challenge, no matter how phrased. The language 'explains the evidence and arguments that lead some scientists to question the adequacy of Darwinian explanation' is as straightforward, upfront, and clinical as it gets. Mere opposition is not bias and prejudice, or else the First Amendment and freedom of speech have no meaning.

Of course, true to their hypocrisy and betrayal of the search for truth, the AIBS adds in the next immediate Paragraph: "Science education advocates everywhere should remain vigilant in order to thwart attempts by anti-science advocates to introduce "Explore Evolution" as a required or supplemental text in their state biology curricula."[397]

---

396 AIBS State News, supra, at p. 29 of 67.
397 Ibid.

(Emphasis added.) Applied, this kind of exhortation is not a lot different than what would be expected from dictatorial regimes such as Hitler and Stalin's, where only the "party line" can be published. It is quite evident that the AIBS and its cohorts are more interested in "brainwashing" the public with distortions, half-truths and outright lies than in risking the exposure of inferior, contrived macro arguments to the light of day.

For those who think brainwashing is too extreme a word, let us look into some Internet definitions. One source defines it as: "1. <u>Intensive, forcible indoctrination</u>, usually political or religious, aimed at destroying a person's basic convictions and attitudes and <u>replacing them with an alternative set of fixed beliefs; 2. The application of a concentrated means of persuasion</u>, such as an <u>advertising campaign</u> or <u>repeated suggestion</u>, in order to develop a specific belief or motivation."[398] (Emphasis added.)

The behavior and influence of the AIBS and NCSE fits quite well with these brainwashing descriptions, which is why the AIBS has a mail list to keep the cause flowing, and has updates with the "State News on Teaching Evolution" that has also been discussed. <u>Opposing ideas are urged to be quashed from the attention of our school students</u>. Their influence, of course, extends also to the mainstream press. How often do you read where, when a fossil of any type is discovered, that millions of years of age are attached to it without qualification from that news article? It is virtually a given and yet there is plenty of young earth evidence to belie those numbers or at least make the age of the earth a respectable topic of debate. <u>When the flow of information is controlled through the textbooks and the news media, most of the ballgame has been decided</u>. Jefferson's words in this regard seem more riveting than ever. When school board election influence is exercised, this is a form of group social pressure. From the legalistic point of view, words such as "duress" and particularly "undue influence" come to mind with these forms of brainwashing. "Fraud" and "fraudulent concealment" come to mind as to forms of undue influence.

In his 1998 book <u>Cogs in the Soviet Wheel: The Formation of Soviet Man</u>, translated by David Floyd London, Mikhail Heller wrote: "It is not hard to imagine the effect which 'education' and 're-education'

---

[398] Answers.com, http://www.answers.com/topic/brainwashing, at p. 1 of 24. [7/12/09.]

has upon the Soviet citizen, who is exposed from the day he is born to 'brainwashing', bombarded every day, round the clock, by all the means of propaganda and persuasion."[399] That is not a lot different from what we Americans are exposed to today. Macro propaganda has infiltrated both the schoolroom and the news media. This is one of the very realities Jefferson and Madison tried so mightily to avoid and what was truly what they had in mind in endorsing the First Amendment. While this is not in any way to be confused with prisoner of war torture tactics, it has traces of it. Information is deliberately withheld unless it does not contradict the macro fantasy.

In essence, the goal of any true education is not only encompassed within common sense and fundamental fairness, but also within the vision of our forefathers, and is not targeted to distinguish the supernatural from the natural, but rather to promote the truth by expanding the student's viable empirical database to make his own independent decision as to possible derivations and origins. <u>Macros do not fear the supernatural for purposes of separation of church and state, whose principles they have distorted to their own convenience; they fear the revelation of the truth that will expose their own baseless dogma to their own economic and political detriment</u>. Otherwise, they wouldn't pervert and conceal the material facts behind their assumed phenomena the way that they do. Their pitiless game is perversion and concealment. They apply philosophy first and then contrive and falsify evidence and reject credible, contradictory evidence to fit that philosophy, which again, to express it kindly within the parameters of a family show, is as <u>dogmatic</u> as it gets.

<u>Science, Evolution and Creationism</u> also states: "Science's domain is to explore nature. God's domain is in the spiritual world, a realm not possible to explore with the tools and language of science. It must be examined with the heart, the mind, and the soul."[400] A more disingenuous statement as applied would be a challenge to find. "Science" as applied today does much more than <u>explore</u> nature. It perverts it by imputing blind abilities to it that defy logic. As Wallace put it, natural selection is an end result rather than an independent

---

399 Heller, Mikhail (1988) <u>Cogs in the Soviet Wheel: The Formation of Soviet Man</u>, translated by David Floyd London: Collins HarvillISBN 0-00-272516-9; quoted in answers.com, http://www.answers.com/ topic/brainwashing, at p. 7 of 24. [7/12/09.]

400 http://books.nap.edu/openbook.php?record_id=11876&page=15; taken from Francis Collins, director of the Human Genome Project & of the National Human Genome Research Institute at the National Institute of Health, excerpted from his book, <u>The Language of God: A Scientist Presents Evidence For His Belief</u>, at p. 6. [7/8/09.]

creative force. Especially during Darwin and Wallace's time, even the cell was poorly understood, and thought to be more of an amorphous blob than the immensely powerful, highly dynamic system we know it is today. The integrated machine system and purveyor and conveyor of information that is DNA/RNA were also unknown to them. And again, God expresses Himself through His natural laws. To better know those is to better know God, though by no means is that the total expression of Him.

Modernly, science describes these complex systems as if they are self-actuating without giving us a clue as to HOW they are so. Normally, the more complex and synchronized a machine is, the more sophisticated the inventor of it is presumed to be. Why is it any different here? And if the spiritual world is something beyond the equipped scope of science, then what right does science have to eliminate it as an explanatory tool if it admits it is too advanced and science is too limited to understand it? What logical and even ethical right does it have to assume a First Cause of creation of organic life without a Creator? Again, the intellectually honest thing to do is to say it doesn't know HOW these marvelous systems originated, and then study them to ascertain the facts. That is precisely what it DOES NOT DO NOW. It instead squeezes, manipulates and eliminates data in accordance with its preconceived philosophy of a Godless universe where the natural a priori arises out of nothing and though aimless, through natural selection, adapts and makes inheritable "favorable" traits though the process does it innately without a programmer. That's no different than an elementary school kid saying that the automobile, both stylistically and functionally, came into being all by itself. But then again, the kid can't be wrong can he? That is what the adults around him all say about macro.

Francis Collins authored the last statement I have criticized. The current sad state of education and communication concerning macro is well reflected in the events of July, 2009 involving even him. He is of 1990s Human Genome Project fame (and a Theistic macro) and was first considered and eventually named as the new Director of the National Institute of Health. The perceived problem was that Collins claims to be an evangelical Christian geneticist and certain macros such as biologist Jerry Coyne felt he was too public in his faith. Collins (who was converted to Christianity during medical school), as above-referenced, authored the book <u>The Language of God</u> last quoted from, and founded the Bio Logos Foundation, which officially sees no conflict between science and religion; hence his Theistic macro posture.

In a web <u>Newsweek</u> article dated 7/14/09 called "Defenders of the Faith: Scientists who blast religion are hurting their Own cause," Chris Mooney and Sheril Kirshenbaum (co-authors of the book <u>Unscientific America: How Science Illiteracy Threatens Our Future</u>) argue that scientists like Collins are just what the doctor ordered to help relate the cause of science to a doubting public. This effort seems noble enough, to try to show that science and religion are not irreconcilable, and I do not read ill motives into the authors.

But nevertheless, what is disturbing (and very representative of today's prevailing attitude [as well as highly evidentiary of the brainwashing we have discussed]) is that premise that macro is <u>proven</u> science, and that a middle ground between the religious public and science is needed. As they put it, "The idea that science and religion can be compatible is strong on the intellectual merits as well. Granted, it depends how you define your terms: if your religion holds that Genesis must be read literally, then you are <u>in direct conflict with scientific findings about the age of the earth, the diversity of life on the planet</u>, and so on. Yet if we consider religion more broadly—in its own considerable diversity—we find many sophisticated believers who've made peace between their belief and the findings of modern science."[401] (Emphasis added.)

Therein lies the consequence of a distorted, non-disclosure control of information through our education system and media. It is ASSUMED that radioisotope dating is accurate and has conclusively shown an older earth. It is ASSUMED that macro has adequately explained diversity of life on earth, when in fact these are very hotly contested issues for which there is much conflicting evidence. The New Atheists (as epitomized by Richard Dawkins) targeted in the article attack religion with both barrels based on the incompatibility of religious fundamentalism with macro science. However, as we have seen, the highly influential AIBS and NCSE (NOT discussed in the article) find no conflict and represent the official "education" position.

---

401 <u>Newsweek</u>, http://www.newsweek.com/id/206609? from=rss, at http://www.newsweek.com/id/ 206609/page/2. [7/15/09.]

In fact, that and the <u>Science, Evolution and Creationism</u> (NAS) we have just been looking at clearly relate that the supernatural is beyond the province of science entirely and that the two concepts of religion and science suffer no conflict. But this is a non-sequitur because if science takes macro as a given without the Founding Fathers' required debate, it really is in serious conflict with any Genesis-based religion, as well as with the growing list of fully-credentialed scientists who go one step further than Collins, and reject macro totally as a valid scientific concept. For them, there is no proper mixture of the two.

In sum, this article makes the same basic mistake made by most of the modern media, that macro is undisputed, established fact when the total evidence shows it is anything but. The point really isn't in which direction the evidence ultimately leads as Jefferson once exposited to his nephew, but in the proper manner of determining where it leads, the "uprightness" of how it is reached. If the NAS really means that science must be willing to adjust to the facts and be willing to change if the evidence leads in that direction, then an honest, objective opportunity for consideration and implementation in that area must be afforded. That is sadly lacking at this moment.

CHAPTER TWELVE

IS THERE AN ULTERIOR, INSIDIOUS MOTIVE BEHIND THE MACRO AGENDA?

It seems reasonably clear that the macros have an agenda that precludes (censors) evidence of anything that does not support their fairy tale. But these extremes that we have dealt with do raise the question of why? There are four possible answers that will be considered: (1) Too many reputations would be tarnished by the truth; (2) There are too many economic advantages to applying a macro approach; (3) It philosophically provides for Social Darwinism, which allows for laissez-faire economics and politics, and (4) It makes us less accountable for our actions, even to our very lifestyle.

As for answer no. 1, while the scientific reputations of many scientists may seem threatened by a more open discussion of the facts, including those of such luminaries, past and present, as Steven J. Gould, Carl Sagan, and Richard Dawkins (to say nothing of Eugenie Scott), that has never been a reason for suppression of information unless it bucks the prevailing attitude and best interests of those promoting it. E.g., J.D. Whitney, de Perthes and Antony Flew were warmly embraced when they were on the "politically correct" side, and not at all when they were not. While textbooks would have to be rewritten, that is not an insurmountable task. The 1958 legislation made short shrift of that inhibition. While certainly many leading institutions such as the Smithsonian house are greatly influenced by these people, that alone is not powerful enough of a deterrent factor. It is not to be ignored, but seemingly does not qualify as a prime mover, and is regarded here as the least important reason of the four under consideration.

As for answer no. 2, there are certainly major economic influences that would be adversely affected, and this perspective merits serious consideration. E.g., Darwinian biology has supposedly served big pharma very well, and we all know that health care is very, very big business. There is a concentration away from sometimes proven natural remedies (which are hence suppressed) to drugs (prescriptive medicine) that become patentable, and hence highly profitable, to both the AMA and big pharma associated with it. Far more often than not, at best, prescriptive medicine masks or alleviates symptoms, rather than cures the source of the disease. It is more profitable to be continually treating people with prescriptive medicine than it is to cure them.

As for answer no. 3, Social Darwinism provides an entrenched philosophical foundation for laissez-faire politics and economics, and a psychological advantage for justifying exploitation by the moneyed, propertied interests (roughly called the rich) over those much less so (roughly called the poor). This would be a perpetuating myth, of course, rather than a founding one. E.g., the Industrial Revolution was well underway prior to Darwinian theory. In the same token, Darwinian theory is said to have influenced Adolf Hitler and a number of other totalitarian, dictatorial figures. While this is undoubtedly true, it seems a stretch to say that fascism or any other doctrine or movement arose directly from such influence. I would be hard put to say that there would have been no fascist Germany or communist Russia without Social Darwinism or otherwise the macro theory itself. Brutal totalitarian and other dictatorial regimes rose and fell long before Darwin's view of biology ever came into play.

As for answer no. 4, macro does engender the attitude of lack of ultimate accountability for one's actions, and that may be the most singularly imposing reason of all, because what affects lifestyle and attitude manifests itself in multiple ways. Aldous Huxley's quote certainly is most consistent with this observation. While we may jokingly refer to actions we take as being the "animal" in us and certainly not consciously have macro on our minds, nonetheless, the expression itself may easily have derived from the suggestion that we came from primeval slime, and are allowed to regress some times because of it. It is submitted that this is the no. one reason why macro is perpetuated, with no. 3 being a logical offshoot of that.

CHAPTER THIRTEEN

MACRO MUST DEAL WITH THE DECLINING LONGEVITY AND SIZE ISSUES OF MAN, FAUNA AND PROBABLY FLORA

If most macros cling to their position that their beliefs and the Bible are not incompatible, they need to confront the marked disparity in longevity (not only as to length of life, but in maturation as well, as to when child-bearing or making becomes possible) between pre- and post-Deluvial man. For this reason, not only are pre-Noahic flood longevity ages presented, but the age of initial fatherhood also shown. Scripture makes a point of including both, which arguably must not be ignored.

It must, of course, be acknowledged that the Biblical year was 360 days (which has some other historical implications as discussed below). To compensate for that, I have determined that the five-day difference when divided into 365 equals 73, which means that 73 must be divided into the Biblical ages to determine how much younger each biblical person is under today's barometer. E.g., 73 divided into Adam's age of 930 is 12.7, which I have rounded into 13, making Adam comparably 917. Leap year is not considered significant enough of a factor to be included herein and has not been. The same process has been applied to the maturation (child-bearing) age when it effectuates any difference in years as great as 1 or more, even if below 1 rounds to 1. The difference has been expressed in parentheses so as not to misstate the Scriptural account of the ages. The present scaled ages will be used in the main discussion, however.

The Genesis succession (based on age of fatherhood and child born) is: (1) Adam-130 (2) (Seth), 930 (13); (2) Seth- 105 (1) (Enosh), 920 (13); (3) Enosh- 90 (1) (Kenan), 905 (12); (4) Kenan-70 (1) (Mahalalel), 910 (12); (5) Mahalel- 65 (Jared), 895 (12); (6) Jared-162 (2) (Enoch), 962 (13); (7) Enoch- 65 (1) (Methuselah), 365 (not factored because he Scripturally ascended prior to any impending natural death); (8) Methuselah-187 (3) (Lamech), 969 (13); (9) Lamech-182 (2) (Noah), 777, and (10) Noah-500 (7) (Shem, Ham, Japheth), 950 (Noah lived 350 years post-Flood).

Note the sharp post-flood decline: (1) Shem (one of Noah's kids and first-born)-100 (1) (Arpach'shad), 600 (8); (2) Arpach'shad-35 (Shelah), 438 (6); (3) Shelah-30 (Eber), 433 (6); (4) Eber-34 (Peleg), 464 (6); (5) Peleg- 30 (Re'u), 239 (3); (6) Re'u-32 (Serug), 239 (3); (7) Serug-30 (Nahor), 230 (3); (8) Nahor-29 (Terah), 148 (2), and (9) Terah-70 (1) (Abram, Nahor, Haran [who fathered Lot]), 209 (3). At various other locations in Genesis, Abram (who became Abraham), died at 175 (2). Isaac fathered at 60 (Esau, Jacob) (1) and died at 180 (2). Jacob died at 147 (2) and Joseph, his son, died at 110 (2) as the book of Genesis closes.

In almost all instances above, biblical men begat other sons and daughters, as the text itself tells us. Although some of them are specifically named later, in most cases they are not, and except as above-described, their vitals are not mentioned either. The age at death is only once mentioned for women in the Genesis account, which is of Sarah at 127 (2). It is not explained in any way why Eve's age at death is not mentioned. Nor is the event of her death mentioned for that matter. This is just a point of information and is not to be read as implying anything beyond that.

Noah lived another 350 years post-Flood, making his overall total 950. Shem dropped longevity after the Flood, reduced to 600 years (a sharp drop considering the 895 years plus post-Flood and Noah's age when the Flood came). Now translating into modern chronology, we are still left with 950 minus 13 or 937, and for Shem, 600 minus 8 or 592.

There is a definite correlation between declining age for fatherhood and length of life itself shown throughout the Genesis text.

Macros are hence faced with the dilemma of just how to treat this. They must either dispense with these accounts, call them fraudulent or perhaps just allegorical, and hence make no further claim, as many do, to there being no contradiction between Scripture and science (as the macros fallaciously call it) because the Scriptural account can't be trusted at all, OR they must come up with ways to account for these discrepancies on a scientific basis. If it is atmospheric, then that had to be due to a cataclysmic event, arguably the Flood itself, which to make such an immense difference (don't forget the people depicted spread throughout the planet) would have to have been global rather than local. Thus, uniformitarianism is dead and the reality of the Flood itself assumes enormous implications. Everybody everywhere was affected, as we are today.

Dr. Richard J. Hodes, Director of The National Institute on Aging, part of the U.S. National Institutes of Health, has noted that life expectancy in the United States has progressed dramatically from the about 49 years in 1900 to about 76 by the end of the 20th Century.[402] He also stated therein that centenarians are the fastest-growing population segment and that people are living both longer and healthier. Living to 100, it must be observed, however, is still the exception rather than the rule, and it is arguable that most who get there are in very declining health and sustained by prescriptive medicine. There are very definite quality of life issues involved. Nonetheless, even if we are dealing with consistently pushing maximum life spans to 120 years and perfect health in between (which is being very generous), we are faced with an enormous difference in vitality between now and biblical days.

If life cycles are so dramatically effected, how is it that the maturation period is also so dramatically lowered? If atmospheric conditions are to blame, why is there a corresponding maturation decline? Is that not a testosterone vs. estrogen issue? How would atmospheric changes such as further intrusion of Ultraviolet light, elements released in greater or lesser proportion during the Flood's tectonic upheaval, or other atmospheric or natural phenomena play into that? One could see chemical differences entering in, but where did they spring from?

---

[402] "Human Longevity and Aging Research, Statement before the United States Senate, Special Committee on Aging, on 6/3/03, http://www.nia.nih.gov/ AboutNIA/BudgetRequests/HLAgingResearch.htm, at p. 1 of 8. [7/21/09.]

Life spans were presumably considerably lower in pioneer days, for if consistent with the global average, in 1800, the life expectancy at birth was 30 years,[403] but there is no indication the maturation period itself was altered. It appears that young men and women could still become fathers and mothers at no discernible age difference at all to what they can modernly. Austerity and harshness of life by itself is not related to the biological paternity-maternity time clock. <u>Yet the global flood (assuming one for the sake of argument) does appear to have affected maturity as well as longevity, a very sobering thought</u>.

If Genesis is accurate, it speaks of the <u>pre-Deluvial</u> Nephilims, of whom Scripture reports (Revised Standard Version throughout), "…These were the mighty men that were of old, the men of renown," [Genesis 6:4] whom God assigned a life span of 120 years (2) to because he was not with them Spiritually [Genesis 6:3-"Then the LORD said, "My spirit shall not abide in man for ever, for he is flesh, but his days shall be a hundred and twenty years."] It appears clear that because man is of flesh and the spirit has departed, the physical nature of man alone considerably lowers his mortality, at least in terms of the Nephilim. Of course, God wiped out sinful man in the Flood and said He was sorry He had made him [Genesis 6:7], so perhaps man's reversion to sin once again after the Flood was more greatly responsible than atmospheric conditions or other changed conditions, be they geographical or otherwise, were. Could it be that man's age declension and biological decline are more linked to that? No conclusions here, just food for thought and further exploration.

Modern medicine concedes that the human body houses an ongoing battle between free radicals (an electron is missing) and anti-oxidants (which deny them the swiping of an electron from other cells). The desired homeostasis that promotes the proper balance between chemicals and bodily processes for proper overall functioning declines as we age. As the body ages, it manufactures less of those components that combat free radicals and that slack without some kind of human intervention through drugs (we will avoid the other problems these cause), vitamin and mineral supplementation, whatever, allows anti-oxidants to take over and interfere with all important bodily functions, not the least of which is keeping the arteries clean from plaque and

---

[403] Demerath, Ellen W, "Rising Life Expectancy: A Global History,"<u>Human Biology</u>, February 2003, http://findarticles.com/p/articles/mi_qa3659/is_200302/ai_n9188669/ at p. 1 of 2. [7/21/09.]

inflammation. That delicate balance between matter and anti-matter dissipates with age and anti-matter increasingly wins out.

It has been argued that the distance between the Flood inception (2/17) [Genesis 7:11] and abatement of the waters and the settling of the Ark on Ararat (7/17)[Genesis 8:4] was exactly five months. I am uncertain whether the latter two events describe the Ark settlement on Ararat on 7/17 (the way 8:3 and 8:4 blend together, it is unclear to me whether the abatement and settlement are on the exact same day or whether the abatement itself is marked and on 7/17 [sometime thereafter] the Ark then rested on Ararat, marking yet an additional and different milestone: the language at issue is: "…At the end of a hundred and fifty days the water had abated; {4} and in the seventh month, on the seventeenth day of the month, the ark came to rest upon the mountains of Ararat.").

If the abatement and settlement are on the same day (and that does appear to be the better interpretation to me, to set up the settlement because the waters had abated to that point, because we are already told at Genesis 8:3 earlier in the verse that "and the waters receded from the earth continually"), then the 150 days assigned for the abatement by Genesis 8:3 tell us that the lunar calendar was evenly 30 days per month (obviously not the case now), and places authorship of Genesis <u>before</u> the 5th or 6th Century BCE, the placement often given modernly. <u>This suggests that the geological and topographical make-up of our planet was greatly altered, possibly even changing the earth's tilt (in addition to other possibilities)</u>. Only a grand-scale, global catastrophe could have accomplished such an alteration.[404]

This verification of Scriptural accuracy also makes other biblical postulates more plausible. Genesis states that light <u>pre-existed</u> a natural physical stellar source such as we know it now. On the first day (wherein the earth was nothing but water and void and darkness lay upon the face of the deep), God created the lesser and greater lights (evening and morning, which is what marks the day and each successive one in the six-day Creation scenario) before there was an assignable natural source for them, which did not happen until the fourth day with the creation of the celestial bodies. In fact, that was all

---

[404] Bill Cooper, Ph.D., Th.D., "The Calendar and the Antiquity of Genesis," <u>Acts & Facts</u>, ICR, 6/09, p. 19, esp. endnote 2, quoting Morris, J., 2005. "In the Early Earth, Were All the Months Exactly Thirty Days Long?," <u>Acts & Facts</u>, ICR, 34 (12).

that God did that first day at all. It must be important if that is all that He did for an entire day as an omnipotent God.

Based on this account, the light from the first day was all that could sustain the vegetation of the third until the fourth. If this is considered a stretch, then it must be explained how vegetation could survive for the lengthened time (no matter how long) between the third and fourth days. If alleged consistency between Scripture and modern "science" is to be maintained, there is no other way to go with that. For "old-agers" of the earth who are nonetheless theistic macros favoring a great time expanse, this is a profound challenge. For "young-agers" who believe in literal 24-hour days, it's the Australian "no worries."

Hence, presuming Scripture's face value, the provision of life-sustaining light was ab initio. Indeed, there would be no other reason for it. There were no people to service yet. There were no other physical phenomena requiring its support. Not on the first and second days. Hence, the relationship of light to man may well revolve around one of two realities. Either that same original Supernatural light is what services us now (and that is highly plausible by implication) or that while God causes us in our solar system to be serviced by our sun, He projected and extended its initial light to us Supernaturally since many light-years are involved for the sun's rays to reach the earth. While there are other explanations that have been posited from the Creationist camp (and, of course, without dismissing them), it really could be that simple. Just as man, vegetation and other wildlife were created whole in the beginning, the independent light and the after-created sources for it could have been merged by God, though other questions are presented as discussed below in Chapter 14.

Certainly arguments as to Genesis authenticity can be made revolving around this issue. The independence of the light is introduced Scripturally despite no serious attempts being made to measure the speed of light until the middle 17th Century. There was much debate started by the Greeks as to whether light even had a finite speed or was infinite [going back to at least Empedocles (490-430 BCE) and Aristotle (384-322 BCE)] and most certainly the vast grandeur of space and the universe was not fully appreciated until Hubble's telescope in the 1920s. If indeed Moses was the sole author of Genesis, he is usually placed somewhere between the 16th to 18th centuries BCE.

There is authority for there having been writing capacity even then. If so, it is all the more remarkable for that kind of item to be inserted into the Scriptural account at a time when it is doubtful there would have been any serious conjecture concerning it. Certainly this was well before any serious notion of such an expansive universe arose. Could this qualify as a serious hint to divine revelation? As always, this is food for thought, rather than being definitive.

Consistent with the above, the mammoth size of many of the dinosaurs, especially the sauropods, should be of note to macros in terms of scientific implications. It suggests very long ages that they lived (most reptiles do grow throughout life and constantly replace their teeth),[405] which further suggests that atmospheric differences persisted to allow that, or something else altogether was at work. But regardless, if these behemoths lived longer than their descendants of today, does it not lend credence to the longer lives of early Scriptural man? I have yet to see any work that discusses and compares the actual longevity of these various specimens, at least not comprehensively. Would that not be of great scientific value, or has it been done and the results suppressed because embarrassing to the macros? Perhaps the dinosaurs grew for centuries, lending credence to the registered lives of our biblical ancestors having reached well into the upper 800 to middle 900 years, unfathomable in today's world. I.e., maybe EVERYTHING lived longer back then. This might well have included the flora.

In the animal world, the larger the normal size of species, the longer they live.[406] Longer lives for the larger dinosaurs would therefore be expected, and, as reptiles, in part accounts for some of the extreme sizes, e.g., that the sauropods attained.

But the continuing growth of reptiles accounts for only a part of the story. Almost all species were bigger in prehistoric times, suggesting atmospheric conditions almost had to be involved to account for it, because mammals do not enjoy continuous growth throughout life as do reptiles. While, along with man, they may have lived longer, that by itself would not account for greater growth. While more food was presumably available (with flora also being much larger) and greater

---

405 Robert W. Sussman and Audrey R. Chapman, eds. and contributors, The Origins and Nature of Sociality (2004), p. 24.
406 John R. Speakman, "Body size, energy metabolism and lifespan," The Journal of Experimental Biology 208, 1717-1730 (2005) by, http://jeb.biologists.org/cgi/content/full/208/9/1717, at p. 1 of 32. [8/11/09.]

growth can be accounted for partially because of that, that again cannot rationally be the complete picture.

The hornless rhinoceros-like Indricotherium's head top was held 8.2 m high, was 5.5 m at the shoulder, and weighed about 30 tonnes, over 4 times that of the modern elephant. It lived during the Oligocene/Miocene ages.[407] The giant moa bird of the Late Miocene grew up to 4 m. The steppe mammoth of Eurosia, Mammuthus trogontherii, was over 4.3 m at the shoulder. There was a beaver about 2 m long. The great white shark Carcharadon megalodon of the Miocene grew up to 15 m, and weighed up to 25 tonnes.[408] The giant crocodile Sarcosuchus imperator of Africa and the Cretaceous grew between 12 to 15 m long, and weighed almost 10 tonnes.[409] So both on land and water, animals that were directly related to modern species simply grew much larger. Why so?

---

[407] David Pratt, Human Origins, supra, at pp. 1 & 2 of 32.
[408] Id., at p. 13 of 32.
[409] Id., at p. 11 of 32.

CHAPTER FOURTEEN

THE QUESTION OF STARLIGHT

This chapter considers the starlight issue and treats it separate and distinct from the existence of apparently non-stellar light that was created on the first day of the Genesis account. Since one of the lingering bugaboos for the young earth hypothesis has been the seeing of light from objects millions to billions of light years away from us (disregarding the Genesis account and any way that that may be involved in the light we now observe), let's briefly explore competing theories.

It is, first, important to note that there is a light-time dilemma for the big bang theory as well. Hypothetically, based on faith, "religious" scientific concepts have been devised such as dark matter, dark energy and inflation, e.g., to account for the "horizon problem." Even for big bangers, the universe is too big for light to have traveled that far, despite the incredibly high constant speed for it in a vacuum.[410] There have been theories even among macros for accelerated light-speed in the past, but they have been mostly rejected by traditionalists and Creationists alike. It has also been postulated that light is subject to Riemannian geometric space and thereby travels through that medium very quickly, but that argument is largely rejected by all camps today as well.[411]

It does appear that Creationists have presented potentially viable theories relying upon an expansion of space and a concomitant cosmic mass center and recent time dilation. Therein, there is the appearance of billions of years of activities being condensed into a single day,

---
[410] Edward Kolb & Michael Turner, The Early Universe (1988), Ch. 8, Addison Wesley, ISBN 0-201-11604-9.
[411] Christian answers.net, http://www.Christiananswers.net/q_aig_c005.html, p. 1 of 8. [6/25/09.]

which is argumentatively consistent with Einstein's general relativity principles. General relativity has already shown that time can be distorted by both speed and gravity, so that for the latter phenomenon, the lesser-gravity clocks on the tops of tall buildings have been shown to move slightly faster than the greater-gravity clocks at the bottom.[412] Likewise, matter can be so dense that light rays cannot escape and are bent back, a condition known as the "event horizon," wherein time stands still from the perspective of the distant observer.

Creationist astronomer D[avid]. Russell Humphreys' theory (author of <u>Starlight and Time</u> (Green Forest, AR: Master Books, 1994)) presumes the universe to have an edge and a center, with our galaxy and earth near that center. Secular cosmologists reject this under the concept of the "cosmological universe," wherein it is ASSUMED that all galaxies are surrounded by others and are evenly distributed throughout, so that all gravitational effects cancel out to produce no net effect whatsoever. <u>This fiction is maintained despite the universe actually being lumpy rather than evenly distributed</u>. Even NASA contends that the universe is not old enough for gravity to account for the lumpiness, and leaves it very open as to whether dark matter (now who's speculating?) really is responsible for this condition. Big Bang and lumpiness do not have a currently favorable compatibility factor.[413]

A result of an edgy end to the universe that has a center is that certain phenomena such as quantized (in distinct groups rather than random) galaxy red shifts are readily explained, and suggests that galaxies are arranged in concentric shells about a million light years apart. <u>This fits a finite universe but not the conventional infinite one</u>. If this is right, then the earth was formed in a "white hole" condition (opposite of black hole and both allowable per general relativity) and the universe was expanded outward. Time would have been frozen on earth and yet billions of years could have occurred on the outside for light to reach earth, and stars could have aged in the process. Even under Humphreys' model, the time dilation would not be great enough, but it is a promising beginning.[414]

---

412 Scott R. Anderson,: "Lecture 9: Speed of Light and Relativity," <u>Open Course: Astronomy: Introduction</u>, http://www.opencourse.info/astronomy/introduction/09.light_relativity, at p. 7 of 8.
413 "The Lumpy Universe," Goddard Space Flight Center; http://imagine.gsfc.nasa.gov/docs/science/ mysteries_12/lumpy.html, 2 pages. [9/5/09.]
414 "How can light get to us from stars which are millions of light years away in a universe which the bible claims is only thousands of years old?" <u>Christian Answers.net</u>, http://www.christiananswers.net/q-aig/aig-c005.html, at pp. 3 - 6. [1/30/10.]

Dr. John Hartnett even runs the cosmological football a little further by adding a fifth dimension, the velocity of the expansion of the universe, first conceived by Dr. Moshe Carmeli, but supplemented by Hartnett to encompass a universal center of mass. Instead of Humphreys' gravity accounting for time dilation, the immense stretching of space in a short time does it by establishing a <u>cosmological relativity</u>, consistent with starlight being observable during Creation week.[415]

Neither approach depends upon gadgetry such as the aforementioned expansion, dark matter and dark energy, adopted "articles of faith" which are not of an "admitted" religious nature <u>only</u> because of the <u>contrived</u> confines of how "religion" is conventionally defined, and for no other reason whatsoever. <u>But when the current scientific "agenda" is served, consistency and integrity take a back seat, and no double standard is exaggerated enough to be disqualified. Not when it keeps a "fiction" (in the sense of being assumed before realistically established) alive.</u>

Applied, Humphreys and Hartnett's theories should be taught in the public schools right alongside the big bang, and comparisons made, scientific data to scientific data. The Genesis account and any consistencies thereto need not and must not be mentioned at all. What theory best fits the observable data and possibly (though not necessarily) can make testable predictions is all that counts, and nothing else.

From the Creationist standpoint only (and NOT to be included in the public school curriculum), it is submitted that more study needs to be made to reconcile any cosmological theory with the precedence of light without any related physical source that is so clearly laid out in the Genesis account. Besides being informative, its revelation has to be considered purposeful by God, and due diligence should be devoted to determining why, so that all possible scientific and secular value, as well as religious, can be ascertained.

If ever there are public, televised debates on key scientific issues that naturally bring Scriptural aspects into play, this topic would be one of my MUSTS for inclusion.

---

[415] Ch. 5 "How can we see distant stars in a young universe?," <u>Creation Ministries International</u>, http://creation.com/images/pdfs/cabook/chapter5.pdf, at p. 97 (p. 11 of 12). [1/30/10.]

EPILOGUE

It has hopefully been shown that macro is inherently untenable for at least 9 reasons: (1) It not only cannot identify a First Cause, but it is chemically impossible for itself to be a component of that First Cause; (2) Even if a single-celled organism came into existence in a random way, it is not automatic that a means of self-replication would follow, and that self-replication would be more efficient asexually than sexually; (3) Historically, devolution has occurred among all fauna (and probably flora), including man; (4) The genetic code indicates Intelligent Design, not naturalism; (5) Transmutation is impossible even in a controlled setting (breeding-hybridization), let alone in an uncontrolled state; (6) Natural selection development should be constantly upgrading on a grand scale rather than having stopped; (7) Natural selection should lead to commonality, not a variety of kinds; (8) It cannot credibly explain reason, emotion, creativity, higher communication (writing and speaking), etc., and (9) It does not integrate with the terrestrial, solar system, or universe environment in either an <u>inter</u>-disciplinary or <u>intra</u>-disciplinary way.

Micro-Darwinism and micro-evolution in any other stated form, as opposed to adaptation or variation, all reach the same result through a genetic mechanism, but under different auspices, and so do not have the same meaning. Micro-Darwinism assumes random action and adaptation a pre-programmed process. Unlike the micro position, mutations in reality are produced through loss of genetic information, which, of course, further deprives organisms of the ability for transmutation. The genetic code is an example of pre-programming whose mapping deserves a ticker tape parade reception when used to help combat disease and other deleterious effects. However, how memory, emotion, etc. result remains a mystery.

While bias and other motives themselves do not prove or disprove a doctrine (far be it for me to commit a "genetic fallacy" here), they can sometimes indicate how much its initial proposal was based upon objective, clinical science or, instead, upon convenience, wishful thinking, or even desperation. Other than ascribing the mechanism to natural selection, the concept of evolution was familiar territory and had a very long history, including Darwin's own grandfather, Erasmus. We will assume that Darwin and Wallace were the first to subject it to thorough field studies, regardless of whether the purpose was to initially go in that direction or not. The Industrial Revolution was fully underway, creating new means of wealth (in addition to direct landholding) via mass production and mass transportation, and embracing capitalism on a scale hitherto unpracticed. An escape from ecclesiastical dogmatism was rightly being sought. In sum, a change in powerbrokers was desperately being targeted, which, as our Founding Fathers would have observed, became abused. Man's greed to control through pressure groups supported by misplaced wealth took over in a way in which Madison's Federalist no. 10 best intentions for checks and balances could not prevent.

Between Darwin and Wallace, although it is fair to say that Darwin had been working on his theory for far longer than Wallace and thereby at least arguably was better grounded with it, he was also by far the better socially connected, coming from a well-to-do background that was only enhanced by his marriage to Emma Wedgwood, whose grandfather Josiah was an established capitalist who had made his fortune in pottery and its mass distribution. Between these two sources of income, Darwin did not have to be concerned with issues of lack of funding or basic survival. On the other hand, Wallace came from modest means (even though his father started off as a lawyer, it didn't play out well) and would struggle to financially make ends meet for much of his life.

Darwin also was ill and for practical purposes incapacitated for many years prior to his publication of Origin (this statement is not without controversy and is to some extent even doubted by this author, but let's assume it, and he regardless had some physical problems that made him a less than formidable speaker). This made him a rallying point for proponents such as his bulldog, Thomas Huxley. While labeling him a martyr would be a stretch, he could be used somewhat in that direction, and he also had the advantage of avoiding the rigors of direct, on-the-spot debate, which was left in Huxley's capable hands. He could rely on reflection rather than spontaneity, which can be a great advantage in marshaling thoughts in response to macro challenges.

Arguably, the better grounding would not by itself be enough to prefer Darwin over Wallace (although on practical grounds, that could have been how it played out anyway). For that purpose, Darwin could have remained in the background as a consultant. But it is worthy of consideration that Wallace was more dangerous to the economic and political scene than was Darwin. His socialist leanings and social commentary would have made him a liability. He also differed enough theoretically from Darwin to be dangerous to the sanctity of the overall macro doctrine. His view of natural selection itself was more as a descriptive end result rather than the creative force that Darwin espoused. He was critical of sexual selection and of natural selection's inability to explain higher functioning and emotions. He later insisted that there had to be some form of divine intervention (most probably in a Deistic sense) for the First Cause and the higher functions and emotions. The bottom line is that Wallace's approach had to entail some form of an agency behind the overall process, which for him had to invoke supernatural implications. Conceding any form of the supernatural is intolerable to a Darwin-oriented macro.

Further, Darwin had reason to know his theory was weak foundationally. He knew that devolution was an historical truth from the rodent, armadillo and sloth fossils he himself unearthed along his Beagle journeys. He knew that the fossil record to that point did not support the transitional changes that were to be expected under his theory. He also knew that as a breeder of pigeons, crossbreeding could enhance, but could not change, the character of a fauna. It remained the same "kind" of fauna as before. He also knew that his theory did not fit in with the necessary First Cause. While a genuine contribution could have been made by scientifically demonstrating the fall of the Cuvier and Agassiz postulate that kinds were immutable even in terms of variation, Darwin tried to leap the unbridgeable chasm by unjustifiably extending his theory to transmutation. Further, despite his being a former seminary student, the behavior that repulsed him was not even considered in the context of the Genesis fall of man and the doctrine of redemption. How much he would want to get into that debate in the presentation of his theory is itself debatable (though undoubtedly some attention would have to be publicly given it), but how much he needed to consider that before factoring in the offensive behavior is very important. There is no indication that he wrestled with that whatsoever, or that he gave it the honest critical analysis that his background seemingly dictated. A thorough evaluation would have forced him to temper his theory considerably.

In this regard, it is submitted that his correspondences to people such as Hooker, and his public correspondences to newspapers such as the Athenaeum, expose him as not even an agnostic, but actually an atheist. Likewise, the Religious Belief section of his autobiography is disingenuous in stating that he could properly be called a Theist (a misnomer. He would have meant a Deist), and that he entertained such notions while writing Origin of Species. His actions speak otherwise. The fate of this argument has no bearing on the main thesis I have presented herein, but nonetheless it is, in my view, a further extension of Darwin's intellectual dishonesty.

What I find so totally dishonest about Darwin is that he knew the chasm he was leaping from variation to transmutation, and also that diminution (devolution) existed in higher life forms, not just worm-like lower ones. Yet, he projected development toward still more perfect life forms, all basically reactionary to inter- and intra- population struggles between both fauna and flora. It is difficult to conceive how anyone can be privy to refinement such as photosynthesis and yet totally reject the possibility that some directive template must have been inculcated by an intelligence other and immeasurably higher than our own. Included in this calculus would be symbiotic relationships such as the bee cross-pollination scheme, which is seemingly preposterous without a design going far beyond the conscious contemplation of its participants. Even Darwin's awareness of Archaeopteryx should have been tempered with his awareness of other mosaics, such as the gnu and duck-billed platypus. This is the conceptual end that I do not believe Darwin on, even parsed from any considerations of good vs. evil and other teleological considerations.

My final point in considering Darwin's unscientific approach is that it has been argued by Creationists and other anti-evolutionists that if Darwin had been aware of the sophisticated DNA/RNA replication and messaging systems that even the simplest cell enjoys (as opposed to the belief in his time that the cell was essentially an amorphous blob), he probably would have acknowledged at least ID. I do not agree with this assessment. His explanation of altruism, paternal and maternal love, emotion generally, and sexual selection are such that he would doubtless have broken down this entire elaboration as fixed responses of natural selection for the good of the cell. No matter how sophisticated a natural system gets, it would, according to Darwin, be subject to the inexorable law of natural selection or variances of mutation. Because both initially and ultimately, Darwin did not defy the Establishment at all, he went with the surmounting crowd that was creating a new one. As already argued, this is consistent with the reality that he was neither a trailblazer nor a leader but rather, a subservient follower who superficially filled in a gap that scientists, educators, and the liberal clergy were salivating over, and were all too willing to fill while sacrificing empirical science and logic in order to do so.

His own adherents such as Huxley struggled even with the concept of natural selection. Huxley never came to accept it as the driving force during his lifetime. While Darwin himself always said that it was not a full explanation, the theory's initial impetus had little to do with established, objective, clinical science. Huxley and others even admitted how eager they were there to embrace an alternative and blindly accept it on faith. This, of course, is not science at all, and becomes a religion based on faith and dogmatism. Their thinking was that the supernatural must be eliminated at all costs, even though their own doctrine fails to account for much of what we observe in nature.

As has been shown, radioisotope testing is very unreliable, with factors influencing the measurements being largely disregarded, different radioisotope combination tests yielding dramatically different results ignored, and where tests with samples of known age yielding wildly discordant findings are irresponsibly discarded. There is no such thing as a complete stratigraphic column, and the excuses for their lack are highly suspect and reflective of wishful thinking rather than hard, clinical analysis. There is compelling evidence that the radioactive decay rate was accelerated by events of the past, and that the earth may be appreciably younger than currently represented, perhaps as little as 50,000 years or even less. If true, then macro is exposed as a mathematical impossibility and Haldane's Dilemma (among other obstacles) takes center stage. All macro is based on extended time periods of at least millions or billions of years. One suspects that the young age proofs are deliberately suppressed by the NCSE, AIBS and NAS. There is also the general macro deception of misrepresenting the genetic similarity between ape (chimpanzee) and human DNA sequencing, both in terms of percentage and the probative factors involved for comparison.

This also identifies the movement as an agenda rather than a doctrine, and that perpetuates today through our public education system, whose controlling forces are there to shield evolution from all just criticism. In fact, the NCSE was created to combat the "dangerous" influence of Creationism. Seeds of bias and prejudice are evident everywhere. Here the slope gets very slippery, however, because its desire to dominate the education system (whose functioning falls under state action) with a single theme and way of thinking devoid of a consideration of all of the facts, is at odds with the visions of our Founding Fathers (even if it did not fall under state action, which nevertheless it does). Outright fraud is committed in the allowance of Haeckel's woodcarvings and drawings in public school textbooks and of Java Man still being represented as a viable missing link fossil. It seems more than coincidental that "discoverer" DuBois of Java Man (Homo erectus) fame was also a former student of Haeckel's. There is the continuing tendency to allow known tainted evidence to persist as if unchallenged until some other symbolic discovery is available to take its place. Yet these dishonest tactics continue to be rewarded with inclusion in prestigious journals and textbooks.

The legal implications are two-fold. First, the burdens of proof and presenting evidence as to the soundness of its position are placed upon the macros. Second, because of the intent of the First Amendment, the evidence for the First Cause, as well as for the maintenance of our natural order, must be fully exposited and weighed before any conclusions as to the cause and maintenance of our existence and natural order can be made, forcing Intelligent Design information to also be taught in the form of counterpoint to evolutionary principles. When legislative (Constitutional) intent is factored in to explain the meaning of separation of church and state and the free discourse of ideas, it is clear that the deprivation of information pertaining to ID and other scientific challenges to macro is Unconstitutional.

What is at stake on a broader scale is the issue of tyranny vs. freedom. Jefferson and Madison both made it clear that freedom entailed the right and ability not just of the student, but of the general public, to be forming their opinions on any subject under conditions of the dissemination of all relevant information, not just that specially chosen by any interested group, regardless of the leaning of that interest. As Hamilton pointed out (and wherein Jefferson and Madison concur), this is as true of the correct (right) side of an issue (and often that lies in the eyes of the beholder) as it is of the wrong. Aguillard (despite its severe limitations) made it clear that origins issues can be discussed in a public school setting under the infusion of different theories so long as the purpose remains secular and not religious. While the respective curriculum will probably be up to the respective school boards (with hopefully firm federal guidance), it would seem that issues such as the chemical impossibility of life starting in the micro-world apart from a closed system, Haldane's Dilemma, and the fine-tuning and other points raised in books such as Privileged Planet, would alone justify a scientific curriculum whose scope by itself encompasses an impressive panoply of disciplines. Add to that young earth and old earth arguments, and these would comprise a quite impressive scientific package.

The macro mentality is exactly the same as the alleged blind religious zealots they so vigorously attack, and every bit as religious in character, except that they substitute blind faith in unproven assumptions for reasonably foundationed faith that has substantial empirical backing. Applying Hamilton's admonition, they can be as biased, prejudiced, and ill-motived as the alleged wrong. With the stranglehold that the AIBS and NCSE appear to have on the state educational scene, it is paramount that the federal government come forward to regulate the public schools and establish textbook and teaching parameters that are unbiased and recite a full disclosure of all relevant facts for all scientific issues that will inevitably emerge. We cannot and should not tell students what to think, but we most certainly must be vanguards in giving them the appropriate educational armamentarium so that they can make fully informed decisions on their own.

This is why the proposed pedagogy I advance is, I feel, an appropriate one. It is fact vs. fact, the only proper means for comparison. Besides removing any emphases on bias and prejudice that individual <u>factions</u> all to varying extents operate under (again satisfying Hamilton, as well as Madison and Jefferson), it encourages the constant comparison of new findings, and of holding them up to the light of day in the court of public opinion. Macros have operated under the assumption (falsely, I assert, which you are familiar with by now) that their worldview is the proper one, and violate logical fallacy after logical fallacy in force-feeding interpretations based on either insufficient, tainted or outright false information, and that well-known multiple choice alternative, "all of the above."

In law, part of this falls under the objection of "assuming facts not in evidence." Vanquished is the <u>delay</u> (despite the AIBS's misleading pronouncement that science must allow for rejection of the old and insertion of the new, a superficially admirable posture that the macros in fact almost never practice) in abandoning one position that is known to be outmoded until there is enough alleged data to abandon it (with even that decision being made by biased and prejudiced factions). Instead, all propositions are subject to constant re-evaluation in the light of more current information, the accuracy and appropriateness of which a fully informed public is well equipped through total disclosure to decide, effectively diluting the over-influence and improper dominance it was Madison's steadfast mission to counter-balance. And as I have also tried to say throughout, a verdict of "inconclusive" can be as appropriate as a "yes" or "no."

Midgley rightly assails the abuses of Social Darwinism, but under the guise of misuse and abuse of science. She makes the mistake of regarding macro as a science rather than the unproven (and it is submitted here, disproven) religious philosophy that it actually is. Like Hamilton, Jefferson and Madison, she recognizes the foibles of all of those in power, and that checks must be imposed upon them. Of all of the Founding Fathers' contributions to our national fabric, checks and balances (reasonably applied so as to avoid stagnation and lack of responsiveness to the public need and will) may be the grandest of them all.

The Creation v. macro controversy has been shrouded in deception through censorship and through both the perpetuation of and new outright lies as to the status of scientific evidence on these subjects. Like a jury in a court case, the reader can infer from this what he will. But one thing has hopefully been conclusively shown. There is a compelling and growing body of evidence from a growing legion of highly credentialed and credible scientists that disputes and places into doubt macro's basic tenets. Ivanov's deadly experiments show how far macro is willing to go to establish its atheistic foothold (and suppress failure when the desired results are not obtained), as well, of course, as the practices of the AIBS, NCSE and NAS. And, as we have seen with the showing of <u>Privileged Planet</u> and the suppression of fossil findings re the antiquity and physical size of our ancestors, the venerable Smithsonian Institute itself.

But the underlying and seminal issue is not adoption of either philosophical point of view but rather, as Jefferson would put it, how we get there (the "uprightness" of it all). Is it after careful consideration of all relevant, unfiltered observed facts, or is it through a manipulated setting that not only practices censorship (bad enough), but also outright fraudulent misrepresentation of fact? In sum, what is at stake is the exercise of liberty toward the ascertainment of truth, and the Founding Fathers and leading succeeding political figures like Lincoln, FDR, Truman and JFK have shown us that both of these elements sail in the same ship, so that one without the other is an ultimate recipe for subjugation and disaster. Who decides the issue is at the very heart of the controversy, and that by itself serves an enormous SECULAR purpose. Is it the political and educational establishment, or is it the general public that our government is supposed to serve (and who we are historically told is the <u>only</u> body government is supposed to serve)?

From this writer's perch, macro is a fraud, and a like argument can be made for Darwinian application of natural selection (with Wallace's observation being the superior to Darwin's) for even micro activity that is too often conceded under the rubric of adaptation or variation, but that must be ultimately determined by public opinion (if at all) based on the presentation and analysis of material fact. This is why the public school system must present the facts and let the students and other receivers of those facts decide for themselves, that component being the very essence of a free society. Totalitarian and dictatorial systems suppress information, not free societies. Let the people decide, which is what our most treasured Constitutional precepts are designed to promote. Our Founding Fathers had an acute sensitivity to previous regimes (particularly European) whose political and social structures and practices led to tyranny, not just of mind (tragic in and of itself), but also of body. It was their profound desire to see to it that that same destiny did not occur here in this country. Let us act now, before all of the blood, sweat and tears resulting from the ascertaining and application of these principles, is reduced to futility.

Ultimately, this power struggle is symptomatic of a societal disease--the elimination of truth and information to the people. Why did Jefferson say if push came to shove and one entity had to go and the other had to stay, that he would disband government altogether and preserve a free press? The answer is straightforward--for the promotion of truth through the dissemination of ideas. If it is argued that we no longer have a free press, then that too must be corrected. Only an honestly informed public capable of making government accountable for its actions can preserve its freedom. This applies to ALL government levels, whether local, state or federal. All government overreach must be nipped at the bud.

We as a current partially free society must reacquire our full freedom to the extent practicable with reality. We must insist that our school boards present an unbiased approach to science and insist on federal legislation establishing minimum guidelines for state compliance, so that students get the whole truth and nothing but that. There is an acute need for federal leadership, much the same way we needed a stronger central government under principles of federalism that necessitated dispensing with the Articles of Confederation in favor of the U.S. Constitution. Content must not be filled with doctrinal comments, but scientific data and observation only, targeted for allowance of an informed decision.

The macros' current stranglehold on the education system is unsustainable without contradicting and forfeiting this nation's heritage. There has been much talk in this day and age from concerned citizens who feel that our true democratic republic form of government, as Constitutionally intended, is being threatened, or has already been near mortally wounded, and insist on taking our country back. One would be hard-pressed to find a better area in which to start that mission than to peacefully, systematically, and yet assertively, set our education system in order. Knowledge, as precious as that is, is not the only thing at stake. So is freedom and liberty. Too much blood has already been shed to shrink from that responsibility now. My fellow Americans, the ball is now in our court. It is quite conceivable that the future fate of our nation depends on how we handle that ball in controlling educational content, an issue that far transcends that of Creationism or ID vs. evolution. It is, indeed, a power struggle that the American people must now and <u>always</u> win in order to maintain our democratic republic. If we lose this battle and future ones of similar ilk (provided we are in a position to have future battles of similar ilk rather than having already lost the war), we also lose ourselves, which is perhaps the most frightening prospect of all.

BIBLIOGRAPHY

Addicott, Warron O., Chinzei, Kuyotaha and Stanley, Steven M. (1980) "Lyellian Curves in Paleontology: Possibilities and Limitations." *Geology*, Vol. 8.

Adee, Daniel. *Newton's Prinicipia: The Mathematical Principles of Natural Philosophy*. New York.

Alberts, Bruce and Watson, James. *Molecular Biology of the Cell*. Aldrich, L.T. (1956) "Measurement of Radioactive Ages of Rocks." Science, May 18.

Anderson, G. and Keith, M. (1963) "Radiocarbon Dating: Fictitious Results with Mollusk Shells." *Science*.

Anderson, Scott R. "Lecture 9: Speed of Light and Relativity." *Open Course: Astronomy: Introduction*.

Aristotle (350 B.C.E.) *Metaphysics*.

Austin, Steven (2005) "Discordant Radioisotope Dates." Ch. 7. *Thousands, Not Billions: Challenging an Icon of Evolution, Questioning the Age of the Earth*. ICR.

Austin, Steven (2009) "Darwin's First Wrong Turn." *Acts & Facts*, ICR, February.

Behe, Michael J. (1996) *Darwin's Black Box*. Free Press.

Behe, Michael J. (2007) *The Edge of Evolution: ?The Search for the Limits of Darwinism*. Free Press.

Bell, Charles (1811) *Idea of a New Anatomy of the Brain*. Bellamy, Edward. *Looking Backward*.

Bent, Devin. "Epilogue: James Madison and the Separation of Church and State." http://www.ungardesign.com/websites/madison/ main_pages/Madison_archives/constitu_confe..., at p. 1 of 3. [6/13/ 09.]

Bernstein, Ralph E. (1984) "Darwin's illness: Chagas' disease resurgens." JR Soc.Med. July:77(7).

Berthault, Guy. "Geological Time Scale Questioned."

Bettleheim, Frederick A., Campbell, William H. and Farrell, Shawn O. (2009) *Introduction to General, Organic and Biochemistry*. Brooks/ Cole CENGAGE Learning, Belmont, CA.

Bibby, Cyril (1959) *Scientist Extraordinary: the life and work of Thomas Henry Huxley 1825-1895*.

Birch, L.C. and Ehrlich, Paul R. (1967) "Evolutionary History and Population Biology." *Nature*, Vol. 214 (April 12).

Bohlin, Ray. "The Privileged Planet: An Unwanted Premiere!" Bohr, Niels (1934) *Atomic Theory and the Description of Nature*. Bowler, Peter J. and Morus, Iwas Rhys (2005) *Making Modern Science*. The University of Chicago Press.

Boxhorn, Joseph. "FAQ. Observed Instances of Speciation" Boyle, Robert. "The Sceptical Chymist."

Boyle, Robert (1660) *Seraphic Love*.

Boyle, Robert (1681) *A Discourse of Things Above Reason*.

Brass, Michael (2002) *The Antiquity of Man: Artifactual, Fossil and Gene Records Explored*. PublishAmerica.

Brody, David (2002) "Ernst Haeckel and the Microbial Baroque." Cabinet Magazine, Issue 7 Summer.

Brown, R.H. (1992) "Correlation of C-14 Age with Real Time." *Creation Research Quarterly*, 29.

Browne, Janet E. (2002) *Charles Darwin: vol. 2, The Power of Place.* London: Jonathan Cape.

Chain, Ernst (1970) *Social Responsibility and the Scientist in Modern Western Society.*

Chapman, Audrey R. and Sussman, Robert W. (eds. and contributors) (2004) *The Origins and Nature of Sociality.*

Chatterjee, Sankar (1997) *The Rise of Birds: 225 Million Years of Evolution.* The Johns Hopkins University Press, Baltimore.

Clark, R.W. (1985) *The Life of Ernst Chain: Penicillin and Beyond.* New York: St. Martin's Press.

Clark, W.E. LeGros (1966) *History of the primates: An introduction to the study of fossil man.* Fifth ed. University of Chicago Press.

Cohen, I.L. "Darwin Was Wrong—A Study in Probabilities." *New Research Publications, Inc.*

Colling, Richard G. Random Designer: *Created from Chaos to Connect with Creator.*

Collins, Francis. *Coming to Peace with Science.*

Cooper, Bill (2009) "The Calendar and the Antiquity of Genesis." *Acts & Facts,* ICR, June.

Corliss, William R. (comp.) (1994) *Biological Anomalies: Humans III.* Glen Arm, MD: Sourcebook Project.

Covey, Jon. "The Rise of Birds." Ed. Anita K. Millen, *South Bay Creation Science Association.*

Cremo, Michael A. (1998) *Forbidden Archaeology's Impact.* Los Angeles, CA: Bhahtiveda Book Publishing.

Cremo, Michael A. (2003) *Human Devolution: A Vedic alternative to Darwin's theory.* Los Angeles, CA: Bhaktivedanta Book Publishing.

Cremo, Michael A. and Thompson, Richard L. (1993) *Forbidden Archaeology: The Hidden History of the Human Race.*

Curtis, R. (1993) *Great Lives: Medicine.* New York: Scribner. Dao, Christine (2008) "Man of Science, Man of God: Johann Kepler." *Acts & Facts*, ICR, March1.

Dao, Christine (2008) "Man of Science, Man of God: Robert Boyle." *Acts & Facts*, ICR, April.

Dao, Christine (2008) "Man of Science, Man of God: Isaac Newton." *Acts & Facts*, ICR, May.

Dao, Christine (2008) "Man of Science, Man of God: William Kirby." *Acts & Facts*, ICR, July.

Dao, Christine (2008) "Man of Science, Man of God: George Washington Carver." *Acts & Facts*, ICR, December.

Darwin, Charles (1859) *On the Origin of Species By Means of Natural Selection, or the Preservation of Favoured Races in the Struggle for Life.*

Darwin, Charles (1862) "On the Various Contrivances by Which British and Foreign Orchids are Fertilised by Insects."

Darwin, Charles (1871) *The Descent of Man and Selection in Relation to Sex.*

Darwin, Charles and Carroll, Joseph (2003) *On the Origin of Species by Means of Natural Selection.* Joseph Carroll ed. Broadway Press Ltd., Canada.

Darwin, Francis, ed. (1958) *The Autobiography of Charles Darwin 1809-1882*

Darwin, Erasmus. *Zoonomia.*

Davis, Percival and Kenyon, Dean (1993) *Of Pandas and People: The Central Question of Biological Origins.* Foundation for Thought & Ethics, 2d ed.

Dawkins, Richard. *The Selfish Gene.*

Demereth, Ellen W. (2003) "Rising Life Expectancy: A Global History." *Human Biology*, February.

Denton, Michael. *Evolution: A Theory in Crisis.*

Desmond, Adrian and Moore, James (1991) *Darwin.* London: Michael Joseph, Penguin Group.

DeYoung, Don (ed.) (2005) *Thousands, Not Billions: Challenging an Icon of Evolution, Questioning the Age of the Earth.* ICR.

Dolan, Brian. *Wedgwood: The First Tycoon.* Viking/Adult.

Dort, W. (1971) "Mummified Seals of Southern Victoria Land." *Antarctic Journal of the U.S.*, June.

Duck, Mark. "Evolution and the Second Law of Thermodynamics—Detecting Truth." http://www.detectingtruth.com/?p=19. [7/29/09.]

Dudley, H.C. (1975) "Radioactivity Re-Examined." *Chemical and Engineering News*, April 7.

Edwards, Frank (1959) *Stranger than Science.* New York: Lyle Stewart.

Eisenhaler, Frank and Schleiffer, Alexander. "Gregor Mendel, The Beginning of Biomathematics." *IMP Bioinformatics Group.*

Eldridge, Niles (1985) *Time Frames.*

Etkind, A. (2008) "Beyond Eugenics: The Forgotten Scandal of Hybridizing Humans and Apes." *Studies in History and Philosophy of Biological Sciences.* 39(2).

Faul, Henry (1954) *Nuclear Geology.*

Federer, W.J. (1994) *America's God and Country Encyclopedia of Quotations.* Coppell, TX: FAME Publishing.

Fetzer, James H. (2007) "Reclaiming History: A Closed Mind Perpetrating a Fraud on the Public." *Assassination Research*, Vol. 5 No.1 June.

Fleet, Elizabeth (ed.) (1946) *Madison Detached Memoranda. William & Mary Quarterly.*

Flew, Sir Antony (1950) *Theology and Falsification.*

Flew, Sir Antony (1961) "Miracles and Methodology." *Hume's Philosophy of Belief: A Study of His First Inquiry*. London: Routledge and Kegan Paul.

Flew, Sir Antony (1966) "The Credentials of Revelation: Miracle and History." *God and Philosophy*. New York, Dell.

Flew, Sir Antony (1967) "Miracles." *Encyclopedia of Philosophy*. Ed. Paul Edwards. New York, Macmillan.

Flew, Sir Antony (1984) *Darwinian Evolution*. A second edition was published in 1997 by Piscataway, NJ: Transaction.

Flew, Sir Antony (1985) "The Impossibility of the Miraculous." Hume's Philosophy of Religion. Winston-Salem N.C.: Wake Forest University Press.

Flew, Sir Antony (1985) Introduction to *Of Miracles* by David Hume. La Salle, IL: Open Court.

Flew, Sir Antony (1997) "Neo-Humean Arguments About the Miraculous." *In Defence of Miracles: A Comprehensive Case for God's Action in History*. Ed. R. Douglas Geivett and Gary R. Habermas. Downer's Grove, IL: Inter Varsity Press.

Flew, Sir Antony and Varghese, Ray Abraham (2007) *There Is a God: How the World's Most Notorious Atheist Changed His Mind*. Harper One.

Floyd, Chris. "Science & Spirit, Eyes Wide Open: An Interview with Owen Gingerich." http://www.science-spirit.org/article- detail.php?article_id=144, at pp. 1&2 of 5. [7/27/09.]

Foard, James M. (1996) *The Nebulous Hypothesis: A Study of the Social and Historical Implications of Darwinian Theory*.

Gaustad, Edwin S, (ed.) (1982) *A Documentary History of Religion in America*, Vol. I (To the Civil War). Grand Rapids: William B. Eerdsman Publishing Company.

Gilroy, Rex (1976) "And There Were Giants." *Psychic Australian*, October.

Gilroy, Rex (1999) "Giants of the Dreamtime." *Australasian Ufologist Magazine*, Vol. 3, No. 3, 3rd Quarter.

Gingerich, Owen. *The Book Nobody Read: Chasing the Revolution of Nicolas Copernicus.*

Gonzalez, Guillermo and Richards, J.W. (2004) *The Privileged Planet: How Our Place in the Cosmos is Designed for Discovery.* Washington, D.C., Regnery Publishing, Inc.

Gould, Stephen Jay (1977) *Ontogeny & Phylogeny.* Cambridge: Belknap Press.

Gould, Stephen Jay (1991) *Bully for Brontosaurus.* London: Penguin.

Gould, Stephen Jay (2000) "This View of Life." *Natural History*, March.

Gray, Asa. "Natural Selection is not Inconsistent with Natural Theology."

Gregory, W.K. (1927) "Hesperopithecus apparently not an ape nor a man." Science 66.

Gunst, R.H. and McDonald, K.L. (1965) "An Analysis of the Earth's Magnetic Field from 1835 to 1965." *ESSA Technical Report IER 46-IES.* U.S. Government Printing Office, Washington, D.C.

Habermas, Gary R., (ed.) (2005), "My Pilgrimage from Atheism to Theism." Interview. *Philosophia Christi, the Journal of the Evangelical Philosophical Society.*

Hamilton, Alexander. *Federalist No. 1* ("Defects of the Articles of Confederation.")

Heller, Mikhail (1998) *Cogs in the Soviet Wheel: The Formation of Soviet Man.* Translated into English by David Floyd London.

Helmenstine, Anne Marie. "Scientific Hypothesis, Theory, Law Definitions: Learn the Language of Science." http://chemistry.about.com/od/chemistry100/a/lawtheory.htm, at p. 1 of 2. [9/13/09.]

Hitching, Francis (1982) *The Neck of the Giraffe—Where Darwin Went Wrong.* New York: Tickner and Fields.

House, H. Wayne (ed.) (2008) *Intelligent Design 101: Leading Experts Explain the Key Issues.* Kregel Publications.

Humphreys, D. Russell (1994) *Starlight and Time.* Green Forest, AR: Master Books.

Hunt, Kathleen. "Horse Evolution." TalkOrigins.com Hunter, George (1914) *Civic Biology.*

Hutcheon, Pat Duffy (1997) "What Lucretius Wrought." *Humanist in Canada* (Winter 1997/98).

Huxley, Aldous (1966) "Confessions of a Professed Atheist: Aldous Huxley." *Report* (June).

Huxley, Leonard (1900) *The Life and Letters of Thomas Henry Huxley.* 2 vols.

Huxley, Thomas Henry (1896 ed.) *Discourses: Biological and Geological.*

Jackson, Nick (2008) "Against the Grain: There are Questions that Science Cannot Answer." *The Independent*, January 3.

Jensen, J.A. and Padian, K. (1989) "Small pterosaurs and dinosaurs from the Uncompahgre fauna." *Jornal of Paleontology*, 63:372.

Johnson, Phillip E. and Lamoureux, Denis (1999) *Darwinism Defeated? The Johnson-Lamoureux Debate on Biological Origins.* Regent College.

Keith, Arthur (1925) *The Antiquity of Man.* London: Williams and Norgate.

Kepler, Johann (1619) "Harmonies of the World." Kepler, Johann (1619) "Proem."

Kerkut, G.A. (1960) *Implications of Evolution.* New York: Pergamon Press.

Kinkaid, Cliff (2004) "Former Atheist Says God Exists." *Insight on the News.*

Kirby, William and Spence, William (1815-1826) *An Introduction to Entomology: or Elements of the Natural History of Insects.*

Kirby, William (1835) *On the Power, Wisdom and Goodness of God. As Manifested in the Creation of Animals and in Their History, Habits and Instincts.* Bridgewater Treatises.

Kirshenbaum, Sheril and Mooney, Kris. *Unscientific America: How Science Illiteracy Threatens Our Future.*

Kirshenbuam, Sheril and Mooney, Kris (2009) "Defenders of the Faith: Scientists who blast religion are hurting their Own cause." Newsweek.

Kolb, Edward and Turner, Michael (1988) *The Early Universe.* Addison Wesley.

Kollatz, Harry Jr. (2003) "The Huguenots-They fled their homes for religious freedom." *Richmond Magazine*, April.

Laboissiere, Michael C. *Nizkor Project.*

Laing, S. (1893) *Problems of the Future.* London, Chapman and Hall.

Laing, S. (1894) *Human Origins.* London, Chapman and Hall. Lamarck, Jean Baptiste de (1809) *Zoological Philosophical Work.* Lambert, Frank L. "The Second Law of Thermodynamics and Evolution." http://www.2ndlaw.com/evolution.html. [7/29/09.]

Larson, Edward (2004) *Evolution: The Remarkable History of Scientific Theory.* Modern Library.

Lax, Eric (2004) *The Mold in Dr. Florey's Coat: the story of the penicillin miracle.* Henry Holt and Company, LLC.

Leff, David. "What were some of his physical attributes?" *AboutDarwin. com: Dedicated to the Life and Times of Charles Darwin* (started on 2/12/00). http:www. Aboutdarwin.com/Darwin/ WhoWas. html, at p. 2 of 13. [9/24/09.]

Lewin, Roger (1987) *Bones of Contention: Controversies in the Search for Human Origins.*

Lewin, Roger (1999) *Human evolution: an illustrated introduction.* Blackwell Publishing Ltd.

Linnaeus, Carl (Carolus) (1735) *Systema Naturae.*

Lucas, J.R. "Wilberforce & Huxley: A Legendary Encounter." http://users.ox.oc.uk/jrlucas/legend.html. [1/30/10.] Lyell, Charles (1830) *Principles of Geology.*

Macalister, R.A.S. (1921) *Textbook of European Archaeology.*

Madison, James (1785) "Memorial and Remonstrance Against Religious Assessments."

Malthus, Thomas (1798) "Essay on the Principle of Population"

Maranto & Brownlee (1984) "Why Sex?" *Discover*, Vol. 5, No. 2 (Feb.).

McCombs, Charles (2009) "Chemistry by Chance: A Formula for Non-Life." *Acts & Facts*, ICR, Vol.38, No. 2, February.

McMurray, E. (1995) *Notable Twentieth-Century Scientists.* Detroit, MI: Gale Research, Inc.

Mendel, Gregor (1866) *Experiments on Plant Hybridization. Proceedings of the Natural History Society of Brunn.*

Midgley, Mary (1979) "Gene Juggling," *Philosophy*, Vol. 4. Midgley, Mary (1985) *Evolution as a Religion: Strange Hopes and* Stranger Fears

Midgley, Mary (1992) *Science as Salvation.*

Midgley, Mary (2002) Introduction to reprint of *Evolution as a Religion: Strange Hopes and Stranger Fears*

Miles, Sarah Joan (2001) "Charles Darwin and Asa Gray Discuss Teleology and Design." *Perspectives on Science and Christian Faith*, 53.

Miller, Merle (1974) *Plain Speaking: An Oral Biography of Harry S. Truman.*

Milton, Richard (1997) *Shattering the Myths of Darwinism.* Park Street Press.

Milton, Richard (2001) Critique of Brass's *Antiquity of Man.* Milton, Richard (2002) Reply to Brass's Milton critique.

Moore, John and Slusher, Harold S., ed. (1970) *Biology: A Search for Order in Complexity.* Zondervan Publishing House, Grand Rapids, Michigan.

Morris, John (2005) "In the Early Earth, Were All the Months Exactly Thirty Days Long? *Acts & Facts*, ICR, 34.

Morris, Simon Conway. *Life's Solution: Inevitable Humans in a Lonely Universe.*

Newport, Frank. http://www/gallup/poll/114544/darwin-birthday-believe-Evolution.aspex, at p. 1 of 6.

Newton, Isaac (1825) *General Scolium.* Translated by Motte, A. Nietzsche, Friedrich Wilhelm (1887) *On the Genealogy of Morals, a Polemical Tract.*

Orrego, Fernando and Quintana, Carlos (2006) "Darwin's illness: a final diagnosis." *The Royal Society-Notes & Records.*

Owen, Richard. Fossil Mammalis Part 1, The zoology of the Voyage of the H.M.S. Beagle. Ed. C.R. Darwin. London: Smith, Elder and Co.

Paulos, John Allen (1989) *Innumeracy: Mathematical Illiteracy and its Consequences.* Wang Hill.

Paulos, John Allen (2006) "What's Wrong with Creationist Probability?" ABC News.

Paulos, John Allen (2008) *A Mathematician Explains why the Arguments for God Just Don't Add Up* . Wang Hill.

Pennisi, E. (1997) "Haeckel's embryo: fraud rediscovered." *Science.* Peth, Howard (1990) *Blind Faith: Evolution Exposed.*

Pittack, Richard B. (2007) *The Archaeopteryx Controversy.* Walden Computer Services.

Poling, Jeff. "Geologic Ages of the Earth." http://www.dinosauria.com/dml/history/htm, pp. 1-4. [7/2/09.]

Pratt, David. "Exploring Theosophy: The Synthesis of Science, Religion and Philosophy." http://davidpratt/info.

Quigley, Ian (2002) "Haeckel's Law of Recapitulation." *Animal Sciences.*

Ragazzoni, Giuseppe (1880) "La collina di Castenedolo, soltoil rapporto antropologico, geologico ed agronomico." *Commentari dell'Ateneo di Brescia,* April, 4.

Remine, Walter J. (1993) *The Biotic Message: Evolution versus message therapy.* Saint Paul, MN: St. Paul Science.

Richards, M. (2008) "Artificial Insemination and Eugenics: Celibate Motherhood, Eutelegenesis and Germinal Choice." *Studies in History and Philosophy of Biological and Biomedical Sciences.* 39(2).

Richardson, M.K. (1998) *Haeckel, Embryos, and Evolution. Science* 280:983-985.

Rossiianov, Kirill (2002) "Beyond Species: Ilya Ivanov and His Experiments on Cross-Breeding Humans with Anthropoid Apes." *Science in Context.*

Roughgarden, Joan (born Jonathan Roughgarden) (2006) *Evolution and Christian Faith: Reflections of an Evolutionary Biologist.* Hardcover ed. Washington, D.C.: Island Press.

Russell, Bertrand (1946) *History of Western Philosophy.* Schiefelbein, Susan (1992) "Beginning the Journey." *The Incredible Machine* (Third Printing). *National Geographic Society.*

Schiefelbein, Susan (1992) "The Powerful River." *The Incredible Machine* (Third Printing). *National Geographic Society.*

Schindewolf, O.H. (1957) "Comments on Some Stratigraphic Terms." *American Journal of Science*, vol. 255.

Schroeder, Gerald (1998) *The Science of God: The Convergence of Scientific and Biblical Wisdom.* New York: Broadway Books.

Seldes, George (ed.) (1983) *The Great Quotations.* Secaucus, New Jersey: Citadel Press.

Sheldrake, Rupert (1991) *The Rebirth of Nature: The greening of science and God.* New York, Bantam Books.

Shermer, Michael (2002) *In Darwin's Shadow: The Life and Science of Alfred Russel Wallace.*

Slotten, Ross A. (2004) *The Heretic in Darwin's Court: The Life of Alfred Russel Wallace.*

Smith, Charles H. (2005) "Alfred Russel Wallace, Past and Future." *Journal of Biogeography* 32(9).

Smith, George H. (1980) *Atheism: The Case Against God.* Prometheus Books.

Snelling, A.A. (1998) "The Cause of Anomalous Potassium-argon 'Ages' for Recent Andesite Flows at Mt. Nguaruhoe, New Zealand, and the Implications for Potassium-argon 'Dating.'" *Proc. 4th ICC*.

Sonntag, Richard E. (1966) *Fundamentals of Statistical Thermodynamics.*

Sonntag, Richard E. *Introduction to Thermodynamics, Classical and Statistical.* Barnes & Noble.

Sonntag, Richard E. *Thermodynamics and Transport Properties.* Sonntag, Richard E. and Van Wylen, Gordon J. *Fundamentals of Classical Thermodynamics.* (2d ed.) Barnes & Noble.

Speakman, John (2005) "Body size, energy metabolism and lifespan." *The Journal of Experimental Biology 208.*

Stenger, Victor. *The Comprehensible Cosmos: Where Do the Laws of Physics Come From?*

Sulloway, Frank J (1982) "Darwin and His Finches: The Evolution of a Legend." *Journal of the History of Biology* 15 (1):1-53.

Sutherland, Luther. *Darwin's Enigma.*

Thomson, Keith Stewart (1988) "Marginalia Ontogeny and phylogeny recapitulated."

Tiner, J.H. (1975) *Isaac Newton: Inventor, Scientist and Teacher.* Milford, MI: Mott Media.

Tipler, Frank (1994) *The Physics of Immortality.* New York, Doubleday.

Varghese, Ray Abraham. *The Wonder of the World: A Journey from Modern Science to the Mind of God.* Tyr Publishing.

Varghese, Ray Abraham (2004) "Academics viewing the universe through a narrow scope should rethink assumptions." *Dallas Morning News*, 12/15.

Viegas, Jennifer (2009) "Darwin's pianist wife influenced theories." *Endeavour*, Vol. 33, Issue 1, March.

Wallace, Alfred Russel (1869) *The Malay Archipelago*.

Wallace, Alfred Russel (1881) *Land Nationalisation: Its Necessity and Its Aims*.

Watson, R.A. (1982) "Absence as evidence in geology." *Journal of Geological Education* 30.

Wetherill, G.W. (1957) "Radioactivity of Potassium and Geologic Time." *Science*, September 20.

Wilder-Smith, A.E. *The Creation of Life: A Cybernetic Approach to Evolution*.

Wilkins, Harold T. (1952) "The Secret Cities of Old South America." Williams, George C. (1992) "Evolution v. Message Theory." *Natural Selection: Domains, Levels and Challenges*.

Wood-Martin, W.G. (1902) *Traces of the Elder Faiths of Ireland*. London: Longmans, Green and Company.

Woodmorappe, John (1999) "The Geologic Column: Does It Exist?" *Creation Ex Nihilo Technical Journal* 13(2).

Wright, Richard T. (2003) *Biology Through the Eyes of Faith*. Rev. Ed. San Francisco: HarperSanFrancisco.

Zheng, Y.F. (1989) "Influence of the Nature of Initial Rb-Sr System on Isochron Validity." *Chemical Geology*, 80.

INDEX

Accelerated decay, 153-156
Acquired characteristics, law of, 81, 86
Adaptive radiation, 55
Ad Hominem, Ad Hominem Abusive, 66
Agassiz, Louis, 1, 81, 279
Aldrich, L.T., 154
Ameghino, Carlos, 134
American Association for the Advancement of Atheism, 227
American Institute of Biological Sciences (AIBS), 4, 19, 50, 164, 167, 168, 169,
221, 225, 250, 255, 256, 259, 282-285
Amino Acids, 179, 180
Anagenesis, 55
Anaximander, 80
Anderson, Kevin, 186, 187
Anglican Church, 9, 64, 65, 89
Appeal to Consequences of a Belief, 246
Appeal to Ignorance, 132
Appeal to Mockery, 66
Appeal to Novelty, 67
Appeal to Ridicule, 66
Appeal to Spotlight, 66
Archaeopteryx, 5, 26, 36-39, 249, 252, 254, 280
Aristotle, 76, 213
Articles of Confederation, 167, 170, 286
Athenaeum, 75
Austin, Steven, 91-94, 151-153

Ayala, Francisco J., 60, 83, 121
Baumgardner, John, 155, 156
Begging the Question, 83, 104, 111, 114, 208, 232
Behe, Michael J., 172-174
Bell, Charles, 98-100, 229
Bell, Graham, 198
Bellamy, Edward, 68
Bergman, Jerry, 227
Birch, L.C., 219
Bohlin, Ray, 32
Bohr, Niels, 115, 171, 232
Bonner, E.C., 44, 67
Booker, Christopher, 187
Boyle, Robert, 97
Brace, C. Loring 141
Brass, Michael, 143, 144
Bridgewater series, 99
Bronn, Heinrich George, 150
Brown, R.H., 157
Butler Act, 142
Calderon, Gus, 27
California Evidence Code, 117-120
Camp Darwin, 91
Carbon-14, 155, 156, 157, 159
Cardiff giant, 146
Carmeli, Moshe, 275
Carver, George Washington, 94
Catherine, Empress of Russia, 72
Chaffin, Eugene, 151, 153
Chagas disease, 104, 105
Chain, Ernst Boris, 102, 103, 162, 229
Charlotte, Queen of England, 72
Chatterjee, Sankar, 38
Chirality, 179-182
Chmielnitzki massacres, 52
Circular reasoning, 5, 149
Cladogenesis, 55
Clark, W.E. LeGros, 141

Clementson, Sidney P., 154
Cohen, I. L., 185
Collins, Francis, 258-260
Constitution of the United States (U.S. Constitution), 25, 193, 286
Copernicus, Nicolai, 29, 83, 98
Correns, Carl, 87
Coyne, Jerry, 258
Cremo, Michael A., 133, 135-139, 143-145
Crohn's disease, 104
Crookshank, F.G., 227
Cuvier, Georges, 1, 81, 279
Darrow, Clarence, 142
Darwin, Annie, 104, 108
Darwin (Charles), Darwinian, Darwinism, Darwinist, 1, 2, 7, 11, 14, 15, 17, 18, 58, 60, 61, 64, 65, 74-85, 87-95, 97, 99-110, 122, 143-145, 159, 166, 171-173, 176, 189-192, 201, 202, 219, 223, 233-235, 239-244, 252, 253, 255, 258, 262, 277-281, 284, 285
Darwin, Charles Waring, 105
Darwin (Wedgwood), Emma, 69, 70, 72, 73, 108, 278
Darwin, Erasmus, 68, 80, 89, 278
Darwin, Mary, 104, 105
Davis, Percival, 36
Dawkins, Richard, 66, 222, 223
Dawson, Charles, 62
Declaration of Independence, 20, 124
Denton, Michael, 54, 61
De Perthes, Jacques Boucher, 36, 135, 148, 261
De Quatrefages, Armand, 136, 139
Deshayes, Paul, 150
De Vries, Hugo, 87
DeYoung, Don, 151
DNA, 15, 53, 121, 180, 183-187, 192, 232, 282
DNA/RNA, 179-181, 188, 235, 258, 281
Douglas, Stephen, 131
Dubois, Eugene, 133, 282
Duck, Mark, 203-205, 208-210
Dudley, H.C., 154
Edwards v. Aguillard, 10, 34, 35, 160, 162-166, 193, 213, 250, 283

Egerton, Rev. Francis Henry, 99, 100
Ehrlich, Paul, 219
Einstein, Albert, 30
Eldridge, Niles, 39, 150
Empedocles, 270
Eohippus, 56, 248, 254
False Dilemma, 114, 115
Faul, Henry, 154
Federal Rules of Evidence, 117
Federalist Papers no. 1, 22, 167
Federalist Papers no. 10, 21, 160
Fegan, J.W.C., 65
First Amendment (Establishment Clause), 3, 8, 9, 123, 124, 163, 165-167
First Cause (Causation), 18, 76, 80, 98, 122, 179, 221, 258, 277, 279, 282
First Law of Thermodynamics, 203
Fiske, John (James), 44
Fitzroy, James, 67, 89
Fleet, Elizabeth, 49
Fleming, Sir Alexander, 102
Flew, Sir Antony, 18, 22, 36, 77, 80, 107, 189-195, 213, 261
Florey, Howard, 102
Foard, James M., 61
Forbidden Archaeology: The Hidden History of the Human Race, 133, 138, 143, 144
Fourteenth Amendment, 124
Fox, William Darwin, 64
Genetic Fallacy, 32, 220, 278
Gicking v. Kimberlin, 122
Gilroy, Rex, 147
Gingerich, Owen, 21, 33-35, 170-172
Gish, Dwayne, 23, 161
Gish "gallop", 161
Glyptodon fossils, 74
Gonzalez, Guillermo, 30, 31, 33, 102, 148
Gould, John, 89
Gould, Stephen J. (Jay), 39-42, 246, 261

Gray, Asa, 44, 70
Habermas, Gary R., 189-194
Haeckel, Ernst, 5, 39-44, 65, 221, 254
Haldane, J.B.S., 86
Haldane's Dilemma, 27, 86, 282, 283
Hale v. Venuto, 122
Hamilton, Alexander, 8, 20, 35, 167, 168, 255, 283, 284
Hartnett, John, 275
Heller, Mikhail, 256
Henslow, John Stevens, 64, 67, 74
Heppell, David, 144
Hermitage Museum, 72
His, Wilhelm, Sr., 43
Hitching, Francis, 57
Hitler, Adolf, 256, 262
Hodes, Richard J., 267
Holmes, W. H., 140
Homeotic genes, 184
Hooker, Joseph, 67, 71, 76, 77, 90, 280
Huguenots, slaughter of, 52
Humanist Manifesto I, 224
Humanist Manifesto III, 225, 226
Humanist Manifestos, 224, 226, 246
Humphreys, D. Russell, 151, 155, 254, 274, 275
Hunt, Kathleen, 38, 58-61
Hunter, George, 142
Huxley, Aldous, 220, 251, 262
Huxley, Thomas Henry, 65, 66, 73-75, 89, 110, 163, 219, 220, 251, 281
Industrial Revolution, 63, 88, 101, 262, 278
Inherit the Wind, 142
Institute for Creation Research (ICR), 22, 23, 91, 227-229
Integration Principle, 53, 232, 236
Ionization, 179
Ivanov, Ilya, 226, 227, 285
Java Man, 140, 141, 282
Jefferson, Martha Wayles Skelton, 109
Jefferson, Thomas, 8, 22, 35, 41, 74, 124, 126-130, 163, 166-168, 176, 255, 257, 284-286

Jensen, James A., 37
John Muir Trail, 43
Journal of the Royal Society of Medicine, 105
Judicial Council of California Civil Jury Instructions (CACI), 122, 169
Keith, Arthur (Antiquity of Man), 134, 140
Kennedy, John F. (JFK), 131, 285
Kenyon, Dean, 35, 36, 148
Kepler, Johann, 97
Kerkut, G.A., 57
Kirby, Greg, 141
Kirby, William, 95, 99, 229
Kirshenbaum, Sheril, 259
Kitzmiller v. Dover Area School District, 174, 175
Labossiere, Michael C., 113, 132
Lamarck, Jean Baptiste de, 81, 85, 88, 202
Lambert, Frank L., 205, 206, 208, 209
Lang, Andrew, 3
Leakey, Louis, 147, 148
Le Chatelier's Principle, 180
Lincoln, Abraham, 50, 131, 285
Linnaeus, 80
Logical Fallacy(ies), 5, 100, 113-115, 145, 149, 193, 208
Lucretius, 80
Lucy (Australopithecus afarensis), 5, 140, 141, 213, 249, 252
Lyell, Charles, 67, 85, 90, 93, 150
Macalister, R.A.S., 137
Madison, James, 8, 20, 35, 41, 47, 48, 50, 74, 129, 130, 163, 167, 168, 255, 284
Madison Detached Memoranda, 48, 50
Magendie, Francois, 98
Malthus, Thomas Robert, 84, 86
Mass action, law of, 180
McCombs, Charles, 181
Megaltherium fossils, 90
Mencken, H.L., 142
Mendel, Gregor, 87, 88
Midgley, Mary, 222-224, 284
Mikelson, Jan, 186, 187

Mill, John Stuart, 68
Milton, Richard, 143, 144
Mitochondrial DNA (mt DHA), 158, 159
Moir, J. Reid, 134
Mooney, Chris, 259
Morris, Henry M., 25
Morris, John, 244
Morris, Simon Conway, 21, 33-35, 170-172, 244
Morse, Samuel F.B., 109
Mt. Darwin, 44, 67
Mt. Fiske, 44
Mt. Haeckel, 44
Mt. Lamarck, 44
Mt. Mendel, 44, 88
Mt. Spencer, 43
Mt. Wallace, 43
Murray, John, 67
Musk ox carcass (Alaska), 157, 159
National Academy of Sciences (NAS), 4, 19, 50, 225-227, 249, 253, 260, 282
National Center for Science Education (NCSE), 4, 19, 50, 282, 283
National Institute on Aging, 267
National Institutes of Health, 267
National Science Teachers Association, 162
National Society of Genetic Counselors, 108
Natural selection, 82-84, 89, 100, 101, 232, 239-243, 277-279, 281, 285
Nebraska Man, 3, 5, 141, 221, 249, 252
Newton, Sir Isaac, 96, 97, 229
Nietzsche, Frederich, 19
Nizkor Project, 113, 115
Noahic flood, 50, 85, 149, 156, 157
Novella, Steven, 246
Nucleotide, 179, 180
Opitsch, Eduard, 37
Ostrom, John, 37
Orthogenetic, 55
Owen, Richard, 65, 74, 75, 90

Padian, Kevin, 38
Pasteur, Louis, 89, 95, 229
Paul, the Apostle, 44-47
Paulian Principle of Atonement, 51
Paulos, John Allen, 214
Peth, Howard, 198
Piltdown Man, 3, 5, 55, 62, 136, 221, 249, 252
Pittack, Richard, 25, 26
Plato, 213
Poisoning the Well, 145
Polymer, 179, 180
Pope, Alexander, 96
Powell, Lewis F., 163
Pratt, David, 147, 187
Prime Mover, 76, 213
Privileged Planet: How Our Place in the Cosmos is Designed for Discovery, 30, 32-34, 35, 213, 285
Punctuated equilibrium, 39
Quigley, Ian, 42
Radioisotope (radio-) dating, 151, 153, 154, 157, 159, 160
Ragazzoni, Guiseppe, 136-139
RATE Project, 151, 152, 154-157
Reactivity, 179, 180
Rehnquist, William H., 163, 224
Res ipsa loquitur, 121, 122
Richards, Jay W., 30, 21, 33
Richardson, Michael "Mik", 40, 42, 43
Rives, William Cabel, 49
RNA (also DNA/RNA), 15, 18, 121, 180, 181, 185, 187, 188, 232
Roosevelt, Eleanor, 109
Roosevelt, Franklin D., 109, 285
Russell, Bertrand, 224
Sagan, Carl, 262
Santa Cruz River, 91-93
Scalia, Antonin, 162, 175, 224
Schaeffer, Roy L., 26
Schiefelbein, Susan, 53

Schindewolf, O.H., 150
Scopes, John, 142
Scopes Trial, 22, 141, 142
Scott, Eugenie, 51, 160, 161, 225, 261
Second Law of Thermodynamics, 16, 203, 205-207, 209, 210
Selection and Elimination, 104, 113, 193, 232
Selectivity Barrier, 179, 180
Sergi, Giuseppi, 136-139
Seuss Effect, 157
Sheldrake, Rupert, 188
Slotten, Ross A., 106
Smith, George H., 216
Smithsonian Institute, 146, 261
Snelling, Andrew, 151, 153
Socrates, 11, 12
Solomons, Theodore, 43, 44, 67, 88
Solubility, 179
Sonntag, Richard E., 210
Special Pleading, 165-167, 232, 236
Spence, William, 95
Spencer, Herbert, 44
Spinoza, Baruch, 70
Stalin, Joseph, 256
Stanley, Steven, 150
St. Bartholomew's Day massacre, 52
Stenger, Victor, 31
Strand Magazine, 146
Sugar, 179
Tautology, 5
Theosophy, 147
Thompson, Richard L., 133, 138, 139, 143-145
Tipler, Frank, 188
Torcaso v. Watkins, 224
Truman, Harry S., 131, 285
Unreactivity, 179
Van Wylen, Gordon J., 210
Vardiman, Larry, 151
Varghese, Ray, 192, 194

Wallace, Alfred Russel, 14, 67-72, 106, 171, 221, 242, 244, 257, 258, 278, 279, 285
Wallace "effect", 69
Watson, James, 42
Watson, R.A., 149
Wedgwood, Josiah, 72
Weidenreich, Franz, 62
Wells, Jonathan, 184
Whitney, J.D., 36, 140, 148, 261
Wilberforce, Samuel, 65, 66
Wilder-Smith, A.E., 36
William & Mary Quarterly, 49
Williams, George C., 86, 198
Woodmorappe, John, 148
Worth, Eugene R., 43
Zentz v. Coca Cola Bottling Co. of Fresno, 122
Zheng, Y.F., 158
Zuckerman, Lord Solly, 141

www.ingramcontent.com/pod-product-compliance
Lightning Source LLC
LaVergne TN
LVHW091530060526
838200LV00036B/552